CONSTRUCTION LAW IN CONTRACTORS' LANGUAGE

McNeill Stokes

CONSTRUCTION LAW IN CONTRACTORS' LANGUAGE

McGraw-Hill Book Company

New York   St. Louis   San Francisco   Auckland   Bogotá   Düsseldorf
Johannesburg   London   Madrid   Mexico   Montreal   New Delhi
Panama   Paris   São Paulo   Singapore   Sydney   Tokyo   Toronto

Library of Congress Cataloging in Publication Data

Stokes, McNeill.
  Construction law in contractors' language.

  Includes index.
  1. Engineering law—United States. 2. Engineering—
Contracts and specifications—United States. I. Title.
TA223.S76   1977   343'.73'078   76-57752
ISBN 0-07-061635-3

1234567890 KPKP 786543210987

The editors for this book were Jeremy Robinson and Tobia L. Worth,
the designer was Elliot Epstein, and the production supervisor
was Frank P. Bellantoni. It was set in Century Schoolbook
by Monotype Composition Company.

Printed and bound by The Kingsport Press.

This book is dedicated to the construction industry and to the men and women who built our country.

CONTENTS

PREFACE

Legal problems are inherent in every stage of general contractors' and subcontractors' daily business. No matter how conscious contractors may be about referring legal matters to their attorneys, expense and time provide natural limitations when it is not feasible or desirable that the contractors' everyday business be submitted to an attorney's scrutiny. Everyone associated with the building industry necessarily must be armed with some basic acquaintance of the legal problems involved in each situation as it develops. It is therefore important that general contractors and subcontractors generally be aware of their legal rights and liabilities.

One of the purposes of this book is to make general contractors and subcontractors more deeply conscious of facets of the law that affect their day-to-day business. Contractors must be aware of situations in which they can benefit from the law and also recognize certain legal pitfalls in sufficient time to safeguard their interests. Sometimes contractors' knowledge of the law is adequate to dispose of the problems as they arise. However, when legal questions of immediate or potential importance are presented, a lawyer should be consulted. The law constantly haunts general contractors and subcontractors and presents a continuing challenge to their everyday activities.

General contractors must be knowledgeable about the legal effect of provisions and clauses in their general contracts and in the general and special conditions which usually accompany the general contract. Naturally the general contractor should seek a fair and reasonable contract with the owner. Unfortunately, general contracts which are sought in the bidding process, including government contracts, seldom permit flexibility or modification of their terms. However, it is vital that the contract terms be studied to permit a complete understanding of the requirements for pricing a knowledgeable bid.

The ancient practice of the master builder who directly hired the labor and purchased the materials to build an entire building has given way in recent years to the modern general contractor who subcontracts practically all the work on the construction project to subcontractors who are experienced in performing specialized portions of the total work. General contractors have largely become construction managers or construction brokers by subdividing the construction project into many parts and subcontracting each part to subcontractors who actually perform the work by hiring the labor and purchasing the materials. The change in the role of the general contractor from the master builder to the present construction manager or construction broker began in the Depression, developed during World War II, and accelerated during the last two decades. More than 80 percent of the construction work in the United States is now actually performed by specialty subcontractors who have expertise in their portion of the work and specialized labor forces to perform it.

Subcontracting is a risk-shifting device whereby a general contractor can shift the legal responsibility for the performance of a portion of the work to subcontractors who become responsible to the general contractor for the performance of their portions of the work. By subcontracting, the general contractor can also fix the cost of the subcontracted portions of the work at the time the subcontracts are made. This is normally the time of bidding or in the early stages of the construction project. The risk-shifting device of subcontracting portions of the work has caused general contractors to rely more and more on the legal aspects of dealing in subcontracts rather than dealing in labor and material.

Subcontractors must be aware of the legal and practical effects of subcontract provisions that typically appear in subcontracts. Too often, subcontractors sign subcontract forms which are furnished them by general contractors without having any knowledge of the very serious legal implications of many of the subcontract clauses that give general contractors unnecessary legal and practical advantages. Many subcontractors fail to read the subcontract carefully, or if they do read it, they fail to appreciate fully the implications and consequence of much of the language which create unsuspected liabilities to the subcontractor. This has become increasingly a problem as subcontracts have become more and more lengthy, complicated, and deliberately devised to protect the interest of the general contractor at the expense of the subcontractors. To avoid unnecessary financial risk and burdensome legal involvement, subcontractors must read every subcontract carefully and be aware of the legal and practical effects of clauses which give the general contractors unnecessary legal and practical advantages.

General contractors and subcontractors must have a working knowledge of the practical legal problems that they may encounter during performance of construction contracts, which may increase their cost of performance of the contract. Extra work or changes beyond the contract requirements may arise in many forms which entitle contractors to an increase in their contract price. Legal knowledge is essential for the contract rights to claim and be granted increases in the contract price and time extensions. Ultimate success in obtaining an increase to the contract price for extra work or changes depends upon the contractors' prompt recognition of the facts which give rise to the claim and preserving those facts for ultimate presentation in support of a claim for increase in the contract price. Until a contractor has sufficient legal knowledge to recognize and identify the situations for which he is entitled to extra compensation or extension of time, he cannot obtain any relief for performing additional work or extras.

The cash-flow needs of both general contractors and subcontractors require that they vigorously pursue their right to payment. It is the nature of the financing of the construction work that general contractors and subcontractors perform dollar volumes many times in excess of their working capital. The subcontractors and those general contractors who actually perform work must pay for their labor weekly and for their materials and overhead on a current basis. If they are unable to collect payment currently, they will have immediate cash-flow problems. It is, therefore, incumbent upon contractors to understand the various remedies that are available in the construction industry for general contractors and subcontractors to collect their money for work performed.

General contractors and subcontractors should know their legal rights concerning the problems that may be encountered in scheduling of the work, excusable delays, extra costs for acceleration, and damages for delays. Contractors must also be keenly aware of their rights in the very common practice of bidding in the construction industry. They must be aware of the legal doctrines which dictate when their bids become binding, when their bids are not responsive, and when they may revoke their bids.

General contractors and subcontractors must know the special risks of financial loss which may be covered by insurance, and they must be aware of the additional hazards of construction which require special insurance endorsements to a general liability policy.

Contractors must plan their legal relationship with material suppliers so that they may be adequately protected if materials do not conform to the plans and specifications or are delayed in being furnished.

The chapters of this book are designed to point out some of the many realities that occur on a construction project concerning the legal aspects of construction general contracts, subcontracts, and their performance. Unfortunately, attorneys suffer from the handicap of 3 years of intensive training in law school to learn how to murder the English language. This book is an attempt to treat the subject in a practical manner in plain language so that it may be readily understood by general contractors, subcontractors, owners, engineers, and architects as well as attorneys. The text is based on actual cases decided by courts and contracting agencies. The material facts and contract provisions are generally set forth, as well as illustrative cases, so that the reader will obtain a general understanding of the fundamental principles of law involved in construction.

The legal doctrines and exceptions discussed herein may vary according to applicable law and contract clauses. The statements made herein are not intended to be substituted for legal advice from an experienced attorney in a specific fact situation.

MCNEILL STOKES

ACKNOWLEDGMENTS

I would like to acknowledge the invaluable contribution of the many associations and individual clients who have helped me gain an insight into the specialized field of construction law. In particular, I wish to thank:

American Subcontractors Association;

National Roofing Contractors Association;

International Association of Wall & Ceiling Contractors/Gypsum Drywall Contractors International;

National Electrical Contractors Association, Atlanta Chapter;

Association of Mechanical Contractors of Atlanta, Inc.; and

Consulting Engineers Council of Georgia.

I am also grateful to the American Institute of Architects (AIA) for their permission to reprint portions of their Documents. These may be obtained by writing to AIA, 1735 New York Avenue, N.W., Washington, D.C., 20006.

In addition, I would like to express my gratitude for the individual assistance of:

Mr. Bernard B. Rothchild, member and former chairman of the American Institute of Architects Documents Board;

Mr. Thomas J. Barfield of Otis Elevator Company;

Mr. Walter J. Derk of Fred S. James & Company;

Mr. J. L. Jerden of Pritchard & Jerden Insurance Agency;

Mr. David Henritze of Insurance Underwriters, Inc.; and

Mr. J. Ben Shapiro, Jr., Mr. Herman L. Fussell, and Mr. Thomas J. Wingfield of Stokes & Shapiro.

Finally, I would like to show my appreciation for the many hours of legal research contributed by:

Stephen C. Carlson, while a student at Yale University Law School, and

Claudia D. Thurman,

Chilton D. Varner, and

Jeffrey E. Young, while students at Emory University Law School.

1 BIDDING

INTRODUCTION

The science and art of estimating a construction contract is the first step in the construction process. The skill and preparation put into an estimate will have a tremendous effect on the performance of the work. The financial position of the contractor depends on his estimate, which is the blueprint for the control of costs and flow of cash through the performance of the contract. Carelessly underbidding puts the contractor in a financial bind for the entire project and creates fertile ground for the growth of disputes. Understanding and applying the basic legal rules pertaining to bidding is a necessary part of bid preparation. When the owner is a governmental body or public authority, the legal considerations of bidding may be complicated by special rules regulating the activities of the public owner with respect to construction contracts.

There are three parties involved in construction bidding: (1) the owner, who calls for bids on his project; (2) the general contractor, who coordinates and brokers the bids for the specialized parts of the entire job; and (3) the subcontractors, who are specialists in certain fields (for example, plumbing or roofing) and who bid only on a part of the project. The general contractor receives bids from many subcontractors and computes the lowest bid feasible; he uses either the lowest responsible bid from each specialty or sometimes even lower bids he anticipates procuring in post-award negotiations with subcontractors. The owner awards the general contract to the lowest responsive bidder among the general contractors.

Both general contractors and subcontractors must be aware of their rights under the very common practice of bidding in the construction industry. They must know the legal doctrines which dictate when their bids are responsive and when they have a legal right to revoke their bids. General contractors must be particularly aware of the procedures for bidding to owners, which may be either governmental or nongovernmental. Subcontractors who sometimes bid directly as specialty contractors to the owner must also be aware of the procedures for bidding directly. In addition, subcontractors must have a working knowledge of the treacherous legal framework of bidding as a subcontractor to general contractors in the construction industry.

For a long time bidding in the construction industry has presented unique and troublesome problems for general contractors, subcontractors, lawyers, and courts, largely because all the traditional concepts of contract law cannot be easily reconciled with modern business practices.

BIDDING DIRECTLY TO THE OWNER

When an owner decides to use the bidding process to locate and select a general contractor to do the desired work, he notifies general contractors and also potential subcontractors by advertising for bids. Advertising for bids creates no legal obligation on the part of the owner. A bid submitted by a general contractor to an owner is an offer to enter into a construction contract, and the owner's acceptance of a bid completes the offer and acceptance necessary for there to be an enforceable contract.

Where the general contractor submits his bid directly to the owner, there are certain considerations which, if not observed, can prevent receipt of the award even if the contractor should be the lowest bidder. It is the purpose of this section to examine those considerations and to establish some standards to guide the general contractor in submitting his direct bid. The same principles would apply to a specialty subcontractor who submits a bid directly to the owner.

Advertising for Bids

The owner will usually distribute a formal invitation for bids containing the terms and conditions on which the owner is willing to contract, detailed plans and specifications on which the contractor may base his price, and a list of information about the general contractor required by the owner. To submit a bid, the general contractor generally fills out the invitation for bids, signs it, and submits it to the owner before a specified date and time.

In the case of public owners, the law usually requires that the invitation be clear and unambiguous so that all bidders are on an equal footing and free competition is maintained. Similar regulations may apply to ensure that the actual advertising for bids is fair. Taxpayers, unhappy over the way their money is being spent, may also get into the act when a public contract is advertised.

Illustrative Case

In one case, a Louisiana drainage district commission advertised for bids for a contract to build and supply the equipment for four pumping stations. Chiro, a taxpayer, challenged the advertisement for bids, which called for the bidder to design the buildings and furnish specifications and provided for charges and prices to be agreed upon between the contractor and the district. Chiro claimed that these terms were too uncertain to allow competitive bidding between bidders all on the same footing. The court, however, found that the clauses related only to minor changes and that the advertisement for bids was valid. [1]

Responsive Bidding

The key element of a bid on a construction contract is that it must be "responsive" to the invitation for bids. When a public contract must be made by competitive bidding, the award will be made to the lowest responsible, *responsive* bidder. An owner who must select the lowest responsible bid need not even consider a responsible bidder whose bid is not responsive.

A bid is nonresponsive if it places qualifications or conditions in the contract different from those in the invitation for bids or if it offers performance which varies from the invitation with respect to the method of performance, time of performance, or nature of the work required to be done.

Illustrative Case

The advertisement for bids on a Nebraska county highway project made it clear that the time of performance was an essential part of the bid, but the contractor's bid omitted a time of performance. The court held that the bid was incomplete and that the award made to the contractor was invalid. [2]

Submitting the bid after the deadline set by the owner may make a bid nonresponsive.

[1] Chiro v. Fourth Jefferson Drainage Dist., 159 La. 471, 105 So. 556 (1925).
[2] Root v. Douglas County, 105 Neb. 262, 180 N.W. 46 (1920).

Illustrative Cases

An invitation for bids on a government contract contained a closing date for receipt of bids which coincided with the official day of mourning for President Kennedy. The bidder, mistakenly assuming that this was an official holiday, submitted his bid the next day. The bid was rejected for lateness.[3]

A bid was hand carried to the appropriate government office the afternoon prior to bid opening but could not then be delivered because the office closed at the early hour of 4:00 P.M. The bid was accordingly delivered the next day but was rejected for lateness.[4]

A bid may be nonresponsive for failure to obtain a performance bond of the type required by the invitation or for failure to provide all the information required by the invitation. Using a bid form other than the invitation itself may be risky because the bid must contain all the terms of the invitation to be responsive. However, the owner should not be allowed to "nit-pick" by using minor inconsistencies to avoid accepting a proper bid.

Illustrative Case

The contractor, P. H. Porter, placed a condition in his bid on a contract to build a drain to the effect that the county should provide a free building place and a free right of way for the necessary hauling. Although this was a variance from the advertisement, these conditions were necessarily implied in the contract and so they did not invalidate the bid.[5]

The responsiveness of a bid is a contract formality which may be waived by the owner. The contractor may not assert his own nonresponsiveness to invalidate a bid which has been accepted.[6] That is, if the owner chooses to ignore the lateness of a bid or the failure to meet a bonding requirement and accepts a nonresponsive bid, the contractor is bound to perform in accordance with the contract specifications.

Each bidder is entitled to fair consideration and review of his bid because such consideration is necessary to preserve the integrity of the bid system. Notification of award is generally made by written document and may be followed by execution of a formal contract between the owner and the general contractor.

A federal government contracting officer or owner may reject *all* bids. The power to reject all bids should not be used arbitrarily but only in the owner's interest; since such rejection tends to undermine the integrity of the bidding system, it should be based on persuasive cause. Examples of

[3] Comp. Gen. Dec. B-152999 (Mar. 11, 1964), 9 CCF ¶ 72, 498, 2 G.C.R. ¶ 3405.4061.

[4] Comp. Gen. Dec. B-155666 (Jan. 21, 1965), unpublished.

[5] Porter v. Moore, 200 Ky. 95, 252 S.W. 97 (1923).

[6] General Bronze Corp. v. United States, 88 Ct. Cl. 612 (1939).

acceptable reasons for such across-the-board rejection are ambiguity of specifications, revision of specifications, or the case where all bids represent unreasonable prices.

Awarding the Contract

Although there is no general rule of law that the owner should award the contract to the lowest bidder, many laws require governments or public authorities to award the contract to the lowest responsible bidder. For instance, the federal statute dealing with armed forces procurement states at 10 USC Section 2305(c):

... Awards shall be made ... to the responsible bidder whose bid conforms to the invitation and will be most advantageous to the United States, price and other factors considered. However, all bids may be rejected if the head of the agency determines that rejection is in the public interest.

The selection of the lowest responsible bidder is left to the discretion of the public owner, and the courts generally do not disturb the award unless it is obtained by fraud or collusion or the owner's discretion is exercised in the interest of the successful contractor rather than the interest of the public.

Illustrative Case

A Michigan county drainage commissioner awarded a drainage contract to the next to lowest bidder because the lowest bidder, Charles H. Montague, who had demonstrated his financial responsibility, was a stranger to him, while he knew how the next to lowest bidder, Woolman Construction Company, would perform. The court stated that the commissioner's discretion must be exercised in the interest of the public and overturned the award.[7]

As well as the financial responsibility of the bidders, the owner may consider their ability to perform the particular work and the comparative qualities of different materials offered for the money.

Bid Protests

If the owner must use competitive bidding, the award may be vulnerable to the challenge of an unsuccessful bidder on one of three basic grounds: (1) The invitation for bids was so ambiguous that free competition was impossible; (2) the accepted bid was nonresponsive; (3) the award was not made to the lowest responsible bidder.

---

[7] Lowell Township v. Patterson, 214 Mich. 528, 183 N.W. 214 (1921).

Illustrative Case

A board of supervisors rejected the lowest bid on a highway project on the ground that the next lowest bidder offered a better quality of gravel for the project. The court held that the award should have gone to the lowest bidder, Standard Highway Company, who challenged the award because the Louisiana parish was fully protected by the specifications for kind and quality of gravel.[8]

When a federal government bid is protested, the Comptroller General, in reviewing a protested award, may decide that although the action of the agency is challengeable, the fact that the award has already been made controls; the result is not a voiding of the award but rather an admonition, which is of little comfort to the protesting bidder.

Avoiding the Consequences of Bid Mistakes

Bidding contractors are well aware of the inevitable presence of human error in the calculation and preparation of bids on construction projects. Mistakes may be made in determining exactly what work is called for by the contract, or they may be arithmetical or clerical. The necessity for double-checking and avoiding mistakes is imperative because the bidder may have to perform his mistakes. However, a contractor who makes a mistake which the owner knew about (or should have known about) may be able to revoke his bid legally, and his bid bond or bid deposit will not be forfeited.

A contractor who makes a mistake in a bid need not resort to the tactics of one desperate contractor who made a substantial mistake on his first bid on a government contract. The contracting officer, after opening the bids, read the contractor's name as the apparent low bidder and asked the contractor to verify his signature on the bid and bid bond. The contractor stood alone before the contracting officer and inspected his bid and bid bond for an agonizingly long time; then he suddenly crumpled up both papers and ate them. Where the error in the bid is a clerical one which occurred despite ordinary precautions, the courts have allowed contractors to rescind.

Illustrative Cases

E. J. Kastorff, a building contractor, received at the last possible moment a plumbing subcontract bid which was $3,000 below his lowest bid. Erroneously thinking he had already entered the previously low bid in his total column and included that sum in his total bid, he deducted $3,000 from the total amount of his bid and entered the resulting total on his bid form as his bid for the school construction. Thus, the total included no allowance whatsoever for the plumbing work and was approximately 7 percent below what should have been his bid. At the bid opening, the contractor was asked to check his figures. He confirmed them, whereupon the board voted to award him the contract. The next morning, in checking his worksheets, Kastorff discovered his error and immediately informed the awarding authorities, asking to be released from his bid. The

[8] Standard Highway Co. v. Police Jury, 158 La. 294, 103 So. 819 (1925).

school board then gave the contractor written notification of the award of the contract. When he refused to perform, the board sought to recover the difference between the mistaken bid and the next lowest bid. The court held that because (1) the error was an honest one, (2) there was no substantial injury to the school board, and (3) the contractor had given prompt notification of the error, the contractor would not be held to the mistaken bid. [9]

In transposition of figures for a sewer project from "work sheets" to the "final accumulation sheet," a contractor, M. F. Kemper Construction Company, inadvertently omitted an item of $301,769, resulting in a bid one-third lower than the other bids. The error was caused by the fact that the contractor and his assistants were exhausted after working long hours under pressure; the entry was made at 2:00 A.M. Upon discovery of the error after the bid opening, Kemper immediately notified the awarding authority of its mistake and offered evidence of its error. The court found the mistake to be excusable and honest and of a material character. Noting that not all carelessness constitutes neglect of legal duty, the court said it would not penalize the contractor for a clerical error (as opposed to an error in judgment in calculating costs). [10]

There is no magic formula for ascertaining the precise situations in which the courts will allow a contractor to withdraw a mistaken bid. The results seem rather to turn on a case-by-case determination and involve an assessment of the circumstances which led to the error, the possible damages to both parties, and the conduct of the bidder upon discovering the mistake.

Illustrative Case

Mattefs Construction Company submitted a mistaken bid for construction of a building on an Idaho state college campus. In allowing the contractor to withdraw the bid, the court held that one who errs in preparing a bid for a public works contract is entitled to rescission if he can establish that: (1) the mistake is material (here it was 14 percent); (2) enforcement of the contract pursuant to the terms of the erroneous bid would be unconscionable; (3) the mistake was not the result of culpable negligence on the part of the bidder; (4) the party to whom the bid was submitted will not be injured except by loss of his bargain; and (5) prompt notice of the error was given. [11]

The degree of error does not in itself seem to be determinative. The courts have agreed only that it must be "material"; but their definition of that term has varied widely, for example, from 7 to 50 percent in the few cases discussed here.

Even when a contract has been entered into, there are circumstances under which it will not be enforced because of a unilateral mistake by the contractor. If the owner knows the contractor has made a mistake and tries to take advantage of it, or if the owner should have discovered that a mistake was made by examining the contractor's bid, the contractor will not be forced to perform according to the terms of the contract. If no work has been done, the contractor may rescind the bid and recover any deposit given to the owner as a condition of bidding. Neither the

[9] Elsinore Union Elementary School Dist. v. Kastorff, 54 Cal.2d 380, 353 P.2d 713, 6 Cal. Rptr. 1 (1960).

[10] M.F. Kemper Constr. Co. v. City of Los Angeles, 37 Cal.2d 696, 235 P.2d 7 (1951).

[11] Boise Junior College Dist. v. Mattefs Constr. Co., 92 Idaho 757, 450 P.2d 604 (1969).

contractor nor his surety would be liable on a bond given to the owner to ensure that the contractor would perform the work if this bid were accepted.

Illustrative Case

The State of Connecticut advertised for bids to construct the substructure of a bridge, and F. H. McGraw & Company responded with a bid that was $60,000 less than the next lowest bid. The State noticed the discrepancy and conferred with the contractor, and it was determined that McGraw had mistakenly based its bid on one method of performance when the invitation for bids required a more expensive method. No doubt McGraw at this point wished it could turn the clock back to the day it worked out the bid calculations. Knowing of the mistake and knowing that the contractor would refuse to perform because it would take a loss, the State accepted the contractor's bid (which was irrevocable as a condition of bidding). Then upon McGraw's refusal to perform, the State awarded contract to the next lowest bidder and sued McGraw for the amount of the security bond given by the contractor to ensure performance if its bid was accepted. The court held that McGraw made a bona fide mistake and was not so negligent as to be held responsible, and the State had not been prejudiced before it knew of the mistake. The State's claim on the bond was denied and the contract declared legally ineffective. [12]

The ramifications of the defense of mistake in subcontract bid are examined more thoroughly in a later section.[13]

SUBCONTRACT BIDDING

The initial requirement for any contract is that the parties demonstrate to each other their mutual assent to the same bargain at the same time; this mutual assent normally takes the form of "offer" and "acceptance." One party makes a definite proposal, or bid, and a contract is conditioned on the other party's agreement of acceptance in return. In the construction context, the subcontractor's bid is the offer; when he submits a bid, he is promising to render a stated performance, provided the general contractor will accept and likewise bind himself to pay the bid price on the requested terms.

It is important to realize the general principle of contract law that even after the offer is made, either party can change his mind and withdraw from the bargain *so long as there has been no acceptance*. Subject to a few exceptions where a subcontractor has submitted a bid with which he is later dissatisfied, the subcontractor is free to withdraw it at any time so long as no acceptance has been communicated. The general contractor's mental determination to accept is not enough; since there is no way of

---

[12] Connecticut v. F.H. McGraw & Co., 41 F. Supp. 369 (D. Conn. 1941).

[13] *See* p. 15 *infra*.

ascertaining a man's secret thoughts, the general contractor must actually communicate his acceptance before the contract is fixed and the subcontractor's power to withdraw is eliminated.

It is from these mechanics that the problems plaguing construction bidding arise. Generally there is no formal contract at law until after the awarding authority lets the general contract to the contractor. The general contractor will usually not accept a subcontractor's bid until then because he does not want to be bound should he not receive the contract. Thus, at common law the subcontractor's offer or bid is always revocable until formally accepted by the contractor. Similarly, the general contractor is not bound to award the subcontractor the job, even though he uses the subcontractor's bid in computing his own total bid, unless he has formally accepted. This situation clearly leaves a considerable amount of room for disappointed expectations on both sides.

Practically speaking, however, informal commitments are often made prior to the award of the general contract, and the increasing number and size of those commitments have led the courts to reexamine the traditional concepts of offer and acceptance, with the result that they have sometimes recognized a legally binding contract as arising under something other than formal acceptance. It should be noted, however, that the courts remain wary of straying too far from the traditional concepts, and the concepts and cases examined in this discussion reveal a recurrent preoccupation with the question of acceptance. Was there an act which the courts could justifiably recognize as constituting acceptance so that the parties are bound? At exactly what point did it occur? Should the act have been recognizable by both parties as signaling such acceptance?

Once the general contractor has garnered the lowest possible bids from his subcontractors, it is of paramount importance to him that he be able to hold the subcontractors to those bids. It is, after all, the underlying theory of the bidding process that free competition among subcontractors will allow the general contractor to produce the best construction at the lowest possible price. Once the general contractor has obtained the contract, it is critical to his position that a subcontractor on whose offer he has relied in making his prime bid sign a subcontract and perform at the indicated price.

Situations sometimes arise, however, in which a subcontractor finds himself unwilling to sign a subcontract at the bid price—for example, the situation where he has made a mistake in computing his bid or where there has been a marked change in the availability and price of his supplies between the time of bid and the time of performance. In the absence of fixed-price supply contracts, a subcontractor may avoid some of these problems by use of a carefully worded bid proposal form, which allows adjustment of subcontract price to reflect general market-price increases; however, such a proposal form may not be acceptable to the general contractor and will not cover all situations.

The general contractor who attempts to hold a subcontractor to his bid must come to grips with the troublesome fact that it is rare that a clearly recognizable and bona fide contract is concluded prior to the letting of the overall bid to the general contractor. As a result, the courts have been concerned with whether the general contractor has communicated to the subcontractor the acceptance of the subcontractor's bid which is necessary to establish a contract. Where the general's acceptance of the subcontractor's bid has been oral, the contract may still not be enforceable if performance (including any warranties) will take longer than a year;[14] and the general contractor is usually reluctant to bind himself by a written subcontract before he knows whether he has won the general contract. Because of these problems, general contractors who have attempted in court to hold low-bidding subcontractors to their bids have met with mixed results. Their actions have been based on three different legal theories: justifiable reliance, acceptance by use of the subcontractor's bid, and bilateral contracts.

Justifiable Reliance

The theory of justifiable reliance has provided general contractors with their greatest success in forcing subcontractors to perform because the theory conveniently sidesteps the whole question of whether the general contractor has formally accepted the subcontractor's bid. Instead, if the general has justifiably relied on the subcontractor's bid (for example, he has used it in computing his own bid) and if he would be irreparably injured should the subcontractor refuse to perform at his bid price, some courts have held that the subcontractor must perform at the price he indicated in his bid. This doctrine of justifiable reliance is legally termed "promissory estoppel."

However, because contract law is so firmly rooted in the concept that a contract represents an objective "meeting of the minds" and is a voluntary, *mutual* undertaking, other courts have been reluctant to offer relief when one party has clearly withdrawn before formal acceptance and no longer wishes to go forward with the bargain. A subcontractor's success in refuting a claim based on justifiable reliance will depend on how far the courts in his state have come. In a state like California, whose courts have led the way in applying this doctrine in construction cases, his chances will be accordingly diminished. In a more conservative state where courts are reluctant to go outside the traditional offer-acceptance framework, the subcontractor may well be successful in avoiding the alleged obligation.

---

[14] For a fuller discussion of problems in enforcing oral contracts, *see* p. 19 *infra.*

Illustrative Cases

A subcontractor, Gimbel Brothers, sent unsolicited "firm" bids for supplying linoleum to all generals known to be interested in a proposed job. After its bid was used by the winning general, James Baird Company, Gimbel discovered a considerable error in the bid and withdrew its offer immediately by telephone and letter. Baird nonetheless formally accepted the subcontractor's original bid. Gimbel refused to perform. The court found that the fact that the offer had purported to be "firm" was of no consequence because it was unsupported by consideration and because Gimbel had withdrawn his bid before it was formally accepted by Baird, there was no enforceable contract. [15]

A subcontractor, Mesa Electric Company, submitted an erroneous bid to K. L. House Construction Company, a general contractor, for the construction of a building on the campus of the University of New Mexico. The court ruled that House's reliance in using Mesa's bid did not constitute acceptance and thereby give rise to an enforceable contract, even though House had also asked Mesa to proceed with preliminary planning. The subcontractor was allowed to revoke and substitute a more expensive bid. [16]

The preceding cases reflect the traditional viewpoint that the subcontractor's bid is an offer which is freely revocable so long as the general has not communicated his formal acceptance, a viewpoint which is still good law in many jurisdictions.

In recent years, however, an increasing number of courts have resorted to the doctrine of justifiable reliance as a way around those problems arising from an application of strict contract concept to construction negotiations. These courts have appreciated the flexibility the doctrine offers. A court can view those issues that are presented and determine on which side the equities lie—in effect, what the fair result would be—without worrying about the trappings of whether and when a formal acceptance occurred. The important consideration for those courts applying the doctrine has seemed to be that the loss should fall on the subcontractor who made the error rather than on the contractor who merely relied on the subcontractor's bid.

Illustrative Case

Star Paving Company, a subcontractor, submitted a last-minute telephoned bid for paving on a school job to the winning contractor, William A. Drennan, who used it in his bid and listed the subcontractor as required by state law. Upon discovery of an error in its computations, Star revoked its bid before Drennan notified it formally of acceptance. The California court applied the doctrine of justifiable reliance, holding that the offer included an *implied* subsidiary promise not to revoke for a reasonable length of time. It was found that Drennan had accepted the subcontractor's offer before that "reasonable time" had expired. [17]

[15] James Baird Co. v. Gimbel Bros., 64 F. 2d 344 (2d Cir. 1933).

[16] K.L. House Const. Co., Inc. v. Watson, 84 N.M. 783, 508 P.2d 592 (1973).

[17] Drennan v. Star Paving Co., 51 Cal.2d 409, 33 P.2d 757 (1958).

The preceding case was one of the first major cases to squarely challenge the traditional view; it has served as a model for those states that have chosen to apply the doctrine of justifiable reliance to construction cases. There are two facts in the case which can be important to the subcontractor who is attempting to avoid any obligation flowing from a mistaken bid. First, the general, as required by state law, had listed all subcontractors whose bids he had used. The practical effect of the listing was to greatly foreclose the general contractor's ability to "bid shop" after the award. Indeed, the opinion expressly conditioned relief on the general contractor's continued abstention from shopping or demanding a lower price from the subcontractor. (In a situation where the general has not so bound himself, it can be argued that the doctrine should not apply.) Second, the court noted that had the subcontractor made his bid specifically revocable, the court could not have read in the implied promise to hold the bid open for a reasonable time. This finding suggests several ways in which the subcontractor can avoid being bound by an application of the doctrine of justifiable reliance: (1) The subcontractor can expressly state that his offer is revocable until accepted in writing. (2) The subcontractor can state that his bid is an offer open for acceptance for a limited time (for example, 10 days); if the bid has not been accepted by then, it may be withdrawn or be subject to revision. (This approach might be the most acceptable to the general contractor while giving him less time to bid-shop.) (3) Of course, should the subcontractor begin work, the general contractor's acquiescence will be construed as acceptance of the subcontractor's bid.

Those courts which have applied the doctrine of justifiable reliance have insisted that certain elements must be present for the doctrine to apply: There must be a promise which reasonably leads the promisee to rely on it to his detriment; injustice must be unavoidable if the subcontractor should withdraw his bid; there must be a reasonably foreseeable likelihood of reliance by the person receiving the offer, and the reliance must be "justifiable."[18] The subcontractor or the general contractor should examine the facts of his own case very carefully to determine if one or more of those elements is missing. Perhaps the element most vulnerable to attack by the subcontractor is: *Should the general contractor have reasonably relied on the subcontractor's bid without binding himself in a conditional contract?* In the construction industry, where commitments are so tenuous up to the time of the award of the contract and where bids are offered and withdrawn with some frequency, should the general contractor justifiably expect the subcontractor's bid to remain open for a reasonable time? The general contractor has the option of entering a contract with the subcontractor whose bid he uses and making that contract exclusively contingent on his winning the general contract;

[18] N. Litterio & Co. v. Glassman Constr. Co., 319 F.2d 736 (D.C. Cir. 1963).

in the absence of such a conditional contract, it may be argued that the customs of the industry should belie such reliance by a general contractor.

Acceptance by Use of the Subcontractor's Bid

This theory is not the most promising one on which to base a general contractor's lawsuit because one must first construe the subcontractor's bid as an offer calling for acceptance by use in the general contractor's bid; such acceptance is usually not intended by the subcontractor. Even should the contractor be able to establish the subcontractor's intent, the subcontractor may still be able to defeat the action on the grounds that it is often impossible to determine which subcontractor's bid has been used unless the awarding authorities require that subcontractors be listed in the general contractor's bid. The general contractor's unadorned figures do not prove use (and thereby acceptance) of a particular subcontractor's bid.

Bilateral Contracts

The theory of bilateral contracts has its own drawbacks for the general contractor because a bilateral contract is one which requires a return promise to become binding. In response to the subcontractor's promise to do the job at a stated price, the contractor must promise to pay him a stated amount and award him the subcontract. But in practice it is quite rare for a general contractor to accept a subcontractor's bid prior to the letting of the general contract; he usually does not wish to be bound before he is awarded the contract. Occasionally, a court has found that such a contract exists, as in the following case. But more often, the courts have refused to find a bilateral contract where no formal agreement has been reached by the parties.

Illustrative Case

Douglas L. Cox Plumbing & Heating, Inc., submitted a bid for plumbing to Wargo Builders, Inc., the general contractor, only to submit a subsequent, higher bid. There was evidence that when Cox submitted the higher bid, it knew the contractor had won the contract. Shortly thereafter, Wargo wired Cox demanding performance of the subcontract at the originally stated price. The court found the circumstances sufficient to show an acceptance of (and not merely reliance on) the subcontractor's original offer. [19]

ESCAPING THE SUBCONTRACT

There are two situations in which defenses have been successfully argued by subcontractors wishing to avoid signing subcontracts, even in those

---

[19] Wargo Builders, Inc. v. Douglas L. Cox Plumbing & Heating, Inc., 26 Ohio App. 2d 1, 268 N.E.2d 597 (1971).

.jurisdictions that are willing to apply the doctrine of justifiable reliance: where the subcontract contains additional, unnegotiated terms, and where a mistake should have been noticed by the general contractor.

Additional Subcontract Terms

As has been discussed, normally a subcontractor will not be asked to sign a formal, written subcontract until after the general contractor has been awarded the prime contract. When the formal subcontract form is presented to the subcontractor for execution, he may find that it contains provisions not previously discussed by the parties. If the subcontractor wishes to avoid being held to his bid, he should argue that if a contract existed, it consisted only of the bid and those terms actually discussed at the time of the bid. He should argue that the law does not require him to agree to all the additional terms of the written form; indeed, the law has traditionally viewed a purported acceptance which contains such unnegotiated terms as constituting a mere counteroffer rather than a true acceptance.

The law has recognized that such a qualified or conditional acceptance proposes an exchange of obligations different from that proposed by the original offeror. Should the subcontractor decline to accept the counteroffer, the law would not permit the general contractor to demand performance of the subcontractor's original offer; the making of a counteroffer ordinarily terminates the general contractor's power of acceptance of the subcontractor's original bid. Court decisions endorse the usual understanding of bargainers that one proposal is dropped when another is taken under consideration.

Illustrative Cases

The general contractor, C. H. Leavell and Company, solicited a subcontractor's bid which was later orally reduced and used in the general's bid. Both parties entered into an oral agreement that they were bound. Upon receiving the contract, the general asked the subcontractor, Grafe and Associates, Inc., to confirm in writing the reduction. It also requested that the subcontractor confirm the posting of a performance bond, an item upon which there had been no previous agreement. Grafe refused to post the bond. The court held that no binding contract had been reached because the dealings between the parties amounted only to a series of offers and counteroffers.[20]

A general contractor, Debron Corporation, brought suit in connection with a quotation submitted by a subcontractor, National Homes Construction Corporation, for steel erection for a university building project. The court held that the contractor had failed to establish that it had indeed relied upon the original quotation submitted to it because when Debron mailed the purchase-order confirmation, the quoted price had been reduced and additional specifications added; the starting date had been changed; and eleven new "Terms and Conditions" had been added. On this basis, the court found it clear that no contract had ever been entered into.[21]

[20] C.H. Leavell & Co., v. Grafe & Associates, Inc., 90 Idaho 502, 414 P.2d 873 (1966).

[21] Debron Corp. v. National Homes Constr. Corp., 362 F. Supp. 341 (E.D. Mo. 1973).

The subcontractor should note that in order to successfully plead this defense of additional terms, he must be able to show that his refusal to sign the subcontract is indeed based on the presence of the additional, unnegotiated terms in the contract. Should the court be able to determine that the refusal to perform is based not on the presence of the additional terms but rather on a low price, the subcontractor will not be relieved of his obligation to perform.

Illustrative Case

N. Litterio & Company, a masonry subcontractor, submitted a bid which was used by Glassman Construction Company, the prime contractor, in its bid. After Glassman was awarded the contract, it sent Litterio a written proposed subcontract which contained additional terms. By this time Litterio had discovered that its bid was too low and it refused to sign the subcontract. The court found that the subcontractor's refusal was based not on the presence of the additional subcontract terms but rather on the mistaken price, and refused relief to the subcontractor. [22]

Of course, if the general contractor attaches to the invitation for bid a subcontract form which includes any special provisions, the subcontractor will be precluded from later claiming that the formal, written subcontract adds anything new to the subcontract negotiations.

Mistake

To minimize the possibility of a bid containing a mistake being submitted to a general contractor, subcontractors should establish office procedures which ensure that bids are checked by at least one person other than the estimator who originally put the bid together. If possible, additional checks should be made on the bid by checking the price by a different method of computation. For example, if the original bid was calculated by a detailed time and material take-off, then a bid check should be made by calculating the bid using unit prices based on previous cost experience. The chances of an erroneous bid being sent out are reduced the more times that a subcontractor checks the bid.

But where a mistake *does* occur, the subcontractor can sometimes avoid being held to his bid. Where the subcontractor submits a bid which is so far out of line with the other bids that the general contractor should be alerted to the probability of a mistake, the courts will not force the subcontractor to perform.

Illustrative Cases

Due to an error in computation, Ingersoll-Rand Company submitted a bid to supply air-conditioning machinery that was 50 percent low. The contractor, Robert Gordon, Inc.,

[22] N. Litterio & Co. v. Glassman Constr. Co., 319 F. 2d 736 (D.C. Cir. 1963).

used the bid in preparing its own bid. Upon hearing testimony of other contractors that they had discarded the supplier's bid as clearly mistaken, the court refused to give relief to the contractor. Because of its experience, Gordon was not allowed to claim justifiable reliance on the supplier's price. [23]

T. T. Watson, Inc., a Florida subcontractor, submitted a bid for steel fabrication that was substantially less than three other bids received. The contractor, Southeastern Sales and Service Company, asked if the bid included everything in the specifications. Upon receiving an affirmative answer, Southeastern used the amount in submitting its bid for the general contract. On the following day the owner's architect was informed of the name of the steel fabrication subcontractor. An hour later Watson discovered its error and advised the general it was withdrawing its bid. The court held that because the bid was so far out of line, it would not force the subcontractor to perform. [24]

Thus bids can be revoked under appropriate circumstances even if a general contractor uses the subcontractor's bid containing a mistake in calculating the bid to the owner. As a general rule, the use of a subcontractor's bid by the prime contractor in his own bid is not an acceptance of the subcontractor's bid because acceptance must be directly communicated to the subcontractor. Aside from some exceptions under the laws of some states, the subcontractor can revoke his bid containing a mistake even after his bid is used in the general contractor's bid to the owner. Even where the bidder does not realize that there has been a mistake in his bid until after the bid is accepted or even after the contract or subcontract is signed, the bidder is not bound where the bid is so obviously wrong that the general contractor or owner should have caught the error.

It will be noted from the cases that if a bid which contains an error is transmitted to the general contractor or to the awarding authority, the bidder should *notify* the proper parties of the error immediately and revoke the bid containing the mistake. A bid is an offer to make a contract; but before a binding contract comes into existence, the bid must be accepted by the general contractor. If the bidding party revokes the erroneous bid before acceptance, then ordinarily there is no binding contract. Whether the erroneous bid is oral or written, the bidder should immediately revoke the bid orally and confirm the revocation in writing either by letter or telegram addressed to the offeree. If the bidder waits an unreasonable length of time before revoking his bid, his inaction may be deemed to be a ratification of the mistake.

A subcontractor or general contractor who has submitted a bid containing a mistake should be cautious in submitting a corrected bid because after he commences the job, the other party might take the position that the first erroneous bid was binding and pay only the amount of the erroneous bid. [25] This would force the bidder to take the legal offensive in order to collect the full payment due under his corrected bid, and the bidder would have to convince the court that the erroneous bid should not be binding.

[23] Robert Gordon, Inc. v. Ingersoll-Rand Co., 117 F.2d 654 (7th Cir. 1941).

[24] Southeastern Sales & Service Co. v. T.T. Watson, Inc., 172 So.2d 239 (Fla. App. 1965).

[25] Wargo Builders, Inc., v. Douglas L. Cox Plumbing & Heating, Inc., 26 Ohio App. 2d 1, 268 N.E. 2d 597 (1971).

Revocation of a bid or subcontract because of mistake presents a tricky legal situation, and the subcontractor or general contractor should always consult an attorney immediately upon discovery of the mistake.

HOLDING THE GENERAL CONTRACTOR TO HIS PROMISE

The prime contractor occasionally finds himself forced into court by a disgruntled subcontractor who, because of negotiations, had expected to be awarded a subcontract only to see it go to another. These cases by subcontractors against shopping contractors generally have been based on two theories: (1) that the contractor by his actions (primarily by using the subcontractor's bid in computing his own total estimate) has accepted the bid of the subcontractor and has thereby entered into a contract; or (2) that preaward conversations and negotiations constitute an oral contract. The courts have been notably unsympathetic to both theories, and a subcontractor entering upon any such action can do so with the melancholy assurance that his will be an uphill battle.

Acceptance by Use of the Subcontractor's Bid

Courts generally require something more than mere use of a subcontractor's bid before finding that acceptance of the subcontractor's bid has occurred.

Illustrative Case

Lionel F. Favret, an electrical subcontractor, required that if his estimate were relied on in the prime's bid, he must be wired on the date of the bid opening that his bid had been used. His bid was indeed used and Joe Williams, the prime, so wired Favret; but the court found that even the exchange of telegrams did not constitute the requisite acceptance for an enforceable contract to arise. [26]

Bid-listing requirements[27] provided additional examples of how stringently the courts interpret the necessity for a clear and unequivocal acceptance before allowing the subcontractor to recover for loss of the subcontract.

Illustrative Cases

Corbin-Dykes Electric Company had been listed by Burr & Sons Construction Company, the general contractor. When Burr subsequently awarded the subcontract to another subcontractor, Corbin-Dykes brought suit. The court held that the acceptance necessary for an enforceable contract to come into existence could not be established either by the general contractor's use of the bid in his own prime bid or by reference to trade custom that the listed subcontractor would receive the contract. The court ruled that trade custom and usage are admissible only where an existing agreement is ambiguous as to the intent of the parties; here, there was no mutual agreement between the parties to interpret. [28]

[26] Williams v. Favret, 161 F.2d 822 (5th Cir. 1947).

[27] See p. 28 infra.

[28] Corbin-Dykes Electric Co. v. Burr, 18 Ariz. App. 101, 500 P.2d 632 (1972).

The general contractor, Merritt-Chapman and Scott Corporation, listed subcontractor Gunderson Brothers Engineering Corporation in its bid for construction of a dam; further, it advised Gunderson in an unsolicited communication that its bid had been used. Negotiations about additional equipment and obligations were undertaken, and in the prime contract as finally executed by MCS, Gunderson was again named as supplier of all the particular equipment involved. A month later the subcontract was awarded to another bidder. The court would not allow Gunderson to recover, on the basis that the contractor had never clearly accepted Gunderson's offer but instead had been involved in further negotiations which amounted merely to a counteroffer. The listing of Gunderson was of no legal effect. [29]

An exception to this rule arises in a situation where a subcontractor, on the basis of such negotiations and informal agreements, proceeds with the work with the full knowledge and apparent consent of the general contractor.

Illustrative Case

Milone & Tucci, Inc., an Illinois subcontractor that was listed as electrical subcontractor, was subsequently asked by Bona Fide Builders, Inc., the general contractor, to lower its bid. When Milone & Tucci refused, Bona Fide filed with the GSA a request to change the subcontractor; the request was denied. The subcontractor eventually commenced work with the knowledge and consent of the general contractor. When Bona Fide claimed that their dealings had been only negotiations and that no contract could arise because there had been no meeting of the minds, the court held that Bona Fide's actions had unambiguously indicated the existence of a contract. [30]

Under the limited fact situation where a contractor has allowed and perhaps encouraged a subcontractor to perform, the contractor will not be permitted to evade his obligation by claiming that he had not formally accepted the subcontractor's offer. Neither a written offer and acceptance nor the oral counterparts are essential to establishing a contractual relationship where unambiguous conduct clearly manifests an intention to contract.

To the subcontractor, there seems an obvious unfairness in allowing a prime contractor to hold the subcontractor to his bid price on the basis of justifiable reliance (promissory estoppel) while denying the subcontractor the right to prevent the prime contractor from changing to another subcontractor. The courts have admitted the unfairness but have justified it on the basis of reliance. Reasoning that the subcontractor, when making a bid, should reasonably anticipate that if his bid is the lowest, the prime will use it and rely on it, the courts have found that such reliance requires that the subcontractor honor his bid. On the other hand, the subcontractor is not the victim of any such reliance because in the normal situation he has no idea of whether the general contractor will win the award or whether his own bid will be the lowest. The absence of such reliance removes the compulsion for enforcing the contract. When the subcontractor can prove reliance, as in the case discussed previously

[29] Merritt-Chapman & Scott Corp. v. Gunderson Bros. Engineering Corp., 305 F.2d 659 (9th Cir. 1962).

[30] *Accord,* Milone & Tucci, Inc. v. Bona Fide Builders, Inc., 301 P.2d 759 (Wash. 1956).

where he has entered upon performance or at least commenced substantial preparations for performance, the courts will generally bind the general contractor.

Existence of Oral Contracts

The reluctance of courts to accept preaward communications between prime contractor and subcontractor as anything more than mere negotiations has already been discussed.[31] However, even should the subcontractor and the prime contractor reach full oral agreement on all terms of their arrangements and enter into an oral contract, problems would still exist should the subcontractor wish to go to court to enforce the contract. In most states there are laws, generally referred to as the "Statute of Frauds," which require certain types of agreements to be in writing before the courts will enforce them. Generally, these statutes preclude enforcement of any contract if it cannot reasonably be performed and completed within one year. The Statute of Frauds is primarily intended to require evidence of oral contracts where the parties may later disagree as to exactly what was decided. The reason usually advanced for the exception of contracts to be performed within one year is that contracts to be performed within a short time offer less opportunity for memories to become clouded and disputes to arise.

Illustrative Case

Premier Electrical Construction Company, a subcontractor that had bid on part of a project at the Argonne National Laboratories in Illinois was told orally that its bid was "very interesting," but Miller-Davis Company, the general contractor, also intimated that it wanted some "protection" on the subcontractor's price. Premier agreeably submitted higher bids to the contractor's competitors, seeking to ensure that Miller-Davis would get the contract. There were continuing conversations in which the subcontractor was assured that his bid was low and that he would be awarded the subcontract. He sued when the contractor awarded the subcontract to another firm. Although Miller-Davis's official admitted that there had been an "agreement," the court found that the dealings between the parties did not possess requisites of a formal contract. The court reiterated what seems to be the feeling of virtually all courts which have considered the problem: In a contract where performance, together with any warranties, would last longer than a year, enforceable acceptance of a subcontractor's bid generally occurs only when a written contract specifically setting out the terms of the agreement is executed.[32]

Most construction contracts include a provision for a one-year warranty, and if the parties have indeed reached agreement on all the material terms (a requisite for finding that an oral contract exists in the first place), they most likely will have agreed to such a warranty. The time for performance plus the one-year warranty which begins on completion

[31] See p. 8 supra.

[32] Premier Elec. Constr. Co. v. Miller-Davis Co., 422 F.2d 1132 (7th Cir. 1970).

of the work puts virtually all construction contracts beyond the exemption and thus makes them unenforceable should one of the parties later renege on its obligations.

The Uniform Commercial Code (UCC), which applies to a supplier who furnishes only goods and not services,[33] also has a Statute of Frauds provision of which the subcontractor should be aware. It provides:

> Except as otherwise provided in this section a contract for the sale of goods for the price of $500 or more is not enforceable by way of action or defense unless there is some writing sufficient to indicate that a contract for sale has been made between the parties and signed by the party against whom enforcement is sought or by his authorized agent or broker. A writing is not insufficient because it omits or incorrectly states a term agreed upon. The contract is not enforceable under this paragraph beyond the quantity of goods shown in such writing.[34]

Because of these limitations, in every situation where it is possible the subcontractor should obtain some sort of writing. Although the most complete protection is obviously the executed formal contract, something less than an elaborate document can be used in certain cases to establish the existence of a sufficiently specific agreement for enforcement. A short letter or memorandum signed by the party listing the agreed price and any other major terms not included in the specifications, drawings, and statement of conditions, together with a copy of the bid documents, should make the contract enforceable against the prime contractor. In the case of a supplier of goods, the UCC provides that should the supplier send some written confirmation of the oral contract to the purchaser (for example, a purchase order), that writing is sufficient to establish an enforceable contract unless written notice of objection to its contents is given within 10 days after receipt.[35]

As discussed previously, even a purely oral contract can be enforced should the subcontractor (with the full knowledge of the general contractor) commence the work agreed on.

The subcontractor and the general can give some structure and stability to their negotiations if the subcontractor will submit his bid on a carefully drawn bid-proposal form. Such a form should specifically list the conditions governing the bid and should detail those circumstances which will constitute acceptance of the bid, for example, beginning work.

It should be obvious from the foregoing discussion that the effectiveness of the individual subcontractor in holding the general contractor to an anticipated contract is minimal at best. The more promising solution seems to be in such collective action of the subcontractors as the bid-listing procedures, which will be examined next.

---

[33]See note 38 infra. p. 23
[34]Uniform Commercial Code § 2-201(1).
[35]Id., § 2-201(2).

BID SHOPPING

The building construction industry has changed greatly from the time when the general contractor performed most of the construction work as a master builder who directly hired employees of the various crafts to do the work. Today the general contractor performs almost no work directly with his own forces but subcontracts practically all the work to specialty subcontractors who actually perform the construction; he has become, in effect, a broker of construction subcontracts.

It is the theory of the present system that procurement of construction contracts is based on a competitive bidding system in which the lowest responsible bidder will be awarded the subcontract by the general contractor. Unfortunately, the actual result is often different because of the controversial practice known as "bid shopping." Upon being awarded the contract, the general contractor has vastly improved his bargaining position; he now completely controls the market for that particular project. The superior position of the general contractor after the award has been made to him was summed up by a federal judge of the United States Circuit Court of Appeals for the Fifth Circuit, whose opinion explains:

The prime contractor is in peculiarly favorable position to impose upon those who would enter into subcontracts with him burdensome agreements as to arbitration. The number of subcontractors from which the prime contractor may choose is limited only by the scope of the industry, while would-be subcontractors must seek the nod of a single prime contractor, who is in that respect a complete monopolist.[36]

After the award of the general contract the general contractor has made a commitment to do the total job at the given price, and it is to his financial advantage to bid-shop for subcontract prices lower than those he received prior to determining his total contract price. Any lower prices that the general contractor may receive in this process of shopping his lowest bid from subcontractor to subcontractor represent windfall profits which will accrue to him alone because the savings will not be passed on to the awarding authorities.

Subcontractors sometimes voluntarily attempt to meet or better the lowest subcontract price submitted without waiting to be shopped. These activities are typically labeled "bid peddling." Practically speaking, bid shopping and bid peddling often coexist in the same situation and are but different sides of the same coin.

It is clear that there are situations in which the prime contractor may engage in bid shopping for reasons which go beyond a mere wish to increase the profitability of the project. For example, the contractor may desire to deal with a particular subcontractor who has not previously submitted a bid, or he may find that his lowest bid comes from a subcontrac-

---

[36] Electronic & Missile Facilities, Inc. v. United States *ex rel.* H.W. Moseley, 306 F.2d 554, 559 (5th Cir. 1962).

tor of borderline reliability. Indeed, the contractor may have *anticipated* bid shopping and computed his bid on prices lower than those he received. In such a situation, his bid price may approximate what he will actually have to pay out to his subcontractors and he will enjoy no resulting "windfall profits." Some general contractors and authorities go further and defend bid shopping as being a form of vigorous price competition in keeping with national antitrust policies. It should be pointed out, however, that the practical results of the procedure, in fact, greatly impair the efficiency of the bidding system as a means of market competition. The adverse results of bid shopping can be categorized as follows:[37]

1. Subcontractors who are involved in situations where shopping is permitted often quote higher prices on subcontracts because they know they are likely to be shopped. This method of pricing does not represent the subcontractor's real price which would be based directly on his estimated cost of labor and materials plus a reasonable markup for overhead and profit; the total bids have instead been distorted by an artificial inflation because of padded subcontract bids.

2. The preparation of a bid involves the time and cost of analyzing the requirements of the project and of estimating the price of materials and labor. Bid shopping increases the risk of loss of that investment of time and money since parties engaged in bid shopping or peddling may use bid quotations prepared by others for bargaining purposes without troubling to prepare their own independent quotations. Apart from the unfairness to one who has gone to the expense of preparing his own bid, this practice of submitting what is essentially a blind and uninvestigated bid can be a matter of excessive and unwise risk to the subcontractor bidder.

3. General contractors are desirous of obtaining subcontractor bids in sufficient time to prepare their own bids for submission to the awarding authority; however, the fear of preaward bid shopping frequently causes subcontractors to withhold their bids until the last moment, thus handicapping the general contractor in preparation for his own bid. This practice can also lead to errors in bids.

4. Some subcontractors refuse to submit bids on those jobs on which they expect bid shopping. To that extent, competition among subcontractors is reduced and the result may be higher subcontract prices.

5. The subcontractor who is the victim of successful bid shopping may well be forced into a choice between doing the job at a loss or resorting to substandard workmanship. The owner—or the public, in the case of government contracts—may receive shoddy construction from a subcontractor motivated by shopping procedures to cut the cost of construction below that which he originally anticipated. In terms of ultimate cost, a low price below the sale price standard may turn out to be the highest price of all. Cutting prices to the point where they are below cost is in most circumstances proscribed by the antitrust laws; but it is clear that this legal remedy has often been inadequate to protect subcontractors from being victimized by the price cutting of their competitors.

[37] Schueller, *Bid Depositories*, 58 MICH. L. REV. 497 (1960); Comment, *Bid Shopping and Peddling in the Subcontract Construction Industry*, 18 U.C.L.A. L. REV. 389 (1970).

In any system which tolerates substantial bid shopping, the owner does not receive the benefit of competitive prices offered on the bid date. It is the price of the subcontracts which ultimately determine the cost of the project. The general contractors merely add competitive percentages to cover their overhead and profits. It is the subcontractors who add contingencies into their contract bids, which may widely vary the costs. It is the subcontractors' bids which dictate whether the owner can realize an economic savings on the cost of the construction. Where bid shopping prevails, it is the general contractor who gets the benefit of the subcontractor's ultimate price rather than the subcontractor's arbitrary price submitted on the bid date in anticipation of shopping. The price agreed upon after all the shopping is over is purely an arbitrary price and may or may not approach the subcontractor's best price. Whether the final price is above or below the subcontractor's best price, the owner has been victimized by what is essentially an inefficient system. If the ultimate price is too high, it simply means that the owner is paying more than he should for the particular work. If the ultimate price is below the fair subcontract price standard, the loss may be greater because of the substandard workmanship which may accompany the low price.

Even if the general contractor, in anticipation of bid shopping, bases his bid on what he thinks the ultimate prices will be for the various subcontractors, this method of pricing is arbitrary and never represents the subcontractor's real price based upon estimated cost of labor and materials plus a reasonable markup for overhead and profit.

Negotiations for bid shopping and bid peddling, which may go on for days, weeks, and even months after the bid date to the owner, effectively mitigate against realistic competitive bidding on the bid date.

THE CURES FOR BID SHOPPING

There have been various attempts in the industry to suppress or prevent the practice of bid shopping. Those efforts, with their successes and limitations, will be discussed below under three headings: individual ethics; bid depositories; and federal and state legislation, which may take the form of required bid listing, bid filing, or separate contracts.[38]

---

[38] Although some commentators have suggested the Uniform Commercial Code as a solution for those problems troubling the formation of construction contracts, this suggestion is not treated here because its usefulness is severely limited by two considerations: (1) the UCC regulates only the sale of *goods* whereas the vast majority of construction contracts involve services as well; (2) the UCC's most effective strictures are dependent on the existence of a signed writing, a requirement which is often lacking where subcontract bids are telephoned in at the last moment.

Ethics

The Associated General Contractors of America have in the past condemned bid shopping as unethical in their Code of Ethical Conduct.[39] The pertinent provisions regarding subcontracts read, in part, as follows:

Ethical conduct with respect to subcontractors and those who supply material requires that:

1. Proposals should not be invited from anyone who is known to be unqualified to perform the proposed work or to render the proper service.

2. The figures of one competitor shall not be made known to another before the award of the subcontract, nor should they be used by the contractor to secure a lower proposal from another bidder.

3. The contract should preferably be awarded to the lowest bidder if he is qualified to perform the contract but if the award is made to another bidder, it should be at the amount of the latter's bid.

4. In no case should the low bidder be led to believe that a lower bid than his has been received.

Apparently subparagraphs 2 to 4 draw no distinction as to when the bargaining occurs; shopping is condemned whether it occurs before or after the award of the contract to the prime contractor. Subparagraph 4 criticizes what is generally conceded to be the most flagrant abuse of proper bidding practices, that is, the case where a prime contractor misrepresents that he has a bid lower than a particular subcontractor's bid and in an effort to win the subcontract the subcontractor reduces his price in reliance on the misrepresentation. The American Architect's *Handbook* has in the past similarly disapproved of bid shopping.[40]

Unhappily, it is obvious that adherence to such canons of ethics is voluntary and that ethics in an industry such as construction will be situational at best. The question of sanctions for violators of such codes, which have been seen by some as restricting price competition, is a thorny one; there are antitrust problems in trying to coerce contractors into bidding a certain way. The result of these difficulties has been that such intraindustry codes have been largely ineffective in halting the problems arising from bid shopping. Individual subcontractors have been able to mitigate bid shopping by simply refusing to submit bids to those contractors known to be bid shoppers.

Bid Depositories

Perhaps the earliest organized approach to curb bid shopping was the creation of local "bid depositories" for subcontractor bids. The depositories are aimed at eliminating bid shopping completely, both before and

---

[39] Code of Ethical Conduct (1947).

[40] III American Institute of Architects, *Handbook of Architectural Practice* 702 (1958).

after the awards to the prime contractor. A bid depository, though its details may vary with the group creating it, is essentially a facility created and operated by a trade association (or occasionally by an independent agency such as a bank) to collect subcontractor bids and make them uniformly available at a stated time to general contractors.

The mechanics of the operation of the bid depository capitalize on the combined bargaining strength of the subcontractors. Bids for any given project are sent to the depository a short time prior to the date set by the general contractor or awarding authority for the opening and award of subcontracts. The depository keeps the submitted bids confidential until the time of the bid opening, when it opens and tabulates the quotations. The bids are then made known to all subcontractors participating in the depository, with the result that any subsequent bid shopping and bid peddling will be obvious. This form, which is the more common, is known as a "pigeon-hole" depository. A "publishing" depository publishes a list of the subcontractor bid prices which were submitted. This increase in bargaining strength, which bid depositories afford, however, has frequently been challenged as a restraint of free competition under the antitrust laws. Although the prevention of bid shopping and bid peddling may be desirable, the courts and commentators have consistently pointed out some of the legal pitfalls endemic in less ethical depositories, such as price fixing, boycotts, and allocating markets or customers.

Since the 1950s it has been established that a subcontract depository may involve interstate commerce and thus be subject to federal regulation under the Sherman Act. Should a depository be found violative of the antitrust laws, it may be subject to several types of legal proceedings:

1. Civil or criminal action by the Federal Trade Commission or the Antitrust Division of the Department of Justice;

2. Proceedings by state enforcement agencies where state law provides for such sanctions;

3. Treble damage suits by competitors who claim to have been harmed by the activities of the depository.

In the cases where the Antitrust Division has challenged these bid depositories, certain features or effects of the depositories' operations have been repeatedly cited as unreasonable restraints of trade.[41] In the formation of a bid depository, care should be taken to avoid any of these characteristics.

Restraints on Free Price Competition

Depository participants have been prosecuted at various times for flatly agreeing on a fixed price, agreeing to exchange bids to permit price com-

[41] Schueller, *supra* note 37.

parison, using a formula to obtain uniform prices, permitting the depository to eliminate certain low bids, and conspiring to monopolize the market. Wherever depository procedures, either by their own terms or through their effect, result in direct interference with independent, competitive pricing, the bid depository is clearly vulnerable to attack under the antitrust laws.

Coercion or Boycott

Depository regulations have frequently prohibited general contractors who use their services from procuring bids from any other source. Alternatively, they have imposed fines or other penalties upon nonconforming contractors. These regulations have been aimed directly at eliminating bid shopping among nonmember subcontractors. However, since group boycotts to exclude others from a market are per se illegal under the Sherman Act, such exclusionary or compulsory provisions which exclude nonparticipants from at least part of the market will be found offensive. A depository arrangement which is compulsory on members may be open to attack on a principle announced by the U.S. Supreme Court: freedom of trade for the individual to conduct business in his own way. Wherever the effect of a combination is to limit and restrict the right of each of the members to transact business in his ordinary way, the combination is vulnerable to attack.[42]

Allocation of Markets or Customers

If subcontractors reach a determination in advance as to which subcontractor is to serve certain markets or specific customers, there is obviously no opportunity for truly competitive bidding. Such an agreement is virtually certain to be adjudged a per se violation of the Sherman Act because it is both exclusionary and in restraint of trade.

Participation by Other Groups in Restraint of Trade

Depositories have often buttressed the collective strength of their own members with that of their suppliers, customers, or labor groups. Where a depository has persuaded other groups to withhold their services from contractors failing to obey the depository rules, the restrictive effect is obvious and challengeable.

In a recent discussion with a client who was trying to formulate procedures to govern a proposed bid depository, the author was vainly trying to explain these pitfalls and the sometimes complicated legal theories behind them. On being met with protestations from the client that he could not understand the theories, the author offered a simplified ex-

---

[42] Addyston Pipe & Steel Co. v. United States, 175 U.S. 211 (1899).

planation: "What I am saying is that if you do these things, you'll go to jail." Came the reply: "Now *that* I understand."

The question remains of whether an effective bid depository may be formed which avoids the anticompetitive results discussed previously. The consent decrees issued in the majority of litigated cases have prohibited continued operation of the depositories *in a manner which objectionably restrains competition;* that is, they stop short of prohibiting depositories completely. These decrees can be read as conceding at least a possibility that some form of bid depository might be designed which would escape prosecution under the antitrust laws. Indeed, in one civil antitrust case[43] a depository operation at first judged restrictive was modified and resubmitted to the court for its approval. The depository succeeded in modifying its plan to meet the objections of the court and accordingly received approval.

But perhaps the more representative cases illustrate the pitfalls in attempting to create a totally legal, yet effective, bid depository.

Illustrative Case

Harold Christiansen, a member of the Mechanical Contractors Bid Depository, became dissatisfied with the rules of the depository and resigned. Later, after losing a subcontract to a depository member whom he had underbid, he brought suit under the Sherman Act against the depository for treble damages. The depository argued that its purpose was to prevent bid shopping and bid peddling, not to eliminate competition. The court found fault with the regulation that general contractors could not accept bids from a source other than the depository and that there could be no direct negotiations between subcontractors using the depository and prime contractors. The sanctions for disciplining violators—expulsion or fines for subcontractors and refusal of service for prime contractors—also came under attack. The court found that the depository's rules constituted an agreement in restraint of interstate commerce and an attempt to monopolize part of the interstate commerce in violation of the Sherman Act, and awarded the petitioner treble damages.[44]

It becomes clear from the discussion above that the bid-depository concept involves extremely serious antitrust problems. The practical consequence which concerns most subcontractors is that those provisions subject to antitrust challenge imbue the depository with its real effectiveness. If those provisions are deleted in order to avoid becoming entangled with antitrust litigation—for example, if the depository depends upon public knowledge rather than penalties to ensure compliance and if there is no requirement that persons deal exclusively through the depository— the depository's success in combatting bid shopping is weakened. It is for that reason that depositories represent a less than comprehensive answer to the problem.

[43] United States v. Bakersfield Associated Plumbing Contractors, Inc., 1958 TRADE CAS. ¶ 69,087, *modified,* 1959 TRADE CAS. ¶ 69,266.

[44] Mechanical Contractors Bid Depository v. Christiansen, 352 F.2d 817 (10th Cir. 1965), *cert. denied,* 384 U.S. 918 (1966). *Accord,* People v. Inland Bid Depository, 233 Cal. App. 2d 851, 44 Cal. Rptr. 206 (1965).

Subcontractors have regularly pushed for federal construction legislation which would control bid shopping. However, any such federal bills have been strenuously and consistently opposed by general contractors with the result that no legislation has succeeded in passing. In the awarding of contracts by the federal government, the General Services Administration (GSA), the Department of Health, Education and Welfare, and the Department of the Interior by regulation require the listing of subcontractors in the bids of general contractors. The pertinent sections of the GSA requirement are as follows:

Section 5B-2.202-70   Listing of subcontractors.

(a) Except as otherwise provided in paragraphs (b) and (c) of this section, invitation for bids shall require the bidder to name the principal subcontractors (or his own firm when it will perform the work). Contracting officers shall determine the categories of work for which subcontractors' names are to be submitted. The mechanical, electrical, and elevator and/or escalator divisions of the project specifications shall be included in the subcontractor listing by title and section numbers. In addition, such listing shall include, by titles and section numbers, all other general construction categories of work in the project specifications which, individually, are determined by the contracting officer to comprise at least three and one-half percent of the estimated cost of the entire contract; categories estimated to cost less shall not be included. . . .

(b) The requirement to name subcontractors is not applicable to separate contracts for phased construction where individual categories of work are bid separately. . . .

(c) The requirement to name subcontractors shall not be included in invitations for bids on new construction contracts not estimated to exceed $150,000 or on alteration contracts not estimated to exceed $500,000. It may be omitted from invitations for bids on contracts estimated to exceed such amounts if determined by the contracting officer to be clearly inappropriate, provided that such determinations are documented and retained in the contract file.[45]

Then, in a lengthy clause, the GSA regulations prohibit substitution of subcontractors except under limited conditions; but that clause also contains a disclaimer that the listing clause creates any property rights or cause of action for the prime contractor or the subcontractor. Several states also have legislation requiring the listing of subcontractors whose bids have been used.[46] These listing requirements are primarily aimed at curbing bid shopping.

The Comptroller General has actively enforced the listing requirement. He has refused to award a contract to the low bidder where the contractor failed to list his subcontractors;[47] and on an even closer question,

[45] 41 C.F.R. § 5B-2.202-70 (1976).

[46] See, e.g., Cal. Gov't. Code § 4104 (West Supp. 1976); Mass. Ann. Laws ch. 149, §§ 44A-E (1976); N.J. Stat. Ann. § 52:32-2 (Supp. 1976); N.Y. State Fin. Law § 138 (McKinney 1940).

[47] 43 Comp. Gen. 206.

where the general contractor accidentally failed to name one subcontractor for a specific category of work, the Comptroller General determined that the omission was of a material nature and sufficient to cause the bid not to be responsive.[48]

The state and federal regulations limit shopping to some degree because the consent of the awarding authority is required for any change; but the courts have generally agreed that the statutes confer no legal rights upon the subcontractor who is so listed. The statutes have been interpreted as intended to protect the public and the awarding authority rather than the subcontractor.

Illustrative Case

An insulation subcontractor, Cortland Asbestos Products, Inc., was listed in the general's bid only to be later informed that the subcontract was being awarded to someone else. He sued the general contractor, J. & K. Plumbing & Heating Company, for the bid price. The court refused relief, noting that any communication by the general contractor about the subcontractor's bid had been only to the awarding authority and not to the subcontractor. Because J. & K. had not notified Cortland directly of acceptance of its bid, no contract arose merely because of the listing.[49]

California is a state which has allowed the subcontractor substantive rights under the listing provision. Although early decisions follow the traditional interpretation that listing of subcontractors was not aimed at conferring rights on the subcontractor but at protecting the public and the awarding authority, a later case holds that where a listed subcontractor is denied the contract for any reason other than that he is unable or unwilling to perform, a cause of action arises against the prime contractor.[50] It is important to emphasize, however, that the court based its opinion on a California statute, the Subletting and Subcontracting Fair Practices Act,[51] which specifically stated that its provisions, including a listing requirement, were intended to end bid shopping and protect subcontractors. States which do not have such a specific statute may be reluctant to adopt this liberal California view; but the California legislation offers a model for other states who wish to offer more protection to subcontractors.

Although some subcontractors have faulted bid listing as an incomplete remedy because it has no effect on preaward bid shopping, for that very reason it is immune from the antitrust challenges which have so plagued bid depositories. Listing does not impede normal competition between subcontractors or interfere with negotiations prior to the award of the contract to the general contractor.

[48] 46 Comp. Gen. 156.

[49] Cortland Asbestos Products, Inc. v. J. & K. Plumbing & Heating Co., 304 N.Y.S.2d 694 (App. Div. 1969).

[50] Southern California Acoustics Co. v. C.V. Holder, Inc., 456 P.2d 975, 79 Cal. Rptr. 319 (1969).

[51] Cal. Gov't. Code §§ 4100–13 (West 1966 Supp. 1976).

Another statutory approach to reducing bid shopping and bid peddling on public contracts is required bid filing with the awarding authority. Massachusetts and Connecticut have such laws.[52] Under these systems, sub-bidders file their bids with the awarding authority, which rejects any nonresponsive bids. The awarding authority sends the general contract bidders a list of the acceptable sub-bidders and the amounts of their bids. The sub-bidders are bound by the submitted figure to every general bidder not specifically excluded; any variance from that bid is void. The general bidders then use the sub-bids they choose and list them on their bid forms. Substitutions must be agreed to. Only if there is no sub-bid for a particular category may the general bidder list an indefinite sub-bidder. This approach combines the features of bid depositories and bid listing.

The third statutory method of curbing bid shopping in public contracts is to invite separate bids on certain portions of the project. The awarding authority thus deals directly with the various phases to be separately contracted. Bid shopping is entirely eliminated for the separately awarded specialty contracts. Under the North Carolina statute[53] for contracting totaling over $20,000 separate specifications must be prepared and a separate bidding procedure must be used for the following specialties: (1) heating, ventilating, and air conditioning; (2) plumbing and gas fittings; (3) electrical installations; and (4) refrigeration for cold storage. If the allocation for any category is less than $2,500, then it may be combined with the general contract.

Separate contracting directly with specialty subcontractors is widely used by private owners. Although at present the state and federal legislation affects only public construction, it should be possible to adapt the government listing or bid filing requirements to the circumstances of private construction. Should subcontractors succeed in so expanding the scope of the listing requirement, it may offer the most acceptable weapon against bid shopping. Listing is a practical approach which solicits the actual ultimate price of the subcontractors on the bid date and ensures that this real price will be passed on to the awarding authority at the time of the bid. Experience has shown that whatever its limitations, in actual practice bid listing does inhibit bid shopping to a considerable degree because the awarding authority typically does not agree freely to substitutions.

[52] Conn. Gen. Stat. Ann. § 4–1373–f (West 1969 Supp. 1976); Mass. Ann. Laws ch. 149, § 44A (Michie/Law. Co-op 1976).

[53] N.C. Gen. Stat. § 143–128 (1974 Supp. 1975).

2 GENERAL CONTRACTS

INTRODUCTION

In recent years the role of many general contractors has evolved from that of master builder, who actually built an entire project by directly hiring the labor and purchasing and installing the materials, to that of manager and coordinator of all the different types of construction work that must go into a project. The construction work itself is now performed substantially by specialty contractors and subcontractors. Today's general contractor no longer attempts to be an expert in all the different trades, and he parcels out much of the work to separate subcontractors, each specializing in his own particular trade. By subcontracting, the general contractor also shifts the legal responsibility for performance of each portion of the work to the specialty subcontractor and establishes a firm price for each portion of the subcontracted work.

There are several areas of basic concern to a general contractor which should be covered in his contract with an owner. The general contractor must have an adequate amount of money due and payable at the proper time to enable him to finance the work of each of his subcontractors as well as the work which he will perform directly. The general contract must specify the amount, method, and time of payments to be made by the owner to the general contractor and the percentage of retention (if any) to be withheld from progress payments by the owner. The general contract must also specify accurately the scope of the work to be performed and the time within which the work must be completed. In addition, provisions are necessary to establish fair and precise procedures for handling changes in the work to be performed. Other provisions may include a definition of the rights of both parties upon a default or termination of the contract.

Two critical questions about the payment clause of particular importance to the general contractor are "How much money and when do I get it?" An even more important question is "Does the owner have the money available to pay when due?" Therefore, the ultimate consideration of a general contractor must be "Does the owner have adequate construction and permanent finances to meet all of the payments under the contract?"

It is common for the owner to require that the general contractor obtain a performance and payment bond to ensure the availability of funds for completion of the work and for the payment of bills in the event of a default by the general contractor. The general contractor has a similar need to know that the owner will be able to perform his obligations under the contract. He should therefore verify the source of funds required to make payments under the contract, including an allowance for change orders. The general contractor should virtually undress the owner to see if he has adequate financing available to pay for the construction, including change orders.

The contract should provide that the general contractor has the right to satisfactory financing evidence from the owner. For example, the information clause of the American Institute of Architects (AIA) General Conditions, Document A201 (1976 ed.), Article 3.2.1, provides:

3.2.1 The Owner shall, at the request of the Contractor, at the time of execution of the Owner-Contractor Agreement, furnish to the Contractor reasonable evidence that he has made financial arrangements to fulfill his obligations under the Contract. Unless such reasonable evidence is furnished, the Contractor is not required to execute the Owner-Contractor Agreement or to commence the Work.

In addition, Article 3.2.2 requires disclosure of information directed toward protecting the contractor's lien rights and alerting him to any restrictions he may overlook. This clause is of particular importance where the owner possesses the land under an option contract or a ground lease.

3.2.2 The Owner shall furnish all surveys describing the physical characteristics, legal limitations and utility locations for the site of the Project, and a legal description of the site.

In answer to the question "How much is the contractor to be paid?" the general contract must specify the total amount of payment to which the contractor will be entitled for performance of the construction. Although there are variations in payment clauses, there are three basic ways of calculating the compensation that the contractor will receive under the contract: a lump sum or fixed price, unit pricing, and cost plus a fee.

The construction work required to be performed by a contractor under the scope of work provision of the contract is the other side of the payment coin since the two are always joined together. Thus, a contractor must pay as much attention to those provisions in the general contract defining the scope of work as he does to those provisions concerning payment.

The question "When is the contractor paid?" involves progress payments, retention, and final payment. These payment terms govern whether the contractor will have an adequate amount of cash flow to cover his current costs and expenses during construction.

More recently the role of the general contractor, which evolved from master builder to construction broker, has evolved, on selected projects, to consultant employed by the owner as a construction manager. A construction manager normally is employed from the inception of the project and gives valuable advice to the owner concerning the design of the project, plans and specifications, and construction feasibility, as well as time, labor, materials, costs, and methods which will be needed. A construction manager may also supervise and coordinate the work of specialty contractors during the building of the project.

This development has special implications for the specialty contractor because, on a project with a construction manager, the specialty contractor may have a direct contractual relationship with the owner, and thus he must be aware of the legal considerations of construction general contracts. This chapter, therefore, is addressed to both general and specialty contractors.

Similarly it is important for subcontractors to be well informed about the provisions contained in contracts between the owner and the general contractor because quite often these provisions are made a part of subcontracts by reference; that is, the general contractor binds his subcontractors to all the obligations he assumes to the owner for the subcontractor's portion of the work. Subcontractors normally insist upon receiving the rights and remedies that the contractor has under his contract with the owner before agreeing to accept the responsibilities.

FIXED-PRICE CONTRACTS

The most common form of general contract is a lump-sum agreement in which the owner and general contractor agree to a fixed amount to be paid to the contractor for the performance of the entire contract work. The contractor takes the risk of being able to perform all the work for the amount specified in the contract. The general contractor's profit, if any, is realized by the difference between the lump-sum contract and the cost of the construction, including overhead and indirect costs. Therefore, the contractor must add an adequate amount to cover the risk of increased costs.

In estimating work under a fixed-price contract, the bidding contractor considers the worst conditions that might affect costs and relates those to the price he considers necessary to obtain the work through the low bid process. The owner normally pays lump-sum prices which are guarded to varying degrees maximum anticipated costs, whether or not the maximum costs are actually incurred. The contractor cannot usually receive any escalation of the contract prices for inflated costs if there is no escalation clause in the contract. However, this does not preclude the contractor from sustaining a claim for equitable adjustment in the event that his costs are increased by changes in the contract requirements, or by other acts of the owner and his agents.

Illustrative Case

A contractor, Blount Brothers Corporation, negotiated a labor agreement with the IBEW during the performance of a construction contract which increased its labor costs. Blount Brothers sought an increase in the contract price, claiming that the government

had promised to adjust the price. However, since there was no provision for escalation in the fixed-price contract, the contractor had to absorb the increase.[1]

To the extent competitive conditions allow, this risk factor must be contained in the general contractor's price to the owner. An owner typically desires a fixed-price general contract if he needs to fix a specific financial commitment for financing the project. A commonly used lump-sum contract is the AIA Standard Form of Agreement between Owner and Contractor, Document A101 (1974 ed.), which contains a lump-sum payment clause which simply states:

The owner shall pay the Contractor for the performance of the Work, subject to additions and deductions by Change Order as provided in the Conditions of Contract, in current funds, the Contract sum of _____.

Lump-sum payment provisions may be used in conjunction with a variety of flexible payment combinations. For example, the contract may provide that the fixed price be reduced if the contractor does not meet certain performance requirements, such as not completing the work within the contract time; or the contract may provide that the fixed price be increased if the contractor exceeds a performance standard.

When in 1908 the federal government wrote a contract for its first airplane, the performance specifications required that a "heavier than air flying machine" should fly 40 miles per hour carrying two passengers with a combined weight of 350 pounds and carry enough fuel for 125 miles. Payment was to be made on a lump-sum basis with an incentive that the lump sum would be increased 10 percent for every mile an hour that the plane flew in excess of 40 miles per hour or that the lump sum would be decreased by 10 percent for every mile an hour that the plane flew under 40 miles per hour. The Wright Brothers got the contract and built the plane, which flew 42 miles per hour. The government accepted and paid for the plane, and then the plane crashed.[2]

UNIT-PRICE CONTRACTS

Under unit pricing of construction general contracts, the general contractor is paid a fixed amount for each unit of work performed. To avoid disputes over how much work has in fact been performed, each "unit" of work must be precisely defined.

In using the unit-price method, the owner assumes the risk of the *amount* of work that is to be done. This includes the risk that the estimates of prospective work made by the owner or the architect are accurate and therefore that the total cost of the construction is accurately

[1] Appeal of Blount Bros. Corp., 1964 B.C.A. ¶ 4422 (1964).

[2] U.S. Signal Corp. Specification #486 (1908).

predicted. The contractor bears the risk that the *cost of each unit of work* will not rise above the unit prices specified in the contract.

When the general contractor bids on the units of work, he bases his price on the cost of performing the quantity of work anticipated. If, during the course of performance, the number of units of a particular type of work is substantially decreased, the cost per unit to the contractor will normally be much greater than contemplated. Conversely, if the amount of a particular unit of work is substantially increased, the contractor's cost per unit performed may decrease so that the original unit price becomes unfairly high. Some contract provisions, such as AIA General Conditions, AIA Document A201 (1976 ed.), in Article 12.1.5, call for an adjustment of unit prices when quantities to which the unit prices are applicable vary substantially:

12.1.5   If unit prices are stated in the Contract Documents or subsequently agreed upon, and if the quantities originally contemplated are so changed in a proposed Change Order that application of the agreed unit prices to the quantities of Work proposed will cause substantial inequity to the Owner or the Contractor, the applicable unit prices shall be equitably adjusted.

A construction contract may combine a basic lump-sum-payment method with a supplemental unit-price arrangement for certain types of work, such as rock excavation.

Illustrative Case

A contractor was engaged by the City of Jefferson, Missouri, to construct the parking facility for a lump sum, but the specifications also called for the use of unit prices if rock was encountered in the excavations. The bidders were to include "300 cubic feet of rock as part of the base bid . . .," and the contractor had bid a unit price of $2 per cubic foot for rock excavation of more than 300 cubic feet. The contract also contained the following clause: "Where the quantities originally contemplated are so changed than an application of the agreed unit of price to the quantity of work performed is shown to create a hardship to the owner or the contractor, there shall be an equitable adjustment of the contract to prevent such hardship." The City had been granted a directed verdict by the trial court on the basis of its argument that the contractor had failed to follow the procedures under the change clause of the contract in presenting its claim for rock excavation over 300 cubic feet. The appellate court reversed this directed verdict, holding that the contractor should be allowed to present evidence showing that the contract contemplated the use of unit prices outside of the formal change-order procedure.[3]

In order to obtain larger payments early during a construction project to help finance the remainder of the work, contractors sometimes bid disproportionately high unit prices on the work to be performed early and correspondingly low unit prices on subsequent work. The use of this practice may return to haunt the contractor in certain circumstances. If the owner decides to reduce the number of units of the early work, the

[3] Cure v. City of Jefferson, 396 S.W.2d 726 (Mo. 1965).

contractor will lose the entire unit-price compensation on the eliminated work, including the amount he had shifted to the early work from the later work. The owner may also use a change order to rearrange the work, which could upset the financing plans of the contractor.

COST-PLUS CONTRACTS

Under a cost-plus-a-fee-compensation arrangement, the owner pays the general contractor for costs necessarily incurred in the construction and either a fixed fee or a fee based on a percentage of the cost of construction. Using the cost-plus-a-fee contract, an owner assumes the risk of greater construction costs than originally estimated. The owner may desire to set an outside limit on this risk by requiring the general contractor to guarantee the maximum cost of the contract and thereby fix a limit on the amount of the owner's investment in the project. The cost-plus-a-fee contract is also useful to the owner who does not know at the time of contracting whether or not a construction project will be completed in full or who wishes to begin on the construction before the plans and specifications are finally completed. This method normally allows the contractor to accept a smaller profit margin than under a lump-sum contract because the contractor does not have to assume the risk of cost increases.

The addition of a maximum guaranteed cost provides a sharing of this risk by the parties, and the contractor must be able to determine from the plans and specifications if he can perform the work within the guaranteed maximum cost. Generally speaking, the contractor should expect the "upset price" to be higher than on a fixed-price basis because without a clause giving the contractor a share of the savings, these "not to exceed" contracts work solely for the benefit of the owner. Where there is no maximum-cost guarantee, the contractor's fixed or percentage fee simply reflects other factors such as management costs for the type of work and the hazards that are involved in its performance.

Another clause which may be inserted along with the guaranteed maximum cost is the savings clause. Using this combination the contractor is paid upon completion of the contract a certain percentage of the amount by which the actual cost of performance falls below the guaranteed maximum cost. This incentive is a bonus in addition to the contractor's fee. The contractor should be aware that legally there does not have to be a savings clause in a contract with a guaranteed maximum cost.

The main questions which should be resolved are proper language in the cost-plus-a-fee construction contract for identification of those costs that are reimbursable, those that are not reimbursable, and those that are included in the base figure from which the percentage fee is calculated. The reimbursable cost figure and base figure from which the percentage fee is calculated are not necessarily identical.

A cost-plus-a-fee contract must be very specific in setting out which costs are or are not included in the costs which the owner must reimburse the contractor. The costs to be reimbursed typically are specified to mean those necessarily incurred in the proper performance of the work, which include: wages, payroll taxes, and fringe benefits; cost of all materials, supplies, and equipment incorporated in the work, including transportation charges therefor; payments to subcontractors; rental and maintenance charges for all necessary equipment, trucks, and hand tools; cost of salaries for contractor's employees stationed at the field office or while they are expediting production or transportation of materials or equipment; proration of reasonable travel, meals, and hotel expenses of the officers or employees of the contractor directly incurred with the work; premiums of all bonds and insurance, seals, and use taxes related to the work; permit fees; minor expenses, such as telephone and telegraph costs, cost of temporary site facilities and removal of debris; and losses and expenses not compensated by insurance which result from causes other than the fault or negligence of the contractor.

Typically the costs not to be reimbursed are stipulated as: salaries or other compensation for the contractor's officers and employees while working at the contractor's main office or branch offices; expenses of the contractor's principal or branch offices other than the field office; any capital expenses including interest on the contractor's capital and any additional capital required to perform the work; all general overhead expenses; and costs due to negligence of the contractor, subcontractors, or anyone directly employed by the contractor.

The contractor should specify in great detail which costs are to be reimbursed, which costs are not reimbursable, and which costs and services are covered in the fee. The reason such care is necessary becomes apparent upon the examination of cases where the contract covered the matter in general terms only, such as "The contractor shall be paid the cost of the building plus 10 percent." The courts vary widely in what they consider the undefined term "costs" to mean. A frequent source of discrepancy is whether overhead is a cost or whether it is covered by the fee. Some courts consider the various components of overhead to be chargeable as costs,[4] whereas others reason that it is an indirect expense which is difficult to compute and should therefore be recovered through the fee.[5] Most courts do not consider general overhead to be a cost.

Labeling of items such as taxes and insurance is frequently a source of disagreement.

Illustrative Cases

The contract provided that the owner, Fireside Coffee Shop, pay the contractor, Herre Brothers, Inc., the actual cost of all labor, materials, and other proper charges specified in the contract plus 17 percent. The contract did not specify whether social security taxes, unemployment taxes, premiums on liability and workmen's compensation insur-

[4] Herre Bros., Inc. v. Rhoades, 208 Pa. Super. 357, 222 A.2d 486 (1966).
[5] Kubela v. Schuessler Lumber Co., 492 S.W.2d 92 (Tex. Civ. App. 1973).

ance, and union welfare contributions were costs within the meaning of the contract. Neither did the contract specify whether Fireside would be entitled to the benefit of cash discounts secured by the contractor for prompt payment of his bills and for quantity purchases of material. The trial court ruled that all of these items would not be reimbursed by the owner because they were not listed in the contract. The appellate court, however, stated that a new trial was necessary so that the intent of the parties could be determined on the subject of whether or not these items were to be reimbursed as costs.[6]

A cost-plus contract provided that "the contractor shall not be entitled to reimbursement for any amount for said overhead . . . ." The owner, Prom Town House Motor Inn, Inc., contended that taxes and insurance were part of overhead and that it was not obligated to reimburse the contractor, J. J. LaPuzza Construction Company, for these expenses. The court, however, considered that this contract provision was ambiguous in its meaning, and, therefore, construed it against the drafter, Prom Town House. The court stated: "Without specific reference in the contract we consider F.I.C.A. taxes, unemployment insurance, health and welfare insurance, and employer's contributions to pension funds within the ambit of wages and allowable as costs."[7]

Another problem area is the cost of subcontracted work where the owner pays the subcontractors directly. The issue is whether the general contractor may use this cost, which he did not pay, as a basis for computing the percentage fee. Where the general contractor does pay the subcontractors, the question arises whether the contractor may use the total price of the subcontract for computing his fee, or whether he must base his fee on the subcontract price minus the subcontractor's profit. In this area, the contractor usually, but not always, wins in court.

Illustrative Cases

The owner, F. E. Anderson, contended that under the terms of their agreement the contractor, B. F. Churchill, was to be paid only 10 percent of the cost of labor and materials used by him in performing the work which he did not subcontract. However, the court upheld the contractor by ruling that "the cost of the building" included the full cost of work performed by subcontractors.[8]

A contractor, J. J. Walsh & Sons, was allowed to charge a percentage of the actual material and labor furnished by subcontractors, but not of the profit of the subcontractors. The court held that otherwise the owner would be required to pay double commissions for profits.[9]

Another court held to the contrary of the previous case and allowed the general contractor to assess his percentage on the entire amount paid to subcontractors when the work was performed on a cost-plus basis.[10]

There is often controversy about which of the contractor's managerial employees' salaries are reimbursable as costs.

[6] Herre Bros., Inc. v. Rhoades, 208 Pa. Super. 357, 222 A. 2d 486 (1966).

[7] LaPuzza v. Prom Town House Motor Inn, Inc., 191 Neb. 687, 217 N.W.2d 472 (1974).

[8] Churchill v. Anderson, 128 F. Supp. 425 (W.D. Ky. 1955).

[9] Grafton Hotel Co. v. Walsh, 228 F. 5 (4th Cir. 1915).

[10] Hamilton v. Coogan, 28 N.Y.S. 21 (1894), aff'd, 148 N.Y. 753 (1896).

The general contractor, Clark County Construction Company, refused to pay the salary of the subcontractor's general manager who supervised the construction of the work, claiming that his compensation was covered by the subcontractor's fee. The court found that it was customary for the general contractor to reimburse the subcontractor for the salaries of those who superintended the construction work, and that if the general manager had not superintended the work, the contractor would have been forced to hire a supervisor whose salary Clark would have had to reimburse.[11]

The contractor, B. F. Churchill, contracted with Andy Anderson to build a theater, a drugstore, and three store buildings on a cost-plus-10-percent basis. In a suit for the balance due, Churchill claimed that he was entitled to recover as a cost the wages he paid to his son, Charles Churchill. Anderson claimed that because Charles was the contractor's son, he should be paid out of the contractor's 10 percent fee. The court, however, found that because Churchill was a working supervisor, his wages were reimbursable costs.[12]

The likelihood of disputes as to reimbursable expenses may be reduced significantly by setting forth in the contract, in very detailed terms, those items which are reimbursable costs. The AIA Cost Plus Contract, AIA Document A111 (1974 ed.) may be used as a guide. For example, Sections 8.1.2 and 9.1.1 specify that salaries of the contractor's employees who are stationed at the principal office or branch offices may not be charged to the owner, but that salaries of employees stationed at a field office, at shops, or on the road when expediting the performance of the contract, are chargeable as costs. Article 10 allows the contractor the benefit of cash discounts if the contractor obtains these with his own funds. If the owner provides the contractor with the funds to obtain the discount, however, only the discounted price and not the full price is used to compute the percentage fee. Trade discounts, rebates, and refunds, however, accrue to the owner, and the contractor is obligated to obtain them on behalf of the owner.

Another issue covered by the AIA Cost Plus Contract is whether casualty losses are reimbursable costs. Section 8.1.12 stipulates that losses and expenses that are not compensated by insurance or otherwise sustained by the contractor in connection with the work are generally to be reimbursed by the owner unless they are caused by the fault or negligence of the contractor. Thus, the contractor would not be reimbursed for defective work or property damage which he caused. Insured losses which are not the fault of the contractor are reimbursable. However, they are not included in the cost of the work for the purpose of determining the contractor's fee. The cost of reconstruction made necessary by such a loss would be included in the base cost for calculating the fee.

The primary advantage of a cost-plus contract to the contractor is that the owner, not the contractor, bears the risk of rising prices or unanticipated expenses for material and labor. The contractor need not be pre-

[11] Winston & Co. v. Clark County Constr. Co., 186 Ky. 743, 217 S.W. 1027 (1920).
[12] Churchill v. Anderson, 128 F. Supp. 425 (W.D. Ky. 1955).

occupied with inflation or with cutting costs in order to realize a profit. In fact, the effect is exactly the opposite where the fee is a percentage of the costs rather than a fixed sum—the higher the cost of construction, the greater profit the contractor makes. This lack of motivation by some contractors to minimize costs has given rise to the legal principle that a contractor may not charge the owner for any unreasonable expenses. Normally in cost-plus contracts there is a contractual statement that only reasonable and necessary costs will be reimbursed to the contractor. The owner has the right to expect the contractor to do the work efficiently and not to waste the owner's funds.

Illustrative Cases

K. P. Builders, engaged by Mr. and Mrs. Gilt to remodel their home, sued the owners for $6,650.76 allegedly due under a cost-plus contract. The court found that the entire amount of the claim represented the cost of "repetitive work caused by the ineptitude of the workmen . . ." and these costs were therefore unreasonable. The court held that the owners were not obligated to pay for such unreasonable costs.[13]

When Theodore Westendorf, the contractor, arbitrarily and unnecessarily raised the wage of a carpenter from $2.75 to the outrageously high wage (in 1905) of $3 per day, the court held that Westendorf could not charge the owner, Feral C. Dininny, for the increase because the contractor was bound to make the best terms he could for the repair of Dininny's house.[14]

The contractor, Thompson-Starrett Company, hired by Max Pam on a cost-plus-a-fee basis, performed construction work inefficiently with incompetent employees. The court stated that the contractor had done the work "in reckless disregard" of its obligation to use the same skill and ability as for work where its profit was dependent upon its ability to do the work at a cost less than the contract price. The court held that Thompson-Starrett would be paid only *reasonable* costs for performing that work plus a percentage.[15]

Section 8.1 of the AIA Cost Plus Contract requires that costs, to be reimbursable, must be "necessarily incurred in the proper performance of the Work."

In the absence of a challenge to the reasonableness of costs or to their proper categorization as costs, however, the owner is obligated to pay the total agreed price regardless of how high it is.

Illustrative Case

RCR Leasing and Harpring Sales and Erectors entered into a contract to construct the building for a car dealership. The contract called for the owner to pay Harpring its cost plus 10 percent and did not stipulate an upset price. Although costs rose far above RCR's expectations, they were required to fulfill their part of the bargain.[16]

[13] Kerner v. Gilt, 296 So. 2d 428, 432 (La. App. 1974).

[14] Westendorf v. Dininny, 103 App. Div. 593, 92 N.Y.S. 858 (1905).

[15] Title Guarantee & Trust Co. v. Pam, 155 N.Y.S. 333 (1915), aff'd, 182 N.Y.S. 824, aff'd, 232 N.Y. 441, 134 N.E. 525 (1922).

[16] RCR Leasing, Inc., v. Harpring Sales & Erectors, Inc., 474 S.W.2d 870 (Ky. App. 1972).

In order to place some of the risks of increased costs on the builder, some cost-plus contracts also set a maximum allowable figure, or an upset price. If the cost to complete the building exceeds this maximum, the contractor, not the owner, must pay the difference.

Illustrative Cases

Robinhorne Construction Corporation, Orin L. Robson, and Red Arrow Construction, Inc., a joint venture, undertook to construct a Howard Johnson motel and restaurant in Urbana, Illinois, for Jack Snyder. The contract provided for the contractors to be paid their cost plus 6 percent plus an additional fee. A maximum price of $1,018,700 including the 6 percent but excluding the fee was agreed upon. The joint venture encountered financial difficulties and extensive delays in their performance. It became clear to Snyder that they would not be able to complete the job within the maximum price set. For this reason and because of the delays and financial problems, Snyder terminated the contract and took over completion of construction. When the contractors challenged this action, the court upheld both the maximum price provision and the owner's right to terminate the contract. Snyder was awarded the difference between his actual costs incurred on the project and the agreed maximum price. [17]

Baldi Construction Engineering agreed to construct a building for Wheel Awhile, Inc., on a cost plus basis. Although no definite plans or specifications were included in the contract when it was executed, the parties had a verbal understanding that the contract price would be in the $160,000 range. Baldi proceeded to begin certain preliminary work on the construction. After the final plans and specifications were furnished to the contractor, Baldi presented the owner with an estimate of $230,651 for the project. Wheel Awhile thereupon canceled the project. When Baldi brought suit to enforce its right to perform the contract, the court held that the owner had been justified in cancellation because Baldi's estimate breached the agreement as to a maximum price. Baldi was allowed to recover only the fair value of the work that had already been done on the project. [18]

By contrast, unless the maximum price is clearly agreed upon as binding, the contractor may recover costs exceeding that amount.

Illustrative Case

J. E. Hathman, Inc., agreed to construct a fraternity house for Sigma Alpha Epsilon for cost plus 6 percent. The contract provided for an "[e]stimated maximum cost of . . . $300,000 . . ." and allowed the maximum cost to be adjusted in accordance with any changes ordered. Hathman completed the building in accordance with the contract and billed SAE for $413,276.97. SAE contended that the limit of its liability to Hathman was $300,000 plus 6 percent, or $318,000. Hathman, however, claimed that the maximum price was only an estimate and therefore was not binding. The court agreed because the meaning of "estimated" was unambiguous. [19]

PROGRESS PAYMENTS

The method of payment to the general contractor by the owner for work performed and the timing of such payment is naturally a vital consideration for the general contractor. The normal method is through monthly

[17] Robinhorne Constr. Corp. v. Snyder, 113 Ill. App. 2d 288, 251 N.E.2d 641 (1969).

[18] Baldi Constr. Engineering, Inc. v. Wheel Awhile, Inc., 263 Md. 670, 284 A.2d 248 (1971).

[19] J.E. Hathman, Inc. v. Sigma Alpha Epsilon Club, 491 S.W.2d 261 (Mo. 1973).

"progress payments" by the owner to the general contractor, representing the value of materials delivered and construction completed up to the time of submission of monthly requisition by the general contractor. The architect is often designated as the party to certify the amount of construction completed and money due the general contractor each month.

The general contractor is not expected to finance the entire construction by waiting until project completion for the entire contract sum to be paid, but neither is the owner expected to put the entire contract sum into the hands of the general contractor before the work has been completed. The methods of payment and timing of progress payments represent a balance between these competing interests. The construction industry operates on the premise that the buyer of the construction, the owner, substantially finances the construction. However, when we consider that contractors, subcontractors, and fabricators must often pay their workmen and material suppliers long in advance of reimbursement, they are, in fact, providing a large amount of construction financing.

There must be a provision in the contract that specifically entitles the contractor to receive progress payments. Without such a provision, the courts have held that the contractor has a right to payment of the lump sum of the contract only after completion of all the work.[20]

Under most construction contracts the contractor is entitled to receive progress payments from the owner as material is delivered and field labor performed. At the beginning of a project, the owner and contractor agree on a billing schedule containing dollar values for major components of the work. Payments are normally calculated on the basis of percentages of material and labor completed. If the contract compensation is on a cost-plus-a-fee basis, progress payments are made periodically based on direct costs incurred by the contractor plus some portion of the contractor's fee as negotiated by the parties.

The contract should provide a specified date on or before which the contractor will be paid each month. The contract should clarify whether the progress payments provision includes payment, not only for the percentage completion of the work in place, but also for materials and equipment suitably stored at the site or at an off-site location agreed to by the owner. A contractor who discovers belatedly that the progress payment clause in his contract does not include payment for stored materials and equipment may have a serious cash-flow problem. His material and equipment suppliers will expect payment as soon as materials are shipped to the jobsite. Yet, the contractor would not yet be entitled to progress payments covering these items and, therefore, would have to pay for stored materials and equipment with his own funds. This is particularly serious in those cases where a project falls well behind schedule, and a contractor must wait for a long period to install the material. It is doubly frustrating to a contractor who manufactures his

---

[20] Appeal of Emsco Screen Pipe Co., 69-1 B.C.A. ¶ 7710 (1969).

material because he has already financed the fabrication period and must then wait even longer to recover his out-of-pocket costs.

To obtain a progress payment, the contractor is generally required to submit to the architect or the owner a monthly requisition supported by detailed information to establish the contractor's right to payment consistent with the method called for in the contract. To aid the architect and owner in evaluating applications for payments, before submitting any application for progress payments, the contractor normally prepares a schedule of values of the various portions of the work. This schedule is used by the architect and owner as a basis for evaluating monthly applications for payment. The schedule of values may show that the contractor has used unbalanced bidding or other techniques to claim for unduly large progress payments at the beginning of construction, and the architect may adjust these to the extent he considers appropriate, thereby reducing early progress payments.

A typical progress payment provision is contained in the AIA General Conditions, AIA Document A201 (1976 ed.), Sections 9.3 to 9.5, which set out the contractor's obligation to submit applications for payment at least 10 days before each progress payment is due, together with substantiating information required by the architect or the owner. These sections also prescribe the architect's obligation to issue a certificate of progress payments properly due and the owner's obligation to make the payments certified by the architect:

9.3 Application for Payment

9.3.1 At least ten days before the date for each progress payment established in the Owner-Contractor Agreement, the Contractor shall submit to the Architect an itemized Application for Payment, notarized if required, supported by such data substantiating the Contractor's right to payment as the Owner or the Architect may require, and reflecting retainage, if any, as provided elsewhere in the Contract Documents.

9.3.2 Unless otherwise provided in the Contract Documents, payments will be made on account of materials or equipment not incorporated in the Work but delivered and suitably stored at the site and, if approved in advance by the Owner, payments may similarly be made for materials or equipment suitably stored at some other location agreed upon in writing. Payments for materials or equipment stored on or off the site shall be conditioned upon submission by the Contractor of bills of sale or such other procedures satisfactory to the Owner to establish the Owner's title to such materials or equipment or otherwise protect the Owner's interest, including applicable insurance and transportation for those materials and equipment stored off the site.

9.4 Certificates for Payment

9.4.1 The Architect will, within seven days after the receipt of the Contractor's Application for Payment, either issue a Certificate for Payment to the Owner, with a copy to the Contractor, for such amount as the Architect determines is properly due, or notify the Contractor in writing his reasons for withholding a Certificate as provided in Subparagraph 9.6.1.

9.4.2 The issuance of a Certificate for Payment will constitute a representation by the Architect to the Owner, based on his observations at the site as provided in Subparagraph

2.2.3 and the data comprising the Application for Payment, that the Work has progressed to the point indicated; that, to the best of his knowledge, information and belief, the quality of the Work is in accordance with the Contract Documents. . . .

9.5   Progress Payments

9.5.1   After the Architect has issued a Certificate for Payment, the Owner shall make payment in the manner and within the time provided in the Contract Documents.

If the owner fails to pay progress payments due the contractor, it may be considered a breach of the contract justifying the contractor to stop work if the payments missed represent a significant amount in relation to the entire contract.[21] The contractor, however, must follow the progress-payment application procedures in order to be entitled to his monthly payment.

Illustrative Case

A contractor, Moore & Morris Building Company, was engaged to build a theater under a contract which specified that progress payments would be made monthly in the amount of 85 percent of the architect's estimates of all materials delivered and paid for and which were incorporated in the building. These estimates were to be based on invoices presented to the architect by the contractor. Instead of presenting invoices, the contractor had given the architect approximations of the value of labor and material which may reasonably have been incorporated in the building. The court held that in order to satisfy the requirements of the contract, invoices were required rather than mere approximations.[22]

The owner may have the right to withhold progress payments otherwise due to the contract under certain circumstances enumerated in the contract or when liquidated damages for delay have accrued against the contractor. An issue often arises as to whether the owner may withhold progress payments in addition to the normal retention when the retention is of sufficient amount to protect the owner.

Illustrative Cases

Austin-Griffith, Inc., a contractor engaged by the Goldbergs to construct a building, failed to complete the building within the stipulated time, and liquidated damages at the rate of $50 a day began to accrue. The Goldbergs began to withhold progress payments after the completion date of the contract had passed. Even though the contract apparently contained no authorization for the owner to withhold progress payments, the court held that it would be inequitable to require the owner to pay the contract price to Austin-Griffith after the contractor had breached the contract by delaying performance and after the Goldbergs had suffered damages as a result of that delay. The court held that the owners were justified in withholding payments.[23]

---

[21] Guerini Stone Co. v. P. J. Carlin Constr. Co., 248 U.S. 334 (1919). The right to stop work for missed progress payments is discussed more thoroughly in the chapter on Remedies.

[22] Hall v. Union Indemnity Co., 61 F.2d 85 (8th Cir. 1932).

[23] Austin-Griffith, Inc. v. Goldberg, 79 S.E.2d 447 (S.C. 1953).

A contract for the construction of a hotel contained a provision for withholding progress payments, including a provision that payments might be withheld "to such extent as may be necessary to protect the owner from loss. . . ." The contract also provided for 15 percent retention of progress payments. The architect refused to issue certificates for progress payments because he found that there was defective work not remedied, that there was a reasonable doubt as to whether the contract could be completed with the unpaid balance of the contract price, and that the contractor, Elmer Montgomery, had failed to make payments to materials suppliers. Montgomery asserted that the architect's refusal was unreasonable and arbitrary and the amount withheld far in excess of that required. The court held that the architect's refusal to issue certificates for progress payments was reasonable and within the rights of the architect and owner.[24]

A more equitable result would have been obtained if the contract, in the last illustrative case, had contained the wording of the most recent A201 provision for withholding payments. Section 9.6.1 states that the architect "may withhold his Certificate *in whole or in part,* to the *extent necessary* reasonably to protect the Owner . . ." (italics added). This language more clearly limits the architect's power to withhold payments. If the normal retention already withheld from progress payments is fully sufficient to protect the owner in a situation where defective work is uncorrected or material suppliers are unpaid, then it should not be necessary to withhold any further progress payments. Surely the owner should not be able to withhold a $100,000 progress payment on a large project because of a $1,000 defect that was not corrected. This problem could be partially remedied by inserting into the contract the following language which is similar to Article 9.6.1 of the AIA General Conditions (A201, 1976 ed.):

If the architect is unable to approve an application in its entirety, he shall immediately notify the contractor to resubmit the application. If agreement cannot be reached upon the amount due, the architect shall issue a certificate of payment for the amount for which he is able to make representations to the owner.

This clause would prevent the owner's withholding the entire progress payment, but it would not prevent duplication by withholding the normal retention and also a current amount from progress payments.

Another factor which may bring into question the "necessity" of withholding progress payments for the protection of the owner is the possible presence of surety bonds secured by the general contractor and furnished to the owner to guarantee the performance of the job and payments to subcontractors, laborers, and material suppliers. A clause found in some government contracts, ASPR 7-104.21, prohibits the withholding of progress payments if the amount authorized to be withheld is less than the amount of retention already withheld. In other words, progress payments are not withheld if the owner is already protected. The Comptroller General of the United States has issued an opinion[25] in which he states that the contracting officer should not set progress payments off against liqui-

[24] Montgomery v. Karavas, 45 N.M. 287, 114 P.2d 776 (1941).
[25] 45 Comp. Gen. 484 (1966).

dated damages even when those damages exceed the retention. First, the government is protected by a performance bond; second, the possibility may exist that suspension of progress payments might make it impossible for the contractor to continue to work. This is an enlightened position because a performance bond adequately protects an owner.

RETENTION

Historically retention of about 10 percent has been withheld from construction contract progress payments for the following ostensible purposes: to provide partial financial security for the owner if work is not completed in accordance with the contract; to provide practical leverage against the contractor to ensure that the contract is fully performed; to discourage financially irresponsible construction contractors from attempting to perform a contract; and to save the owner the cost of paying construction interest on the amounts retained. Retention is generally withheld by providing in the construction general contract that only 90 percent of each progress payment due to the general contractor will be paid.

These reasons for retention are not valid in the modern construction industry, and the retention system which is unique to the construction industry has become increasingly inequitable and counterproductive. Retention is one of the major obstacles to the free flow of funds to the construction process. An adequate flow of funds is necessary to ensure that each party involved in performing a contract will be able to complete his obligations with good quality work and in a timely fashion. A reduction or elimination of the financial burdens placed on the general contractor and subcontractors when funds are withheld is to the benefit of all the parties, including the owner.

Subsequent to the historical implementation of retention to provide partial financial security to owners, insurance companies developed surety bonds which guaranteed full contract performance and provided a 100 percent guarantee of financial security to the owner. In the underwriting process, the surety companies also weeded out financially unstable contractors. However, even after the advent of surety bonding, the retention system was continued. Thus, under the present system which requires both bonds and the withholding of retention to ensure performance, an owner has the double protection of a 100 percent surety-bond guarantee and a 10 percent guarantee in the form of a retention holdback. In addition, there are express and implied warranties required under the contract documents. Overlapping protection is not needed to ensure completion because the owner has recourse to the bonding company in the event of default by the contractor. Also the multiple protection is unduly costly to the owner and inequitable to the general contractor and subcontractors who perform work with their own forces.

Most of the construction work is actually performed by specialty contractors who are subcontractors. In pricing their work, these subcontractors ultimately determine the cost of buildings and projects to the owners. General contractors who supervise and coordinate but do little work with their own forces add a competitive percentage for overhead and profit to their subcontractors' prices for the major portion of the work. Contractors and subcontractors must pay for their labor weekly and their materials monthly or even more frequently to obtain vendors' cash discounts. They also have current indirect costs which must be covered with an overhead and profit markup. The contingencies added to the contract price by the subcontractors often dictate whether an owner can realize an economic saving on the cost of the construction.

If the owner holds back a 10 percent retention in the general contract, the general contractor will normally hold back the same percentage retention from the subcontractors. Contractors and subcontractors must fund 100 percent of their costs of labor, materials, and indirect cost currently each month. Therefore, they must cover the 10 percent retention holdback either by increasing their prices to compensate for all or a portion of the retention holdback, borrowing the money from financial sources to replace the retention or funding the retention out of working capital.

The cost of construction has become so enormous that most contractors and subcontractors simply do not have the working capital to fund the 10 percent retention. The use of working capital to fund the retention results in a continuing withdrawal of the working capital because as each contract is performed and the retention paid to the appropriate contractor, another contract will normally take its place with a similar or greater amount of retention. The end result is to withdraw completely from the effective working capital of the contractor performing the work an amount to cover retention. Borrowing the money to cover retention from banks is often impractical because the interest rate is usually far above the prime rate and funds are not available in sufficient quantity to finance the large amounts retained.

Thus, a substantial proportion of the 10 percent retention must be covered by contractors and subcontractors who perform the work by increasing their contract prices. The practice of withholding the 10 percent retention holdback from progress payments creates a serious negative cash flow to those performing work, which becomes progressively burdensome as the project advances. The effect is particularly acute after a subcontractor has completed his work. Those persons who perform the work must recoup a portion of this negative cash flow by increasing the price of the construction. They do not have sufficient working capital or borrowing power to cover the larger amounts of retention, nor is it good business to tie up working capital or borrowing power indefinitely in nonproductive retention.

The magnitude of the problem is shown by the results of a survey by the American Subcontractors Association in 1974 which showed that on the average subcontractors each must cover approximately $200,000 in outstanding retainage. The financial burden of retention is particularly heavy in the case of the subcontractors who finish their contract work in the early phases of a construction project. Early finishing subcontractors such as the grading, foundation, steel erectors, and roofing contractors must endure a 10 percent retention until the entire general contract is completed; they sometimes wait one or two years for their retention. Because they simply cannot wait so long to collect the 10 percent retention, they often calculate their prices by providing for overhead and profit which will be paid currently out of the 90 percent progress payments and substantially discount the retention that they will not receive until a year or two after the entire project is completed. Although the subcontractors who perform work over the entire length of the general contract do not have to wait as long after they finish their portion of the contract to receive retention, the effect is still quite severe because they must fund the 10 percent holdback progressively over the entire length of the contract.

Owners could obtain substantially lower contract prices if no retention is withheld on construction general contracts. The survey by the American Subcontractors Association in 1974 showed that owners would realize an average cost savings of 3.7 percent if subcontractors had no retention to consider in establishing their prices. Thus, the owner would be in a better position to save on the contract price than if he withheld the retention and collected interest on it. The federal government's General Services Administration has found that by eliminating any retention, it has been able to save substantially on the contract prices and still obtain good job results. Other agencies of the United States government similarly have eliminated retention.

The argument that retention is a necessary club for the owner and architect to wield in order to get punch-list items finished and the building completed is illusory. Retention has just the opposite effect. When the full retention on the general contractor is withheld until all punch-list items are completed by the general contractor and all subcontractors, individual subcontractors simply are not motivated to perform their punch lists quickly because they know that the work of the other contractors will delay payment of retention to them for an indefinite period. However, if the subcontractors know that final payment of their retention will be made when they complete their individual punch lists, then they have strong incentive to complete their punch lists as quickly as possible.

The interest of the owners, general contractors, and subcontractors actually run parallel on the elimination or reduction of retention because the owner may save substantial sums of the principal costs of the project and the contractors who perform their work may eliminate the negative cash flow created by the holdback of the 10 percent retention. It is also in the interest of all parties to complete the building and punch lists as quickly as possible and to receive final payment.

Retention on contracts may be reduced on a graduated scale based on a percentage of completion so long as the contract progresses satisfactorily. When the project nears 50 percent completion, a significant reduction may be made in retention by one of the three basic methods as the work proceeds: hold the full percentage retention until the total work reaches 50 percent completion and then pay one-half of the retention being held to the general contractor with retention on the future progress payments cut to one-half of the original percentage; hold the full percentage retention until the work reaches 50 percent completion and then eliminate withholding of further retention from the progress payments for the rest of the general contract; hold the full percentage retention for each work category performed by the subcontractors and reduce the retention as each subcontract work category reaches 50 percent completion.

In the *Guide to Supplemental Conditions,* published by the American Institute of Architects, AIA Document A511 (1973 ed.), options are provided for the reduction of retention when the work project is 50 percent completed. This can have the inequitable result of retaining a full percentage of retention on early finishing subcontractors and a reduced retention on later finishing subcontractors. If the basic retained percentage for the first option is 10 percent, a reduction in payment upon completion of 50 percent of the general contract would be to 5 percent. On all subsequent progress payments, a 5 percent retention would be withheld. The clause providing for this type of retention reduction at the 50 percent stage is quoted in the *Guide to Supplemental Conditions,* AIA Document A511 (1973 ed.):

Until the Work is 50 percent complete, the Owner will pay _____ percent of the amount due the Contractor on account of progress payments. At the time the work is 50 percent complete, if the manner of completion of the Work and its progress are and remain satisfactory to the Architect, and in the absence of other good and sufficient reasons, the Architect shall [on presentation by the Contractor of Consent of Surety for each application] authorize any remaining partial payments to be paid in full.

The modern method of reducing and paying a retention is to reduce it equally for all subcontract work categories as each subcontractor satisfactorily completes 50 percent of his work and to release retention when the work category is completed. The general contractor is paid the retention reduction to be passed on to each subcontractor as the subcontract work category reaches 50 percent completion, and the full retention is paid upon completion of the subcontractor's work. This is known as "line-item payment" of the retention. The retention withheld on subcontractors who finish work early in the life of the project is released by the owner upon completion of that work. It is inherently unfair to continue to withhold retention from early finishing subcontractors who have substantially completed their work. Language similar to the following will provide line-item reduction and payment of retention:

If the manner and completion of work and its progress are and remain satisfactory to the architects, in the absence of other good and sufficient reasons, for each work category shown to be 50 percent or more complete in an application for payment, the architect shall, without reduction of previous retention, certify any other remaining progress payments for each work category to be paid in full.

When the work in each work category has been substantially completed and is satisfactory to the architect and in the absence of other good and sufficient reasons, all funds previously retained for each work category shall be paid in full to the contractor who shall make payment of retention to the subcontractor performing such work category less the amount determined by the architect to be equal to one and one-half times the cost of completing or correcting any items not completed in accordance with the contract documents.

A system of line-item reduction of retention in which the 10 percent retention for each work category is reduced after 50 percent completion and the payment of retention in full upon completion of work in each work category benefits owners because of faster completion of buildings at a reduced cost.

There are some who contend that it is impractical to ascertain when each trade has substantially completed its individual portion of a project. For example, there are inherent difficulties involved in determining that a steel contractor has fully complied with the plans and specifications until other trades have fitted in their work at a later time. In such a case, it may be necessary to delay the confirmation of the completion of the steel work for a short while, but there is absolutely no reason to hold back the final payment until the grass is mowed twice and the structural steel cannot even be seen to be inspected.

FINAL PAYMENT

Upon completion of the contract requirements, the contractor is entitled to final payment including any retained sums. Many contracts specify that the decision as to whether there has been completion of the project rests with the architect or engineer. Usually the contract will require that the architect's decision as to completion be evidenced by a certificate of completion and that no final payment may be made until the certificate is issued. Conversely, once a certificate is issued, the contract may preclude the owner from claiming that the contractor has not completely performed. However, in order for the contract provision for an architect's certificate to have the latter effect, the contract must state unequivocally that the issuance of the certificate is final and binding on the owner. Absent such a provision, the owner may be able to sue the contractor for failure to perform in accordance with the contract requirements even after issuance of such a certificate.

Illustrative Case

A contractor, John M. Bickerstaff, sued to foreclose a lien for materials and labor furnished to the Fraziers under a contract for constructing a home. The Fraziers counterclaimed for damages resulting from the contractor's alleged breach of the contract. Bickerstaff contended that the owners' claim was barred because of the certificate of completion issued by the architect. The court disagreed, however, holding that the architect's certificate of completion does not bar the owner as a matter of law from claiming damages for the contractor's failure to perform the contract. [26]

Even in such cases, though, issuance of the certificate is strong evidence in the contractor's favor that he has completed construction.

Problems arise more often when the architect refuses to issue the certificate than when the certificate is issued and the owner fails to abide by it. The issue becomes whether the certificate is a prerequisite to final payment. The contractor may feel that he has complied with the contract and that the architect is unreasonable in deciding to withhold the certificate.

There are cases in which the courts have held that an honest decision by the architect not to issue a certificate will prevent recovery by the contractor if the decision is not a gross mistake, even if it is unreasonable. In other cases, however, the courts have held that an unreasonable refusal by the architect to issue a certificate entitles the contractor to final payment without the certificate.

Illustrative Case

MacKnight Flintic Stone Company, a contractor, agreed to "make water-tight the boiler room, coal room, cellar, etc., of the courthouse and prison . . . in the manner and under the conditions prescribed and set forth in the annexed specifications. . . ." Although the contractor performed the work in strict accordance with the specifications, the cellar leaked, and the superintendent refused to issue the certificate required for payment. The court held that because MacKnight Flintic had completely fulfilled his obligation under the contract, the superintendent's refusal was unreasonable and the contractor could recover without the certificate. [27]

Another recognized ground for entitling the contractor to final payment in the absence of a required certificate occurs when the failure to issue a certificate is the fault of the owner and not the contractor. A typical fact situation is that the owner or the architect withholds the certificate in spite of the architect's honest opinion that the contractor has completed construction.

[26] Bickerstaff v. Frazier, 232 So. 2d 190 (Fla. App. 1970).
[27] MacKnight Flintic Stone Co. v. City of New York, 160 N.Y. 72, 54 N.E. 661 (1889).

A contractor, Haugen, brought suit against the owner, Raupach, for the balance due under the contract. Raupach complained that the contractor had not complied with the contract and had not obtained an architect's certificate. The contractor showed that the architect was of the opinion that Haugen had substantially complied with the contract's requirements and had withheld the certificate solely at the insistence of the owner. The court held that under these circumstances failure to obtain the certificate of completion was excused, and Haugen recovered the balance due.[28]

George Steffek Construction Company agreed to construct a color photography processing plant for Robert A. Wichers and Professional Photographers Color Corporation. When the building was near completion, the architect certified the building for a progress payment of $10,059.86. The owners, however, paid only $5,000, claiming that the contractor had already been overpaid. Wichers had no complaints with the quality of the workmanship. When the color lab was 98 percent complete the owner moved into the building and began color processing. The architect, however, failed to issue a certificate of completion. In a suit by the contractor for the balance due, Wichers claimed that final payment was not due because the building was only "substantially" complete and the contractor was not yet entitled to a certificate of completion. The court, however, found that Wichers had waived the requirement of a certificate by refusing to pay the previous amount certified as due, by moving in and accepting the benefit of the contractor's work, and by delaying in calling for a final inspection by the architect. The contractor was held to be entitled to the full balance due.[29]

The acceptance of final payment has important legal consequences for both the owner and the contractor. It may operate to cut off claims by either party against the other which were or should have been discovered before final payment.

The AIA General Conditions (AIA Document A201, 1976 ed.) provide that final payment constitutes a waiver of all claims by the owner except unsettled liens, faulty or defective work appearing after substantial completion, failure of the work to comply with the contract documents, or the terms of any special warranties. Conversely, the acceptance of final payment by the contractor under the AIA General Conditions constitutes a waiver of all claims by the contractor except those previously made in writing and identified by the contractor as unsettled at the time of the final application for payment. Those claims which are not reasonably discoverable until after final payment may usually be made after final payment.

Even after making final payment upon completion or upon substantial completion, the owner is normally protected by the contractor's warranties that all work is of good quality, free from faults and defects, and in conformance with the contract documents. For equipment and building systems requiring maintenance, specialty contractors normally provide a guarantee as well as maintenance and callback service during a prescribed period following the date on which the equipment is placed into operation.

[28] Haugen v. Raupach, 260 P.2d 340 (Wash. 1953).
[29] Steffek v. Wichers, 211 Kan. 342, 507 P.2d 274 (1973).

Illustrative Cases

Jacobson Construction Company contracted to construct a large building on sloping ground for Zion's Cooperative Mercantile Institution. The contractor was aware that the shoring subcontractor's work was faulty and would likely rupture the water lines in the adjoining alleyway. However, Jacobson did not order additional bracing to the shoring piles. The water main ruptured, the shoring collapsed, and the jobsite was damaged to the extent of $49,003.57. The owner filed suit against the contractor to recover this amount. The Cooperative subsequently made final payment to Jacobson pursuant to a contract provision that "[t]he making and acceptance of the final payment shall constitute a waiver of all claims by the owner, other than those arising . . . from faulty work appearing after final payment . . . and of all claims by the contractor except those made previously and still unsettled." The court found that the suit was not barred by final payment because the legal action had been instituted before final payment. Jacobson was held liable for the damages. [30]

Mr. and Mrs. Ramonas entered into a contract for remodeling work with Kerelis Construction Company that provided that the contractor remedy defects due to faulty materials or workmanship appearing within a 1-year period after contract completion. In addition, the contract required that "final payment shall constitute a waiver of all claims by the owner, other than those arising from . . . faulty work appearing thereafter. . . ." The Ramonas discovered that certain work was carelessly performed and did not comply with the building code. Because they gave notice of the defects within 1 year of final payment, Kerelis was obligated to remedy the faulty work. [31]

An important concept related to final completion and final payment is that of substantial completion. When a contractor has not completed, and even refuses to complete, every detail of the contract, he is entitled to a final payment of a reduced amount. The contractor is generally entitled to the contract price reduced by "an amount necessary to account for the difference between what the owner got by the actual performance as compared to what he bargained for." [32]

Illustrative Cases

A contract for a prefabricated garage for a home called for payment "upon completion." Because of several defects in the workmanship, primarily cracks in the concrete floor, the homeowners, the Allens, contended that there was no completion and that the contractor, Bullock Company, was not entitled to payment. The contractor asserted that he was entitled to the value of his work. In holding that the contractor was entitled to recovery, the court stated "a building is complete and the builder may recover the contract price, less sums necessary to correct defects, when the builder's performance is substantially in compliance with the contract." Because the contract also contained a specific disclaimer for liability for cracks, Bullock was held to be entitled to the full contract price. [33]

John W. Ryan engaged Jimmie Thurmond Construction Company to construct a building for $294,000. The contract called for the building to be substantially completed by January 10, 1968, and to be completed and occupied by February 10, 1968. The building,

[30] Zion's Cooperative Mercantile Inst. v. Jacobson Constr. Co., 27 Utah 2d 6, 492 P.2d 135 (1971).

[31] Ramonas v. Kerelis, 102 Ill. App. 2d 262, 243 N.E.2d 711 (1968).

[32] Watson Lumber Co. v. Guennewig, 79 Ill. App. 337, 226 N.E.2d 270 (1967).

[33] Bullock Co. v. Allen, 493 S.W.2d 5 (Mo. App. 1973).

however, was not substantially completed and occupied until May 28, 1968. At that time the owner paid the contractor $274,600. The contractor sued for the balance due claiming that he had fully performed the contract. Ryan counterclaimed for loss of rental value and for interest he had paid on money borrowed to complete and finance the building. In addition, Ryan claimed that Thurmond had never fully completed the required construction work. In its opinion, the court stated: "[A] strict and literal performance of a building and construction contract is not absolutely essential to entitle a contractor to recover on his contract. If the contractor has substantially performed, he may recover the contract price less the reasonable costs of remedying trivial defects and omissions . . . ." Because the contractor claimed that he had fully performed, the appellate court remanded the case to the trial court to decide the issue of whether there had been full performance of the contract. [34]

The contractor has a right to receive the retained percentage when he completes the project and complies with the contract procedures for obtaining final payment. However, most courts have construed retention to be for the purpose of protecting or indemnifying the owner, and therefore the owner may not permanently retain amounts beyond the extent of its damages.

Illustrative Case

When Fenner & Shea Construction Company presented its final draw request to the financer, Empire Savings and Loan Association, it was denied pursuant to instructions issued by the owner, Kenneth H. Wadkins. In a suit by Fenner & Shea for the retained amount, Wadkins claimed that the contractor had breached the contract by performing certain portions of the work in an unworkmanlike manner and that Wadkins was therefore entitled to keep the unpaid balance. The court disagreed, holding that because Fenner & Shea had substantially performed the contract, Wadkins was entitled to retain only that amount necessary to complete the performance required by the contract. By refusing to return the difference, *Wadkins* had breached the contract. [35]

SCOPE OF WORK

The amount of work which the general contractor is required to perform under his contract is directly related to the payment clause. It is but the other side of the same coin. Invariably, contractors verify that the total amount of money is correctly stated in the payment clause, but they often neglect to verify the accuracy of the scope of work description. If the scope of work is expanded beyond that which the contractor contemplated in his bid, then the amount of money may be drastically inadequate.

The scope of work which the general contractor must perform in order to fulfill his contract obligations must be legally defined by the general contract. The contract normally incorporates general and special conditions as well as plans and specifications by specific reference. The complex nature of plans and specifications for construction projects make it necessary for the contractor to study these carefully in order to include all

---

[34] Ryan V. Thurmond, 481 S.W.2d 199 (Tex. App. 1972).

[35] Fenner & Shea Constr. Co. v. Wadkins, 511 P. 2d 924 (Colo. App. 1973).

parts of the work in his bid. For the same reason, it is very important for the general contractor to be sure that the final version of the plans and specifications (including all addenda) includes only work which was contemplated when he made his bid.

The contract should contain a definite and concise statement of the work to be done rather than general language as to the nature of the project under construction. Contractors should never sign contracts containing so-called dragnet clauses which some owners use as catchalls to require that the work for accomplishment of an intended purpose is covered by the contract. Such a clause might say, for example, "and all other things and services necessary or desirable" or "and all work incidental to the work specified in the plans and specifications." Such language in the contract might be seized upon by the owner in an attempt to require the contractor to do whatever is needed to accomplish the result desired by the owner rather than the work outlined by the detailed plans and specifications. By including specific language describing the work to be done, the contract leaves the responsibility for design with the architects and engineers where it belongs. To determine the scope of the work under a construction contract, the plans and specifications and the contract itself must be clearly written. The more clarity and specificity built into the plans and specifications and into the contract clause describing the work to be done, the less likely it is that disputes will arise concerning their interpretation.

The contract generally gives initial authority for interpretation of the plans and specifications during performance of the contract to the architect or to the contracting officer in the case of a government contract. The proper general standard to be applied in interpreting the contract language is to choose meanings for words that will be attached to them by reasonably intelligent persons acquainted with all the operative usages and customs of the trade and knowing all the facts and circumstances existing prior to and at the time of the making of the contract.[36]

In addition to the work explicitly required by the specifications, the scope of the contract will be interpreted to include work which, although not mentioned in the specifications, is obviously indispensable to the completion of the project. This will also be true when a reasonable site inspection would have informed the contractor that such work was indispensable. In case of any doubt, clarification should be obtained by a contractor prior to submitting his bid.

Illustrative Case

Ambrose-Augusterfer Corporation agreed to perform all work required to install a new air-conditioning system at a United States Post Office as shown on the contract draw-

---

[36]*Restatement of Contracts* §§ 230–36. The areas of contract interpretation are discussed in detail in Chap. 5, under "Constructive Changes."

ing. To accomplish this, it was necessary to remove 2,000 light fixtures in the building and later replace them. The court concluded that the contractor had a duty to carry out a reasonable site inspection which would have clearly indicated that the light fixtures would have to be removed. Since this was required to do the work, it was by implication an indispensable part of the contractor's obligation. Therefore the contractor was not allowed to recover any additional compensation for the removal, rehanging, and rewiring of the fixtures. [37]

Items of work not mentioned in the contract or specifications may be added to the scope of the work by a custom or usage of the trade if the work would normally be performed, including the omitted item. Such a trade practice must be well established and known by the parties or must be so common that they should have known it.

Illustrative Case

The Coast Guard provided Ahern Painting Contractors, Inc., with specifications which gave no method for preparing surfaces to be painted with a special acrylic paint. However, the evidence given in the case established that it was accepted trade usage to provide a fine coat of oil-base paint before applying acrylic paint to exterior wood surfaces. The contractor, following the specifications and ignoring the trade practice, applied the acrylic paint with a primer. When the paint peeled from the buildings, it was held that Ahern was responsible for the expense of repainting the buildings. Their inexperience cost them more than 10 percent of the contract price. [38]

On the other hand, usage of the trade may restrict the scope of work.

Illustrative Case

M. B. Kahn Construction Company laid the foundation for housing units at an Air Force Base with 12-inch cement block, under a specification which required bricks to be laid with completely full mortar joints. The contracting officer directed Kahn to fill in the holes in the cement blocks with mortar, and the contractor sought extra compensation for this work. It was held that the language of the specification could not require the contractor to fill in holes in the concrete blocks because the contractor showed that where the holes in the cement blocks were to be filled it was customary for the specifications to provide for it expressly. [39]

Thus, if the extra work ordered by the owner is beyond the general scope of the contract, that is, if it cannot be regarded as fairly and reasonably within the contemplation of the parties when the contract was entered into, then it may be within the contractor's rights to refuse to perform the extra work. [40] This allows the contractor to use labor and equipment on a more profitable job. If the owner insists on extra work

---

[37] Ambrose-Augusterfer Corp. v. United States, 394 F.2d 536 (Ct. Cl. 1968).

[38] Appeal of Ahern Painting Contractors, Inc., 68-1 BCA ¶ 6949 (1968).

[39] Appeal of M.B. Kahn Constr. Co., 1964 BCA ¶ 4272 (1964).

[40] Luria Bros. & Co. v. United States, 369 F.2d 701 (Ct. Cl. 1966). A further analysis of this section is contained in the discussion concerning performance of contracts, in Chap. 5.

beyond the general scope of the contract, the contractor can quite rightly ignore him.

CHANGE CLAUSES

Any construction contract for a project of significant size should include a change clause which gives the owner a unilateral right to alter the work within the scope of the contract.

If the owner requires work to be done which is in excess of that required by the original contracts but is still within the general scope of the project, the contractor must perform the work and he should receive extra compensation under the formal change procedure in the contract or under the constructive change doctrine.

Generally, the owner may adjust the specifications within the general scope of the contract, parameters of the work, methods of performance to be used by the contractor, and sequence of performance to the work. Thus, the owner is able to react to changing financial or physical circumstances and to take advantage of developing technology. The change clause also provides a means by which suggestions by the contractor may be incorporated into the work.

In addition, the change clause provides the procedure for the contractor to assert his claims for additional compensation beyond the original contract price covering extra work done at the direction of the owner, whether express or implied. Providing an administrative remedy within the contract for pursuing claims benefits both the owner and the contractor because they might otherwise have to settle such claims in court. This points out the necessity for the change clause to be accompanied by an equitable and efficient disputes clause which outlines the procedure for settling claims when the parties do not agree. Quick, reliable disputes procedures are essential because a contractor normally must proceed with the work while his claim is pending, which can disrupt his cash flow.

The general contractor should be aware of any provisions in the contract for processing changes. Since most changes will actually be performed by subcontractors, the normal procedure is for the general contractor to add markups to the subcontractors' prices for changes, which are passed on to the owner. Some general contracts will stipulate that changes are to be compensated at a cost with fixed percentage markups on changes. It is important to the general contractor to determine if the percentage(s) apply to the total cost of the performance of the change, whether the general contractor directly performs the extra work or subcontracts it. The general contractor's percentage of markup necessary to cover his overhead cost is normally higher if the general contractor performs the work with his own forces than if subcontractors perform the changed work. Some general contracts stipulate varying percentage markups depending on whether the work is actually performed by the general contractor's forces or it is subcontracted.

Problems which may arise in change procedures during performance of a contract are discussed in Chapter 5, as well as typical contract change clauses. Contract dispute clauses are discussed in Chapter 7.

Most construction contracts call for withholding a percentage retention of the total contract price until completion of the work. When a change order for extra work is issued, the contract price is adjusted upward. At the time a contractor applies for a progress payment which includes compensation for the extra work, the question arises as to whether the owner is entitled to withhold the percent of retention from the payment allocable to the extra work as well as from the portion allocable to the base contract work originally contemplated. The courts have generally interpreted typical construction contracts to apply the retention amount to all the work under the contract, including work added by change order.

Illustrative Case

In holding that the owner had withheld more than the retention specified in the contract, the court stated:

> [The contract], by express terms, made the price of extras or changes a part of the contract price; in other words, it made the agreed price of the changes and extras a part of the cost to be added to the original price named in the contract, the $13,000. Therefore on the date of the last advancement to the contractors, the contract price for the erection of the building was $13,232, which was as binding upon [the owner] as if it had been so written in the original contract. It is thus seen that [the owner, by withholding more than the proper retainage on $13,232] had in its hands more than the portion of the contract price it had agreed to retain until the building was completed. [41]

The contract should provide that no retention be withheld on change orders. If changes are made to the contract during the performance, contractors must perform these changes with current funds and they should be paid in full for all changes. Even under a reduced system of retention, large amounts are withheld in the base contract. To permit further retention on change orders for work not originally contemplated by the parties or to allow additional time before payment of the base-contract retention becomes due because of change orders is inequitable to contractors. The processing or performance of change orders should not hold up either the reduction of retention or the final payment of retention for work performed under the base contract.

TIME OF COMPLETION

One of the most important provisions in a construction general contract is that covering the job progress schedule, including the date on which the

---

[41] Illinois Surety Co. v. Garrard Hotel Co., 118 S.W. 967, 969-70 (Ky. App. 1909).

general contractor promises to have the work completed. If the general contractor fails to prepare his time estimate carefully and does not allow enough time to complete the work, he may be liable to the owner for liquidated damages for delay. The work generally must be substantially complete by the date set for completion. Substantial completion is normally defined as the date the architect certifies when the owner may occupy the project for its intended use.

If a general contractor encounters excusable delays so that his actual performance is extended beyond the original contract time, he must be able to establish sufficient evidence of such delays and their impact on job progress if he is to avoid possible default for failure to complete the contract within the original completion date and to avoid the assessment of liquidated damages.

In order to obtain an extension of the contract time for excusable delays, there must be a clause in the general contract or in the general conditions which permits such an extension time. Without an excusable delay clause, the general contractor is bound to perform the contract on time unless it becomes impossible to do so because of an act of God, the law, or fault of the other contracting party. The general conditions of most construction general contracts contain an excusable delay clause.

The excusable delay clause of the AIA General Conditions, Document A201 (1976 ed.), is contained in Article 8.3.1, which states:

8.3.1   If the Contractor is delayed at any time in the progress of the Work by any act or neglect of the Owner or the Architect, or by any employee of either, or by any separate contractor employed by the Owner, or by changes ordered in the Work, or by labor disputes, fire, unusual delay in transportation, adverse weather conditions not reasonably anticipatable, unavoidable casualties, or any causes beyond the Contractor's control, or by delay authorized by the Owner pending arbitration, or by any other cause which the architect determines may justify the delay, then the Contract Time shall be extended by Change Order for such reasonable time as the Architect may determine.

The excusable delay clause generally permits a time extension where delays are the fault of neither party to the contract or where they are the fault of the owner or his representatives. The effect of such clause, which grants an extension to the contract time of performance, is that the owner may not declare the contractor to be in default for finishing late, assess liquidated damages, or demand that the contractor accelerate performance to finish on time. Caution must be exercised to ensure that any notice requirements contained in an excusable delay clause are complied with in a timely manner. Excusable delays are discussed in more detail in Chapter 5.

If a construction contractor breaches the contract by failing to perform his obligations under the contract, the general rule is that the owner may recover damages from the breaching party sufficient to compensate the owner for its losses resulting from the breach in order that it may be placed in the same financial position as if the breach had not occurred.

The parties may, however, choose to estimate or "liquidate" the damages to be paid by the breaching party when they execute the contract. In construction contracts, the general practice is for "time is of the essence" to be stipulated, and accordingly the construction contractor promises to complete the work within a specified period of time. Often the contractor and owner will stipulate in the contract that the contractor will be liable for a specified amount for each day beyond the date set for completion. The following is a typical liquidated damages clause in a construction contract:

The contractor shall complete the work hereunder within _____ days, excluding Saturdays, Sundays, and holidays. From the compensation otherwise to be paid, the owner may retain the sum of $_____ for each day, Saturdays, Sundays, and holidays not included, that the work remains uncompleted beyond the specified period, which sum is agreed on as the proper measure of liquidated damages that the owner will sustain per diem on the failure of the contractor to complete the work in the time stipulated, and this sum is not to be construed in any sense as a penalty.

The parties may also specify a maximum amount of damages to which the per diem assessments will be allowed to accumulate. Often the contract requires that certain steps in the work be completed at certain dates, and the owner may have the power to assess liquidated damages or demand performance on overtime at the contractor's expense if the contractor is delayed in completing the particular steps of the work. The assessment of liquidated damages prior to final payment may be accomplished by withholding part of the progress payments due to the contractor at the completion of each step if the contract so provides.

Illustrative Case

The Department of the Interior engaged Union Paving Company to construct various piers and abutments for a bridge. The contract required that each pier and abutment be completed by a certain interim completion date and provided for the assessing of liquidated damages in the sum of $100 per day for each day of delay in completing the various portions of the work. When the contractor was late in attempting to meet four of the interim completion dates, $24,000 per diem assessments were withheld from the progress payments. When Union Paving completed the entire job within the time required by the contract, he sought to have the liquidated damages assessed for delays in meeting the interim completion dates returned. The court, however, held that liquidated damages were appropriate for delays in completing various portions of the work because the timely completion of portions of the work was essential to coordination of the entire project, and it would be difficult, if not impossible, to determine what actual damage might result if delays were encountered.[42]

Regardless of the result in the illustrative case, a smart owner would write the liquidated damages clause to forgive the contractor who makes

---

[42] Union Paving Co. v. United States, 115 F. Supp. 179 (Ct. Cl. 1953).

the final completion date. This provides an incentive to the contractor to catch up on lost time.

The parties to a contract may not establish the amount of per diem liquidated damages at just any arbitrary figure. To establish a valid and binding liquidated damages clause, the amount must be spelled out specifically in the contract, and parties must have made a genuine attempt to establish the actual damages which would be expected to result from a breach of the contract. In addition, the contract must be of such a nature that the damages expected to result from a breach would be difficult to ascertain with certainty at the time of the contract.[43]

The damages awarded by a court for a breach of contract must be compensatory, not punitive, and therefore the courts will not enforce a liquidated damages provision which is intended to penalize the breaching party or to be used as a club to force one party to perform the contract. Therefore, if the amount fixed as liquidated damages appears to be a penalty rather than a good-faith estimate of the expected damages, the courts may disregard the provision and award the injured party the actual damages suffered as a result of the breach. However, the courts normally recognize the parties' estimate of damages in cases where the actual damages would be particularly difficult to ascertain. The courts have reasoned that the parties are in the best position to know what the damages are likely to be, and simply enforcing a liquidated damages clause allows the court to avoid the difficulties of trying to ascertain the amount of actual damages at a trial. The more uncertain the damages are, the greater is the courts' tendency to let the estimate of the parties stand. If the damages to be expected from a breach of contract are obvious and of a fixed amount, the contract situation is not an appropriate one for the assessment of liquidated damages. However, these situations seldom arise in the construction industry.

To determine whether a liquidated damages clause was intended to be a penalty or a valid pre-estimate of the damages, the court will consider the language of the contract and circumstances existing at the time of the execution of the contract. If a contract may be breached in different ways which would give rise to different amounts of actual damages, the presence in the contract of the same fixed amount of liquidated damages for different breaches may result in an unenforceable penalty. For instance, if a contractor is engaged to build both a house and a garage, it would be expected that the damages the owner would suffer if the completion of the house were delayed would be much more than the damages he would suffer if the completion of the garage were delayed. If there were a single liquidated damages figure in the contract based on the damage for delay in completion, and the contractor completed the house on time but not the garage, the owner should not be able to collect that amount for the num-

---

[43] Sun Printing & Publishing Ass'n v. Moore, 183 U.S. 642 (1902); United States v. Bethlehem Steel Co., 205 U.S. 105 (1907); *Restatement of Contracts* § 339 (1932).

ber of days beyond the contract completion date the garage was not completed.[44]

The contractor's breach of a construction contract often takes the form of delay in the completion of the project, and therefore the owner's damage generally consists of loss of use of the structure being built and accompanying problems. The amount of liquidated damages in construction contracts, therefore, usually begins with the rental value of a structure and also includes any other justifiable cost which would be expected to result because of the particular circumstances of the parties. For instance, if the completion date is near the onset of cold weather and the owner has a special need to occupy a structure, damage resulting from delay would not be restricted to the mere rental value of the structure.[45]

Illustrative Case

Robert McMullan & Son, Inc., agreed to paint several buildings for the government. Under the contract the liquidated damage provision set a fixed amount of damages for each day that all the buildings were not completely painted. Obviously, if some of the buildings were completed and the government was able to use them, the actual damage would not be expected to include the rental value of occupied buildings. The contractor challenged the validity of the liquidated damages provision, claiming that it was a penalty. But the government either had a terrific lawyer or uncanny luck because the sum set in the contract was derived by computing the monthly expense of administering the contract rather than upon the rental value of buildings not completed. This cost did not vary according to how many buildings were completed and therefore was a valid liquidation of the damages.[46]

In applying a valid liquidated damages clause which is not a penalty, the courts will enforce the contract according to its terms. Ordinarily, the owner cannot recover both liquidated and actual damages for breach of contract by the contractor if the contract contains a liquidated damages clause. However, it may be that the parties inserted a liquidated damages clause which was meant to cover only one type of breach of contract. In such a case, if some other breach occurs, or if more than one breach occurs and not all are covered by liquidated damages, the owner could recover for both actual and liquidated damages.

If the actual damages suffered by the owner are either more or less than the amount of liquidated damages provided for in the contract, the parties must accept the amount of liquidated damages and cannot normally introduce evidence to show actual damages in an attempt to increase or decrease the recovery. Some courts have applied this general rule even if the contractor can show that the owner has suffered no actual damages at all as a result of the contractor's delay.[47] Other courts,

---

[44]See Corbin on Contracts § 1066 (1964).

[45]Ross v. Loescher, 152 Mich. 386, 116 N.W. 193 (1908).

[46]Appeal of Robert McMullan & Son, Inc., 71-2 B.C.A. ¶ 9106 (1971).

[47]Southwest Engineering Co. v. United States, 341 F.2d 998 (8th Cir. 1965).

however, have taken the view that if no harm has been suffered by the owner, the mere presence of a liquidated damages clause should not allow the owner to recover.[48]

Illustrative Case

Massman Construction Company was engaged by the city of Greenville, Miss., to construct four bridge piers in the Mississippi River within 350 days under a contract in which the parties liquidated the damages for delaying completion at $250 per day. The contractor's performance was late, but the city suffered no losses because not a single car could cross the bridge the day it was completed—there was no road up to the bridge! The court stated, "Even though we assume that the contract provided for liquidated damages instead of a penalty, nevertheless, the intent and purpose of the provision was to guard the city against the delay in opening the bridge, and against only such losses as the parties anticipated would be caused by a delay in completion of the contract." The court held that under all the facts and circumstances of the case, the assessment of liquidated damages would be unequitable and unreasonable and would amount to a penalty.[49]

Similarly, some courts have refused to enforce liquidated damages when the amount of liquidated damages turns out to be grossly in excess of the actual damages suffered. Such a gross difference may also be taken as persuasive evidence that the parties intended a penalty rather than an estimate of the expected actual damages.[50]

In drawing up contracts, many contractors guard against inclusion of any liability for consequential damages such as loss of use, loss of revenue, and loss of profits. This is on the theory that if losses are to be anticipated as a result of delays, they should be handled through liquidated damage provisions where a specific completion date, per diem damages, and basis for excusable delays can be agreed upon in advance. If a contract is silent concerning consequential damages, an owner may still institute action to collect such damages. Thus, the safest step to take is to include a written provision in the contract to the effect that neither party shall hold the other liable for consequential damages.

DEFAULT AND TERMINATION

Construction general contracts often contain a provision which authorizes the owner to terminate the employment of the contractor and take over the completion of the work using the contractor's materials and sometimes even his equipment and tools. A typical termination paragraph providing that the owner must obtain a certificate from the architect stating the termination is justified and that the owner must give the contractor and his surety written notice of his intention to terminate is

---

[48] *Restatement of Contracts* § 339, comment (1932).

[49] Massman Constr. Co. v. City Council, 147 F.2d 925 (5th Cir. 1945).

[50] 5 *Corbin on Contracts* § 1063 (1964).

found in the AIA General Conditions, AIA Document A201 (1976 ed.), Section 14.2.1:

14.2.1 If the Contractor is adjudged a bankrupt . . . , or if he persistently or repeatedly refuses or fails, except in cases for which extension of time is provided, to supply enough properly skilled workmen or proper materials, or if he fails to make prompt payment to Subcontractors or for materials or labor, or persistently disregards laws, ordinances, rules, regulations or orders of any public authority having jurisdiction, or otherwise is guilty of a substantial violation of a provision of the Contract Documents, then the Owner, upon certification by the Architect that sufficient cause exists to justify such action, may, without prejudice to any right or remedy and after giving the Contractor and his surety, if any, seven days, written notice, terminate the employment of the Contractor and take possession of the site and of all materials, equipment, tools, construction equipment and machinery thereon owned by the Contractor and may finish the Work by whatever method he may deem expedient. In such case the Contractor shall not be entitled to receive any further payment until the Work is finished.

The parties are free to agree to such clause in a construction contract, and the courts have generally upheld the owner's right to remove the contractor from the job if the conditions specified in the termination clause are present. The contractor, therefore, should avoid termination clauses which allow the owner to take over and complete the job when the contractor has committed only a minor violation of his contractual obligation.

Illustrative Cases

Robinhorne Construction Corporation agreed to construct a motor lodge for Jack O. Snyder under a cost-plus-6-percent contract which included a guaranteed maximum cost and a termination clause similar to the AIA clause quoted previously. The contractor failed to complete the contract within the time specified, and 6 months after the original completion date notified the owner that it expected his costs to go beyond the guaranteed maximum. At this point work on the project was virtually stopped. The court held that the evidence amply supported a finding of failure of Robinhorne to comply with contract provisions regarding the completion date and delays, failure to have sufficient workmen on the job, and failure to comply with the guaranteed maximum contract price. Snyder was justified in terminating the contract and taking over completion of the work because Robinhorne had materially breached the contract. Therefore, the contractor's suit to enjoin the owner from taking over the completion failed. The owner recovered on his counterclaim for the difference between the cost incurred by him in completing the work and the agreed maximum contract price.[51]

J. W. Mercur & Company, a contractor constructing a building, went bankrupt before final completion and therefore failed to complete the building within the specified time. The owner, Pennsylvania Institution for the Instruction of the Blind, followed the procedure set out in the termination clause in the contract for taking over the work and was justified in terminating the employment of the contractor and completing the work. The owner argued that by breaching the contract, Mercur had forfeited his right to any further payment. The court held, however, that under the terms of the contract, after the owner had completed the building, the contractor could recover the balance due under

---

[51] Robinhorne Constr. Corp. v. Snyder, 113 Ill. App. 2d 288, 251 N.E. 2d 641 (1969).

the contract minus the cost of completion and any damages resulting to the owners from the contractor's default.[52]

It is desirable to insert additional wording in the contract stating that the contractor shall be allowed a reasonable time in addition to written notice to remedy any deficiency before the termination provisions become effective.

Because the exercise by the owner of his rights under the termination clause completely ends the contractual relationship, the courts are very strict in applying the procedural requirements of the clause. In particular, the owner must follow strictly the requirements for obtaining an architect's certificate and for providing the contractor with the proper notice of the owner's intent to terminate. Furthermore, the architect's certificate must be issued in good faith.

Illustrative Cases

The owner, Emma Butler, assumed that the contractor, American-Hawaiian Engineering Construction Company, had failed to diligently prosecute the work and consequently terminated the contract and undertook to complete the work. However, the termination clause in the contract required the owner to give the contractor 3 days notice before termination, and Mrs. Butler had not notified American-Hawaiian. The court held that Mrs. Butler was not authorized to take charge of the work and that the contractor was justified in resisting her attempt to remove it from the jobsite and take over the work.[53]

After M. J. Daly & Sons had substantially completed the construction of a hotel, the architects issued a certificate under the termination clause in the contract for not totally completing the work on time, and the owner, New Haven Hotel Company, took over completion of the work. At the time of termination, $500 worth of work remained to be done on the $80,000 contract. The court held that the architect's certificate of default had not been made in good faith and that the contractor had substantially performed the contract. Thus, Daly had a right to enforce a lien for payment on the project.[54]

Federal government contracts contain a clause giving it the right to terminate a contract for convenience when its completion would not be in its best interest. Most government contracts now contain a termination-for-convenience clause, and private owners also often place such a clause in a construction contract. The government termination-for-convenience clause found in Standard Form 23-A, Section 37, and ASPR Section 8-701 is a typical termination-for-convenience clause:

The performance of work under this contract may be terminated by the government in accordance with this clause in whole, or from time to time in part, whenever the contracting officer shall determine that such termination is in the best interest of the government. . . .

[52] Hunn v. Pennsylvania Institution for Instruction of the Blind, 70 A. 812 (Pa. 1908).

[53] American-Hawaiian Engineering & Constr. Co. v. Butler, 133 P. 280 (Cal. 1913).

[54] M.J. Daly & Sons, Inc. v. New Haven Hotel Co., 99 A. 853 (Conn. 1917).

A termination-for-convenience clause may be validly used when the owner simply wishes to withdraw from the contract. The major advantage of the termination-for-convenience clause to the owner is that the contractor agrees under the clause to accept only his costs incurred and a profit on the work actually performed rather than the total anticipated profit which the contractor could recover normally for the wrongful termination of the contract.

Illustrative Case

Nolan Brothers, Inc., undertook to construct for the Corps of Engineers two rock jetties out into the Gulf of Mexico in Texas. When about one-third of the work was done on the $9 million contract, the government exercised its contract right to terminate performance for the government's convenience. The parties' attempts to negotiate a termination settlement were unsuccessful, and the government issued a payment determination in the amount of $5 million out of the $8 million sought by the contractor. Nolan Brothers appealed this amount to the Board of Contract Appeals and then to the Court of Claims, contending that the government had breached the contract by providing defective specifications and therefore should not be allowed to terminate the contract for convenience, thereby depriving the contractor of his total anticipated profits. The court upheld the government's right to terminate the contract, whether or not it had previously breached the contract.[55]

[55] Nolan Bros., Inc. v. United States, 405 F.2d 1250 (Ct. Cl. 1969).

3 SUBCONTRACTS

INTRODUCTION

Too often subcontractors sign subcontract forms which are furnished them by general contractors without having any knowledge of the very serious legal implications of many of the subcontract clauses that give the general contractors unnecessary legal and practical advantages. Many subcontractors only check to see that their name is spelled right and that the money is correct before they sign subcontract forms which create unsuspected liabilities on the part of the subcontractors.

Subcontractors must read each subcontract carefully and completely to discover the legal pitfalls of such clauses. When confronted with an unfair or one-sided contract, a subcontractor should refuse to sign it and should insist on either substituting a subcontract form with neutral terms or modifying the general contractor's subcontract in order to eliminate the oppressive and objectionable portions.

Through education programs sponsored by the chapters of the American Subcontractors Association and other specialty subcontractor trade associations, many subcontractors have become aware of the practical problems and legal pitfalls of subcontract clauses and are negotiating changes in the clauses which are unduly harsh to the subcontractors. In many cases subcontractors substitute a more neutral standard subcontract form sponsored by the American Institute of Architects or the standard subcontract form sponsored by the Associated General Contractors of America and the Associated Specialty Contractors, Inc., which will be referred to as the AGC subcontract form. If a subcontractor is presented with a loaded subcontract form which is devised to protect the interests of the general contractor, the subcontractor should retype the special contract terms on an AIA or AGC standard form subcontract and present it to the general contractor for execution of this neutral standard subcontract form.

Subcontractors should become conscious of the problem areas in subcontracts and negotiate with the general contractors to strike out or modify the clauses which give the general contractor unfair advantage. In many cases all the subcontractor has to do is merely ask the general contractor to modify such loaded clauses. When subcontractors point out the objectional clauses to the general contractors, the general contractors often state, "I don't blame you; I wouldn't sign that either."

BATTLE OF THE FORMS

The construction industry has changed greatly from the time when the general contractor performed most of the construction work as a master builder who directly hired employees of the various construction crafts to do the work and directly purchased the materials. In the modern-day construction industry the general contractor performs almost no work directly with his own forces but subcontracts practically all the work to specialty subcontractors; these subcontractors actually perform the overwhelming majority of the construction work with their own forces and purchase most of the materials necessary. Many general contractors obtain a general contract and then merely manage the contract by brokering practically all the work to subcontractors.

Subcontractors are not only faced with harsh and strict provisions imposed on them by the terms of the general contract, but also they are often faced with additional harsh provisions in loaded subcontract forms, which give the general contractors unnecessary legal and practical advantages. These subcontract forms have typically been intentionally drafted by the general contractors' attorneys to obtain maximum legal and practical advantages over the subcontractors, and the subcontractors may fail to fully appreciate the legal implications and consequences of much of the language. These loaded subcontract forms have become increasingly more lengthy and more complicated, and they are deliberately devised by attorneys to protect the interests of the general contractors at the expense of the subcontractors.

These loaded subcontract forms drafted for general contractors contain clauses which would literally make a subcontractor build his own scaffold, tie his own noose, and then give the general contractor total discretion to trip the trap door to hang the subcontractor without notice. And after it is all over, there is authority usually built into the loaded subcontract forms to allow the general contractor to backcharge the subcontractor's estate for the cost of the rope and the scaffolding.

As an alternative to the loaded subcontract forms devised by general contractors, subcontractors should substitute more neutral standard subcontract forms such as those sponsored by the American Institute of Architects and the Associated General Contractors of America. A standard form sponsored by the Associated General Contractors was developed in conjunction with several subcontractors associations in 1966, and this more or less neutral form has come into wide use by general contractors and subcontractors.

In 1967, the American Institute of Architects followed very closely the terms and conditions of the AGC standard subcontract form in the AIA standard subcontract form agreement (AIA Document A401). In 1972, the author had the pleasure of negotiating certain additional changes in the AIA standard subcontract form which strengthened some of the subcontract terms and conditions for the benefit of the subcontractors. However, both the AIA and the AGC standard subcontract forms contain similar neutral provisions.

It is a sound approach for subcontractors to substitute either the AIA or the AGC standard subcontract form in lieu of any subcontract forms devised by individual general contractors. If a subcontractor is presented with a subcontract form that is obviously devised to protect the interest of the general contractor, then the subcontractor should retype the special contract terms on either an AIA or an AGC standard subcontract form and present it to the general contractor for execution as a neutral agreement. General contractors have readily accepted these two neutral forms, and they have come into wide national use. Copies of the AIA subcontract form can be obtained either from AIA national headquarters or from virtually any blueprint company for a very minor charge. Copies of the AGC subcontract form may be obtained from the national or local chapters of Associated General Contractors of America or from the national or many of the local chapters of the American Subcontractors Association or many other construction specialty associations.

When a subcontractor is presented with an obviously loaded subcontract form, he could call the general contractor and say, "How about substituting the American Institute of Architects Standard Subcontract Form A401?" However, when orally approached, the general contractor will initially be inclined to say no because he may not be familiar with the terms of this standard subcontract form or know how to fill out the form, and he may feel that consideration of this standard subcontract form would require substantial legal review by his lawyer. So the general contractor is initially inclined to simply say no to an oral proposal to substitute a more neutral subcontract form.

The wise subcontractor takes another more practical approach by filling out the terms and conditions of an AIA Standard Subcontract Form A401 and sending filled-out copies to the general contractor with a polite letter proposing to substitute the form in lieu of the original obviously loaded subcontract form. The subcontractor might sign the filled-out neutral form or await the general contractor's signature before signing and request that the general contractor sign all copies and return one copy to the subcontractor. More often than not, the subcontract form is returned in the mail signed by the general contractor without comment. The difference in using this last approach is that the general contractor can readily see that the filled-out Standard Subcontract Form A401 is more or less neutral and protects the general contractor and subcontractor equally. All the general contractor then has to do to the filled-out standard subcontract form to have a legally binding subcontract is sign his name.

However, when the general contractor responds to the subcontractor saying that he cannot accept the AIA Standard Subcontract Form A401, the subcontractor is in an excellent position to propose the AGC standard subcontract form as a compromise. More often than not, the AGC subcontract form is a very acceptable compromise with both the general contractor and the subcontractor. The AGC subcontract form is more readily accepted by general contractors than the AIA subcontract form because the AGC's form is sponsored and approved by the general contractor's own national association. In any event, either the AIA or the AGC standard subcontract form contains terms that protect both the general contractor and the subcontractor, and both forms are certainly more neutral in respect to the subcontractors than the loaded subcontract forms devised by the general contractors.

Many subcontractors also include stipulations in their bids that the subcontractor's bid be conditioned upon use of an AIA or AGC standard subcontract form between the parties if their bid is accepted. If the subcontractor's bid is accepted, the use of the stipulated standard form subcontract is then legally required to be used by the general contractor. Many subcontractors are also drafting either the AIA or the AGC subcontract form and initially sending the form to the general contractor after the general contractor has indicated that the subcontractor's bid has been accepted.

A subcontractor should not be complacent and blindly sign the general contractor's form, which is obviously loaded against the subcontractor. If a subcontractor signs a loaded subcontract form, he may need the services of a preacher rather than a lawyer to pray that nothing happens on the construction job.

PAYMENT TERMS

Typically, "contingent payment clauses" appear in subcontract forms devised by general contractors, and provide that the subcontractors will not be paid until the general contractor is paid by the owner or until the architect approves the work. Under a contingent payment clause the general contractor has shifted the risk of nonpayment by the owner from the general contractor to the subcontractor. Many things may happen on a construction project that are totally beyond the control or responsibility of the subcontractor and that may cause payment by the owner or certification by the architect to be substantially delayed or even permanently prevented. Under contingent payment clauses general contractors often deny responsibility for paying the innocent subcontractors if anything occurs which causes the job not to be certified by the architect or causes the owner not to pay the general contractor.

A subcontractor may *never* get paid if he signs a subcontract which makes payment to him contingent upon payment by the owner to the general contractor. An example of a contingent payment clause is:

Contractor agrees to pay the subcontractor 30 days after completion of work, certification by the architect, and payment by the owner to the contractor.

By signing a payment clause that is contingent upon the owner paying the general contractor, the subcontractor has assumed the owner's credit risk and he has shifted the risk of nonpayment to himself instead of the general contractor. If something happens on the job that is beyond the control and responsibility of the subcontractor and that causes the owner not to pay the general contractor or the architect not to approve the work, then the general contractor may attempt to deny any responsibility to pay the subcontractor for work that is properly completed.

Illustrative Case

On a construction project the architect refused to certify the job, and the owner refused to make final payment to the general contractor, Peacock Construction Company. Peacock denied any further liability to the subcontractor, West, relying on the failure of the architect to certify the entire job and the failure of the owner to pay it. West was not involved in any defective work and sued Peacock for his contract balance. The court denied the subcontractor's right to recover for the work that admittedly had been properly performed by West on the grounds that West had agreed to make his payment contingent upon final certification of the job by the architect and payment by the owner to the general contractor, which never happened. The subcontractor had not presented to the court a legal excuse for overriding the contingency payment clause. [1]

The opinion in the preceding illustrative case stressed that the court reached this result in the absence of the subcontractor showing a legal excuse that the language of the contingent payment clause should not be held to be a condition precedent to the subcontractor's right to recover. Fortunately, in a number of recent decisions by the courts of Massachusetts, Maryland, North Carolina, New York, Florida, and California, contingent payment clauses have been interpreted to allow recovery by subcontractors even though the general contractor is not paid by the owner. Typically, contingent payment clauses provide that a subcontractor will be paid after the general contractor receives payment from the owner. These recent cases have uniformly construed the contingent payment clauses as not barring a subcontractor's right to recover and that the payment by the owner is not a condition precedent to the subcontractor's right for the payment after a reasonable length of time. In other words, in recent cases courts have construed the contingent payment language as an intermediate timing device to defer the subcontractor's payment for a reasonable length of time, but typical contingent payment clauses do not ultimately bar the subcontractor's right to recover from the general contractor.

[1] Peacock Constr. Co. v. West. 111 Ga. App. 604 (1965).

A contingent payment clause which was signed by A. J. Wolfe Company, a subcontractor, provided that the subcontractor shall be paid "within 10 days after . . . (the owner's) payment of such monthly progress payments . . . (has) been received by the general contractor." The general contractor, Baltimore Contractors, Inc., contended that the receipt of payment from the owner was a condition precedent to the subcontractor's right to payment and that Baltimore Contractors, in fact, had not been paid for the work for which Wolfe sought payment. The court interpreted this contingent payment clause as not requiring payment from the owner to the general contractor as a condition precedent to payment to the subcontractor; the court ruled that the contingent payment clause should be viewed as postponing payment from the general contractor for only a reasonable length of time and, allowed the subcontractor to recover.[2]

In another case the subcontractor, Atlantic States Construction Company, was allowed to recover its final payment because the court construed the contingent payment clause not to require payment by the owner to the general contractor, Drummond & Company, as a condition precedent to recovery of payment by the subcontractor. The contingent payment clause provided: "Final payment shall be made within 30 days after completion of work included in this Subcontract, written acceptance of same by the Architect and Owner, or their authorized representatives, and *full payment* therefore by the Owner." The court allowed the subcontractor to recover even though the general contractor had not been paid because of the owner's insolvency.[3]

The North Carolina Court of Appeals ruled that a contingent payment clause did not forestall the time for payment to the subcontractor until the general contractor received payment from the owner in spite of a contingent payment clause which provided: "Final payment will be paid within 15 days of acceptance of and payment for the entire contract by the Owner. . . ." A dispute between the general contractor and the owner had delayed payment to the general contractor, Chaney & James Construction Company. The court found that the subcontractor, Howard-Green Electrical Company, had a contract solely with the prime contractor, not a contract for the credit of the owner, and that the subcontractor did not accept responsibility for any part of the building other than the electrical work which was subcontracted.[4]

As seen in the preceding illustrative cases, the dynamics of the law relating to contingent payment clauses are moving rapidly toward the subcontractor's position, upholding the subcontractor's right to recovery of payment after a reasonable time in spite of the lack of payment from the owner to the general contractor. The courts are particularly prone to allow the subcontractor to recover when the reason for the lack of payment to the general contractor from the owner is the general contractor's own fault.[5] There is a strong thread that runs through the law that a party cannot benefit by his own fault and that the general contractor should not be allowed to raise a contingent payment clause as a bar to

---

[2] A.J. Wolfe & Co. v. Baltimore Contractors, Inc., 355 Mass. 636, 244 N.E.2d 717 (1969).

[3] Atlantic States Constr. Co. v. Drummond & Co., 251 Md. 77, 246 A.2d 251 (1968).

[4] Howard-Green Elec. Co. v. Chaney & James Constr. Inc., 12 N.C. App. 63, 182 S.E.2d 601 (1971). Similar results were reached in the case of Thomas J. Dyer Co. v. Bishop Int'l. Engineering Co., 303 F.2d 655 (6th Cir. 1962); Midland Engineering Co. v. John A. Hall Constr. Co., 398 F. Supp. 981 (N.D. Ind. 1975); Schuler-Hass Electric Corp. v. Aetna Casualty & Surety, 649 App. Div. 2d 260 (N.Y. 1975).

[5] Standard Asbestos Mfg. Co. v. Kaiser, 316 Ill. App. 441, 45 N.E.2d 75 (1942).

payment of the subcontractor when the reason that the owner did not pay the general contractor was the general contractor's own fault.

However, the last thing that a subcontractor wants is to have to resort to a court case to attempt to override a contingent payment clause that he has signed. Even if the subcontractor may ultimately be able to successfully vindicate his right to payment in court when the owner does not pay the general contractor, the general contractor will read the language literally and initially stand on the contract language to deny payment to the subcontractor. The best approach is for the subcontractor to add a savings clause which clearly establishes that the subcontractor will be paid if the general contractor is not paid by the owner or the architect does not certify the work for any reason that is not the fault of the subcontractor. General contractors typically accept such savings clauses, and a subcontractor should never sign a contingent payment clause unless language similar to the following savings clause is included:

If the architect fails to issue a certificate for payment or the contractor does not receive payment for any cause which is not the fault of the subcontractor, the contractor shall pay the subcontractor, on demand, progress payments and the final payment.

The preceding clause is essentially the language included in Article 12.5 of the AIA Standard Subcontract Form A401. If a subcontractor substitutes the AIA standard subcontract form, he automatically includes the savings clause.

The AGC standard subcontract form does not make the subcontractors' payment contingent upon payment by the owner, but it does make subcontractors' payment contingent upon payment certificates issued by the owner or the architect. The following is the AGC payment clause, Article 20:

The Contractor shall pay the Subcontractor within 7 days, unless otherwise provided in the Contract Documents, upon the payment of certificates issued under the Contractor's schedule of values, or as described in Article IV herein. The amount of the payment shall be equal to the percentage of completion certified by the Owner or his authorized agent for the work of this Subcontractor applied to the amount set forth under Article IV and allowed to the Contractor on account of the Subcontractor's work to the extent of the Subcontractor's interest therein.

A subcontractor who signs a clause making payment contingent upon certification by the architect is assuming the risk that all other work on the job will be performed satisfactorily; if the work of another subcontractor or the work of the general is defective, the architect may never certify the job. Thus the subcontractor may never be paid even though he has performed his work completely and satisfactorily and even though the defective work is not his responsibility. If payment is contingent upon certification by the architect and/or contingent upon payment by the owner to the general contractor, then an additional savings clause should be inserted in the subcontract which is similar to Article 12.5 of the AIA Standard Subcontract Form A401, quoted previously.

The AGC standard subcontract form contains a savings provision similar to the one in the AIA subcontract form, which gives the subcontractor the right to demand progress payments if payment certificates are not issued for any cause not the fault of the subcontractor; however, there is an added requirement that the failure of the architect to certify the work must also be caused by the fault of the contractor. It is questionable whether the AGC form permits a subcontractor to obtain final payment if the owner or architect does not issue a certificate for payment. The AGC clause states in Article X (22):

The Contractor shall pay the Subcontractor on demand for his work and/or materials as far as executed and fixed in place, less the retained percentage, at the time the payment should be made to the Subcontractor if the Architect or Owner's authorized agent fails to issue the certificate for any fault of the Contractor and not the fault of the Subcontractor or as otherwise provided herein.

It is recommended that the words "and final payment" be inserted in this clause in AGC forms to ensure the subcontractor's right to final payment and that the words "for any fault of the contractor and" be deleted to avoid having to establish the fault on the general contractor to ensure payment to the subcontractor.

In many cases the owner delays payment to the general contractor for months, and then under a contingent payment clause the general contractor attempts to pass this delay back to the subcontractor for an equal number of months or for an even greater period of time. Contingent payment clauses relieve the general contractor of the necessity for working capital and allow him to shift the financial burden for nonpayment of the work to the subcontractors, who have legal obligations to pay for their labor, material, and indirect costs on a current basis. The general contractor, who has a profit anticipation from the owner, should also have the financial risk and responsibility necessary for financing the project. By signing contingent payment clauses the subcontractor is putting himself in the banking business by providing part of the construction financing of a project.

If a subcontractor does not want his right to payment contingent upon events that take place beyond his control, the subcontractor should add the previously quoted AIA payment savings clause or the subcontractor should strike the words in the payment clause which make payments contingent upon final certification by the architect and payment by the owner. The subcontractor should modify the contingent clause by striking out the italized portion of the following clause:

Payment shall be due 30 days after completion of the work, *final certification by the architect and payment by the owner.*

By striking out those contingencies or adding the contingent payment savings clause, the subcontractor no longer bears the risk of nonpayment because of events that occur that are not his own fault.

RETENTION

Subcontractors must get out of the banking business. Subcontractors are in the business of building construction and should not be required to finance construction projects in whole or in part. The subcontractor is providing a part of the construction financing to the extent of any retention withheld from progress payments for his work. Two factors of vital importance to the subcontractor concerning retention are how much retention and when does the subcontractor receive payment of his retention.

Retention is ostensibly withheld to ensure that performance of the work will be completed by the subcontractor. After a subcontractor has completed his work, then the reason for withholding retention ceases. In practice, almost all subcontract forms which are drafted by general contractors allow the general contractors to hold retention until the entire construction project has been completed. Under such retention clauses, those subcontractors who complete their work at an early stage of the total construction work on the project, such as clearing, grading, foundation, roofing, and steel erection subcontractors, may have to wait many months and even years for their retention. Of course, for those subcontractors in the finishing trades, who work on the project until its final completion, delays in receiving final payment of retention are not as prolonged.

For a subcontractor to avoid having to wait until completion of the entire project to receive his subcontract retention, the payment clause should be modified to state:

Final payment shall be due 30 days after completion of the work by the subcontractor.

Under this language the subcontractor does not have to wait until after final acceptance of the project to receive full payment for his work. The subcontractor's warranty is adequate to protect the general contractor against problem items that might arise after completion of the subcontractor's work.

No retention should be held on subcontracts which have performance and payment bonds. When bonds are furnished by the subcontractor and retention is also withheld to ensure performance to the general contractor, the general contractor has double protection which is inequitable to the subcontractors and unduly expensive. The general contractor has recourse to the bonding company in the event of noncompletion by the subcontractor.

The modern trend is also to begin to reduce retention when a subcontractor's work is 50 percent completed and to pay subcontractor his retention in full when the subcontractor's work is completed. This method of paying retention is called "line-item reduction of retention" and "line-item payment of retention." The early finishing subcontractors should be paid their retention when they finish their work.

One of the traps against which subcontractors must guard is ensuring that the general contractor does not withhold a greater percentage retention on the subcontractor than is withheld from the general contractor by the owner. If the general contractor has his retention reduced at the 50 percent completion stage to 5 percent and continues to hold 10 percent retention on the subcontractors until completion of the job, a tremendous pool of working capital is created for the general contractor's use if he contractually does not have to reduce retention to the subcontractors because they have signed subcontracts agreeing to a full 10 percent retention until completion of the entire job. Consequently, when a general contractor is withholding 10 percent retained funds from subcontractors and the owner is withholding only 5 percent retention, the general contractor will not be very motivated to finish the work because it will actually cost the general contractor money to finish the work by reason of having to pay out more retention to the subcontractors than he has coming from the owner. The following is a case in which the author was involved which illustrates the abuses that are often reaped by general contractors when subcontractors fall into the trap of allowing a general contractor to hold more percentage retention on the subcontractors than is withheld from the general contractor by the owner.

Illustrative Case

A general contractor, John Hall Construction Company, had retention reduced to 5 percent after it had completed 50 percent of the general contract required work. The general contractor's printed form subcontracts contained a provision that 10 percent retention would be withheld from all subcontractors until final completion of all work on the project. The result was that during the latter stages of the job, the owner of the project owed the general contractor less than the general contractor owed to the subcontractors. Several years after the project had been completed and occupied for school purposes, the general contractor continued to withhold retention from subcontractors and further continued to be involved in disputes with the owner. These disputes resulted in delaying the final payment to the general contractor. The subcontractors filed suit in federal court seeking to recover the retained amount, and the general contractor contended that it was not required to pay the subcontractors until the project had been "completed" and final payment made from the owner to the general contractor. The court rejected this argument, holding that a contingent payment clause in the subcontracts could not be the basis by which a general contractor indefinitely withholds monies due subcontractors. The court went on to hold that when the subcontractors completed their work they were entitled to final payment regardless of continuing disputes between the general contractor and the owner.[6]

[6] Midland Engineering Co. v. John A. Hall Constr. Co., 398 F. Supp. 981 (N.D. Ind. 1975).

To avoid the trap of allowing the general contractor to hold more retention from the subcontractors than is withheld from the general contractor by the owner, the subcontractor should always insert a clause that states:

The general contractor will withhold no more percentage retention from the subcontractor than is withheld by the owner from the general contractor for the subcontractor's work.

There are many legendary general contractors who made full use of the practice of holding the subcontractors' retention to provide their own working capital. One of the more widespread stories in the construction industry is about the notorious general contractor who on his deathbed called in his family and named eight subcontractors that he wanted to be his pallbearers. The family was surprised and asked him why in the world he wanted these eight subcontractors to be his pallbearers and he replied, "Well, they carried me this far. They might as well carry me the rest of the way."

One of the more famous lawyers representing general contractors, in a recent briefing paper, instructed how to hold more retention from subcontractors than was withheld by the owner from the general contractor:

In many instances, however, it is provided in the prime contract that no sums will be retained from monies earned after 50 percent of the work is performed. But, unless the *subcontract* expressly provides the prime may *continue* to retain a percentage on *all* earnings of the sub until the completion and acceptance of the *entire* work. This frequently leads to controversy.[7]

By signing a clause which delays payment of retention until final acceptance of the entire construction project by the owner or the architect, the subcontractor may have waived his lien rights for the final retention. Under the lien laws of many states, a subcontractor must file a lien within 3 months after completion of his work, and if the completion of the subcontractor's work is more than 3 months prior to the final acceptance of the job, then the subcontractor legally might not be able to claim retention until his lien rights have expired. Therefore, final payment and retention clauses should state that final payment and retention shall be paid within 30 days after completion of the subcontracted work. The following clause has been inserted into subcontracts to ensure final payment by the general contractor after completion of the subcontractor's work:

Final payment shall become due 30 days after completion of the Subcontractor's work. Inspection for acceptance (if acceptable) shall be made within 1 week following request by Subcontractor. In the event completed work is not acceptable, deficiencies must be listed and mailed to Subcontractor within 1 week of inspection. After correction of deficiencies, Subcontractor may then request additional inspection as described above.

Holding the retention on each subcontractor until after the entire general contract work is completed increases the cost of the building to the owner and also delays completion of the total construction project. The

[7] Max E. Greenberg, *Construction Subcontract Terms—Critical Areas of Coverage, Briefing Papers— The Government Contractor,* June 1972.

subcontractors must pay for their labor, material, and indirect cost on a current basis and therefore must fund any retention held for a long duration either out of working capital, borrowed funds, or by increasing their subcontract prices. Subcontractors simply do not have sufficient working capital to fund the vast amounts required for retention, nor do they have the capacity to borrow these huge amounts. Therefore, a portion of the retention is funded by the subcontractor simply by increasing his contract price. A recent survey by the American Subcontractors Association surveying some 1,200 subcontractors throughout the United States indicated that the average increase in a subcontractor's price is 3.7 percent of the subcontract amount or 37 percent of the 10 percent retention. Paying the subcontractor's retention on a line-item basis as he completes his work significantly reduces the tendency of a subcontractor to increase his price in order to fund the retention over a long period of time.

Holding retention on subcontractors until the general contractor finishes the entire building actually delays completion of the building because the subcontractors simply are not motivated to rapidly finish their punch-list items. For example, if a subcontractor has punch-list work to complete and his retention is to be held until the general contract is totally completed, the subcontractor will not be motivated to rapidly finish his punch-list work because he knows that other subcontractors and the general contractor will drag out the completion of their punch lists. If this subcontractor puts up a maximum effort to complete his punch list rapidly, it will not benefit him because his retention will not be paid until all other work is completed. However, if a subcontractor knows that as soon as he has completed the punch list on his portion of the work that he will receive his retention, he will complete his punch list as rapidly as possible in order to receive the retention. Each subcontractor, in turn, will be similarly motivated to receive their retention on a line-item basis as soon as they complete their work, and, therefore, the entire building will be rapidly completed.

Illustrative Case

Three school buildings in New York City had not been finally completed for over 3 years after the owner had moved into and taken occupancy of the buildings. The subcontractors proposed to the owner that the owner pay each subcontractor's portion of retention when each subcontractor completed its work on a line-item basis. In 2 weeks each of the three buildings were totally punched out and completed.

The interests of the owners, general contractors, and subcontractors run parallel to pay retention by line item as each subcontractor completes his work and to reduce retention by line item when each subcontract category reaches 50 percent completion. Payment of retention to subcontractors when each subcontract category of work is completed will contribute greatly to a faster completion of an entire building, and the owner and general contractor will have adequate protection by guarantees and maintenance agreements by the subcontractors.

SCOPE OF WORK

Subcontractors should be extremely careful not to sign a subcontract which amplifies or expands the scope of the work beyond that which was anticipated in the subcontractor's bid. The subcontract should contain a very definite and concise statement of the work which is limited to the exact work contemplated by the subcontractor.

The clause in a subcontract document describing the work to be performed is one of the most important clauses in the subcontract. The description of the subcontractor's work must be precise. Otherwise, the subcontractor may find himself having to perform work he did not contemplate when he bid the job or negotiated his subcontract.

Subcontractors should take pains to make sure that there are no ambiguous or dragnet clauses that would require the performance of any work other than that specifically included in the subcontractor's bid. Furthermore, if certain work is excluded in the subcontractor's bid, he should make sure that the work is also excluded in the subcontract. If it is not excluded in the subcontract, the subcontractor may have to perform the work even though it was excluded in his bid.

The description of the work should begin with the denomination of the type of work that the subcontractor is going to perform, e.g., mechanical, electrical, roofing, plumbing, grading, structural, concrete, rebar, scaffolding, tile or terrazzo, etc. The description should be precise and use words that exactly define the type of work the subcontractor is going to do. In the next part of the description of the work, the subcontract scope of work should denominate exactly the plans by sheet numbers, date, and date of last revision. If the subcontractor does not describe the work in detail, he may find that he has bid on a version of the plans and specifications which were later revised and signed a contract which specified a later revision date that has materially changed his work. The next part of the description should state that the work shown on the plans will be in accordance with denominated sections of the specifications. If the subcontractor bids only part of a trade, e.g., the plumbing work as part of the mechanical, then he should make sure to break out and list those specifications sections that relate to plumbing work. A good example of a precise description of the work in a subcontract document is as follows:

The Subcontractor shall furnish the labor, materials, equipment, and supervision necessary to construct the mechanical work shown on drawings numbers M-1 to M-8, dated March 1, 1974, and last revised August 14, 1974, and drawings numbers M-9 to M-12, dated March 1, 1974, and last revised August 10, 1974, in accordance with specifications sections 15a and 15b (mechanical only).

Subcontractors should avoid dragnet clauses, which provide that a subcontractor will perform the work of his trade, regardless of what section the specifications or on which drawings that the work might appear. Frequently, architects will place work in a different category of drawings than that in which the work is normally encountered. The following type of dragnet clause should not be agreed to by the subcontractor to define the scope of the work:

. . . all mechanical work shown on the plans and specifications.

The following illustrative case shows what can happen if a subcontractor agrees to perform the work of his trade regardless of where it was shown in the plans and specifications.

Illustrative Case

Acousti Engineering Company, acoustical subcontractor, signed a contract that stated that the subcontractor agreed to do all acoustical work called for in all the plans and all the specifications after viewing only a set of architectural plans of the general contract which provided for an additional new wing to be constructed on a hospital. The subcontractor priced the ceiling work from the architectural drawings of the new wing and bid the job accordingly. In addition to the new wing addition, the general contract also included in the mechanical and electrical plans and specifications air-conditioning of the old hospital building, which required tearing out and replacing ceilings for mechanical and electrical work of the old hospital. Both the electrical and the mechanical contractors had specifically excluded from their bid the replacement of the ceilings they were to tear out and replace in the old hospital, and the estimator for the general contractor forgot to sub-out the remedial ceiling work for the electrical and mechanical work in the old hospital. Subsequently, the general contractor, Robert E. McKee, attempted to stick the remedial ceiling work on the acoustical contractor, pointing to the broad language of the scope of work of the acoustical subcontract which stated that it covered all acoustical work in all the plans and specifications of the general contract.

Miraculously, the arbitrator ruled in favor of the subcontractor, probably because he realized that the general contractor was trying to stick this work on the subcontractor with the broadest language in his scope of the work.[8]

Subcontracts also frequently contain language which broadly binds the subcontractor to do all the work that is required by the owner of the general contractor, such as:

It is understood and agreed that whatever is required of the contractor by the owner is required of the subcontractor.

If this clause were interpreted literally, the subcontractor would be obligated to perform the entire job for which the general contractor is obligated rather than furnishing only work that was intended under the subcontract. If the subcontractor is bound to the general contractor as the general contractor is bound to the owner, it should only be in relation to portions of the work covered under his subcontract and this clause should at least be modified by adding the following words:

. . . as applicable to the work covered in this subcontract.

[8] Acousti Engineering Co. v. McKee, Am. Arb. Ass'n, Arb. No. 32100062-71 (1972).

Also to be avoided are dragnet clauses which provide that the subcontract will perform work not expressly called for in the plans and specifications, such as:

. . . and all other things and services necessary or desirable.

. . . and other related items.

. . . in all respects as is therein required of the contractor and all work incidental thereto.

Such dragnet clauses have the effect of making an architect and engineer out of the subcontractor. They may very well bind the subcontractor to furnish any item or any system or any amount of labor that is required to make the system work, whether or not these things were required by the original plans and specifications. Remember that the responsibility for design rests with the architect and engineer, the responsibility for coordination and supervision rests with the general contractor, and the responsibility to supervise and construct only a narrow portion of the work rests with each subcontractor.

Occasionally, architects also place the same requirements under more than one heading, and the result may be that more than one subcontractor is required to perform the work, which can lead to disputes or litigation. Therefore, a subcontractor should be very careful to determine if work of his trade is required in other specifications or if the contract specifications are ambiguous so that such duplications can be eliminated. It is in the interests of the subcontractor to attempt to limit the scope of the work to that on which the subcontractor actually based his bid. One method to avoid expanding the subcontractor's scope of the work in the subcontract is to incorporate the subcontractor's bid into the subcontract as the definition of the scope of the work.

It is unthinkable that a subcontractor would not check to see that the subcontract contains a precise statement of the amount of money that the subcontractor is to receive under the subcontract, and yet subcontractors tend to ignore or be sloppy in defining the scope of the work, which is the corollary to the payment clause. The scope of work is the other side of the payment coin. It is just as important that the subcontractor be precise in defining the scope of the work as in stating the amount of money he is to receive under the subcontract.

CONDUIT CLAUSES

The general contractor naturally will be motivated to bind the subcontractors to the general contractor as the general contractor is bound to the owner. Conversely, the general contractor should be willing to provide the subcontractors with the same rights, redress, and remedies which the general contractor has against the owner. "Conduit clauses," also called "flow-down clauses," provide that the subcontract incorporates the general contract provisions which are applicable to the subcontractor's work. If conduit clauses are used, the same rights and duties should flow equally from the owner down through the general contractor to the subcontractor as well as from the subcontractor up through the general contractor to the owner. Both the AIA Standard Subcontract Form A401 and the AGC standard subcontract form contain conduit clauses which provide that the subcontractor is bound to the same responsibilities and duties as the general contractor has to the owner which are applicable to the subcontracted work; in turn, the subcontractor has the same rights, redress, and remedies against the general contractor that the general contractor has against the owner. AIA Standard Subcontract Form A401 contains the following conduit clause, Article 11.1:

The Subcontractor shall be bound to the Contractor by the terms of this Agreement and of the Contract Documents between the Owner and Contractor, and shall assume toward the Contractor all the obligations and responsibilities which the Contractor, by those Documents, assumes toward the Owner, and shall have the benefit of all rights, remedies and redress against the Contractor which the Contractor, by those Documents, has against the Owner, insofar as applicable to this Subcontract, provided that where any provision of the Contract Documents between the Owner and Contractor is inconsistent with any provision of this Agreement, this Agreement shall govern.

Often subcontract forms drafted by the general contractors contain a conduit clause which ties the subcontractor to the general contractor's obligations but conspicuously omits the corresponding rights by the subcontractor, such as the following:

Contractor shall have the same rights and privileges as against the Subcontractor herein as the Owner in the General Contract has against Contractor.

Subcontractor acknowledges that he has read the General Contract and all plans and specifications and is familiar therewith and agrees to comply with and perform all provisions thereof applicable to Subcontractor.

It is patently unreasonable for the general contractor to attempt to bind the subcontractor to the provisions of the general contract while the general contractor does not give the corresponding rights, remedies, and redress to the subcontractor.

If a conduit clause is used in the subcontract, then it is imperative that the subcontractor inspect all plans and specifications and all contract documents, including all general and special conditions, the general contract, and all modifications and addendums, because the subcontractor is agreeing to be bound by the terms and conditions in the subcontract that are contained in the general contract and plans and specifications applicable to the general contract. If the general contractor is unwilling to allow inspection of the general contract, then the general contract should be excluded from the operation of the conduit clause.

CHANGES

The changes article in a subcontract must be studied to determine the extent to which the general contractor may unilaterally direct increases or decreases in the work, suspend performance of the work, or otherwise direct changes without being limited to changes within the general scope of the subcontract. If the change clause in a suggested subcontract includes provisions which will allow the general contractor to add quantities at his unilateral discretion, the subcontractor may not desire to have the pricing for the increased work predicated upon the pricing for that of the original subcontract. If the subcontractor should happen to be performing the original subcontract at reduced profit or at a loss, his loss may be expanded.

The subcontractor is motivated to complete the work promptly in a good workmanlike manner and to release his workforce for other jobs. The cost of performing changes which extend the time of performance may be much more than the contemplated cost of the original work.

A subcontractor should retain flexibility on the pricing of the changes in order to ensure that he has the requisite funds to meet the burdens of the performance of changes. Clear provisions should be obtained in the subcontracts which allow the subcontractor to price his work either on a cost-plus formula or at a negotiated price.

Both the AIA and the AGC standard subcontract forms provide that the subcontractors must make changes in the work when directed in writing by the general contractor, and the subcontractor is tied to the same rights, remedies, and redress for payment of the change as contained in the general contract and general conditions. The AIA Standard Subcontract Form A401, Article 11.13, provides the authority for the general contractor to direct the subcontractor to make changes. Article 11.4 provides the conduit procedure for the subcontractor to make claims under the provisions of the general contract documents.

11.13 The Subcontractor shall make any and all changes in the Work from the Drawings and Specifications of the Contract Documents without invalidating this Subcontract when specifically ordered to do so in writing by the Contractor. The Subcontractor, prior to the commencement of such changed or revised work, shall submit promptly to the Contractor written copies of the cost or credit proposal for such revised Work in a manner consistent with the Contract Documents.

11.4 The Subcontractor shall make all claims promptly to the Contractor for additional work, extensions of time, and damage for delays or otherwise, in accordance with the Contract Documents.

In subcontracts containing authority under which the general contractor can unilaterally direct the subcontractor to perform the work as changed, even though the parties do not agree on the price for the changed work, the subcontractor must have a remedy which will quickly meet his financial needs in deciding the price for the changed work. Such a remedy may be a provision for an expeditious arbitration proceeding under which the cost is shared equally between the general contractor and the subcontractor. Arbitration proceedings must be subject to speedy resolution insofar as the subcontractor is concerned. Otherwise, he will be out of pocket for the costs of his required performance for a substantial period of time.

The AIA contract documents provide an arbitration procedure both in Article 14 of AIA Standard Subcontract Form A401 and in Article 7.10 of the General Conditions. The AIA General Conditions, in Article 12, govern the procedure for changes in work and permit the owner to direct changes in the work of the general contractor, which, in turn, may be transmitted to the subcontractor, which is within the scope of the work of the subcontract. The AIA changes clause provides for payment of changes by either an agreed lump-sum negotiated price, unit prices, a cost plus a percentage, or fixed-fee pricing of the change. Or, if none of the methods can be agreed upon, the disputes clause provides that the architect must initially determine the cost of the changed work based upon the reasonable expenditures plus a reasonable amount for overhead and profit; or if there is a savings, a determination for a deductive change is made by the architect for only the cost of the work without deduction for overhead and profit. If the contractor or subcontractor disputes the value of the work certified by the architect, then the contractor or subcontractor can demand arbitration.

The subcontractors and general contractor should be aware that the AIA General Conditions changes clause requires the architect to certify and the owner to pay at least the value of the change as determined by the architect. The subcontractor should not allow the architect or the owner to attempt to starve the general contractor or subcontractor into agreement. The owner must pay at least what the architect says is the value of the work. Then the contractor and subcontractor can argue about the difference in what the architect certifies the value of the work to be and the claim by the contractor or subcontractor.

A common subcontract changes clause provides that the subcontractor may be paid for extra work only when it is authorized by an officer of the general contractor in advance and in writing. Although the subcontractor's foreman may be tempted to perform extra work upon an oral demand by the general contractor's field superintendent, this is a very unwise practice. The general contractor may dispute the reasonable value of the work performed, or he may reject the claim entirely because it was not authorized in advance in writing by the proper officer, as required by the contract.

Where such claims have been presented to the courts, the subcontractor may be awarded the reasonable value of the work, despite the contract requirement of proper authorization, where the subcontractor is able to prove both that there was an oral order to perform the work and that the general contractor accepted the benefits of the work. Similar results have been reached by the courts when the owner accepts the benefits of the work.[9]

Illustrative Case

Orndorff Construction Company was directed by an unauthorized representative of the government to do certain work not included in the original excavation quantities in the contract. The contractor performed this work without obtaining a written authorization from an authorized representative, as required by the contract. Orndorff's claim of a change was upheld because it was shown that the authorized representative knew that the changes in the work were being made without written authorization from him.[10]

However, there are also cases in which circumstances have denied recovery to the subcontractor for work performed on oral order. The outcome of each case depends both on the adequacy of the proof of oral order and acceptance of the benefits and on the law in that jurisdiction. A subcontractor, therefore, should not assume that he is entitled to the fair value of extra work. Instead he should make it a strict rule not to perform any extra work unless it is properly authorized in writing.

Another problem area sometimes encountered with payment for extra work is a subcontract provision that the subcontractor will be paid for extra work only when and to the extent that the general contractor is paid for the extra work by the owner. The general contractor may have been obligated to perform this work under the general contract and would therefore not receive any extra compensation for it; or the owner may contest the general contractor's authority to proceed with the extra work. In either case, the general contractor does not receive payment for the work as an extra, and the clause attempts to insulate the general contractor from any obligation to pay the subcontractor.

LIEN RIGHTS

A subcontractor should *never* sign a contract which contains a provision that waives any of the subcontractor's "lien rights," or the right to proceed on any general contractor's payment bond. If the subcontractor signs a subcontract which has a clause waiving his lien rights, then under the lien laws of many states, his lien rights are gone. The legislatures of several states have recognized that no waivers of liens should be permitted, and Massachusetts and New York have recently passed laws invalidating any purported waivers of liens.[11]

A subcontractor should not sign a subcontract with a waiver of lien rights clause, and if a waiver of lien rights clause appears in the sub-

---

[9] Lindbrook Constr., Inc. v. Mukilteo School Dist. No. 6, 458 P.2d 1 (Wash. 1969); Bailey v. Martin, 101 Ga. App. 63, 112 S.E.2d 807 (1960).

[10] Appeal of Orndorff Constr. Co., 67-2 B.C.A. § 6665 (1967).

[11] *Ann. Laws of Mass.*, Chap. 254 § 32 (Supp. 1975); *N.Y. Consolidated Laws Ann.*, Book 32 § 34 (McKinney's, Supp. 1975); *N.Y. Acts 1975* (Bill No. S. 947-A).

contract, the subcontractor should strike it out. Many subcontractors follow the policy of eliminating waiver of lien rights clauses from subcontract forms, and they seldom encounter any objection from general contractors. Any general contractor who insists upon a subcontractor waiving his lien rights is acting unreasonably. If a subcontractor chooses to proceed with a subcontract containing a waiver of his lien rights, then the subcontractor will be proceeding on a job with an unreasonable general contractor without any recourse to obtain payment should the general contractor be unable to pay.

A subcontractor who waives his lien rights not only loses his right to file a lien but also may have to remove at his own cost and expense any liens which may have been placed against the property as a result of his work. The subcontractor may have to remove those liens placed by his materialmen and subcontractors because in another clause in the subcontract he may have agreed to indemnify the general contractor and the owner from liens arising out of the subcontractor's work. In this situation the general contractor could fail to make payment to the subcontractor, and yet the subcontractor would have agreed not only to waive his lien rights but also to idemnify the owner and general contractor against any liens placed by persons subordinate to the subcontractor.

Lien laws are unique to the United States law and are without parallel in English common law or European civil law. They were developed in the days of Jefferson and Madison to foster the building of the United States. They have served their purpose well, and the same reasoning that prompted these leaders to develop lien laws and has proliferated lien laws throughout the fifty states is still valid today. The basic policy behind the lien law is that the labor and material furnished by general contractors, subcontractors, material suppliers, or mechanics become affixed to the real estate and improve the value of the land and cannot be reclaimed by them. Just the opposite is true with personal property because it can be reclaimed by the creditor or delivery can be made simultaneously with payment. This is not the case with construction. Payment is usually made after the labor and materials have been incorporated in the real estate. Therefore, the only manner in which protection can be afforded a general contractor, subcontractor, or material supplier for payment is to give them a meaningful security interest in the land to secure their payment for the value of the labor and materials that they have previously furnished to improve the land.

All fifty states have made the determination that it is basically inequitable to allow the owner to ultimately receive the benefit of a general contractor's, subcontractor's, material supplier's, or mechanic's work without ultimately bearing the responsibility of ensuring that the labor and material are paid for. Subcontractors are secured creditors in most states to the extent of the owner's equity on any private construction job. Although lien laws vary from state to state, in many states subcontractors may become secured creditors by notifying the owner and filing a notice on the deed records where the property is situated of a claim of lien against the property within a specified time from the completion of his work. If the subcontractor is not paid, then in many states he must file suit to commence legal action for the recovery of the amount of his claim and foreclosure of his lien within a specified time, which is usually between 3 months to 1 year.

Lien rights are lost by many subcontractors merely because they do not file their liens within time limitations provided in the lien laws. It is not an insult to a general contractor or owner to file a lien to protect your legal rights. If the situation were reversed, the general contractor would be filing for his lien rights. A subcontractor should allow his attorney several weeks lead time so that he can obtain a proper legal description of the property involved. Also, if he has some lead time, the attorney possibly may obtain payment without the necessity of filing the lien.

A subcontractor can lose his lien rights if he signs a lien waiver or an affidavit stating that he has been paid when, in fact, he has not been paid. A subcontractor should never sign a waiver of lien or affidavit stating that he has waived his lien rights or acknowledge that he has been paid all money due him when, in fact, he has not been paid. The waiver of lien or affidavit should be made contingent so that it is not effective until the subcontractor actually receives his payment for whatever amount is due. Most waivers of liens for final payment can simply be modified by adding the contingent words, "Upon receipt of $_____," followed by the waiver of lien language in which the subcontractor waives his lien rights and acknowledges receipt of all monies due him. With the contingent language added, if the subcontractor does not receive the payment due him, then the lien waiver and acknowledgment of receipt of monies due him is not effective and will not waive his lien rights or bar his right to recovery.

On the interim waiver of liens, subcontractors should be very careful not to waive their lien rights until their money has been received, and they should be careful to waive their lien rights only to the extent that they have received payment, not to waive their lien rights for future work. An interim standard waiver of lien that has been recommended by both the Associated General Contractors of America and American Subcontractors Association and that covers the problem of interim waiver of liens is as follows:

Furthermore, in consideration of the payments received, and upon receipt of the amount of this request, the undersigned does hereby waive, release, and relinquish all claim or right of lien which the undersigned may now have upon the premises above described except for claims or right of lien for contract and/or change order work performed to extent that payment is being retained or will subsequently become due.

In some states, a general contractor can also waive a subcontractor's lien rights if the general contractor signs a final affidavit stating that all materialmen and subcontractors have been paid and this affidavit will act to discharge a subcontractor's lien. However, a general contractor who signs a false affidavit stating that all bills have been paid when they have not been paid is breaking the criminal laws.

If the owner has little or no equity because of a high mortgage and the owner defaults in the mortgage payment, there is a risk of the mortgage holder foreclosing for the amount of the mortgage and wiping out all subcontractors' liens. A prior first mortgage holder who forecloses has priority over the lien holders in many states.

A subcontractor can become a secured creditor of the owner should the general contractor not pay him merely by filing a lien within the specified time provided by law if he has not waived his lien rights. Why should he neglect his lien rights and become an unsecured creditor and risk non-payment by the general contractor? Guarding lien rights is one of the subcontractor's best insurances for collecting his money.

BOND RIGHTS

Liens cannot be claimed against property owned by governmental entities. To protect the subcontractor's right to payment, both federal and state laws require the general contractor to secure a "payment bond" signed by an authorized surety company. Under the federal statute, commonly termed the "Miller Act," a subcontractor who has not been paid within 90 days after payment is due may file suit on the general contractor's payment bond in federal district court, so long as recovery is sought within 1 year after the subcontractor furnished the last labor or material. This right to sue on the bond has an additional requirement if the subcontractor is a second-tier subcontractor and does not have a direct contractual relationship with the general contractor: The subcontractor must give formal written notice to the prime contractor within 90 days after he furnished or supplied the last labor or material for which he is making a claim, giving the name of the party with whom he contracted and stating the amount of the claim with substantial accuracy.

The House of Representatives of the United States Congress has recently recognized that waiver of Miller Act bond rights should not be permitted under the Miller Act and has approved a bill which would be of great benefit to subcontractors and material suppliers, amending the Miller Act to prohibit waiver of lien rights.[12] The proposed amendments also provide that claimants of the Miller Act may be entitled to attorneys' fees if the bonding companies require that they pursue to litigation and defend in bad faith. However these Miller Act amendments were not acted on by the Senate and are not yet enacted into law.

Most states also have a statute similar to the Miller Act which gives subcontractors who work on state, county, and municipal projects the right to sue on the general contractor's payment bond. Subcontractors

[12]H. R. 11691 (1974).

should be sure to consult their attorneys to learn exactly what time limitations and notice requirements exist for recovery on payment bonds in the state where the work is situated.

On more and more private jobs the owners require the general contractors to furnish a payment bond. The purpose of these bonds is to ensure payment for all labor and material used in the performance of the contract. Subcontractors must follow necessary steps to protect themselves under the provisions of the bonds. Subcontractors should follow these procedures to protect their bond rights on *all* jobs:

1. At the initial construction stage the subcontractor should determine if he is working on a bonded job. Often subcontractors work on bonded jobs and do not even know it.

2. When the job *begins,* the subcontractor should obtain a copy of the bond from the owner. The insurance company that underwrites the bond sends the bond directly to the owner. The owner is usually very cooperative in furnishing a subcontractor with a copy of the bond.

3. If the subcontractor is not paid on time, he should do *exactly* what is required by the terms of the bond and within the time stated in the bond. If the bond requires that notice be given to the insurance company within a specified time of any default by the general contractor and that such notice must be sent by certified mail to a particular address, then all of these conditions must be complied with or the subcontractor may lose his right to payment under the bond.

Some state laws provide that bond claimants can require a surety or insurance company to pay a penalty and claimants' reasonable attorneys' fees if the surety or insurance company refused in bad faith to honor its obligations under a payment bond within a period of time after receipt of a notice of default. Since this law was passed in Georgia providing for a 25 percent penalty and attorneys' fees, surety companies have been much more responsive to paying off their obligations under payment bonds.[13]

If a subcontractor is working on a bonded job, he must be sure not to waive his bond rights and to follow the procedures for pursuing payment under the bond.

HOLD HARMLESS AND INDEMNITY PROVISIONS

The contractual liability created by a "hold harmless agreement" is the assumption by contract of another's liability. The "indemnitor" is the party to the contractual agreement who assumes the obligation to hold the "indemnitee" harmless for liability. A hold harmless agreement is a contract for indemnity which normally protects the indemnitee against the consequences of an act. In general, hold harmless agreements are not illegal as long as they do not protect against a crime or are not declared contrary to public policy either by court or legislation. Hold harmless agreements indirectly conflict with the common-law concept that a man

[13] Ga. Code Ann. § 103–210 (1968 Supp. 1976).

must be responsible for his own wrongs, and it is against public policy to allow him to stipulate against his own negligence or wrongdoing.

Hold harmless and indemnity clauses in subcontracts should be strictly limited to injury or damages arising out of the subcontractor's work and caused by the negligence of the subcontractor, his agents, and employees. It is not unreasonable for subcontractors to agree to indemnify and hold harmless the general contractor and owners for damages which are caused by the subcontractor's negligence because the subcontractor is normally responsible for his negligence. However, in recent years, these hold harmless provisions have been broadened in scope to require the subcontractor to indemnify the owner, general contractor, and/or architect against any and all liabilities arising out of the job, including the negligence of the owner, general contractor, and/or architect.

Those hold harmless clauses which are limited in scope to the subcontractor, agreeing to indemnify and hold harmless the owner, general contractor, and architect against the subcontractor's negligence are called "limited-form" hold harmless clauses, and typically they have the following language:

Subcontractor agrees to indemnify and hold harmless the General Contractor against claims, damages, bodily injury, or property damage arising out of the Subcontractor's work and caused by any act or omission of the Subcontractor, his agents, and his employees.

A "broad-form" hold harmless clause, which is very objectionable, is an agreement under which the subcontractor agrees to indemnify and hold harmless the general contractor, owner, and/or architect against all claims arising out of the work, including any claims resulting from the negligence of the general contractor, owner, or achitect. A severe example of a broad-form hold harmless clause is as follows:

The Subcontractor shall indemnify and hold harmless the Contractor and all his agents and employees from and against all claims, damages, losses, and expenses, including attorneys' fees, arising out of or resulting from the performance of the Subcontractor's work whether it is caused in part or in whole by a party indemnified hereunder. In any and all claims against the Contractor, or any of his agents and employees by any employee of the Subcontractor, anyone directly or indirectly employed by him or anyone for whose acts he may be liable, the indemnification obligation under this Paragraph shall not be limited in any way by any limitation on the amount or type of damages, compensation, or benefits payable by or for the Subcontractor under workmen's compensation acts, disability benefit acts, or other employee benefit acts.

A third type of hold harmless clause is the "intermediate-form" hold harmless clause, which requires the subcontractor to indemnify and hold harmless the contractor against all losses arising out of the work and resulting from the negligence of the subcontractor even though the party indemnified may also be negligent. An example of an intermediate-form hold harmless clause appears in Article 11.20 of AIA standard subcontract form:

11.20   The Subcontractor shall indemnify and hold harmless the Contractor and all of his agents and employees from and against all claims, damages, losses, and expenses including attorneys' fees arising out of or resulting from the performance of the Subcontractor's Work under this subcontract, provided that any such claim, damage, loss, or expense (a) is attributable to bodily injury, sickness, disease, or death, or to injury to or destruction of tangible property (other than the Work itself) including the loss of use resulting therefrom, and (b) is caused in whole or in part by any negligent act or omission of the Subcontractor or anyone directly or indirectly employed by him or anyone for whose acts he may be liable, regardless of whether it is caused in part by a party indemnified hereunder.

11.20.1   In any and all claims against the Contractor or any of his agents or employees by and employee of the Subcontractor, anyone directly or indirectly employed by him or anyone for whose acts he may be liable, the indemnification obligation under this Paragraph 11.20 shall not be limited in any way by any limitation on the amount or type of damages, compensation or benefits payable by or for the Subcontractor under workmen's compensation acts, disability benefit acts or other employee benefit acts.

11.20.2   The obligations of the Subcontractor under this Paragraph 11.20 shall not extend to the liability of the Architect, his agents or employees arising out of (1) the preparation or approval of maps, drawings, opinions, reports, surveys, Change Orders, designs or specifications, or (2) the giving of or the failure to give directions or instructions by the Architect, his agents or employees provided such giving or failure to give is the primary cause of the injury or damage.

A subcontractor who signs a broad-form hold harmless clause has become an insurance company because he has agreed to insure other parties against their own negligence and fault. By signing a broad-form hold harmless clause, a subcontractor undertakes the obligations of paying for damages for which he would not otherwise be legally responsible. When a subcontractor signs a broad-form hold harmless clause, he is undertaking a contractual liability as distinguished from a general liability for his own negligent acts. Contractual liabilities are not covered by a subcontractor's general liability insurance. Unless a subcontractor's insurance program specifically includes coverage of contractual liability under hold harmless clauses, the subcontractor must pay out of his own pocket any losses that are incurred under the broad-form hold harmless clause arising from damages caused by the fault of someone else. It takes only one substantial uninsured loss to put most subcontractors out of business.

Illustrative Case

A specialty contractor, Cleveland Consolidated, Inc., was required to defend and ultimately assume liability for a serious personal injury which was solely the fault of Kraft Foods, the owner. An employee of a subcontractor, Johnson Service Company, was injured when an employee of Kraft negligently drove a tow motor into scaffolding on which he was working. The specialty contractor was not even on the job at the time. The injured employee sued Kraft for the negligence of its employee, and Kraft vouched the Cleveland Consolidated into the case to defend and to ultimately pay for judgment. The court enforced the broad-form hold harmless clause against Cleveland Consolidated, and Kraft did not have to assume any of the financial burdens for which it was solely at fault. The specialty contractor did not have contractual insurance coverage or hold harmless insurance, and consequently it had to pay the very substantial damages for the serious injury out of its pocket. [14]

[14] Kraft Foods v. Disheroon, 118 Ga. App. 632, 165 S.E.2d 189 (1968).

There are many other recent cases in which subcontractors who were not at fault had to pay very substantial losses and legal expenses because they signed broad-form hold harmless clauses and agreed to insure not only the owners, but also the architects and engineers against their own professional negligence.

These recent cases have caused much concern to subcontractors, and, through the efforts of associations representing subcontractors, laws have been passed declaring broad-form hold harmless clauses to be invalid as against public policy. In twenty-six states laws have been passed which either prohibit, nullify, or modify[15] a subcontractor's liability under hold harmless provisions when the injury or damage arises from the sole negligence of the party indemnified under the hold harmless clause, normally the general contractor, owner, and/or architect. The Tennessee hold harmless law (*Tennessee Code Annotated,* Section 62-624) is representative of the statutory attempts to declare void or unenforceable hold harmless agreements in the construction contract, and it states:

Section 1.   A convenant, promise, agreement or understanding in, or in connection with or collateral to a contract or agreement relative to the construction, alteration, repair or maintenance of a building, structure, appurtenance and appliance, including moving, demolition and excavating connected therewith, purporting to indemnify or hold harmless the promisee against liability for damages arising out of bodily injury to persons or damage to property caused by or resulting from the sole negligence of the promisee, his agents or employees, or indemnitee, is against public policy and is void and unenforceable.

These laws generally invalidate broad-form hold harmless clauses but usually do not invalidate intermediate-form hold harmless provisions

---

[15] California (*Calif. Civil Code* § 2782–84 (West 1974));
Delaware (*Del. Code* tit. 6 § 2704 (1975));
Florida (*Fla. Stat. Ann.* § 725.06 (West 1969 Supp. 1977));
Georgia (*Ga. Code Ann.* § 20–504);
Hawaii (*Haw. Rev. Stat.* § 431–453 (1968));
Idaho (*Ida. Code* § 29-114 (1967 Supp. 1976));
Illinois (*Ill. Ann. Stat.* ch. 29 § 61 (Smith-Hurd 1969 Supp. 1977));
Indiana (*Ind. Stat. Ann.* §§ 26-2-5-1, 26-2-5-2 (Burns 1974 Supp. 1976));
Maryland (*Md. Cts. & Jud. Proc. Code Ann.* S 5-305 (1974 Supp. 1976));
Michigan (*Mich. Stat. Ann.* § 26–114(1) (1974));
Mississippi (*Miss. Code Ann.* § 31-5-41 (1972 Supp. 1972));
New Hampshire (*N.H. Rev. Stat. Ann.* § 338A: 1 (1955 Supp. 1975));
New Mexico (*N.M. Stat. Ann.* § 28-2-1 (1954 Supp. 1975));
New York (*N.Y. Gen. Oblig. Law* § 5-322.1 (McKinney's 1964 Supp. 1976));
North Dakota (*N.D. Cent. Code* § 9-08-02.1 (1975));
Ohio (*Ohio Rev. Code Ann.* § 2305.31 (Page 19—Supp. 1976));
Oregon (*Ore. Rev. Stat.* § 30–140 (1975));
Pennsylvania (*Pa. Stat. Ann.* tit. 68 § 491 (Purdon 1965 Supp. 1976));
Rhode Island (Bill no. 76-S-2324, June 3, 1976);
South Dakota (*S.D. Compiled Laws Ann.* § 56-3-16 (1967 Supp. 1976));
Tennessee (*Tenn. Code Ann.* § 62–624 (1976 Supp. 1976));
Texas (*Tex. Civil Stat.* § 249d (Vernon 1973));
Utah (*Utah Code Ann.* § 13-8-1 (1973));
Virginia (*Va. Code* § 11-4.1 (1950 Supp. 1976));
Washington (*Wash. Rev. Code Ann.* § 4.24.115 (1962 Supp. 1975));
West Virginia (*W.Va. Code* § 55-8-14 (1966 Supp. 1976)).

where the subcontractors are jointly liable with the parties indemnified under the hold harmless provisions. If a subcontractor and the party indemnified under a broad-form hold harmless clause were both negligent, then even after the passage of this statute, the subcontractor may be required to pay all losses. In the states which have these laws, intermediate-form contractual liability insurance will still be required to insure the circumstances under which the subcontractor may be jointly negligent with the party indemnified by the hold harmless clause. It is questionable whether the subcontractor's general liability policy may cover such losses in spite of the fact that the loss arises, at least in part, from the subcontractor's own negligence. Each subcontractor must check with his individual insurance agent to verify whether he is covered under a specific hold harmless clause.

Courts generally do not allow a party to limit his liability by stipulating against his own negligence. Some courts take the position that no agreement could avoid the liability for one's own negligence and that to allow a party to indirectly avoid the responsibility for his negligence in the agreement is also void and contrary to public policy. Other courts reason that freedom of contract requires upholding agreements even though the agreement indirectly allows a party to avoid responsibility for the consequences of the party's own negligence or fault if the intent of the party is clearly spelled out in the agreement.[16]

However, generally courts bend over backward to avoid construing hold harmless agreements to include an agreement to indemnify the other parties for the indemnitee's own negligence. If the hold harmless clause stipulates that the subcontractor shall indemnify the general contractor for any injury or damage arising out of the work, a court generally has construed this language as not creating a broad-form hold harmless clause and has interpreted this language as holding only the general contractor harmless for those injuries which are caused by the fault of the subcontractor.

Illustrative Case

Georgia Marble Setting Company, a marble subcontractor, had an employee injured because of the negligence of Batson-Cook Company, the general contractor. The injured employee collected workman's compensation from Georgia Marble and sued Batson-Cook for its active negligence. Batson-Cook, in turn, called upon Georgia Marble to defend and respond to any damages under the hold harmless clause which was in the general subcontract form and provided that the subcontractor would indemnify and hold harmless the general contractor for any injury arising out of the work. Although admittedly the injury arose out of the work, the court narrowly construed the language "arising out of the work" as not including indemnification for the general contractor's own negligence and held that the clause did not apply.[17]

---

[16]See, e.g., Kraft Foods v. Disheroon, 118 Ga. App. 632, 165 S.E.2d 189 (1968).

[17]Batson-Cook Co. v. Georgia Marble Setting Co., 112 Ga. App. 226 (1965).

When a subcontract contains a broad-form hold harmless clause, it should be either deleted or modified to a limited-form hold harmless clause. Many contractors will strike out broad- or intermediate-form hold harmless clauses if the subcontractor will just ask. Alternatively, subcontractors should modify broad-form hold harmless clauses to a limited form by limiting the hold harmless clauses to cover all the subcontractor's negligence for which the subcontractor is already legally bound under the law. If the broad-form hold harmless clause is signed, it should be insured against loss with broad-form contractual liability insurance coverage. All hold harmless clauses should be insured with blanket contractual liability coverage.

Subcontractors should read the hold harmless clauses in subcontracts very carefully and check with their attorneys and insurance agents concerning questions about their liability under the clauses. After a subcontractor reviews several hold harmless clauses, he will probably acquire a working knowledge of the various types of hold harmless clauses so that in the future he can spot problem areas of his liability under such clauses.

PROTECTION-OF-WORK CLAUSES

Many subcontracts devised by general contractors contain "protection-of-work clauses" in which the subcontractor agrees to protect or insure his work against any damage and agrees to replace the work if damaged or destroyed; the wording is similar to the following:

The subcontractor shall insure his work against loss resulting from fire, earthquake, flood, water damage, windstorm, hail, explosion, strike, riot, civil commotion, aircraft, vehicles, smoke, vandalism, malicious mischief, theft, or any other cause whatsoever, and neither the contractor nor the owner will under any circumstances, unless otherwise specified, be liable or accountable to the subcontractor for such loss. Subcontractor shall effectually secure and protect the work to be done hereunder and assume full responsibility for the condition thereof until final acceptance by owner and contractor. Subcontractor shall be liable for any loss or damage to any work in place or to any equipment and materials on jobsite, even though the particular work damaged may have been finished by the subcontractor at that time.

The subcontractor should not be obliged to insure his materials after they are stored on the job or installed in the project, at which time they become a part of the construction and should be insured by the owner or general contractor under the so-called builder's risk insurance policies. Literally interpreted, some of the protection-of-work subcontract clauses would require the subcontractor, in the event that the building burned down, to reaccomplish the work without any payment up to final acceptance of the building by the owner. It is doubtful that many subcontractors carry such insurance in their own name, or at least sufficient insurance to cover these losses. The builder's risk insurance policies purchased by the owner or general contractor should cover the work once installed or suitably stored on the premises. Only damage done to the work by the subcontractor or his employees or agents should be his responsibility to replace or repair.

Other types of protection-of-work clauses stipulate that the subcontractor protect his work from damage by other trades during the course of the construction, as follows:

Subcontractor shall protect its work from damage during the construction of the project and any work damaged by Subcontractor or any other contractors until final acceptance shall be repaired or replaced by Subcontractor.

For many subcontract trades it is impossible to protect the work from damage by others. For example, ceiling, walls, or glass contractors would have to erect barricades in front of every ceiling, wall, and window that they build to protect their work from damage during construction. It is the obligation of a subcontractor to install the work once in the correct manner, and then it should be the responsibility of the general contractor to coordinate the job properly so that the work is not damaged or, if it is damaged, to determine the responsible party to charge the cost of the remedial work.

As a general rule, protection-of-work clauses should be deleted by subcontractors because under such clauses the subcontractor is assuming a potentially catastrophic liability. Each subcontract should be read carefully as it pertains to the protection-of-work provisions to make sure that the subcontractor is not agreeing to assume any liability or responsibility that he had not contemplated previously.

WARRANTIES

Subcontractors are well advised to limit warranty clauses to start from the time of completion of their installation rather than from the time of acceptance of the entire project. Warranty provisions in subcontracts usually require that the subcontractor warrant his work for 1 year from final acceptance of the entire project. On jobs where there is extensive site development which may go on for years, the subcontractor would be obliged to warrant his portion of the work well beyond the time he originally intended.

A typical subcontract warranty clause provides:

Subcontractor shall remedy any defects and pay for any damage resulting therefrom which shall appear within 1 year from the date of acceptance by the owner, or a longer period of time if specified in the contract documents.

Under this clause it would be compulsory for the subcontractor to know the exact contents of the contract documents in order to know what the warranty time period may be. It is also possible that in the contract documents between the owner and the general contractor the time might be modified during the course of the contract. Modifications may be agreed upon between the general contractor and owner which the subcontractor would refuse to be bound by or at least prefer not to be bound by because these modifications might increase the subcontractor's responsibilities.

Subcontractors should make sure that the warranties they extend to the general contractor or owner are clearly defined and that they understand the scope of the warranties. In addition, they should make sure that they do not extend the warranties beyond the warranties given to them by manufacturers of products installed, unless they do so knowingly and obtain the work at a price at which they can afford to take and assume such risk.

Not only do subcontractors have to contend with the written or express warranties contained in their contracts for the period of time specified, but also they must be aware of the unwritten warranties which the law implies. The law implies a warranty of merchantability or fitness for a particular use. If the subcontractor's construction or material is defective, the owner or general contractor can rely on the implied warranty for the length of time of the controlling state's statute of limitations, which is normally a length of time considerably longer than the express warranty. Typically, the statute of limitations on implied warranties is 4 to 8 years.

Express warranties contained in AIA Standard Subcontract Form A401 do not exclude implied warranties and stipulate:

The warranty provided in this Paragraph 11.9 shall be in addition to and not in limitation of any other warranty or remedy required by law or by the Contract Documents.

This warranty, which is similar to the warranty provisions that typically appear in the General or Special Conditions of the general contract, specially reserves the implied warranty. Even without the language which stipulates that implied warranties are reserved, the implied warranty would attach to the subcontractor's work unless the implied warranty is expressly excluded by a disclaimer.

Under some circumstances, the implied warranties may be excluded by a disclaimer of all implied warranties. For such a disclaimer, the subcontract should stipulate the following in bold print:

THE EXPRESS WARRANTIES CONTAINED HEREIN ARE IN LIEU OF ALL OTHER WARRANTIES, EXPRESSED OR IMPLIED, INCLUDING ANY WARRANTIES OF MERCHANTABILITY OR FITNESS FOR A PARTICULAR USE.

Unless the subcontractor excludes the implied warranties, legal remedies may be available to the owner or general contractor which can force the subcontractor to rectify defective work or materials far beyond his express warranty.

TEMPORARY SITE FACILITIES

The question of who is responsible for temporary site facilities which are common to all contractors on a jobsite has been a very troublesome area that has led to myriads of disputed backcharges by general contractors charging subcontractors for the temporary facilities. The best way for the subcontractor to avoid backcharges by the general contractor is to settle the question of responsibility for temporary site facilities at the time of the bid proposal and in the subcontract.

Both the AIA and the AGC standard subcontract forms have blank space which is to be filled in to designate the responsibility for furnishing and paying for temporary site facilities. In all subcontracts, the subcontractor should designate the temporary site facilities which he expects the general contractor to furnish at no cost to the subcontractor. These temporary site facilities will normally be those temporary site facilities and services which are common to all contractors on the jobsite and which the general contractor normally furnishes to all subcontractors. To foreclose the general contractor from attempting to backcharge the subcontractors for the cost of these temporary facilities or services, the subcontractor should stipulate that all temporary site facilities and services should be furnished by the general contractor at no cost to the subcontractor, with language such as the following:

Contractor shall, at no cost to Subcontractor, furnish utilities, services and facilities, as listed below, conveniently located at the construction site for use by Subcontractor to install its work, and of sufficient capacity to service Subcontractor's equipment and employees as well as the equipment and employees of all other Subcontractors of Contractors including Contractor on the job: (a) Electricity at each floor rated for small tools, hoists, derricks, scaffolds, and welder's equipment; (b) Toilets; (c) Personnel elevators so positioned that Subcontractor personnel are not required to walk up or down more than two floors to get to or from their place of work at the construction site; (d) Drinking water; (e) Rubbish removal from an area designated by the Contractor at each floor; (f) Accessible and adequate storage area within the building for Subcontractor's materials and equipment; (g) Adequate clear area to enable Subcontractor to perform its work without interference; (h) Should Subcontractor elect to use the Contractor's hoist, such use shall be available during regular working hours at no cost to Subcontractor and at such other times which do not cause any interference with Subcontractor's orderly job progress; (i) Adequate watchman services; (j) in the event that overhead protection is required by Subcontractor to protect Subcontractor's personnel working below prior trades, Contractor will be responsible for furnishing and erecting such protection and moving it as required by Subcontractor; (k) Temporary heat; (l) Perimeter protection and barricade shall be installed in compliance with OSHA regulations at no cost to Subcontractor. Such protection shall not interfere with the normal installation of the work covered under this Subcontract. Where protection or barricades must be removed to allow installation of the work under this Subcontract, it shall be removed and reinstalled by Contractor at no expense to Subcontractor.

The responsibility for furnishing and paying for temporary site facilities is being standardized in many cities by recommended bidding conditions established between local chapters of the American Subcontractors Association and local chapters of the Associated General Contractors of America, Inc. The typical recommended bidding conditions of these local areas designate responsibility for hoist facilities, temporary electrical service, construction water, trash removal, temporary heat, drinking water, toilet facilities, and other necessary temporary site facilities.

These bid conditions normally provide that the general contractor will generally be responsible for furnishing or contracting to furnish at no cost to the subcontractor all temporary facilities. All subcontractors who follow these local recommended bidding conditions would have no responsibility for providing or paying for the stipulated temporary site facilities which are the designated responsibility of the general contractors.

These recommended bid conditions may also settle the question of whether a subcontractor's price should include the additive amount for a payment or performance bond. The recommended bidding conditions may also designate the responsibility for compliance with safety requirements which are common to all contractors on the jobsite, such as the general contractor's responsibility for furnishing perimeter protection and barricades and to comply with first-aid requirements.

These bidding conditions have become a custom of the trade in the areas where they have been established, so that if subcontractors have subcontracts which do not incorporate the bid conditions, they can take the position that the bid conditions are included into the subcontract as a custom of trade unless there is an express provision in the subcontract which is in conflict with the bidding conditions. In order to specifically ensure that the bidding conditions are followed by the general contractor, subcontractors should include in all *bids* and *subcontracts* that "the recommended bid conditions established by the [local area construction council] currently in effect are incorporated by reference." To guard against backcharges for temporary facilities and to ensure that a subcontractor is not required to furnish temporary facilities which the general contractor should furnish under the recommended bid conditions, subcontractors should incorporate the recommended bid conditions into their bids and subcontracts.

The AIA Standard Subcontract Form A401 expressly limits the authority of the general contractor to backcharge a subcontractor for services unless the contractor gives the subcontractor advance notice and confirms the notice in writing within the first 10 days of the following calendar month. Article 12.8 of the AIA Standard Subcontract Form provides as follows:

The Contractor agrees that no claim for payment for services rendered or materials and equipment furnished by the Contractor to the Subcontractor shall be valid without prior notice to the Subcontractor and unless written notice thereof is given by the Contractor during the first 10 days of the calendar month following that in which the claim originated.

The AGC standard subcontract form contains similar language except it does not require advance notice from the contractor to the subcontractor, but it does require a written confirmation of the first 10 days of the following month. Subcontractors should be very wary of clauses which permit the general contractor to backcharge the subcontractor for services rendered.

LIQUIDATED DAMAGES

A subcontractor may be subjected to the "liquidated damages" imposed on the general contractor without being aware of any liquidated damages provision in the subcontract. Such imposition is innocuously done by providing that the subcontractor is bound to the general contractor in the same manner that the general contractor is bound to owner. It may be argued that implicit within such a statement is the fact that if the general contractor were bound to the owner for liquidated damages, the subcontractor would be so bound to the general contractor for liquidated damages. Many times the general contractor loses time in the early phases of the work and attempts to impose unrealistic time schedules upon subcontractors; then he attempts to impose liquidated damages on subcontractors if they do not finish within the unrealistic time schedules. Many subcontracts provide that the subcontractor will meet the time-performance schedules established from time to time by the general contractor. This provision gives too great a latitude to the general contractor.

Subcontractors would be well advised to include in their subcontract that they be allowed a specified number of days within which to perform their work plus extensions for any delays caused which were beyond their control. The subcontractor might also want to specify a number of consecutive days to perform the work to guard against staggered scheduling on a job, which would cost more because of problems of mobilization and demobilization of the job and loss of job momentum.

Both the AIA and AGC standard subcontract forms contain provisions which do not allow the general contractor to assess subcontractors with liquidated damages unless it is specifically stipulated in the subcontract. The following is the language of the AIA Standard Subcontract Form A401, Article 12.7, relating to liquidated damages:

The Contractor shall make no demand for liquidated damages for delay in any sum in excess of such amount as may be specifically named in this Subcontract, and no liquidated damages shall be assessed against this Subcontractor for delays or causes attributed to other Subcontractors or arising outside the scope of this Subcontract.

The AGC subcontract form contains similar language. The scheduling, coordination, and progress of the job is the responsibility of the general contractor. The subcontractors do not have any control over the time periods of construction other than the number of days required for the subcontractor to complete his work unobstructed or without interference by other trades. The subcontractor should not accept any liquidated damage provisions to be inserted into the subcontract unless it is specifically tied to the delays caused by the subcontractor in addition to the number of days stipulated to be required for the work.

DELAYS

Delays caused on jobs by the general contractor or owner can cost the subcontractor damages which can be, and frequently are, very substantial amounts. The subcontractor should avoid waiving his rights in a subcontract to pursue damages for delays against the general contractor and/or owner. The subcontractor should avoid signing clauses which state that the general contractor shall not be liable to the subcontractor for delays or that the contractor shall *only* be required to give the subcontractor an extension to contract performance time.

Often subcontract forms devised by general contractors contain a "no-damage-for-delay" clause, providing that the general contractor will not be liable to the subcontractor for delays of any sort, including delays caused by the owner, general contractor, or other subcontractors. Some courts have relieved the subcontractor of this provision, holding that active interference with a subcontractor's performance of its contractual duty is not covered by a "no-damage" provision. The courts have held that a no-damage provision in a construction subcontract relieving the general contractor from liability for delays is not applicable to delays caused by active interference with the subcontractor's performance by the general contractor,[18] or for unreasonably long delays.[19]

A typical no-damage-for-delay clause which should not be signed is:

Contractor shall not be liable to subcontractor for any delays caused by the owner or architect. Should the contractor delay the subcontractor's work, then, and in such event, contractor shall owe subcontractor therefore *only* for extension of time equal to the delay caused and only then if written claim for the delay is made to contractor within 48 hours from beginning of this delay.

This clause would bar a subcontractor's right to claim and recover his costs for delays, and the subcontractor would be entitled to an extension of contract time only in the event that he notified the general contractor within 48 hours after the start of the delay. This 48-hour restriction is an unreasonably short notification time which is calculated to foreclose the subcontractor's rights to excusable delay and damages for delay.

Many subcontracts do have a notification provision which requires that the subcontractor notify the general contractor and/or the owner within a stipulated time after the commencement of a delay. These notice requirements should be complied with in order to avoid any argument about pursuing the subcontractor's right to submit a claim for his increased costs because of the delay.

Nearly all subcontracts have a specific time limit for completion. If the subcontractor runs past this limit, he may be liable for liquidated delay damages or for a portion of the damages assessed against the general contractor. A subcontractor is extremely vulnerable to liquidated damages because the money can be taken from the subcontractor's progress payments or retention.

Most subcontractors are required by their contracts to make a claim for

[18] Wright & Kemers, Inc. v. State, 263 N.Y. 615, 189 N.E. 724 (1934).
[19] Ippolito-Lutz, Inc. v. Cohoes Housing Authority, 254 N.Y.S. 2d 783 (App. Div. 1968).

an extension of time if the project is delayed for any reason. This claim should be made in order to avoid an assessment of liquidated damages. Again, most subcontracts adopt the procedures outlined in the general contract for claiming an extension of time.

The AGC and AIA standard subcontract forms recognize the subcontractor's right to make claims for extension of time and for damages for delays in accordance with the provisions of the general conditions. Article X (4) of the AGC standard subcontract form provides:

The subcontractor shall make all claims for extras, for extensions of time and *for damage for delays* or otherwise, promptly to the Contractor consistent with the Contract Documents.

In addition to not waiving his right to delay damages, the subcontractor should serve timely notification of his claim for delay and should also keep accurate records to be able to establish the cost of the delay. A job log which outlines the various delays encountered on the job and the reason therefor, coupled with accurate cost records, are invaluable aids in pursuing the claim for damages for delay.

LEGAL JURISDICTION

Many subcontract forms used by national general contractors provide that the subcontract shall be construed under the laws of their home states and that any lawsuits must be brought in their home towns. This may cause a severe burden on local subcontractors who must bring actions in Texas, New York, or California because the cost of litigating lawsuits in distant cities can be prohibitive; without such a clause, jurisdiction for suits would be in the local courts. The national contractors who come to a locality for construction should have to comply with the local law and also be subject to suit in the locality where they are contracting with subcontractors. The following is an example of such a clause, which should be stricken in its entirety:

This contract and all provisions contained herein shall be interpreted by the laws of the State of Texas and jurisdictions of all suits arising under this contract shall be in Harris County, Texas.

A stipulation in the fine print of a subcontract that litigation over disputes must be filed in the locality of the general contractor's home office may block a subcontractor's Miller Act rights to sue the surety and general contractor because the Miller Act case must be filed in the locality where the work is performed.[20]

The AIA General Conditions, Article 7.1, stipulate that "the Contract shall be governed by the law at the place where the Project is located."

[20] 40 U.S.C. § 270b(b) (1969).

Subcontractors are cautioned not to agree to a legal jurisdiction other than the courts and law of the place where the work is performed.

CANCELLATION AND DEFAULT

Subcontracts often provide language which allows general contractors the unrestricted right to cancel a subcontract agreement, such as the following clause:

Contractor reserves the right in its sole and absolute discretion and without cause to terminate this subcontract agreement.

Because a "termination-for-convenience clause" allows the contractor to terminate for any reason whatsoever and does not require the consent or approval of the subcontractor, it is in the subcontractor's best interest to strike out this clause entirely. If, however, this is not possible, the subcontractor must at least ensure that he will be fully compensated for any losses and damages he sustains from cancellation of the contract.

A common termination-for-convenience clause limits recovery by the subcontractor to damages which are a direct result of termination. Some damages provisions may stipulate that indirect damages, such as reimbursement for materials ordered or purchased but not used and loss of anticipated profits, are not recoverable. The subcontractor should insist on including in the termination clause specific language to ensure that he is compensated for work already completed, loss of anticipated profits, and possibility of contractual liability to third parties, such as suppliers.

One of the most ominous clauses that typically appears in a general-contractor-devised subcontract form is the "default clause," under which the general contractor has almost total discretion to declare a subcontractor in default, take possession of his materials, equipment, and tools, finish the subcontractor's work, and then backcharge the subcontractor for the extra cost that will surely follow, including the general contractor's attorney's fees. Under this default clause, the general contractor practically has authority to take, not only the subcontractor's materials, equipment, and tools, but also his house, his wife, his dog, and even the shirt off his back. However, reciprocal rights are never given the subcontractor in such a default clause. The best approach is for the subcontractor to strike out a default clause in its entirety because it is unreasonable; if challenged by the general contractor, the reply should be that the subcontractor wishes to have reciprocal rights to declare the general contractor in default of his subcontract, which, of course, the general contractor would say is unreasonable.

The following is an example of an unreasonable default clause which must be deleted from the subcontract:

Should Subcontractor at any time refuse or neglect to supply a sufficient number of properly skilled workmen or a sufficient quantity of materials of proper quality, or fail, in any respect, to prosecute the work covered by this Subcontract with promptness and diligence, or fail in the performance of any of the agreements herein contained, Contractor may at his option, after 24 hours written or telegraphic notice to Subcontractor, provide any such labor and materials and deduct the costs thereof from any money then due or thereafter to become due to Subcontractor for said work, and shall have the right to enter upon the premises and take possession, for the purpose of completing the work included under this Subcontract, of all the materials, tools, and appliances thereon, and may employ any other person or persons to finish the work and provide the materials therefor; and in case of such discontinuance of the employment by Contractor, Subcontractor shall not be entitled to receive any further payment under this Subcontract until the work shall be wholly finished; at which time, if the unpaid balance of the sum to be paid under this Subcontract exceeds the expenses incurred by Contractor in finishing materials or for finishing the work, such excess shall be paid by Contractor to Subcontractor, but if such expense shall exceed such unpaid balance, then Subcontractor shall pay the difference to Contractor. The expenses incurred by Contractor, as herein provided, either for furnishing materials or finishing the work, and any damages incurred by such default, shall be chargeable to, and paid by, Subcontractor, and Contractor shall have a lien upon the unpaid balance of the contract price, all materials, tools, appliances and equipment of Subcontractor of the premises and used in connection with said work to secure payment thereof, and further to secure performance of Subcontractor.

Should Subcontractor default in any of the provisions of this Subcontract, and should Contractor employ an attorney to enforce any provisions hereof or to collect damages for breach of this Subcontract or to recover on the Subcontractor's bonds, Subcontractor and his surety agree to pay Contractor's attorney reasonable attorney fees, as against the obligations herein contained. Subcontractor and his surety waive all rights of exemption.

The subcontract forms devised by the general contractors always provide for assessment of attorney's fees and interest against the subcontractor for any damage, but never do these subcontracts provide the reciprocal right to the subcontractor to recover attorneys' fees and interest against the general contractor. It is beginning to be a practice among material suppliers to charge interest on unpaid invoices, and the subcontractors should also start following the practice of charging general contractors interest on late payments. The subcontractor should delete from subcontract forms any provisions which allow the general contractor to collect attorneys' fees and interest from the subcontractor, unless the subcontractor is given the reciprocal right to collect attorneys' fees and interest from the general contractor.

4 SUPPLY CONTRACTS

INTRODUCTION

Construction general contractors and subcontractors must direct some careful attention to their contractual relations with their material suppliers. Receipt of quality materials and equipment for a construction project on time and at the prices contemplated at the beginning of the project can easily make the difference between a profitable or a losing contract. Control of the costs of materials and equipment that go into a construction project starts at the estimating stage and must remain throughout the duration of the construction and any warranty periods.

General contractors and subcontractors should have a working knowledge of how to legally nail down fixed-price supply contracts and to avoid a price-supply squeeze. The Uniform Commercial Code, as it applies to the practices used by merchants, has become established over the years and has a great effect in the supply of materials and equipment. A contractor should also know what alternatives to pursue if materials or equipment are not available on fixed-price contracts during periods of performance.

When necessary materials or equipment for a construction project are defective or late, the contractor who is contracting for the materials or equipment generally has recourse against the supplier for breach of contract. This remedy offsets the liability of the contractor to the owner for defects or delays in the construction. In certain circumstances, the contract between the owner and the contractor may allow an extension of the contract time for material shortages, or the contractor may have a right to substitute less expensive but acceptable materials.

The legal doctrines discussed in dealing with supply contracts are applicable to both general contractors and subcontractors because they apply to the contractor who actually purchases the materials or equipment from the supplier.

FIXED-PRICE SUPPLY CONTRACTS

In order to control the costs of materials and equipment which are to be used in the construction, contractors should obtain fixed-price supply contracts with suppliers. Under such a contract, the supplier agrees to deliver the materials at a fixed price as the contract calls for delivery, no matter what happens to the market price or availability of the materials.

Under the Uniform Commercial Code, which is the governing law of supply contracts in most states, certain supply contracts are not enforceable unless they are in writing because the UCC provides, Section 2-201 (1):

Except as otherwise provided in this section a contract for the sale of goods for the price of $500 or more is not enforceable by way of action or defense unless there is some writing sufficient to indicate that a contract for sale has been made between the parties and signed by the party against whom enforcement is sought or by his authorized agent or broker. A writing is not insufficient because it omits or incorrectly states a term agreed upon but the contract is not enforceable under this paragraph beyond the quantity of goods shown in such writing.

A contract for the sale of goods can be an oral agreement developed in a phone conversation. But, in order for an agreement to be enforceable, there must be some writing, some memorandum, indicating that a contract does indeed exist, and it must be "signed" by the party against whom the contract is to be enforced; that is, it must be authenticated in some way. The memorandum may not necessarily be the contract itself but merely evidence of the existence of a contract. Once that evidence exists, any and all competent evidence can be introduced to prove the exact terms of the contract.

Illustrative Case

A general contractor, Southwest Engineering Company, conferred with a supplier, Martin Tractor Company, prior to submitting a bid for the construction of a runway lighting facility at an Air Force base. Martin quoted a price by phone of $18,500 for standby generator equipment. The contractor submitted its bid using this figure and was awarded the contract. After the award, the supplier informed Southwest that the price had risen to $21,500. The contractor agreed to this price and was sent a memorandum jotted down by Martin during this meeting, listing the component parts of the generators and the prices for each item. A few weeks later the supplier contacted Southwest, withdrew its quotations, and refused to supply the generators. When Southwest sued Martin for breach of contract, Martin claimed that there was no contract to be enforced since there was no written agreement satisfying the Statute of Frauds in § 2-201 of the UCC. The court, however, found that the memorandum made at the meeting between the parties was sufficient because it was evidence of a sale of goods, it was signed by the supplier, and it specified the quantity to be sold. The contractor recovered the difference between the price quoted by the supplier and the much higher price he was forced to pay to purchase the generators from another source.[1]

In some cases where the contract could not be enforced because there was no sufficient written memorandum, the partial performance of the contract by the parties may be enough to show the existence of the contract and make it enforceable.

[1] Southwest Engineering Co. v. Martin Tractor Co., 205 Kan. 684, 7 UCC Rep. Serv. 1288 (1970).

Illustrative Case

George C. Christopher & Son, Inc., a structural steel contractor engaged in construction of an airplane-hanger project, made an oral contract with Kansas Paint & Color Company, a paint supplier, to provide primer suitable to use on steel. The paint supplier contended that there was no enforceable contract because none could be created by the contractor's oral acceptance of the supplier's bid for the paint contract. However, Kansas Paint had in fact delivered a large amount of paint to Christopher under the contract, and the partial performance was evidence of the existence of a contract. Therefore, the court enforced the contract and found that there had been a breach of the contract when the primer paint on the steel rusted, peeled, and flaked.[2]

Parties often disagree about what are the actual terms of an oral contract, and sometimes they even disagree about whether a contract has been entered into at all. Misunderstandings easily develop. An old maxim states that an oral contract is "not worth the paper it is written on." For a contractor to protect himself from such disputes and misunderstandings with his suppliers and to ensure that the courts will recognize his actions as having actually created a fixed-price supply contract, the contractor should seek to have as much of the agreement as possible included in writing and signed.

The UCC recognizes letters of confirmation and purchase orders as a normal method of satisfying the written-memorandum requirement, and the UCC provides [Section 2-201(2)]:

Between merchants if within a reasonable time a writing in confirmation of the contract and sufficient against the sender is received and the party receiving it has reason to know its contents, it satisfies the requirements [of a written memorandum] against such party unless written notice of objection to its contents is given within 10 days after it is received.

Section 2-201(2) thus provides that self-executing memoranda prove the existence of a contract even though it is not signed by the other party. It is, of course, to the contractor's advantage to include in a self-executing memorandum as much of the terms of the agreement as is possible in order to facilitate proof of the terms of the supply contract. It is possible, however, under the UCC, for the supplier to object later to any of the specific terms of the memorandum as inaccurate representations of the actual contract.

Illustrative Case

Tiffany Incorporated, a highway contractor, received an erroneous price quotation for highway construction materials over the telephone from the supplier's secretary. Tiffany used this quotation in pricing a state highway construction project and sent W.M.K. Transit Mix, Inc., the supplier, a letter of confirmation. W.M.K. allegedly did not object to its terms within the 10-day limit. When W.M.K. then refused to supply the materials at the quoted but mistaken price, Tiffany sued for breach of contract, claiming the W.M.K.'s failure to object to Tiffany's confirmation letter was the assent necessary to form a con-

---

[2] George C. Christopher & Son, Inc. v. Kansas Paint & Color Co., 523 P.2d 709, 14 UCC Rep. Serv. 1256 (Kan. 1974).

tract. The court, in applying the technicalities of the law, found that the objection of the supplier was timely because the confirmation was received on July 15th, and the objection sent on July 25th and received by Tiffany on July 29th. This timely objection nullified the written confirmation and there was no enforceable contract.[3]

Often, memos that are sent by a contractor to a supplier confirming an oral agreement differ in their terms. Under the UCC, the mere fact that a written confirmation accepting an offer contains different or additional terms does not mean that there is no contract, unless the memorandum specifies that acceptance of the offer is conditioned on assent to the additional or different terms or materially alters the contract.

If an oral agreement is followed by a formal acknowledgment or confirmation and there are *additional terms* or suggestions (for example, "ship by Tuesday" or "rush"), the UCC Section 2-207 says that where the parties are "merchants" (a material or equipment supplier and a contractor purchasing supplies would normally be considered "merchants" for the purposes of a purchase of these materials), additional terms will become part of the contract unless:

1. The offer expressly limits acceptance to the terms of the offer.

2. They materially alter the contract (for example, negating standard warranties, reserving a power to cancel upon minor defaults, or in some way altering normal trade practice).

3. Notification of objection has already been given or is given within a reasonable time after a party learns of the additional terms.

Therefore, if a contractor received a written confirmation of an order or an acknowledgment of an oral discussion and the confirmation contains additional or different terms to which the contractor does not feel he should agree, the contractor should notify the supplier immediately and object to the terms. These terms then merely become proposals for addition to the contract and are not enforceable.

Where a contractor wishes to add terms to an oral agreement, the contractor may do so in his confirmation that is sent to the supplier. Then the shoe is on the other foot, and the supplier has the burden of objecting. Or, as mentioned previously, either party may condition the making of a contract on the other party accepting the additional or different terms.

Illustrative Case

Negotiations between General Bronze Corporation, a construction contractor, and Southeastern Enameling Corporation, a manufacturer of laminated panels, had ended in a tentative agreement between the two parties for the supplying of the panels. Then the contractor sent to the supplier a "confirmation" in which an additional term was added to the effect that any disputes between the parties would be submitted to arbitration. Southeastern Enameling signed this written contract without objecting to the additional term. The court held that Southeastern Enameling was bound by the arbitration

[3] Tiffany Inc. v. W.M.K. Transit Mix, Inc., 10 UCC Rep. Serv. 393 (Ariz. App. 1972).

clause, even though it claimed that it was never actually aware of the presence of the arbitration clause in the contract.[4]

Finally, the case often arises where both parties send confirmations or memoranda, each containing terms that conflict with the other. In such a case, the conduct of the parties may establish a contract despite the conflicting terms; and the contract will then consist of those terms on which the parties expressly agreed, on which the writings agree, and other terms that the UCC automatically includes, such as certain implied warranties.

Thus, the contractor should review all forms and confirmations sent by suppliers and should adopt an affirmation contracting procedure consistent with the preceding discussion to obtain fixed-price supply contracts on his terms.

A letter of confirmation to be used as a self-executing memorandum should confirm at least the following aspects of the purchase: description of the materials or equipment, quantity, price, date of delivery, and allowable substitutions, if any. For example, immediately after an agreement is reached in a phone call with a supplier, a contractor should send the supplier a letter of confirmation such as the following:

This letter will serve to confirm the agreement by _____ of our company, and _____ of your company, during their telephone conversation of this morning.

We have agreed to purchase and you have agreed to sell _____ (describe material and quantity) _____ at _____ (price) for use on the _____ (name of project) construction project described in this morning's telephone conversation. Delivery is to take place at the jobsite according to the following schedule:

[There will be no allowable substitutions.]

Enclosed are two (2) signed copies of our standard purchase order form containing the terms of our agreement which were discussed. Please sign and return one (1) copy of the purchase order.

A contractor is well advised to write letters confirming all his oral contracts, particularly those agreements made with suppliers of materials and equipment that call for fixed prices, firm quantities, and specific delivery dates. Letters of confirmation are important documents having very real legal consequences, and they will also elicit prompt replies from suppliers accepting or rejecting the terms and conditions.

It is imperative that a contractor seeking fixed-price supply contracts from suppliers also use carefully drafted purchase orders to solidify his position when dealing with suppliers. Although a purchase order, by itself, will not create an enforceable contract, a letter of confirmation of an oral agreement that is sent by a contractor to a supplier, unless objected to by the supplier, will operate to satisfy the requirements that contracts for the sale of goods be in writing under the UCC Section 2-201(1)

[4]Southeastern Enameling Corp. v. General Bronze Corp., 434 F.2d 330 (5th Cir. 1970).

and (2). Thus, if an agreement can be proved, the contractor will be able to enforce the agreement. And, if the purchase order is signed by the supplier and a copy of it or an acknowledgment is returned to the contractor, it will become the contract itself governing virtually all aspects of the relationship between the contractor and supplier in that transaction.

After having negotiated a fixed-price supply contract with a supplier, the contractor should send a letter of confirmation to the supplier along with a purchase order such as the model provided specifying the quantity to be supplied, price, and other necessary information. Should the supplier fail to respond within 10 days of receipt of the letter of confirmation and purchase order, the contractor will have a fixed-price supply contract according to the terms agreed upon in the telephone negotiation. Should the supplier sign and return the purchase order, the contractor will have a fixed-price supply contract based on the terms of the purchase order.

A purchase order should be drafted so that it protects all of the contractor's rights to receive the stated quantity of materials which conform to the plans and specifications at a stipulated price on time from his supplier. The purchase-order form and its general conditions on the following pages are a model of the type of provisions a contractor's purchase orders should contain. A contractor should consult his own attorney to draft a purchase-order form that best suits his particular needs.

The typical construction contract contains a warranty clause such as the clause found in the AIA General Conditions of the Contract for Construction, AIA Document A201:

13.2.2 If, within 1 year after the Date of Substantial Completion of the Work or designated portion thereof or within 1 year after acceptance by the Owner of designated equipment or within such longer period of time as may be prescribed by law or by the terms of any applicable special warranty required by the Contract Documents, if any of the Work is found to be defective or not in accordance with the Contract Documents, the Contractor shall correct it promptly after receipt of written notice from the Owner to do so unless the Owner has previously given the Contractor a written acceptance of such condition. This obligation shall survive termination of the Contract. The Owner shall give such notice promptly after discovery of the condition.

Contractors should make sure that the warranties they extend are clearly defined and that they understand the scope of the warranties. Furthermore, since the contractor is generally required to warrant his work to the general contractor and/or owner, the contractor should be certain to obtain guarantees and warranties from his suppliers for the materials they provide. In fact, contractors should be careful that their warranties obtained from the supplier extend to the same duration and scope as the warranties given to the general contractor and/or owner, and that if the warranties given to the general contractor and/or owner extend beyond the warranties given by the suppliers of the materials and equipment installed, then the contractors must realize they have assumed this risk and obtained the work at a price at which they can afford to take the additional warranty risk.

PURCHASE ORDER

TO:

Date _____

Purchase Order No. _____

SHIP TO:

Above purchase order number MUST appear on all inquiries, invoices, packing slips and shipping documents.

Render all invoices in TRIPLICATE

Job _____

Ship via:

_____

F.O.B.

Freight Terms:

SHIP THE FOLLOWING ITEMS AND DO THE WORK IN STRICT ACCORDANCE WITH THE PLANS AND SPECIFICATIONS.

Price:

Terms:

Delivery Date(s) Required:

ALL TERMS AND CONDITIONS AS SET FORTH ON REVERSE SIDE ARE PART OF THIS PURCHASE ORDER.

ACCEPTED: _____   _____
            Supplier   Purchaser

By: _____   _____
            Title   Title

Date: _____

GENERAL CONDITIONS

All material and equipment furnished under this order shall be guaranteed by the Seller to the Purchaser and Owner to be fit and sufficient for the purpose intended, and that they are merchantable, of good material and workmanship and free from defects, and Seller agrees to replace without charge to Purchaser or Owner said material and equipment, or remedy any defects latent or patent not due to ordinary wear and tear or due to improper use or maintenance, which may develop within one year from date of acceptance by the Owner, or within the guarantee period set forth in applicable plans and specifications, whichever is longer. The warranties herein are in addition to those implied by law.

The Seller and all material and equipment furnished under this order shall be subject to the approval of the architect, engineer, or the Purchaser, and Seller shall furnish the required number of submittal data or samples for said approval. In the event approval is not obtained the order may be cancelled by Purchaser with no liability on the part of Purchaser.

All material and equipment furnished hereunder shall be in strict compliance with plans, specifications, and general conditions applicable to the contract of Purchaser with the Owner or another contractor, and Seller shall be bound thereby in the performance of this contract.

The materials and equipment covered by this order, whether in a deliverable state or otherwise, shall remain the property of the Seller until delivered to a designated site and actually received by the Purchaser, and any damage to the material and equipment or loss of any kind occasioned in transit shall be borne by the Seller, notwithstanding the manner in which the goods are shipped or who pays the freight or other transportation costs.

The Seller hereby agrees to indemnify and save harmless the Purchaser from and against all claims, liability, loss, damage or expense, including attorneys' fees by reason of any actual or alleged infringement of letters patent or any litigation based thereon covering any article purchased hereunder.

Time is of the essence of this contract. Should the Supplier for any reason fail to make deliveries as required hereunder to the satisfaction of the Purchaser, or if the materials are not satisfactory to the Architect/Engineer, the Purchaser shall be at liberty to purchase the materials elsewhere, and any excess in cost of same over the price herein provided shall be chargeable to and paid by the Supplier on demand. Should any delay on the part of the Supplier or defects or nonconformance of the materials or equipment with the plans and specifications occasion loss, damage or expense including consequential damages to the Owner or to the Purchaser, the Supplier shall indemnify the Owner and the Purchaser against such loss, damage or expense including attorneys' fees. If for any cause, all or any portion of the materials to be furnished are not delivered at the time or times herein specified, the Purchaser may, at his option, cancel this order as to all or any portion of materials not so delivered.

Seller shall furnish all necessary lien waivers, affidavits or other documents required to keep the Owner's premises free from liens or claims for liens, arising out of the furnishing of the material or equipment herein, as payments are made from time to time under this order.

All prior representations, conversations or preliminary negotiations shall be deemed to be merged in this order, and no changes will be considered or approved unless this order is modified by an authorized representative of Purchaser in writing.

Accordingly, the supplier of a product should be tied into the guarantees and warranties of the contract *and* the *plans and specifications*. The sample purchase order presented previously specifically provides on its first page that the supplier "Ship the following items and do the work in strict accordance with plans and specifications." The warranty provision of the terms and conditions of the purchase order provides:

All material and equipment furnished under this order shall be guaranteed by the Seller to the Purchaser and Owner to be fit and sufficient for the purpose intended, and that they are merchantable, of good material and workmanship and free from defects, and Seller agrees to replace without charge to Purchaser or Owner said material and equipment, or remedy any defects latent or patent not due to ordinary wear and tear or due to improper use or maintenance, which may develop within one year from date of acceptance by the Owner, or within the guaranteed period set forth in applicable plans and specifications, whichever is longer. The warranties herein are in addition to those implied by law.

It is, of course, necessary that the contractor give the supplier copies of the plans and specifications at the time his order for materials is placed in order to facilitate the supplier's compliance with the warranty that the materials be furnished "as per plans and specifications."

The law sometimes implies a warranty of "merchantability" or "fitness for use." Therefore, legal remedies may be available even if the contractor has neglected to write any guarantees and warranties into his purchase order or if the supplier has not provided a warranty of his own. But it is always wise to provide express warranties as much as possible in the supply-contract terms rather than to rely upon the uncertainty that a court will later provide implied warranty protection.

Illustrative Case

In a case between Kansas Paint & Color Company, a paint supplier, and George C. Christopher & Son, a structural steel contractor, when the paint peeled and flaked from the structural steel, Christopher sued Kansas Paint, relying on a theory that there was an implied warranty in the contract that the paint would be fit for priming structural steel. The supplier claimed that it had effectively disclaimed any implied warranty of fitness by language in an invoice sent with the paint to the contractor which disclaimed implied warranties. However, the court found that the intent to disclaimer was ineffective because it was not made conspicuously as required by the UCC. A warranty of fitness was in fact implied in the contract because Kansas Paint had reason to know of the particular purpose for which the paint was required, and Christopher relied on the supplier's skill and judgment to select a suitable paint for the structural steel.[5]

By requiring suppliers to guarantee that the materials and equipment they provide will meet the plans and specifications with which the contractor must comply, the contractor can protect himself from any additional costs that might arise if damages result from the inadequacy of materials or equipment supplied. This type of protection should be sought in all supply contracts. Express warranties may also be contained in representations by suppliers in advertising and statements.

[5] George C. Christopher & Son, Inc. v. Kansas Paint & Color Co., 523 P.2d 709, 14 UCC Rep. Serv. 1256 (Kan. 1974).

Illustrative Case

The advertising brochures given to Hawkins Construction Company by its scaffolding supplier, Matthews Company, contained an express warranty that the scaffolding was designed to safely carry working loads up to 20,000 lb per unit of scaffolding. Hawkins was using the scaffolding to support the roof of a building during the pouring of the roof deck cement. While the contractor's workmen were pouring cement on a portion of the roof deck, the roof and scaffolding suddenly gave way. Luckily, no one was seriously hurt, but there was substantial property damage. The jury's finding that the scaffolding was defective and that this defect caused the collapse of the roof was upheld on appeal, and the contractor recovered from the supplier the cost of repairing the building and replacing the scaffolding on a theory of breach of warranty.[6]

A wise course of action to pursue on major guarantees or warranties of the materials or equipment as per the plans and specifications is to make sure that the warranties are properly made by the supplier in favor of the owner so that if problems arise after the contractor has completed his work, the owner can go against the supplier without necessarily involving the contractor in a legal hassle. Should default on any of the guarantees or warranties become apparent before the contractor completes his work, he should insist on his legally implied warranties and express contractual rights and demand that the supplier either correct the defects or replace the defective material or equipment. Should the supplier fail to do so, the remedies available would be an action for breach of contract.

If a contractor has a firm contract which has been obtained from his suppliers through the use of negotiation, a letter of confirmation acting as a self-executing memorandum, and a purchase order, then he has legal remedy against defaulting suppliers. Some individual contractors have been faced with price increases by suppliers with whom the contractors had unenforceable oral contracts even though the contractors thought their oral agreements would have prevented price increases. Using letters of confirmation as self-executing memoranda and purchase orders is an absolute must for contractors to protect themselves from suppliers reneging on their agreements and prices.

If a supplier fails to deliver the materials or equipment at the time and price specified in the contractual agreement with the supplier, the contractor has an action against the defaulting supplier for breach of contract and damages can be recovered. Under normal principles, the contractor would be entitled to direct money damages measured by the difference between the contractor's reasonable expenses in obtaining other materials or equipment and the contract price with the supplier. For example, if a contractor had contracted with a supplier for 100 items at $45 per item, and the supplier failed or refused to deliver on time, forcing the contractor to purchase all 100 items at the current market price of $95 per item, the contractor's recovery would be the difference in the current price and the contract price for a total recovery of $5,000.

---

[6] Hawkins Constr. Co. v. Matthews Co., 190 Neb. 546, 209 N.W.2d 643 (Neb. 1973).

The contractor would be under a legally imposed duty to mitigate his damages. That is, he could not sit back and let the damages run up against the defaulting supplier any higher than would be reasonably necessary. As soon as it becomes clear that the supplier has breached his contract, the contractor should make a reasonable effort to find the same materials at as low a price as possible. The additional expense of this search for a new supplier may also be recoverable, in addition to the cost to purchase the materials or equipment.

Illustrative Case

American Contractors was awarded a job for installing a plastic pipe water system in a small community using a quotation for the plastic pipe from its supplier, Clow Corporation. Although the agreement between the contractor and the supplier did not specify the times for delivery of the pipe, Clow was late In supplying part of the pipe and American fell behind in the job and suffered delay-associated damages. Ultimately American terminated the contract with Clow, obtained the pipe elsewhere at a higher price, and sued Clow for the difference in prices between the replacement pipe and the pipe which should have been supplied on time initially. Clow argued that the contractor should have mitigated damages by continuing to accept lower-priced pipe from Clow. However, the jury found that American was entitled to cancel the contract with Clow because Clow failed to furnish the material within a reasonable time, and therefore American was able to purchase other materials from another supplier and recover the difference in cost from the original supplier who breached the contract, provided that the purchase of replacement pipe was reasonably necessary and was made in good faith.[7]

A supplier who furnishes equipment to a contractor may be liable on a theory of negligence when he should have known that any defect in the equipment will be likely to result in injury to those using it. The contractor may be able to rely upon a negligence theory if a supplier's negligence results in a defect which causes harm to property on the jobsite or personal injury to the contractor or his employees.

Illustrative Case

George Queen, an employee of Southern-Ferro Concrete Company, a masonry contractor, lost his balance and fell against the guard rail of a scaffold provided by Patent Scaffolding Company. The guard rail broke and Queen fell to the pavement below and was killed. Since it was proven that the guard rail was defective, Patent was held responsible in damages for the death of Southern-Ferro's employee.[8]

Consequential damages are normally not recoverable unless they were within the contemplation of the parties at the time of the formation of the contract. For a contractor to recover consequential damages, such as loss because of delays or loss of profits, it would be necessary to prove that the supplier had reason to know that such loss would result from a failure to

[7] Owens v. Clow Corp., 491 F.2d 101 (5th Cir. 1974).
[8] Queen v. Patent Scaffolding Co., 46 Ga. App. 364 (1932).

perform. The letter of confirmation as well as telephone negotiation would be a good place to set the stage for a possible recovery of consequential damages by explaining any particular circumstances that would cause a major expense or loss of profits if the contractor was delayed and forced to seek another source of supply. In particular, if the contractor is faced with a provision for liquidated damages for delay, this information should be passed on to the supplier so that the cost of paying these damages could be collected from the supplier if his delay in delivery causes delay in the contractor's total performance.

Illustrative Case

Oliver-Electrical Manufacturing Company had a contract to supply spacer fittings for electrical transmission lines being built by I. O. Teigen Construction Company. Oliver-Electrical breached the contract by delivering the parts late. When Oliver-Electrical sued Teigen for the unpaid balance due on the contract, Teigen counterclaimed for consequential damages caused by the initial cost of delay, that is, the increased cost for the actual number of days of delivery caused by the supplier, and also the delay caused by the extension of the work into more costly winter conditions. The court held that the initial delay damages were within the contemplation of the parties at the time of the making of the contract as to special damages which would result from a breach of the contract. However, the court held that special damages caused by winter construction were not within the contemplation of the parties at the time the contract was entered into. Therefore, Teigen recovered the initial delay damages but it did not recover damages resulting from the winter conditions.[9]

If a particular supplier is the only source of unique materials or equipment for which there is no suitable substitute, a court is authorized by UCC Section 2-716, in the right fact situation, to order specific performance on the part of the supplier. That is, the court might issue an order requiring that the supplier deliver the material or equipment. Failure to abide by the order for specific performance could result in finding the supplier in contempt of court along with the payment of damages to the subcontractor.

ALTERNATIVES TO FIXED-PRICE SUPPLY CONTRACTS

If a contractor finds he cannot convince his suppliers to agree to fixed-price supply contracts, the contractor will have to explore the various other means of dealing with possible price instability.

Using Judgment in Selecting Long-Term Construction Contracts

A contractor should consider economic conditions in bidding or negotiating on long-term construction projects and try to accurately predict anticipated price increases over the life of the project. A decision to pass up

[9] Oliver-Electrical Mfg. Co. v. I. O. Teigen Constr. Co., 177 F. Supp. 572 (D. Minn. 1959).

a long-term project would mean short-term hardship for the contractor; but if the alternative is gambling with a reasonable possibility of bankruptcy, it may be a decision that has to be made. The severity of the short-term hardship will, of course, vary depending on the size of the contractor's business, the profitability of the other long-term contracts that the contractor is currently performing, and the profitability of whatever short-term work the contractor can enter into during the period of economic uncertainty. During periods of price instability, contractors have turned to work which can be completed in a short time instead of performing long-term contracts.

Anticipating Future Price Increases in Lump-Sum Prices

If a contractor continues to negotiate or bid fixed-price construction contracts, he should submit prices that include an estimate of the outside maximum increase of materials or equipment prices that he expects to occur between the date of the contract and the date of delivery of the materials. In inflationary periods, however, this can be mainly a matter of guesswork, and the contractor may find himself in a severe price-supply squeeze if he does not gaze deep enough into his crystal ball to forecast price increases.

Having Some Other Party Purchase the Materials

A third alternative to using the fixed-price supply contracts is to shift the risk of price instability of materials or equipment to the owner or general contractor by having one of them directly purchase the materials or equipment. Under such an agreement, the contractor would bid only on the labor required for the particular construction project, leaving the supply aspect to the owner or general contractor. Some contractors will disagree with this approach because of their practice of adding a percentage markup to the total cost of labor and materials. However, there is no reason that the contractor cannot take into consideration the value of materials purchased by others in pricing a labor-only contract.

Purchasing and Storing Materials at the Beginning of the Contract

A fourth alternative to the fixed-price supply contract is for the contractor to purchase the materials and accept delivery at the beginning of the construction contract to hedge against future price increases and to ensure the availability of the materials at the time they are needed in the construction project. The contractor pursuing this alternative of early purchase and delivery of materials and equipment should make sure that he can obtain early progress payments from the owner in order to pay for the materials and equipment purchased at the initial phase of the construction job and to cover the costs of storage.

Early delivery of materials and equipment should be encouraged, even though they are not immediately needed in the performance of the construction. In order to achieve availability and price protection, the construction user should be willing to accept items delivered to an approved storage site and pay for them. If additional expenses for storage or handling charges are incurred, the construction user should also pay the extra costs.

There are two ways in which the contractor can be reimbursed for the additional expenses of extra storage and insurance costs: He can be reimbursed directly by the owner, or he can include the additional expenses of storage and insurance costs in his initial price on the job. To legally bind the owner to reimburse him, the contractor should include in his contract a clause such as the following:

The contractor will immediately undertake to purchase certain materials required by the contract. Contractor will suitably store and insure the materials on the jobsite or at other storage facilities. The Owner agrees to pay for said materials when delivered to the jobsite or other storage facilities and in addition to the contract price to pay for the cost of storage and the costs of insurance for said stored materials.

Including the additional expenses of storage and insurance costs in his price is perhaps the safest method of reimbursement because if the contractor's price is accepted, the additional storage and insurance costs will come out of the contractor's price.

The Board of Directors of the American Institute of Architects has recognized the need to allow payment for early delivery of materials and equipment by declaring in a policy statement of May 17, 1974:

Early purchase and delivery of materials and equipment should be encouraged even though not immediately needed. These should be placed in a storage site approved by the Owner, who, in turn, should make payment as provided in our contract documents on account of the stored items and defray in whole or in part any storage or extra handling charges.

The AIA General Conditions (AIA Document A201) states that payment for materials suitably stored on the site or at some other location may be agreed upon in writing between the parties, and Article 9.3.2 of the AIA General Conditions provides:

Unless otherwise provided in the Contract Documents, payments will be made on account of materials or equipment not incorporated in the Work but delivered and suitably stored at the site and, if approved in advance by the Owner, payments may similarly be made for materials or equipment suitably stored at some other location agreed upon in writing. Payments for materials or equipment stored on or off the site shall be conditioned upon submission by the Contractor of bills of sale or such other procedures satisfactory to the Owner to establish the Owner's title to such materials or equipment or otherwise protect the Owner's interest, including applicable insurance and transportation to the site for those materials and equipment stored off the site.

Under this clause, the contractor must have a written agreement that protects the owner's interest in the stored materials to establish title to the materials and insurance in favor of the owner.

Using Escalation Clauses

Another alternative to fixed-price supply contracts is the use of escalation clauses in the construction contract that the subcontractor signs with the general contractor, which, in turn, might be included in the general contractor's contract with the owner. Such escalation clauses will shift the full risk or part of the risk of price increases to the general contractor or the owner. Although there are many variations of escalation clauses, three basic types of escalation clauses are: day-one–dollar-one escalation clauses, significant-dollar-increase escalation clauses, and delay escalation clauses.

Day-one–dollar-one escalation clauses reimburse the contractor or subcontractor for the costs of any price increases in materials or equipment that occur after the signing of the contract or acceptance of the bid. The owner or general contractor pays the difference in the cost of the materials or equipment between the date of the contract or bid and the time of installation. Under a day-one–dollar-one escalation clause, each dollar increase in materials or equipment is reimbursed from the first day of the contract or bid. A typical day-one–dollar-one escalation clause is as follows:

The prices of materials and equipment contained in this bid or contract are those in effect as of _____ (date); contractor shall be reimbursed for all increases in the cost of material and equipment as of the date of installation, plus _____ percent overhead and _____ percent profit.

The date that should be filled in is the date of the bid or contract, preferably the date of the bid. The percentage for overhead and the percentage for profit should be a reasonable calculation to be filled in according to the individual contractor's anticipated overhead and desired profit.

Significant-dollar-increase escalation clauses are calculated to reimburse the contractor only for the large price increases which occur in materials or equipment between the bid or contract date and the date of installation. This type of clause places the burden of small price increases upon the subcontractor but shifts the risk of significant price increases to the general contractor or owner. A typical significant-dollar-increase escalation clause, which also provides for an extension of contract time due to unavailability of materials, is as follows:

In the event of significant delay or price increase of material, equipment, or energy occurring during the performance of the contract through no fault of the contractor, the contract sum, time of completion, or contract requirements shall be equitably adjusted by change order in accordance with the procedures of the contract documents. A change in price of an item of material, equipment, or energy will be considered significant when the price of an item increases _____ percent between the date of this contract and the date of installation.

The contractor may want to specify that any price increases above 5 or 10 percent an item of materials would be reimbursable. The percentage price increase should be a reasonable calculation of what the owner or general contractor will accept and the maximum increase the contractor is willing to assume.

Delay escalation clauses are calculated to hold a fixed-price contract for a limited period of time but allow the contractor to receive escalation benefits if the job is delayed beyond a given number of days or a specified date. This type of escalation clause seeks to reimburse the contractor for those price increases and expenses that arise during the period of delay. A typical delay escalation clause is as follows:

It is contemplated that the performance of the contractor's work will be completed by _____ (date). In the event that the contractor's work is not completed by that date, through no fault of the contractor, then the contractor shall be reimbursed for all increases in the costs of labor, material, and equipment by reason of said delay, including reimbursement for extended on-site supervision and overhead plus _____ percent general overhead and _____ percent profit.

The parties should agree upon the estimated completion date, and the percentage of overhead and profit should represent a reasonable calculation of the contractor's overhead and desired profit.

When contractors experience difficulty in successfully obtaining open-ended escalation clauses into the contract, they might consider combining an escalation clause with a guaranteed maximum price. This, in effect, would be submitting two prices by combining a price based upon current market prices of materials and equipment to be increased by some form of escalation with a maximum upset price. There are other methods of combining approaches. Some contractors submit one price based upon escalation and another lump-sum price and give the general contractor or owner the choice of either. Whatever the approach the individual contractor chooses to solve the price-supply squeeze on materials in the construction industry, the contractor should make an individual judgment of what is best for his company or what is best in a particular contract situation.

EXTENSION OF TIME FOR MATERIAL SHORTAGES

Generally, the American Institute of Architects standard contract clauses and government contracts seem to permit an excusable delay and allow for extension of time when a contractor cannot obtain materials because of short supply. Article 8.3.1 of the AIA's General Conditions of the Contract for Construction Document A201 (1976 ed.) provides:

If the Contractor is delayed at any time in the progress of the Work . . . by labor disputes, fire, unusual delay in transportation, adverse weather conditions not reasonably antici- patable, unavoidable casualties, or *any causes beyond the Contractor's control*, . . . , or by any other cause which the Architect determines may justify the delay, then the Contract Time shall be extended by Change Order for such reasonable time as the Architect may determine. [Italics added.]

The AIA's General Conditions are incorporated by reference into the AIA's standard subcontract, so that Article 8.3.1 would apply to the sub- contractor as well.

The preceding excusable delay clause is stated broadly enough so that material shortages could be considered an excusable delay. There is some doubt about whether the failure of a manufacturer to produce goods on time is an excusable delay because the contractor could be held to the duty of having found reliable suppliers before entering into a contract.

Illustrative Case

H. B. Nelson Construction Company, engaged in the construction of a sea plane hangar for the Navy, received a shipment of trusses from a supplier which were so badly bent during shipment that the work was delayed 22 days while the trusses were restored to their normal condition. The Navy denied the contractor's request for an extension of time, but the Court of Claims allowed the extension under a typical excusable delay clause because the delay was unforseeable at the time the supply contract was made and the contractor used the usual and long-established methods employed by the commercial world in general to obtain material. Nelson had no cause to suspect that the customary practices would fail to produce supplies for the project on time.[10]

The Board of Directors of the American Institute of Architects has de- clared a policy to its members that material and equipment delays should be considered as a basis of excusable delay and passed the following policy statement on May 17, 1974:

Completion dates should be established based on delivery time of major items needed in the construction process. If liquidated damages are a contract consideration, bona fide delays in manufacturing schedules or shipment should be considered as warranting an extension of time.

Article 8.3.2 of the AIA's General Conditions establishes the procedure for making a claim for extension of the contract time and provides:

Any claim for extension of time shall be made in writing to the Architect not more than twenty days after the commencement of the delay; otherwise it shall be waived. In the case of a continuing delay only one claim is necessary. The Contractor shall provide an estimate of the probable effect of such delay on the progress of the Work.

So, it would be wise for the contractor to make a claim for extending the contract within the 20-day period and preferably as soon as possible after the supply problem arises.

[10] H.B. Nelson Constr. Co. v. United States, 87 Ct. Cl. 375, *cert. denied,* 306 U.S. 661 (1939).

In government contracts the general rule is that a contractor is not in default where his failure to perform his obligations is due to causes beyond his control or without his fault or negligence. The standard default clause excuses failure to perform on time for a whole catalog of reasons. Severe material shortages caused by a foreign government's oil embargo, a worldwide shortage, and government manipulation of the economy may fit within the spirit of the clause.

If a contractor is faced with a material shortage on a federal government job which prevents him from completing his work, he should request and obtain an extension of time for the period of the delay from the contracting officer. This is based upon Standard Form 23-A, General Provisions, Article 5(d) which provides:

The Contractor's right to proceed shall not be so terminated nor the Contractor charged with resulting damage if:

(1) The delay in the completion of work arises from unforeseeable causes beyond the control and without the fault or negligence of the Contractor, including but not restricted to . . . the delays of subcontractors or suppliers arising from unforeseeable causes beyond the control and without the fault or negligence of both the Contractor and subcontractors or suppliers . . . .

The Contracting Officer shall ascertain the facts and the extent of the delay and extend the time for completing the work when, in his judgment, the findings of fact justify an extension . . . .

A notice of delay is required to be filed with the contracting officer within 10 days of the commencement of the delay; but even if the contractor is outside this time limit, he should file a notice because there are certain exceptions to this requirement of timely written notice, such as informal communication of some information pertaining to the delay and the reasons for it, which have been held by courts to be sufficient so long as there was some written communication. Also, since the notice is for the benefit of the General Contractor or Owner, if they have actual knowledge of the delay, the failure to give notice may be excused or waived. The same may be true if the General Contractor or Owner is found not to have been prejudiced by failure to give timely notice.

Illustrative Case

Delays in the performance of a subcontract for the erection of three fuel tanks by John H. Maxwell & Company arose because of defects in property furnished by Macri Construction Company, the general contractor. Maxwell failed to give timely written notice to Macri requesting an extension of time as he was required to do by the subcontract. However, Macri had worked with him in trying to remedy the defects and clearly knew of the existence of the delay. Therefore, the court held that the notice requirement was waived by the general contractor, and the subcontractor was not held liable for liquidated damages for delay.[11]

[11] Macri v. United States ex rel. John H. Maxwell & Co., 353 F.2d 804 (9th Cir. 1965).

However, a subcontractor should be cautioned that the default clauses in the government's standard construction contracts specifically provide that a general contractor's failure to perform due to the default of a subcontractor is excusable only if both the general contractor and subcontractor are free from fault. Applying this concept to the subcontractor-supplier level, a subcontractor may be held liable for a default due to supply problems unless both the subcontractor and supplier were free from fault. Board of Contract Appeal's decisions would also indicate that the subcontractor may still be liable even if the supplier was not negligent in his delay or failure to manufacture if the materials or equipment could have been obtained from another source. In a legal proceeding on a government contract, the burden of proof would be on the subcontractor to demonstrate that neither he nor his supplier is at fault in the material unavailability and that the materials could not be obtained from another source.[12]

Extensions of time for material shortages or failure of a manufacturer to produce on time will have to be negotiated under existing contracts, but additional protective language should be written into future contracts to save the subcontractor the added expense of liquidated or delay damages if he is delayed in his performance due to material or equipment shortages.

RIGHT TO SUBSTITUTE MATERIALS

The right to substitute materials can be used to alleviate the possible price instability on materials or equipment originally specified. If a contractor cannot substitute materials or equipment in order to complete the job on time, he may be stuck with added expense and delays. Therefore, contractors should include provisions giving themselves a right to substitute materials and to be reimbursed for any additional expenses such substitution involves.

If the standard forms of the American Institute of Architects are being used, the contractor should be sure that the Supplementary Conditions of the Contract for Construction include Article 16.1 of the A201 Supplementary Conditions (August 1972 ed.) or equivalent language which provides for substitution of materials and equipment:

16.1.1 Whenever a material, article or piece of equipment is identified on the Drawings or in the Specifications by reference to manufacturers' or vendors' names, trade names, catalog numbers, or the like, it is so identified for the purpose of establishing a standard, and any material, article, or piece of equipment of other manufacturers or vendors which will perform adequately the duties imposed by the general design will be considered equally acceptable provided the material, article, or piece of equipment so proposed is, in the opinion of the Architect, of equal substance, appearance and function. It shall not be purchased or installed by the Contractor without the Architect's written approval.

[12]Cf. Appeal of Anderson, ASBCA 632, 5 CFF ¶ 61182 (1950).

Article 16.1.1 is merely a generalized substitution provision, allowing a substitution of equal material or equipment with the architect's approval. It does not, strictly speaking, apply to the situation of forced substitution of more expensive materials or equipment due to unavailability and reimbursement for the added expense. However, it can be contract authority to which the contractor can look to convince the architect to approve the substitution of materials of equal quality that are cheaper than those originally specified.

In a policy statement of the board of directors of the American Institute of Architects approved on May 17, 1974, the following resolution encourages substitutions when materials or equipment are in short supply, with a corresponding adjustment of the contract prices:

Materials or equipment known to be in short supply should be avoided in design or specifications. If materials or equipment become unavailable during construction, or if delay in delivery will critically impede job progress, the designer should make every effort to find an acceptable substitute, with any contract adjustment—up or down—made accordingly.

The contractor may want to supplement Article 16.1.1 to provide for the situation of forced substitution of more expensive materials and for reimbursement for the added expense he might face due to such substitution.

The Construction Industry Affairs Committee of Chicago lists the following as one of its several suggested solutions to the shortage of materials:

If materials or equipment, which the contractor (prime or sub) is required to supply are not available, due to a shortage or unavailability, then an acceptable substitute must be found and an adjustment in the contract price made accordingly. A delay in obtaining delivery of the substitute item will be a legitimate reason for an extension of the contract time.

This clause could be written into a construction contract in order to give the contractor the right of substitution and the right to adjustment in the contract price.

The following clause is another possible supplement to AIA Article 16.1.1; it could stand on its own in a contract to permit substitutions, an increase in the contract price, and an extension of the contract time if materials or equipment become unavailable:

If materials or equipment which the contractor is required to furnish under the contract become unavailable either temporarily or permanently subsequent to the execution of the contract through causes beyond the control and without the fault of the contractor, then in the case of temporary unavailability, the contract time shall be extended by change order for such period of time as the contractor shall be delayed by such unavailability, and in the case of permanent unavailability, the contractor shall be excused from the requirement of furnishing such materials or equipment. The owner agrees to pay the contractor any increase in cost between the cost of the materials or equipment which have become permanently unavailable, and the cost of the closest substitute which is then reasonably available.

Such substitution provisions are among the most beneficial provisions for future contracts that a contractor could obtain to protect himself from material price instability. A contractor should always be careful that the substituted materials meet the minimum standards called for in the contractual obligations.

5 PERFORMANCE

INTRODUCTION

Too often, general contractors and subcontractors fail to recognize the legal implications of problems that arise during the performance of construction contracts which may increase the cost of performance of the contract. Extra work or changes beyond the contract requirement may arise in many forms, not always apparent to the contractor performing the work, that may entitle him to an increase in the contract price.

Ultimate success in obtaining an increase in the contract price for extra work or changes depends upon the contractor's prompt recognition of the facts for ultimate presentation in support of the claim for an increase in the contract price. Until the contractor recognizes and identifies the situations in which he is entitled to extra compensation, he cannot obtain any relief. The contractor cannot hope to identify all situations in which he is entitled to extra compensation for performing additional work until the key members of the contractor's staff and field personnel have become sufficiently educated to recognize the legal situations in which the contractor may be entitled to extra compensation and bring them to the attention of the contractor and in appropriate cases to the attention of his counsel.

The basis of a claim by the general contractor is the general contract and its accompanying documents, including any general and special conditions and the plans and specifications. The basis for any claim for compensation for a subcontractor is the subcontract and those portions of general contract documents which may be incorporated into the subcontract. General contractors and subcontractors necessarily must be aware of when they are entitled to extra compensation under the terms and conditions of the general contract documents. Subcontractors must also read subcontracts very carefully to avoid signing clauses which give the general contractors unnecessary legal and practical advantages or which waive the subcontractors' rights to ultimately claim compensation for extra costs to which the subcontractors would otherwise be entitled.

The right to extra compensation may arise for the general contractor because of the actions of the owner or the owner's authorized representatives. The right to extra compensation for a subcontractor may arise when actions by the owner or his authorized representatives are transmitted to the subcontractor through the general contractor, or they may arise directly from the actions of the general contractor. The reference to contractors in this chapter is applicable to both general contractors and subcontractors unless otherwise noted.

This short summary is designed to point out some of the legal problems that may occur during the performance of construction contracts. Any generalizations are made for the sake of brevity, and the legal doctrines and exceptions discussed herein may vary according to the applicable law and contract clauses.

CHANGES

As construction technology develops and becomes more advanced and complex, the problem of making changes in projects becomes more complicated and more costly to owners, contractors, and subcontractors. Ideally, many changes can be prevented if enough time is taken in developing, reviewing, and checking the original drawings and specifications. But unfortunately this ideal cannot always be reached, and even on a well-thought-out construction project, the owner, architect, general contractor, and subcontractors may find it necessary to change the original plans.

There are many reasons for issuing a change order. It may be necessitated by the further development of the owner's requirements, incorporation of construction improvements, deletion of unneeded features, equipment changes, unavailability or slow delivery of specified items, correction of contract document errors, resolution of coordination problems, and changes to include applicable code requirements or technological improvements. The result is an increasing number of change orders, and each one opens the possibility of misunderstandings among the contractual parties. This unfortunate situation often occurs because one or more of the parties lacks full understanding or concern about the whole change-order process.

Close cooperation between owners, architects, engineers, general contractors, and subcontractors is an absolute must in the complex arena of modern-day construction. It is imperative that all parties concerned in a construction project have a thorough understanding of change-order procedures and the many elements that go into the pricing of a change order beyond the direct costs for labor and material that enter into the estimated cost for making a change.

When the owner requests a change, the contractor performing the work must evaluate the scope of the change and determine and develop material costs, transportation costs, correct labor costs, the effect of the change on the project time, and the realistic and possible adverse effect of the change on other job conditions. He must also compute the overhead cost, which is the management cost, related to the change and a reasonable profit. The total sum of these items represents the cost to the contractor who performs the change.

If a subcontractor performs the change, the general contractor adds his own cost and a reasonable overhead and profit. Overhead, which is the cost of management of the change, will normally be higher than the overhead and costs calculated for the original project. Profit is a principle reason for doing business, and a reasonable profit must always be assigned to each change order.

The change article in a general contract must be studied to determine the extent to which the owner or his representatives may order a change in the work, and a subcontractor must study the subcontract to determine the extent to which a general contractor or the owner, through the general contractor, may unilaterally direct an increase or decrease in the work, suspend performance of the work, or otherwise direct changes within the general scope of the subcontractor's work. Because the overwhelming amount of the work under a general contract will actually be performed by subcontractors, it is the subcontractors who will be most directly concerned with pursuing extra compensation for changes during the performance of the work. Should a change affect several trades, the general contractor will collect all the subcontractors' estimates, total them, and add his overhead cost of administering performance of the change order. This will be the total cost which is seen by the owner.

Change clauses generally give the owner authority to order changes in the work within the general scope of the contract, establish the procedures for the owner to make a formal change and for the contractor to make a claim that a change has been ordered, and set out methods for calculating an appropriate adjustment to the contract price and an extension of the contract time.

The AIA General Conditions (AIA Document A201, 1976 ed.) provide for changes in the work in Articles 12.1.1 and 12.1.2, which state as follows:

12.1.1   A Change Order is a written order to the Contractor signed by the Owner and the Architect, issued after the execution of the Contract, authorizing a change in the Work or an adjustment in the Contract Sum or the Contract Time. The Contract Sum and the Contract Time may be changed only by Change Order. A Change Order signed by the Contractor indicates his agreement therewith, including the adjustment in the Contract Sum or the Contract Time.

12.1.2   The Owner, without invalidating the Contract, may order changes in the Work within the general scope of the Contract consisting of additions, deletions or other revisions, the Contract Sum and the Contract Time being adjusted accordingly. All such changes in the Work shall be authorized by Change Order, and shall be performed under the applicable conditions of the Contract Documents.

A similar change clause is found in the federal government's Standard Form 23-A Construction Contract, which gives the contracting officer the authority to order changes that are within the general scope of the contract. Usually the change clause in subcontracts incorporates the procedure for processing changes that is contained in the general contract. The change in work clause of AIA Standard Subcontract Form (AIA Document A401, 1972 ed.) appears in Articles 11.4 and 11.13 and incorporates into the subcontract the procedure for changes contained in the AIA General Conditions. These articles provide:

11.4   The Subcontractor shall make all claims promptly to the Contractor for additional work, extensions of time, and damage for delays or otherwise, in accordance with the Contract Documents.

11.13   The Subcontractor shall make any and all changes in the Work from the Drawings and Specifications of the Contract of the Contract Document without invalidating this Subcontract when specifically ordered to do so in writing by the Contractor. The Subcontractor, prior to the commencement of such changed or revised work, shall submit promptly to the Contractor written copies of the cost or credit proposal for such revised Work in a manner consistent with the Contract Documents.

If the general contract requires that a change order be issued in writing by the owner, then the contractor should obtain a written order from the owner or his authorized representative. If a subcontract requires a change order to be issued in writing by the general contractor prior to the performance of the work as changed, the subcontractor involved should be careful to follow the contract procedures of obtaining an appropriate written order from the general contractor or his authorized representative prior to the performance of the changed work in order to avoid problems in subsequently obtaining payment for the performance of changed work.

Often, the general contractor does not follow the procedure set out in the contract for ordering changes and extra work. Instead of a written order in advance by an authorized representative, an oral order from the general contractor's field superintendent may be issued. Although the subcontractor's foreman may be tempted to perform the extra work in expectation that the subcontractor will be paid the reasonable value of the work, he should not perform extra work ordered orally. The general contractor may dispute the fair value of the work performed, or he may reject the claim entirely because it was not authorized in advance in writing by the proper officer, as required by the contract. The subcontractor should abide strictly by the procedure set out in the contract for complying with change orders if he wishes to preserve his right to compensate for extra work performed. Specifically, he should obtain written authorization for the changed work on a form that identifies itself as being an order for changed or extra work.

Many general contractors and subcontractors supply their field supervision with a supply of extra work authorization forms with instructions that their field personnel should not perform any extra or changed work without obtaining the signature of an authorized representative of the party ordering the extra or changed work. If the claim clearly indicates that the scope covers "authorization for extra or changed work" and it is signed by an authorized representative of the party ordering the work, the signed form is the legal basis entitling the contractor to extra compensation for the extra or changed work.

If extra work is directed by an owner's representative who is not authorized to make changes, the courts may refuse compensation to the contractor unless an authorized representative knows and approves of the change. The contractor should not follow the directions of any representative without writing a protest letter to the owner unless the owner has already notified the contractor that the particular person has the authority to make changes. In general, inspectors do not have such authority, and even the architect may lack authority to change the specifications.

Illustrative Cases

The firm of Howell & Goin was reconditioning a school building in Frankfurt, Kentucky. After the basement and first floor were completed, a flood inundated both the basement and the first floor, and the contractor again reconditioned them at the request of the architect. Because the contract required the written authorization of the school board for changes in the work, the court held that no change order had been issued. As it turned out, the flood washed away Howell & Goin's profits as well as its finished work because it didn't stick ito finger in the dike by insisting on a written change order![1]

Montgomery Construction Company failed to damp-proof a wall as required by the specifications and argued that the inspector approved the work without damp-proofing and thus made a change in the contract. However, the contract stated that "no inspector is authorized to change any provision of the specifications without the written authorization of the contracting officer." The government was allowed a credit on the contract price.[2]

When a contractor receives oral instructions from a representative who the contractor is not certain has the appropriate authority, it is a wise course of action to write the owner reporting the field instructions and stating that these instructions require extra work for which the contractor, if required to perform, will claim an extra. The authorized agents of the owner may then tell the contractor not to proceed with the work, in which case the contractor has no further problem; or the owner may acquiesce in these instructions either by affirmatively issuing a written change order or by silence or failure to repudiate the instructions. This notice also fairly alerts the authorized representatives of the owner to the fact that the instructions were issued by operating personnel, which provides the owner with an opportunity to clarify, define, and rescind the instructions before costs are incurred. Writing a letter confirming oral and possibly unauthorized instructions not only preserves the contractor's right to relief but also gives the owner an opportunity to avoid any misunderstandings before work is performed. A written confirmation also avoids any disputes as to the issuance and scope of the instructions.

[1] Goin v. Bd. of Educ., 298 Ky. 645, 183 S.W.2d 819 (1944).

[2] Appeal of Joseph W. Montgomery, 58-2 B.C.A. ¶ 1925 (1958).

If the contract expressly exempts the owner from liability for extra work unless there is a proper written authorization, the contractor may not be permitted by the courts to recover for the extra work. However, if there is adequate proof that there is an oral direction for the work to be done and that the owner has knowingly received and accepted the benefits of the work, the contractor may be awarded the reasonable value for the work notwithstanding the contract provision requiring a written change order.

Illustrative Case

Orndorff Construction Company was directed by an unauthorized representative of the government to perform certain work not included in the original excavation quantities in the contract. Orndorff performed this work without obtaining a written authorization from an authorized representative as required by the contract. Orndorff's claim of a change was upheld only because it was shown that the authorized representative knew that the changes in the work were being made without written authorization from him.[3]

Notice Requirements When the Contractor Claims Extra Compensation

The typical construction contract change clause contains a requirement that the contractor or subcontractor give written notice that he considers a particular item to be a change or extra and that unless this written notice is given within a specified time, the contractor or subcontractor may be barred from claiming additional compensation under the contract. This written-notice requirement is one of the many pitfalls which await an unwary contractor. If the contractor neglects to give the required notice, he may lose a great deal of money performing extra work and be unable to recover, particularly if the other party was prejudiced because of lack of notice.

Illustrative Case

Ten years after the work on a government contract was completed, the contractor that built a research laboratory, Mishara Construction Company, asserted claims for various extra work on the project. The records of correspondence at the time did not show that Mishara had ever notified the government of these claims. It was held that the government was prejudiced because its engineering records were no longer available and the claims could not be evaluated. Therefore, Mishara did not recover.[4]

Many companies give their project managers, superintendents, and foremen detailed instructions on what notices are required by the particular contract for the specific job on which they are working. The jobsite personnel are instructed in the correct contractual method of reporting any changes, extras, and delays. Contractors who establish a methodical system which consistently recognizes circumstances requiring written noti-

---

[3] Appeal of Orndorff Constr. Co., 67-2 B.C.A. ¶ 6665 (1967).
[4] Appeal of Mishara Constr. Co., 72-1 B.C.A. ¶ 9353 (1972).

fication to the owner will not have to absorb the cost of changes because of procedural technicalities in the contract.

The notice provision which a subcontractor should follow may not be in his subcontract. Rather, it may be in the General Conditions, which are a part of the specifications and which are often incorporated into and made a part of the subcontract by reference only. Therefore, in preparing supervisory personnel for commencement of work on a new project, it is not enough to look at only a contract or subcontract. Every part of the subcontracts, general contract, General Conditions, supplementary conditions, plans, and specifications must be examined, and a list must be made of every place in those documents where notice is required.

However, a contractor or subcontractor who performs extra work and is otherwise entitled to be paid for it will not automatically lose his money just because he has failed to follow procedural technicalities in the contract. Experience has shown that the courts hesitate to deny a just claim because of such technicalities. Instead, they have recognized several areas which will allow a general contractor or subcontractor to recover for extra work, changed work, or delays even though no written notice was ever given.

The courts have recognized that these notice requirements serve two functions: (1) They give the owner or architect an opportunity to correct any problem which is going to result in extra cost. (2) They protect the owner from "surprise" claims after the job is over. Since the notice provisions are placed in the contract for the protection of one of the parties, the courts have found that these notice provisions can be *waived* by that party in situations where the failure to give the required notice does not have an adverse effect on the party who was to receive the notice. For example, the courts have found that the owner may waive written notice of extra work, changed work, or delays where the owner had actual knowledge of the circumstances and the contractor considered them to amount to a compensable change in the work.

Illustrative Case

Lindbrook Construction, Inc., entered into a contract with a Washington school district for certain cut and fill work. The plans and specifications showed the work to be performed and made specific representations with respect to the conditions to be encountered, the source and the amount of cut and fill, the depth of required excavation, and the availability of sufficient fill material from specific areas of proposed cuts. The contractor relied on these representations in the preparation and submission of his bid. Once excavation commenced, Lindbrook was required to perform extra work which delayed the entire job because there was an extensive shortage of fill materials, and the contractor was required to open and utilize a borrow pit. Lindbrook did not give the required "written notice" that it was having to perform extra work, but the architect was present on the jobsite and knew of this work. He directed that it proceed. He knew the grading contractor considered it to be "extra" but stated that he, the architect, considered it to be a part of the contract work. When Lindbrook filed suit for the losses caused by this "extra work," the school district attempted to block his suit by showing that he had failed to give the required written notice. The court met this argument head-on and found that notice in writing had been waived. The architect knew this work was being performed and that the contractor considered it to be extra. Since the purpose of the notice provision is to give the architect and owner an opportunity to correct any problems, the school district was not adversely affected by the lack of written notice. If any corrections could have been made, the architect could have made them.[5]

The lack of timely notice may also be waived if the owner has considered the claim on its merits or agreed at sometime to pay the contractor for the work.

Illustrative Case

Fred Clark, a grading contractor engaged to install a drainage system, claimed extra work for the removal of certain muck and dirt. The owner, Belleau, Inc., agreed to pay for the work over and above the contract price. In reliance on this statement, Mr. Clark did not submit a written claim within 1 week of the decision that it was extra work, as required by the contract, because he was told no payment would be made until the engineer estimated the amount of work done. Under these circumstances, recovery was allowed even though timely notice was not given.[6]

Where the owner had knowledge of the circumstances that formed the basis of the claim, the courts and contract appeals boards have then held that compliance with the formal notice requirement is not required. Some decisions have indicated that the notice requirement will not be enforced until the owner shows that it was somehow prejudiced or harmed by not knowing of the claim within the proper time limit.

Illustrative Case

The government's representative required Beacon Construction Company, the contractor, to use a more expensive method of caulking windows than contemplated by the contractor, and the contractor claimed that the change of method was a compensable change. The government initially moved to dismiss the case on the grounds that Beacon failed to notify the contracting officer within 30 days. The government lost its Motion to Dismiss because the government demonstrated no injury or prejudice resulting from Beacon's failure to meet the notice provisions of the contract.[7]

Changes within the General Scope of the Contract

In order for an owner to be able to unilaterally order the contractor to perform a change, the proposed change must be within the general scope of the contract. The line between whether or not a change in work is within the general scope of the contract is a difficult one to define because it is based on the facts of each situation. For a proposed change to be within the general scope of the contract, the change in the work must be one that would be regarded as fairly and reasonably within the contempla-

[5] Lindbrook Constr., Inc. v. Mukilteo School Dist. No. 6, 458 P.2d 1 (Wash. 1969).
[6] Clark v. Belleau, Inc., 14 Ga.App. 587 (1966).
[7] Appeal of Beacon Constr. Co., 68-2 B.C.A. ¶ 7197 (1968).

tion of the parties when the contract was entered into.[8] The elimination or addition of an entire building would not normally be held to be within the scope of the contract, whereas minor structural variations would.

Illustrative Case

The contracting officer attempted to eliminate a $99,000 nurses' quarters from a $911,000 project via a formal change order. The Court of Claims held that such a cardinal change, if allowed, would give the government the unilateral power to completely alter the contract by adding or eliminating entire buildings. It would be almost impossible for a contractor to allocate his resources to a job if the government could drastically change the amount of work to be done.[9]

It is sometimes said that a "cardinal change" is not within the scope of the contract. The Court of Claims described the cardinal change doctrine in the following opinion:

The cardinal change doctrine is not a rigid one. Its purpose is to provide a breach remedy for contractors . . . directed by the Government to perform work . . . not within the general scope of the contract. In other words, a cardinal change is one whiche, because it fundamentally alters the contractual undertaking of the contractor, is not comprehended by the normal Changes clause . . . . [T]here is no automatic or easy formula which can be used to determine whether a change (or changes) is beyond the scope of the contract and, therefore, in breach of it. "Each case must be analyzed on its own facts and in light of its own circumstances, giving just consideration to the magnitude and quality of the changes ordered and their cumulative effect upon the project as a whole."[10]

In the preceding case the contractor built an airplane hangar which collapsed because of defects in the specifications. Even though the reconstructed hangar was essentially identical to the original hangar, the court looked to the undertaking of the contractor rather than the product and held that reconstruction of the hangar was a cardinal change that the contractor could refuse to perform without breaching the contract. Just as one change may be cardinal and thus beyond the scope of the contract, the total effect of a number of changes may also be considered beyond the scope of the contract.[11]

If the contractor believes that a certain change in the work is beyond the general scope of the contract, he has several alternatives. If the extra work order is, in fact, outside the general scope of the contract, the contractor is justified in declining to perform it. Conversely, if the contractor is unilaterally directed to perform extra work that ultimately is proved to be within the general scope of the contract, it is legally a change and the contractor must perform the extra work or be in breach of his contract.

[8] Freund v. United States, 260 U.S. 60 (1922).

[9] General Contracting & Constr. Co. v. United States, 84 Ct. Cl. 570 (1937).

[10] Edward R. Marden Corp. v. United States, 442 F.2d 364, 369 (Ct. Cl. 1971).

[11] J.D. Hedin Constr. Co., v. United States, 347 F.2d 235, 257 (Ct. Cl. 1965).

Illustrative Case

A change order requiring that a foundation be placed on piles was held to be a change beyond the scope of the contract when the specifications did not require piles. The Court of Claims held that the contractor did not breach the contract when he refused to drive piles for the foundation.[12]

The cardinal change doctrine brings to mind the story of the contractor who went out to the jobsite when the building was ready for him to start work. He counted the floors, and exclaimed: *"Four* floors? I thought there were only *three!"* In this situation, if the architect wanted four floors but put only three in the plans, can he force the contractor to do the work on the fourth floor? The contractor wants to complete the three floors fast and move on to a more profitable job; he will not be satisfied with an adjustment to the contract price for the extra work. The answer is arguably no. This extra would make the contractor do one-third again as much work as he had planned, and so this change is beyond the scope of the contract. Of course, if the plans and specifications originally designated four floors, the contractor is really in trouble.

Pricing Changes

The pricing of the changed work may be based on a negotiated price, a cost-plus formula (on a fixed or percentage fee), or unit prices, or the price may be determined under the disputes clause. The contractor who is required unilaterally to perform a change must have a fast remedy under the disputes clause in the contract documents in order to fix the price of the changed work because the financial needs of the contractor require that the price for changed work be determined quickly to ensure that the contractor has adequate funds to meet the financial burdens of performance of the extra work. The procedure in the disputes clause must be subject to speedy resolution insofar as the contractor is concerned; otherwise he will pay out of his pocket for the cost of his required performance for a substantial period of time.

The procedure for determining the price of a change in the work in the AIA General Conditions (AIA Document A201, 1976 ed.) appears in Articles 12.1.3 to 12.1.5, which set out a typical procedure for pricing changes and provides as follows:

12.1.3 The cost or credit to the Owner resulting from a change in the Work shall be determined in one or more of the following ways:

.1 by mutual acceptance of a lump sum properly itemized and supported by sufficient substantiating data to permit evaluation;
.2 by unit prices stated in the Contract Documents or subsequently agreed upon;
.3 by cost to be determined in a manner agreed upon by the parties and a mutually acceptable fixed or percentage fee; or
.4 by the method provided in Subparagraph 12.1.4.

[12] Freund v. United States, 260 U.S. 60 (1922).

12.1.4   If none of the methods set forth in Clauses 12.1.3.1, 12.1.3.2 or 12.1.3.3 is agreed upon, the Contractor, provided he receives a written order signed by the Owner, shall promptly proceed with the Work involved. The cost of such Work shall then be determined by the Architect on the basis of the reasonable expenditures and savings of those performing the Work attributable to the change including, in the case of an increase in the Contract Sum, a reasonable allowance for overhead and profit. In such case, and also under Clauses 12.1.3.3 and 12.1.3.4 above, the Contractor shall keep and present, in such form as the Architect may prescribe, an itemized accounting together with appropriate supporting data for inclusion in a Change Order. Unless otherwise provided in the Contract Documents, cost shall be limited to the following: cost of materials, including sales tax and cost of delivery; cost of labor, including social security, old age and unemployment insurance, and fringe benefits required by agreement or custom; workers' or workmen's compensation insurance; bond premiums; rental value of equipment and machinery; and the additional costs of supervision and field office personnel directly attributable to the change. Pending final determination of cost to the Owner, payments on account shall be made on the Architect's Certificate for Payment. The amount of credit to be allowed by the Contractor to the Owner for any deletion or change which results in a net decrease in the Contract Sum will be the amount of the actual net costs as confirmed by the Architect. When both additions and credits covering related Work or substitutions are involved in any one change, the allowance for overhead and profit shall be figured on the basis of net increase, if any, with respect to that change.

12.1.5   If unit prices are stated in the Contract Documents or subsequently agreed upon, and if the quantities originally contemplated are so changed in a proposed Change Order that application of the agreed unit prices to the quantities of Work proposed will cause substantial inequity to the Owner or the Contractor, the applicable unit prices shall be equitably adjusted.

A contractor is well advised to negotiate the price of a change before the change is performed rather than afterward. This is termed in the construction industry as the "call-girl principle" after another ancient profession in which their services are worth more before the service is performed than after. Negotiating a lump-sum price for a change before the change is performed will give both the party requesting the change and the contractor performing the change assurance of the exact amount of the cost and payment of the change, so that there will be no surprise after the work is performed. Negotiating a lump-sum price before a change is performed will also normally result in the contractor receiving payment for the change more quickly than if the price has to be settled after the work is performed.

The alternative of pricing a change on a cost-plus-a-percentage or a fixed-fee basis requires an agreement as to overhead and profit. Documentation of the costs of the change is essential. General contractors and subcontractors must always check general contract documents to see if the owner has stipulated in the contract the overhead and profit markup for changes. A problem arises if the overhead and profit markup stipulated in the general contract is unreasonably low to cover the overhead and profit of managing the changes. The overhead and profit necessary to cover a change is normally much greater for the contractor who actually performs the changes than the overhead and profit markup necessary to cover the general contractor's overhead and profit if he subcontracts the work. Rather than performing the work himself, the general contractor normally will be motivated to subcontract changed work. A subcontractor performing the work may be able to take the position that an unreasonably low overhead and profit markup, stipulated in the general contract, controls only the markup of the general contractor to the owner on the subcontractor's price but does not limit the subcontractor's markup of overhead and profit for the work performed by the subcontractor.

The AIA change clause provides for an equitable adjustment in unit prices if the unit price quantities are substantially changed beyond those contemplated by the parties. If, under the AIA change clause, the owner and contractor cannot agree on the price of a change, the disputes clause provides that the architect must determine the cost based upon a reasonable cost plus overhead and profit. If dissatisfied with the value assigned by the architect, the owner or contractor may have the option of demanding arbitration. Under the AIA General Conditions, a contractor should not allow an owner to "starve" the contractor into agreeing to the owner's price for a change. The terms of the AIA change clause dictate that the owner must pay at least the amount certified by the architect for the change, so that the contractor may have the use of that amount while the parties work through the final resolution of the dispute.

The typical change clause for government construction contracts in Standard Form 23-A states that the contracting officer shall make an equitable adjustment to the contract price and the time allowed for performance when a change is ordered. Equitable adjustments are based on the contractor's reasonable cost of performance, and the actual cost proved by the contractor should be accepted unless it is shown to be unreasonable.[13]

Illustrative Case

Several change orders were issued to Canon Construction Corporation, a contractor that was paving roads for the government. These ordered changes, concerning relocation of roads and methods of paving, were performed by the contractor at increased cost over the original contract. The government asserted that the equitable adjustment should be based upon engineering estimates of the cost of the work. It was held, however, that the actual costs incurred were reasonable and they would be the measure of damages.[14]

To the contractor's reasonable cost is added an allowance for overhead and profit as part of the equitable adjustment. The circumstances of the extra work under a change order may indicate that the rate of profit allowed should be greater or less than the profit rate for the original contract. Factors such as the complexity and difficulty of the work, the amount or risk assumed by the contractor, and the amount of capital

[13] Bruce Constr. Co. v. United States, 324 F.2d 516 (Ct. Cl. 1963).

[14] Appeal of Canon Constr. Corp., 71-1 B.C.A. ¶ 8780 (1971).

invested by the contractor in the changed work may be used to determine the rate of profit.[15]

The contract lump-sum change order and the cost-plus formula are the most preferred types of pricing because they give the contractor better flexibility to ensure that he has enough funds to perform the additional work. When lump-sum pricing is used, the contractor submits a proposed cost for making a change in the originally specified installation needed by the contractor to make a fair, reasonable, and realistic estimate of the work, including materials to be added or deleted, estimated additional time needed for performance, and detailed estimates of additional costs.

Documentation

Unless the price of the change can be agreed upon in advance, the contractor must preserve the evidence of facts as to the costs and details of the performance of the changed work. Under the cost-plus method or under the disputes clause, for a contractor to be successful in obtaining full compensation for the original contract work as well as the changed work, the contractor must be able to prove his costs. The best evidence of expenses is a complete set of invoices, purchase orders, receipts, and accurate records of wages paid to employees.

Also very helpful in presenting a successful claim for extra compensation for changed work is the existence of a jobsite log in which the job superintendent records anything and everything that may be considered extra work. If a jobsite log is maintained and reviewed daily, the contractor will always be aware of conditions that require quick action, such as directives issued to the job superintendent from a representative of the owner, jobsite delays, or changing site conditions. It is important that every occurrence which might be extra work be documented because there is an inference that circumstances not included in the jobsite log did not occur.

Jobsite logs should be maintained daily by the job superintendent either on a handwritten form or dictated to be transcribed. A jobsite log may be in outline form to aid the job superintendent in making a record of all the important events of each day. It is a good policy to have the daily entries in the jobsite log forwarded to the main office of the contractor daily or weekly in order that the main office can follow the progress of the job and be assured that the jobsite log is being kept up to date.

Notes or memoranda should be kept of oral and telephone conversations. The content of each contract contact with representatives of the owner or other contractors should be noted. Then, as soon as possible, these notes should be translated into written memoranda for the file or a confirming letter to the other party to the conversation. The confirming

[15] See ASPR § 3-808.4.

letters have the dual purpose of implying agreement by the other if he remains silent after receipt of the confirming letter, and also preserving a written record.

In addition to the job log, photographs showing the nature and location of the changed work should also be made part of the file. Photographs can be the ultimate help in documenting the exact factual situation and may even furnish details previously unnoticed or not noted elsewhere. An instant-development type camera is useful, so that additional photographic pictures can be taken before the site conditions are altered, if for any reasons the initial photographs do not clearly depict what needs to be shown.

Depending on the magnitude and complexity of the claim, experts may be needed to produce expert opinions, analyses, and reports on the subject matter of the change. An expert can serve the dual purpose of supporting the claim and advising the contractor on the specifics of the claim. The contractor should not formulate his claim and then hire an expert at the last moment before presenting the claim. Rather, calling in an expert should be among the first steps, when it becomes clear that a substantial claim for extras may exist.

Also relevant in presenting a claim is evidence of the customs and practices of the trade of a particular contracting field. These customs or trade practices amplify plans and specifications and are implicitly incorporated into a contract provided they are not contrary to the expressed provisions of the contract. In addition to "fleshing out" the terms of the plans and specifications, proof of customs and trade practices may be an absolute necessity when questions arise about the standard of workmanship.

Illustrative Case

The government ordered a construction contractor, Stolte-Santa Fe-Bing, to install insulation boards around the interior walls of curbed roof openings because it claimed that the contractor's poor workmanship had resulted in unsightly exposed holes in the concrete and rough metal edges. It was held, however, that the appearance was in accord with good workmanship standards. The government had purchased the standard model and had to pay more for the optional accessories.[16]

Claims Procedure

The contractor should make his claim in writing for extra compensation for a change in work for which a price has not been determined in sufficient detail to clearly and persuasively present the facts necessary to demonstrate his costs and his position that he is entitled to an increase in the contract price for the change in work. No specific form is required for the actual claim. However, it should be logically organized and contain a factual statement of the claim in as much detail as necessary to present the contractor's views persuasively; also, it should contain or

---

[16] Appeal of Stolte-Santa Fe-Bing, 69-1 B.C.A. ¶ 7620 (1969).

refer to the key documents and contract clauses, expert witness reports, and photographs and should contain a discussion of the legal and contractual basis of the claim to demonstrate that the contractor is entitled to the increase in the contract price.

The AIA General Conditions of the Contract for Construction (AIA Document A201, 1976 ed.) contain the following claim clause:

12.3.1   If the Contractor wishes to make a claim for an increase in the Contract Sum, he shall give the Architect written notice thereof within twenty days after the occurrence of the event giving rise to such claim. This notice shall be given by the Contractor before proceeding to execute the Work, except in an emergency endangering life or property in which case the Contractor shall proceed in accordance with Paragraph 10.3. No such claim shall be valid unless so made. If the Owner and the Contractor cannot agree on the amount of the adjustment in the Contract Sum, it shall be determined by the Architect. Any change in the Contract Sum resulting from such claim shall be authorized by Change Order.

This clause requires written notice of the claim 20 days after the event causing an extra cost, but before any work is done. However, if there is adequate proof that the owner knowingly accepted and received the benefits of the work, the contractor may be awarded the reasonable value of the work notwithstanding the written notice requirement. The strict requirements of written notice may be satisfied by substantial compliance with the notice requirement where the owner has knowledge of the circumstances of the claim. (For a detailed discussion of notices, see pp. 132–134.)

Many general contractors and subcontractors have expressed concern at sending notices of claims for fear of creating bad relations with the owner and general contractor. Claims need not cause disputes if they are correctly and tactfully handled and if the other party is made to understand that the notice is required by the contract.

In addition to protecting claims for additional compensation, the general contractor or subcontractor should give notices of claims for extensions of time needed to perform changed work within the specific time limit for completion included in the contract. If the general contractor or subcontractor runs past this limit, he may be liable for liquidated delay damages. A general contractor or subcontractor is extremely vulnerable to liquidated damages because the money can be taken from his progress payments or retention.

Most general contractors and subcontractors are required by the contract to make a claim for an extension of time if the project is delayed for any reason in order to avoid an assessment of liquidated damages. For example, if the owner verbally orders the contractor to do extra work, which will delay completion of the project, the contractor should claim an extension of time within the time limit after he receives the order. The contractor can protect himself by sending one letter to the owner containing two statements:

1. The contractor has been ordered to do extra work (state here the work ordered) for which he will incur extra costs. A claim for extra costs will be forwarded later (or can be made now if known).

2. The extra work will delay completion, and the contractor claims an extension of time to cover the extra work.

Thus, when a project is delayed, two claims are required—one for an extension of time and one for extra cost. A common error of contractors who perform extra work is to claim only an adjustment of the contract price and neglect to claim an extension of time. If the change in the work delays the contractor and he forgets to claim an extension of time, he will be forced to accelerate at his own expense to avoid liquidated damages.

Government contractors must abide by the truth in negotiation provisions of the Armed Services Procurement Act[17] when they submit claims. Under these rules, the contractor must submit cost or pricing data, certifying that the data are accurate, complete, and up to date, and agree to a clause requiring a downward equitable adjustment if inaccurate data submitted result in an excessive equitable adjustment of the claim. Some government agencies have prescribed detailed forms to collect the claims information required by the trust in negotiation rules.[18]

The timely issuance of changes can prevent excessive costs, delays, and hard feelings on the project. To prevent late changes in construction plans, owners can help by continually reviewing the plans and specifications. The architect and contractor can also continue to review work in advance of construction to reduce conflicts and last-minute revisions. The earlier the change is made, the less the cost involved.

CONSTRUCTIVE CHANGES

A formal change order is ordinarily issued in writing by an authorized representative of the owner or by the general contractor to a subcontractor and constitutes a clear admission by the owner or general contractor that it is a change in the contract. A constructive change order differs from a formal change order in that it arises from informal acts and conduct of the owner or his representatives which increase the contractor's cost of performance.

A constructive change order arises when authorized representatives of the owner act in a manner which has the same effect as if a formal written change order had been issued under the change clause. The conduct of the authorized representatives of the owner may be such that they will be considered to have caused or ordered the contractor to perform work beyond that required by the original contract. Such conduct

[17] 10 U.S.C. § 2306(f) (1975) (applied to civilian agencies by FPR § 1-3.808-3).
[18] See DD Form 633-5, ASPR § 16-206.1.

increases the costs of performance of work by the contractor and entitles the contractor to an equitable adjustment of the contract price including a reasonable overhead and profit. Similarly, the conduct of the general contractor may amount to a constructive change and entitle a subcontractor to an equitable adjustment of his subcontract price.

The constructive change may originate with the owner or his representative and bear directly on the general contractor, or it can be transmitted by the general contractor to a subcontractor. On the other hand, a constructive change may originate with the general contractor and bear directly on a subcontractor. The legal doctrines will be similar in either case.

Any conduct by an authorized representative of the owner which has the effect of requiring a contractor to perform work in a manner different from that prescribed in the original contract terms, resulting in an increased cost of performance, may constitute a constructive change order entitling the contractor to relief under the change clause even though no formal change order is issued. A constructive change order may arise from any oral or written act or omission by an authorized representative of the owner which in practical effect requires the contractor to perform work in a different manner than originally specified in the contract. A direction constituting a constructive change order may be implied where the additional work is done with the owner's knowledge and approval, even though no actual direction to do the work is made by an authorized agent of the owner.

Since in such cases there is no formal act of issuing a change order by an authorized representative of the owner, a contractor must recognize and identify the conduct of the owner which constitutes a constructive change order. If a contractor does not do this, the contractor cannot obtain compensation for his increased costs because the burden of proof of the owner's conduct is on the contractor. Architects are famous for remembering things they *intended* to include in the contract. In order to get paid for everything which is truly an extra, therefore, the contractor must follow the old adage: If all else fails, read the contract.

The common types of constructive changes are defective specifications; change in methods of performance; misinterpretation of specifications; overinspection; rejection of conforming work; rejection of "or equal" substitutions; and defective owner-furnished property.

Defective Specifications

A contractor who enters into an agreement to perform work under certain plans and specifications has no right to depart from those plans and specifications. To protect the contractor, the owner who causes the plans and specifications to be drafted is held to give an implied warranty that if the specifications are followed, the work will meet the performance requirements of the contract. This warranty is breached when the specifications prove to be defective, and the increased costs incurred by the contractor in attempting to perform under defective specifications can constitute a constructive change order.

One court considered the contractor's plight when working under defective specifications and concluded: "The contractor is not permitted to vary from the prescribed plans and specification 'even if he deems them improper and insufficient; and therefore cannot be held to guarantee that work performed as required by them will be free from defects . . . or accomplish the purpose intended.' "[19]

The following illustrative cases are examples of constructive changes which occurred because specifications were in error, and therefore defective.

Illustrative Cases

MacKnight Flintic Stone Company agreed to furnish the waterproofing specified and also guaranteed that a New York City building would be watertight. The city engineer prepared the specifications, which were made part of the contract, and supervised the work. No objection was raised at any time as to the quality of the materials furnished or the workmanship. However, the specified waterproofing failed to keep the cellar dry, and the City refused to pay MacKnight Flintic for the work. The court held for the contractor, stating that its promise was not to make the cellar watertight, but to make it watertight by following the plans and specifications prepared by the City.[20]

A plastering contractor followed the specifications for plastering a section of a transcept vaulted ceiling of a large church. The plaster failed to adhere to the ceiling because of a defective specifications in the mix of plaster, a defect unknown to either the contractor or the owner at the time the work was performed. In a private arbitration the contractor was absolved from any responsibility for the failure of the plaster to adhere.[21]

Based on its own analysis of subsurface conditions, the government prepared specifications for the foundation piles for a Veteran's Administration Hospital. The piles were to be encased in a thin steel shell of 0.05-inch thickness. When the contractor, J. D. Hedin Construction Company, drove the piles, the subsurface pressures exerted in driving subsequent piles caused the thin shells on the previously driven piles to collapse. The court held that the contractor should recover all costs resulting from the attempt to perform the piledriving using the defective specifications calling for an inadequate pile casing. The government was held in breach of its implied warranty that compliance with its specifications would result in satisfactory performance. Recovery was granted despite a general clause in the contract which required Hedin to examine the site, check the plans, and assume responsibility for the work until completion.[22]

A contractor has the right to rely without inquiry on the accuracy of plans and specifications. The owner warrants the plans and specifications and the efficacy thereof, and the contractor may rely on them as a correct representation of good and sufficient engineering skill and ability

[19] Coto-Matic, Inc. v. Home Indemnity Co., 354 F.2d 720, 724 (10th Cir. 1965).

[20] MacKnight Flintic Stone Co. v. City of New York, 160 N.Y. 72, 54 N.E. 661 (1899).

[21] Unpublished arbitration case.

[22] J.D. Hedin Constr. Co. v. United States, 347 F.2d 235, 257 (Ct. Cl. 1965).

without independent investigation. The contractor does not assume the risk of extra costs resulting from deficient plans and specifications. If the implied warranty is breached, the contractor is free from liability for failure in the end result and is entitled to compensation for his increased costs in attempting to perform, even if the defective plans and specifications are subsequently remedied and the unattainable requirements are ultimately relaxed to permit performance. The owner cannot cure a breach of the implied warranty simply by extending the time of performance.

Error is one of several ways defective specifications may cause a constructive change. Inadequate detail in the specifications may also lead to a compensable constructive change if the discovery of the omitted detail forces the contractor to incur more costs than the original defective specifications led him to expect.

Illustrative Case

Inadequately detailed specifications failed to show a telephone power feeder line in the path of air-conditioning duct work which the contractor, Markowitz Brothers, Inc., agreed to install. Markowitz was required to relocate the feeder line, and this work was not within the duct-work contract. The Board of Contract Appeals held that the contractor had no duty to make a detailed inspection of the building before submitting a bid, and that it was entitled to an equitable adjustment in the contract price. [23]

If the specifications which indicate the feasibility of doing work in a certain way are so erroneous as to preclude the use of that method, the contractor may recover for unanticipated costs in using a different method. A dimensional error which requires the performance of more work than anticipated also gives rise to a constructive change.

Illustrative Cases

The specifications for the replacement of 20 doors showed the door openings to be 6 feet wide, and so the contractor ordered 6-foot doors. In fact, the door openings were 6 feet, 8 inches wide. It was held that this dimensional error in the specifications amounted to a constructive change. [24]

The height of a crawl space above a ceiling was listed in the specifications as 19 inches when it actually was 10 inches, a space too small to be used by the contractor's workmen. Contractors have been known to be very resourceful in order to get the job done, but they can't be expected to perform miracles. The contractor, Jack Picoult, was required to cut individual access holes for each light fixture support to be installed above the ceiling. He recovered his unanticipated expenses incurred in using the new method. [25]

[23] Appeal of Markowitz Bros., 1964 B.C.A. ¶ 4167 (1964).

[24] Appeal of Ramsley Silk & Woolens, Ltd., 65-2 B.C.A. ¶ 5107 (1965).

[25] Appeal of Picoult, 65-1 B.C.A. ¶ 4543 (1965).

Specifications are defective if they establish unattainable performance requirements. But if performance is possible, the general rule is that when work is covered by the contract and the specifications are not otherwise defective, the contractor cannot recover for difficulties encountered in doing the work.

Illustrative Case

An airport runway contractor, Hyde Construction Company, was required by the specifications to achieve 95 percent compaction of the refill material used in runway construction. The contractor's attempts clearly showed that this compaction standard was a practical impossibility. Hyde was allowed recovery for the expense of adding Portland cement to the top 6 inches of subgrade, a substitute procedure agreed upon by the parties.[26]

Though the general rule is that a contractor fully complies with his obligations under the contract by following the plans and specifications, some courts have recognized exceptions to the general rule in unusual circumstances. If no particular materials or methods are specified in the contract, the general contractor may be required to select a method which will produce the result required by the contract.[27] Similarly, if the contract does not require performance of a particular part of the work necessary to accomplish the desired result, the contractor may be required to perform that work, especially if he had received some notification outside the contract that it had to be done.[28]

When the specifications of a construction contract direct the contractor to perform work which when completed is in violation of building safety ordinances or codes, the contractor should not be liable. It has been held that the code violation is no reason for the owner to refuse to pay the contractor when the contractor was merely following the owner's specifications.

Illustrative Case

Corbetta Construction Company contracted to build a hospital on a new site to replace the one destroyed many years previously in the Great Chicago Fire of 1871. The specifications originally required Corbetta to install U.S. Plywood Corporation's Novoply or an approved equal, but the architect issued and St. Joseph's Hospital approved, in writing, a change order for the substitution of General Electric Textolite. When the building was substantially completed, the City rejected the hospital's application for a license to operate because the wall paneling did not comply with the Chicago Building Code. The hospital ordered Corbetta to correct the deficiency and withheld the contractor's final payment. The hospital obtained court permission to remedy the defect and filed suit against the contractor, the architect, and the paneling manufacturer to recover the cost of removing and replacing the paneling. Corbetta counterclaimed for the payment with-

---

[26] Appeal of Hyde Constr. Co., 1963 B.C.A. ¶ 3911 (1963).

[27] Cannon v. Hunt, 116 Ga. 452 (1902).

[28] Eastern Iowa Light & Power Coop. v. McKenzie, 296 F.2d 295 (8th Cir. 1961); Economy Fuse & Mfg. Co. v. Raymond Concrete Pile Co., 111 F.2d 875 (7th Cir. 1940).

held plus interest. The court, in analyzing the issue, cited 6 *Corbin on Contracts,* Section 1338 at page 394, which states: "If . . . defects in [a building] when completed are caused by . . . defects in plans and specifications supplied by the owner which the contractor was required to follow, the contractor will not be liable for nonperformance and will not be denied a judgment for compensation." The court absolved Corbetta of liability for the cost of altering the building to comply with the Building Code and held that the hospital was liable to Corbetta for the sums withheld.[29]

If the contract contains general language requiring the contractor to follow the building codes, but the specifications describe work which does not meet code requirements, the better rule is that the specific terms of the contract control over general language and the responsibility for altering the work to meet the codes should be the owner's.[30]

When problems occur on a construction contract and the contractor raises the possibility of a defect in the plans and specifications, the owners often attempt to place a financial burden on the contractor by citing the clauses in the contract which generally require the builders to visit the site, check the plans, and inform themselves of the requirements of the work, or by citing the clauses which require the contractor to assume responsibility for the work until completion and acceptance. The courts, however, have not accepted such arguments on behalf of the owners. Following general principles of common law, the courts have held that the specific language of a construction contract, which sets out methods and materials to be used by a contractor, is controlling and is not governed by the more general clauses referring to site visits and responsibility for the work.[31]

Where the specifications require the use of a particular brand of material and the result produced by that material turns out to be unsatisfactory, the specifications are defective, the owner is held to have breached his implied warranty, and the general clauses giving the contractor responsibility for the work do not shift the financial risk to the contractor.[32]

In summary, a contractor has performed adequately if he has followed the specifications, even if they do not produce the desired result. When there is a breach of the owner's implied warranty that compliance with the specifications will produce the desired result, the constructive change doctrine entitles the contractor to an adjustment in the contract price for his increased costs of performance plus reasonable overhead and profit.

Change in Methods of Performance

If a reasonable interpretation of the specifications gives the contractor the right to choose between various methods of performance of the work, the

[29] St. Joseph Hospital v. Corbetta Constr. Co., 21 Ill. App. 3d 925, 316 N.E.2d 51 (1974).

[30] *Restatement of Contracts* § 236(c); 3 *Williston, Contracts* § 619. *But see* Eichler Homes Inc. v. County of Marin, 208 Cal. App. 2d 653, 25 Cal. Rptr. 394 (1962).

[31] United States v. Spearin, 248 U.S. 132 (1918).

[32] Fanning & Doorley Constr. Co. v. Giegy Chemical Corp., 305 F. Supp. 650 (D.R.I. 1969).

contractor has the right to choose the least expensive method. If the owner directs that the work be performed in a manner which is more expensive to the contractor, then a constructive change has been ordered entitling the contractor to recover for the increase in cost of performance by the more expensive method plus the cost of any modification of work completed under the least expensive method. The contractor has the right to choose the method of performance where no particular method of performance is specified in the contract as well as when two or more optional methods are specified. In either case, when the owner directs the contractor to use a method that is more expensive than the least expensive method available, a constructive change has occurred.

Illustrative Case

A contract for the recovering of roofs provided that where fire walls protruded through the roof, bituminous flashings "shall be returned and sealed or capped and sealed to waterproof edges and ends." The roofing contractor, L. F. Still, chose to cap and seal the flashings, but the government demanded that the work be redone by the return-and-seal method, which was more expensive. The court held that the government had no right to demand a more expensive method because the contract unambiguously provided that either method would be acceptable. The roofing contractor was allowed to recover the difference between the cost of returning and sealing the flashings and the cost of the cheaper method as well as the cost of modifying the work he had already completed. [33]

Contract specifications called for the installation of gypsum board to the walls of a barracks, so Dawson Engineering Company started to install the gypsum board vertically. The government directed that it be installed horizontally—a procedure which proved to be more expensive than vertical installation because the contractor had to install nailing strips in the horizontal direction. Dawson was allowed recovery for the additional expense. [34]

The contract requirements for the installation of aluminum windows within precast panels required only that the windows be caulked. No specific method was required for the caulking. The contractor, Beacon Construction Company, desired to install the windows and apply the caulking with a caulking gun, a method which would have properly accomplished the job. The project engineer, however, directed the contractor to use the more expensive "buttering" method. The direction to use a certain method was held to be a constructive change entitling Beacon to an equitable adjustment in the contract price. [35]

A constructive change may also occur when the owner requires the contractor to change the sequence of work, thereby increasing the cost of performance of the contractor's work.

Illustrative Cases

The terms of the contract for making improvements to an office building stated that Mech-Con Corporation was to complete work on the air-conditioning system during certain months and then move on to complete work on the heating system. Before the

[33] United Pacific Ins. Co. v. United States, 497 F.2d 1402 (Ct. Cl. 1974).

[34] Appeal of Dawson Engineering Co., 1963 B.C.A. ¶ 3759 (1963).

[35] Appeal of Beacon Constr. Co., 68-2 B.C.A. ¶ 7197 (1968).

contractor began performance, the government directed that the work on the heating system should be done before the work on the air-conditioning system. The government's reversal of the order of performance was held to be a change in the contract requirements, and Mech-Con was allowed to recover for the increase in the cost of his performance which resulted from the change in the sequence of work.[36]

Hill & Moore Construction Company had agreed to perform exterior improvements on a group of government housing units. The contract allowed the contractor to perform the exterior work on both occupied and unoccupied units, and so Hill & Moore planned to proceed down each street from unit to unit. After the work had commenced, the government directed that no further work was to be done on occupied units. Thereafter, the contractor was forced to skip around the development to units which became unoccupied and were made available by the government. The Board of Contract Appeals held that the direction to perform on a unit-by-unit basis as the units became unoccupied was a constructive change to the contract and that the contractor was entitled to his reasonable increase in costs.[37]

In order to recover for a constructive change because of the use of a more expensive alternative method of performance, there must be a direction by an authorized representative of the owner designating the more expensive method of performance. If the contractor merely voluntarily selects the more expensive alternative method, the contractor cannot recover. This is an exception to the rule for constructive changes by some courts that no actual direction is necessary if the extra work is done with the owner's knowledge and approval.[38] Mere acceptance by the contractor of a suggestion by the owner may not constitute a constructive change.

Illustrative Case

Orndorff Construction Company contended that under the sequence charts which had been prepared work was to proceed to completion upon the Gettysburg Cyclorama Building before work was commenced on a neighboring office building. The contractor contended that the government ordered it to change that sequence and to begin work on the office building before completion of work on the Cyclorama. It was held that even though the contractor was encouraged to start work early on the office building, it was not directed to do so, and in fact changed the sequence voluntarily for its own convenience.[39]

A contractor may not recover if the owner reserves the option of choosing one particular procedure or method of performance over another. Normally, the contractor does not recover if the more expensive method was specified in his bid even if no method is required by the specifications. The method which the contractor asserts that he should have been able to use must be reasonable and feasible for the job; but if the specifications assert that either of two methods is feasible and it is discovered that the

[36] Appeal of Mech-Con Corp., 65-1 B.C.A. ¶ 4574 (1965).

[37] Appeal of Hill & Moore Constr. Co., 1963 B.C.A. ¶ 3709 (1963).

[38] Chris Berg, Inc. v. United States, 455 F.2d 1037 (Ct. Cl. 1972).

[39] Appeal of Orndorff Constr. Co., 67-2 B.C.A. ¶ 6665 (1967).

cheaper method actually was not feasible in the first instance, the contractor may recover the difference in cost between the cheaper and more expensive methods.

Illustrative Case

A contract for the installation of underground utility lines required that Main Cornice Works, Inc., achieve 90 percent compaction of the backfill but required no specific method for the accomplishment of this degree of compaction. The contractor claimed that the government denied permission for the use of the flooding method of compaction forcing the contractor to use more expensive mechanical compaction methods. However, the evidence tended to show that the flooding method was not feasible on this jobsite, and Main Cornice was denied recovery on the grounds that it had not demonstrated that its alternative method was a feasible one. [40]

In addition to showing that he was directed to use a more expensive alternative method of performance, the contractor must also show that the owner's direction to use the alternative method was, in fact, the cause of the increased cost of performance. If some other condition for which the contractor is responsible caused the increased cost, the contractor cannot recover.

Illustrative Case

Baize International, Inc., a contractor that had agreed to resurface airport runways in Korea, claimed that the contract allowed the bags of cement to be stored in large piles. The government required the contractor to stack the bags of cement in rows with spaces in between for inspection purposes. Subsequently, the cement became hydrated and useless. Baize sought compensation for the useless cement claiming that it became hydrated because the method of storing the bags in rows exposed more surface area for hydration. It was held, however, that the hydration was caused, not by storing the cement in rows, but by the inadequate covering material which was placed over the bags of cement. The contractor did not recover because covering the bags was his responsibility. [41]

Misinterpretation of Specifications

If the owner or his authorized representative misinterprets the specifications and requires performance not called for by the contract, the contractor is entitled to an equitable adjustment in the contract price for the contractor's increased cost in performance plus a reasonable profit for a constructive change.

Typically the architect, acting as the authorized representative of the owner, misinterprets the specifications. The problem is often that the architect designs a cow barn and then expects a cathedral. The architect, under the guise of interpretation of the specifications, may state that he had "intended the work to be included." The answer to this assertion is

[40] Appeal of Main Cornice Works, Inc., 65-2 B.C.A. ¶ 5019 (1965).
[41] Appeal of Baize Int'l Inc., 1963 B.C.A. ¶ 3963 (1963).

that the contractors are specification readers, not mind readers. Contractors base their estimates of costs on the work shown on the plans and specifications, not on the architects' intentions to include an additional floor in the building.

The direction by the owner or his authorized representative to perform work beyond the contract requirements may be either oral or in writing. If the contractor is directed to perform in accordance with erroneous interpretation of the contract specifications which differs from the contractor's interpretation, then the contractor is entitled to relief under the change clause for his increased cost of performance which results from the owner's erroneous interpretation.

Illustrative Case

The drawings and specifications given to Brezina Construction Company by the government provided for the installation of sound baffles in the duct work of an air-conditioning system, but the size of the sound baffles was not specified and was not clear from the drawings. The contractor installed one size baffle which was not shown to be inadequate for the performance of the job, but the government directed that these be replaced by baffles of the same dimensions as the ducts themselves. The contract did not baffle the court at all. Brezina's interpretation of the specifications was reasonable and, therefore, the government's directive to install larger baffles was a compensable constructive change.[42]

The contractor cannot convert his misinterpretation of specifications into a compensable change if the owner's interpretation is reasonable and the contractor's is not. To determine whose interpretation is the more reasonable, the courts choose the meaning of the words in the contract that would be attached to the writing by reasonably intelligent persons acquainted with all the operative usages and customs of the trade and knowing all the facts and circumstances prior to and at the time of the making of the contract. Sometimes the application of this general rule will be sufficient to decide the case. For example, if one of the proposed interpretations is inconsistent, illogical, or absurd or produces an impractical or unjust result, it will be disregarded. On the other hand, if one of the proposed interpretations is clearly the logical and natural meaning of the words, the court's analysis need go no further.

Illustrative Case

Blanchard Construction Company agreed to "clear" one portion of government land and to "clear and grub" another portion. The terms of the contract stated that all merchantable timber specified to be "cleared and grubbed" was to remain the property of the government and that all other merchantable timber was to become the property of the contractor. The government claimed that it was entitled under the contract to the merchantable timber from both portions of the tract. The court held, however, that Blanchard's interpretation, that the government was to receive the merchantable timber

---

[42] Appeal of Brezina Constr. Co., 65-1 B.C.A. ¶ 4638 (1965).

from the area which had been cleared and grubbed and that the contractor was to receive the merchantable timber from the land which had only been cleared, was a much more reasonable construction, and so it was adopted. [43]

If the problem cannot be resolved using the general standard of interpretation, certain well-established rules are then applied to interpret the meaning of the contract. [44] There are three primary rules of interpretation: First, technical words are given their technical meaning unless the circumstances or an applicable usage of the trade indicates a different meaning. Second, a writing is interpreted as a whole, and all writings forming part of the same contract are interpreted together. No single word, phrase, or sentence should be interpreted out of context with the rest of the contract. This means that all the provisions of the contract should be read in such a way as to be meaningful, reasonable, and consistent with the rest of the contract. When the contractor reads the contract, he has a duty to determine its meaning by considering the whole contract, not just a single sentence or phrase, but the owner has a duty to clearly express what he intends the contract to mean and to give adequate notice to the contractor of the contract requirements. Third, all circumstances accompanying the transaction concerning the contract between the owner and the contractor may be taken into consideration, with the exception of oral statements made by the parties of what they intended a writing to mean. Discussions prior to the signing of the contract which do not vary or contradict the terms of the contract may be used by the court to interpret or explain the meaning of a word, symbol, or drawing, but such prior discussions may not be used to vary, contradict, or add to the terms of the contract.

Illustrative Case

Construction Service Company contracted with the government to build parts of a dam with reinforced concrete and parts with cheaper gravity concrete. The contractor tried to focus the court's attention on a single sentence of the contract which the contractor argued indicated that the spillway bucket of the dam was to be built with reinforced concrete. Since the rate at which Construction Service had been paid for the spillway bucket was that for gravity concrete, the contractor claimed that the government's interpretation that gravity concrete had been specified was incorrect and that the contractor was entitled to the difference between the cost of the gravity and reinforced concrete. Considering the contract as a whole, the court found that there was no ambiguity in the meaning of the contract and that Construction Service's interpretation was not reasonable while the government's interpretation was reasonable. The contractor did not recover. [45]

There are also other rules applied by the courts when a problem of interpretation cannot be resolved using the primary rules. An interpreta-

[43] Blanchard v. United States, 347 F.2d 268 (Ct. Cl. 1965).
[44] *Restatement of Contracts* §§ 230–236; *see* Randolph Engineering Co., 58-2 B.C.A. ¶ 2053 (1958).
[45] Construction Service Co. v. United States, 357 F.2d 973 (Ct. Cl. 1966).

tion which gives a reasonable and effective meaning to all the language is preferred to one that leaves part of the language unreasonable or meaningless. If the principal apparent purpose of the contract can be determined, the meaning of particular provisions of the contract will be construed to be consistent with the principal apparent purpose.

This whole agreement rule has been applied by the courts to give effect to the entire contract and all of the contract terms. However, where there are clearly unrealistic provisions that are mistakenly included, such as inapplicable boiler-plate language, the inapplicable language must be considered to be of no effect.

If the general provisions of the contract are inconsistent with the specific performance requirements, the specific provisions ordinarily prevail. Similarly, provisions which have been typed onto the contract generally control over the printed boiler-plate terms and conditions of the contract.

Illustrative Case

The general terms of a contract described it as a contract for the painting of water towers. However, the work was required to be accomplished in strict accordance with the specifications and drawings, and these dealt only with the painting of water storage tanks, not with the painting of the towers. Following the government's direction, the contractor, Randall H. Sharpe, painted the towers also. But the contractor knew he had a right to prepare his bid using the specifications, and so he submitted a claim for compensation for extra work. It was held that the specific work details controlled over the general description of the work, and the contractor was allowed an equitable adjustment in the contract price. [46]

Custom and usage of the particular trade is commonly used either to add to the terms of the contract to clarify the contractor's obligations or to clarify an ambiguous provision of the contract. An express term of the contract which contradicts a custom or usage of the trade, however, overrides the custom or usage. For a custom or usage of the trade to be considered, it must be shown that the custom or usage is clear and regularly observed and that it was known or should have been known to both parties. A usage of the trade may be proved by referring to an industry code, such as the National Electrical Code, or by having other contractors in the same trade testify as to the customs and usage of the trade.

One of the most convincing ways a contractor can support his own interpretation is to check with the other bidders who bid on the contract or subcontract to determine how they interpreted the specifications in question. The contractor should then obtain a letter or appropriate statement from the bidders who agree with the contractor's position. If no concurrent interpretations are available from contractors or subcontractors who bid the job to actually perform the work in question, then concurrent

[46] Appeal of Randall H. Sharpe, 1964 B.C.A. ¶ 4124 (1964).

interpretations by other contractors may also be evidence that the contractor's interpretation is reasonable. Of course, any evidence or documentation that shows that the owner or the architect initially interpreted the specification in question similarly to the contractor should be presented.

A final rule of interpretation is that when a court is unable to choose between more than one reasonable meaning, an interpretation is preferred which operates more strongly against the party who drafted the contract. A construction contract and its specifications are usually drafted or caused to be drafted by the owner, and therefore interpretations are most strongly construed against the owner.

Illustrative Case

In a contract to make painting improvements at a post office and courthouse, Gholson, Byars & Holmes Construction Company agreed to paint "all previously painted surfaces." The contractor interpreted the contract not to require the painting of baked-enamel surfaces, but the government directed that all such surfaces be painted. The contractor was able to show that by established custom and usage of the painting trade the baked-enamel surfaces were not considered to be "previously painted." The court held that the trade meaning controlled even if in common language a baked-enamel surface was a painted surface. The contractor had no duty to notify the government of a well-established custom of the trade, and it was reasonable for the contractor to rely on the custom in interpreting the contract. The court said that if there was any ambiguity, it would be construed against the government, who drafted the contract, and the contractor received an equitable adjustment to the contract price for painting the baked-enamel surfaces. [47]

A contractor has a duty to seek clarification of any major patent discrepancy, obvious omission, or drastic conflict in the provisions of the contract. There is no duty to seek clarification where a contractor innocently construes a subtle ambiguity in his favor, but a contractor who deliberately seeks to profit from an ambiguity in the contract which he knows is an error by the drafter may not recover for a constructive change if he has not sought clarification from the owner. If clarification of an ambiguity is sought but is not provided by the owner, the owner will be held to have waived his right to complain of the interpretation placed on the contract by the contractor.

Illustrative Case

Where there was an obvious conflict between the drawings and the contract specifications as to whether the contractor was to weather-strip the windows of the building as well as the doors, the court held that there was an affirmative duty on the part of the contractor, Beacon Construction Company, to call the ambiguity to the attention of the government. Beacon failed to notify the government of the ambiguity and interpreted

---

[47] Gholson, Byars & Holmes Constr. Co. v. United States, 351 F.2d 987 (Ct. Cl. 1965).

the contract in its own favor. The contractor was not permitted to recover his expenses in weather-stripping the windows at the owner's direction.[48]

A contractor may not claim a compensable constructive change when he performs the work according to an interpretation of the contract which is more costly to him in the absence of a direction by the owner to perform the work according to that interpretation and without protesting. The contractor's voluntary performance may be taken to show that both parties intended that the contract be interpreted to require the more costly performance.

Illustrative Case

A contract between the government and Marinell & Campbell, Inc., provided that certain enamel and varnished surfaces were to be repainted but did not specify the type of paints to be used. During the early stages of performance of the contract, the contractor used enamel paint on the enameled surfaces and varnish on the varnished surfaces without protest and without directions from the government to use these paints. Subsequently, Marinell & Campbell asserted that the contract required only a latex emulsion paint, and therefore the contractor claimed an adjustment to the contract price for the difference in price between the latex emulsion paint and the enamel and varnish used. The Board of Contract Appeals disallowed this claim because it found that Marinell & Campbell's actions in proceeding without protest and without directions from the government showed that at the time of the contract both parties intended that enamel be used on surfaces which had previously been enameled and varnish be used on surfaces which had previously been varnished.[49]

If there has been a direction by the owner to perform the work according to an interpretation of the contract that the contractor believes is unreasonable or is contrary to what the parties intended, under the usual disputes clause the contractor must follow the owner's directions and perform the work in that manner. The contractor's recourse is to seek an adjustment in the contract price at a subsequent time. The best practice is to promptly notify the owner that his interpretation of the contract is believed to constitute a constructive change and to file a claim with the owner for recovery of increased costs and an extension of performance time caused by the owner's erroneous interpretation.

Overinspection

Another category of additional requirements changing the nature of the contract terms, and thereby creating a constructive change order, is overinspection by the owner's representatives. Overinspection may take the form of changing the scheduling or frequency of inspections, or requiring as a result of inspection a higher standard of performance.

[48] Beacon Constr. Co. v. United States, 314 F.2d 501 (Ct. Cl. 1963).

[49] Appeal of Marinell & Campbell, Inc., 1963 B.C.A. ¶ 3948 (1963).

Illustrative Cases

A contract between Gordon H. Ball, Inc., and the government clearly provided that the government was to perform x-ray inspection of welds in steel columns at the factory before shipping the columns to the jobsite. The government failed to perform the x-ray inspection at the factory and required the contractor to provide facilities for on-site x-ray inspection at considerable cost to the contractor. The Board of Contract Appeals held that Ball had the right to assume in bidding on the job that it would not have to duplicate any inspection and testing of the welds. Ball was awarded an equitable adjustment in the contract price for its expenses in providing on-site inspection.[50]

Pacific Car and Foundry Company entered into a contract to repair certain boiler components with the U.S. Coast Guard. The contract required the contractor to inspect the work. There were two well-established customary procedures for inspection, one for repair work and another more costly procedure for the inspection of new construction work. Although the government argued that the work was only a modification to new equipment, it was held that the contract expressly described the work involved as repairs, and therefore the government's requirement that Pacific Car and Foundry use the procedure for new construction was a compensable constructive change order.[51]

In order for there to be a constructive change because of overinspection, the inspector must be authorized to issue change orders or his action must be ratified or acquiesced in by an authorized representative of the owner. The owner may not be bound to compensate the contractor for a more expensive manner of inspection than specified in the contract unless it is directed by an authorized representative of the owner or by a representative without authority to issue change orders when an authorized representative of the owner has actual or constructive knowledge that changes in the work are being made. An infrequent exception to this rule that directions by an unauthorized representative must be confirmed by an authorized representative of the owner occurs when a failure to comply with the order of the unauthorized representative would result in materials becoming unusable because of emergency circumstances.

Illustrative Case

An inspector who had no authority to issue change orders directed the contractor, Barton & Sons Company, to use additional epoxy in joining and sealing certain concrete slabs. It was found that the contractor was unable to seek clarification or confirmation from an authorized representative and in fact had no alternative but to comply because the epoxy would have spoiled if not used immediately. The inspector's order was held to be a compensable constructive change order.[52]

Overinspection may also occur if the owner or his authorized representative requires the contractor to meet a standard of workmanship higher than the standard dictated by the customs and practices of the contractor's trade.

[50] Appeal of Gordon H. Ball, Inc., 1963 B.C.A. ¶ 3925 (1963).
[51] Appeal of Pacific Car & Foundry Co., 60-1 B.C.A. ¶ 2505 (1960).
[52] Appeal of Barton & Sons Co., 65-2 B.C.A. ¶ 4874 (1965).

Illustrative Case

Warren Painting Company claimed that the government's inspectors were overly strict in rejecting the work because of slight overlapping of woodwork enamel onto the walls of the houses being painted. The Board of Contract Appeals held that the standard of workmanship required by the contract was the standard generally recognized in the painting trade. It was found that some overlapping of enamel on the wall was a standard painting practice. The orders of the eagle-eyed government inspectors amounted to a change in the work, and the contractor was given an equitable adjustment to the contract price. [53]

Rejection of Conforming Work

A constructive change order can arise when an authorized representative of the owner unjustifiably rejects the contractor's work that conforms to the original contract, requiring the contractor to perform certain rework. But the contractor will not be compensated for additional cost incurred in redoing work to meet standards required by the contract. The owner must properly carry out the inspection procedures required by the contract before rejecting the contractor's work.

Illustrative Cases

Carlin Construction Company, a contractor, completed work on a concrete wall using good workmanship and following the specifications in the contract. The work was rejected, however, because of the presence of discoloration of the concrete called "sand-streaking." The government required the contractor to perform work not authorized by the contract to eliminate this discoloration, and this was held to be a compensable constructive change. [54]

The government rejected the painting work done by the contractor, a joint venture consisting of Day and Zimmermann, Inc., and Madway Main Line Homes, Inc., alleging that the unsatisfactory appearance of the walls painted was the result of the contractors' poor workmanship. They were required to apply a third coat of paint. The Board of Contract Appeals held that the problem was the government paint specifications rather than the contractors' workmanship and held that the contractors were entitled to additional compensation for applying the third coat of paint. [55]

D. R. Kincaid, Ltd., a contractor in Hawaii, constructed a coral and asphalt runway for the government. Although the contract contained numerous test specifications to be performed by the government in each stage of the performance of the contract, the government rejected the runway without performing these tests and without even following the industry-accepted method of inspection. The contractor was compensated for repaving the runway in his attempt to rectify the alleged deficiency. [56]

Not only are the standards of performance required of a contractor governed by the specifications, but also they are amplified by the customs

---

[53] Appeal of Warren Painting Co., 61-2 B.C.A. ¶ 3199 (1961).

[54] Carlin Constr. Co. v. United States, 92 Ct. Cl. 280 (1941).

[55] Appeal of Day & Zimmermann-Madway, 71-1 B.C.A. ¶ 8622 (1971).

[56] Appeal of D.R. Kincaid, Ltd., 65-1 B.C.A. ¶ 4810 (1965).

and practices of the particular contract trade. If the contractor has performed his work under the contract according to the normal customs and practices of his trade, the rejection of his work by an authorized representative of the owner or general contractor who requires a higher standard of workmanship constitutes a constructive change entitling the contractor to an equitable adjustment of the contract price for the costs and a reasonable profit to redo the rejected work. A contract will often require the contractor to follow the specifications using "first-class workmanship," which has been interpreted to mean skillful, average work conforming to industry standards. The determination of whether work was performed in a first-class manner may be influenced by whether or not the contractor followed the manufacturer's recommendations in working with materials. If there is no standard of workmanship expressly stated in the contract, a promise by the contractor to carry out the specifications using good workmanship is implied.

Illustrative Cases

A government contract for the repair of storage tanks required that the contractor, E. W. Sorrells, Inc., install steel liners in seven underground storage tanks and pour grout between the liner and the tank sidewall. Subsequent to the completion of this work, it was discovered that the bottoms of the steel liners had buckled upward, requiring extra work to restore the liners to their proper shape. The evidence presented to the Board of Contract Appeals showed that Sorrells had performed the work in a workmanlike manner according to the specifications provided by the government. The extra cost was caused by a defect in the method of performance specified by the government, not by the workmanship of the contractor, and therefore Sorrells was entitled to compensation for its extra work.[57]

Healy Tibbitts Construction Company, a contractor installing pumps at a salt-water pumping station for the government, did not apply epoxy to the screw threads at the juncture between the steel piping and the bronze pump bowl. After testing in salt water the government observed that corrosion had occurred at the juncture between the piping and the bronze bowl that would not have occurred had epoxy been applied to the screw threads. The specifications did not expressly require that the screw threads be coated with epoxy, but it was held that the installation was not done in a workmanlike manner. That is, by the standard of workmanship of the trade, the contractor should have known that epoxy should have been used on the screw threads. Therefore, Healy Tibbitts was not compensated for recoating the pipe with epoxy and reinstalling the pumps.[58]

The courts may refer to the codes of workmanship standards published by a particular trade if one is available. Often the contract itself will provide that the code, such as the National Electric Code, will govern the performance of the work.

[57] Appeal of E.W. Sorrells, Inc., 70-2 B.C.A. ¶ 8515 (1970).
[58] Appeal of Healy Tibbitts Constr. Co., 73-1 B.C.A. ¶ 9912 (1973).

Illustrative Case

A government contract provided that the provisions of the National Electric Code were to govern the installation of permanent wiring and electrical equipment at a construction site. The National Electric Code provided that junction boxes were to be installed so that the wiring contained in them may be rendered accessible without removing any part of the building and that such junction boxes should be securely fastened in place. The contractor, Mishara Construction Company, installed conduit in front of the junction boxes in such a way as to make them inaccessible, and the junction boxes hung free without attachment to the structure. The government directed rework in the form of repositioning each box and fastening it securely to a structural member of the building. Mishara was not allowed compensation for this rework because the initial installation was found to be a violation of both the standard of good workmanship and the requirements of the National Electric Code.[59]

When a contractor incorporates into a structure work which does not conform to the specifications, the courts must decide whether to make the contractor tear down part of the work to remedy the defect or compensate the owner in some other way. Many courts have adopted the rule that if the contractor in good faith has substantially complied with the contract but made slight deviations, or if the reconstruction would involve unreasonably high expenditures tantamount to "economic waste," the measure of the owner's damages is the difference in value between the work actually done and the work that should have been done according to the specifications.[60]

Illustrative Case

Leonard Hangen, a builder, breached his contract by using wooden lath for his plastering when wire lath was specified in the contract. At trial the jury had awarded the owner, Marie Walter, enough money to have the completed buildings reconstructed—half the original contract price—but the appellate court overturned the award, finding that the trial judge should have instructed the jury to measure the damages by the difference in value of the buildings with wire lath and with wooden lath.[61]

Rejection of "Or Equal" Substitutions

When the specifications permit "or equal" substitutions, the contractor is entitled to make a substitution of materials or equipment which is equivalent or equal to the equipment or materials specified in the contract. If the owner rejects the substitution by a contractor of materials or equipment which are less expensive but equal and directs the contractor to install more expensive equipment, then a constructive change has occurred entitling the contractor to recover the cost difference between the less expensive product and the product which he was directed to install plus a reasonable profit. The submission of an item pursuant to an

[59] Appeal of Mishara Constr. Co., 66-1 B.C.A. ¶ 5308 (1966).
[60] Small v. Lee & Bros., 4 Ga. App. 395 (1908); Jacob & Youngs, Inc. v. Kent, 230 N.Y. 239, 129 N.E. 889 (1921).
[61] Walter v. Hangen, 71 App. Div. 40, 75 N.Y.S. 683 (1902).

"or equal" clause is not the same as a request for a deviation from or change in the contract. In executing the contract, the owner has given the contractor the right to use any item which is equal to the quality and performance of the brand-name standard.

Private owners and developers frequently prefer to demand the use of a single name-brand item. It is perfectly within their contract rights to draft the contract documents to make that demand, and in such a case the contractor will be bound by the contract's language. In public contracts, however, competitive bidding is often statutorily mandated. A demand by a public owner that the contractor use one item would circumvent competitive bidding. The largest contractor in the world, the United States Government, has long adhered to "or equal" clauses; and the administrative boards which rule on federal contract disputes have consistently held that the refusal to approve an "equal" substitution constitutes a constructive change in the contract specifications and entitles the contractor to an equitable adjustment in the contract to cover the increased costs of procuring the more expensive product.[62] The courts interpret an "or equal" clause in a construction contract as creating a valuable contract right for the contractor.

Illustrative Case

The Jack Stone Company agreed to build an addition to the National Institutes of Health at Bethesda, Md. The existing structure contained a fire-alarm system manufactured by Sperti-Faraday. The contract contained the following clause:

1-19 STANDARD REFERENCES

(c) Reference in the specifications to any article, device, product, materials, fixture, form or type of construction by name, make, or catalog number, shall be interpreted as establishing a standard of quality, and not as limiting competition. The Contractor may make substitutions equal to the items specified if approved in advance in writing by the Contracting Officer.

The brand-name standard used in this specification was also Sperti-Faraday. The contractor proposed a fire-alarm system manufactured by ADT which was found to be in all respects equal to and compatible with the existing installation. However, the contracting officer demanded that the contractor install Sperti-Faraday equipment. In holding that Jack Stone was entitled to a judgment for the difference in cost between the two articles, the court reviewed the "standard of quality" clause cited previously and stated that it was designed to discourage the potentially monopolistic practice of demanding the use of a brand-name item or designated article in government contract work. The court stated that the normal understanding of this provision would be that every time a brand-name appears in a specification, it should be read as referring, not only to the particular manufacturer or product which was designated, but also to any equal article or product.[63]

The word "equal" as used in "or equal" clauses does not mean that to be approved the substitution must be identical in every respect to the brand

---

[62] Appeal of Lehigh Chemical Co., 1963 B.C.A. ¶ 3749 (1963); Davies v. Kahn, 251 F.2d 324 (4th Cir. 1958).
[63] The Jack Stone Co. v. United States, 344 F.2d 370 (Ct. Cl. 1965).

named as the standard of quality. The substitution may be "equal" and at the same time have a somewhat different design; equality is to be defined by the quality, performance, and design of the substitution versus the brand-name specified. But "equality" does not mean "identity." If the proffered substitution functions as well as the specified equipment, it should be accepted by the owner as satisfying the "or equal" clause.

Illustrative Case

Sherwin Electric Service, in installing electrical equipment, proposed to substitute a different brand of switch. The specifications of the contract did not identify by name a particular brand of switch but described in minute detail a switch manufactured only by ASCO. The Russelectric switch proposed by the contractor differed from the ASCO switch in that it was a motor-driven switch rather than a solenoid-acctuated switch and it did not have arcing contacts, as did the ASCO switch. The court undertook a factual examination of the merits of the two switches and disposed of the government's contentions that the proffered switch was not equal in quality and performance to the specified switch. The court noted that a good-quality motor will give the same degree of reliability as a solenoid, and that different arc-protection devices were warranted because the two switches differed in the metallurgical composition of their respective contacts. The court found that the evidence produced by Sherwin indicated that the Russelectric switch would have proved as effective and as durable in performance in the contract work as the ASCO switch described in the specifications. In light of this, the court concluded that the contractor was entitled to an equitable adjustment for a change in the work by reason of the contractor being required to install the ASCO equipment rather than the Russelectric switch. [64]

Clauses which provide for the use of a particular brand-name product "or equal" or which provide that brand names are used merely as a "standard of quality" have been common in construction contracts for many years. In construing these clauses, the courts have held uniformly that the contractor has a contractual right, agreed to by the owner, to the use of any product which is "equal" to the brand-name standard in quality and performance. A contractor also has a right to the benefit of an honest judgment by the owner or his representative of the quality of the proposed substitution in relation to the brand-name standard.

Defective Owner-Furnished Property

Additional work required of the contractor because of defective property, equipment, or materials furnished by the owner to the contractor under the contract also gives rise to a compensable constructive change. Therefore, the contractor can recover for his increased cost of performance occasioned by the defective property furnished by the owner. Similarly a subcontractor may recover if the general contractor furnishes defective property.

The owner who contractually agrees to furnish property must furnish

---

[64] Sherwin v. United States, 436 F.2d 992 (Ct. Cl. 1971).

property suitable for the intended use under the contract, which means that the property supplied by the owner must be adequate for the performance of work contemplated by the parties at the time they entered into the contract. If the property furnished is not suitable, then the contractor is entitled to an increase in the contract price for his increased cost of performance in procuring suitable property or for his expenditures required to make the unsuitable property suitable for his performance.

Illustrative Cases

In the late 1800s a contractor, R. D. Wood & Company, agreed to install a system of water works for the city of Ft. Wayne, Ind. Special castings which were to form the connections between large and small pipes were to be supplied by the City from a local manufacturer. When furnished, these castings were defective in size, and the delay and expense to the contractor in remedying the defects amounted to the large sum, in those days, of $750. As a result of this and other problems between the parties, the case was taken to the United States Supreme Court, where Wood was awarded compensation for extra expenditures caused by the defect in the castings supplied by the City. [65]

In a contract for the construction of power lines, Power City Construction, Inc., agreed both to erect the towers furnished by the government and to string the conductors. Costly delay was incurred when government-furnished tower steel proved to be misfabricated and defective. The contractor recovered, not only for the delay in erecting the towers which was directly caused by the defective steel, but also for his increased costs in stringing the conductors on the towers because this phase of the work had to be completed in bad winter weather owing to the previous delay. [66]

The same rule applies to defective owner-furnished models or patterns, erroneous data or information, or erroneously marked parts.

Illustrative Case

Sutton Construction Company agreed with the government to transport the parts of a 75-foot steel tower to an island in Chesapeake Bay and to erect it there. The first problem encountered by the contractor was that, while the government drawings showed that steel reinforcements in an existing concrete base to which the tower was to be attached were no deeper than 2¼ inches from the surface, these reinforcements were encountered as deep as 14 inches. In drilling anchor holes for the tower, therefore, Sutton was unable to use a blow torch to cut through all the steel reinforcements as it had planned and was forced to resort to a very expensive drilling procedure. Then, when the contractor attempted to assemble and erect the tower, it discovered that parts were missing, misfitting, or mismarked. After Sutton spent substantial time and money in attempting to resolve these problems and to erect the tower, the government finally discontinued the project. The contractor recovered for his increased costs which resulted from misleading drawings and the misfitting and mismarked parts. [67]

A contractor may not be allowed to recover for any unreasonable vain attempts to make defective equipment meet the contract specifications.

[65] Wood v. City of Ft. Wayne, 119 U.S. 312 (1886).

[66] Appeal of Power City Constr. & Equip., Inc., 68-2 B.C.A. ¶ 7126 (1968).

[67] Appeal of Sutton Constr. Co., 1963 B.C.A. ¶ 3762 (1963).

When the contractor considers the material furnished by the owner to be unsuitable for use, he should notify the owner at once of the unsuitability and claim a constructive change entitling him to an increase in the contract price for his increased costs plus a reasonable profit. Since the burden of showing the unsuitability of the owner-furnished property is on the contractor, the contractor should establish systems and procedures for educating key personnel regarding the problems of owner-furnished property, for keeping a proper inventory of all property furnished to the contractor by the owner, and for the systematic documentation of any events and problems which occur in connection with owner-furnished materials or equipment.

IMPOSSIBILITY OF PERFORMANCE

When it is impossible to meet the requirements of the plans and specifications, a contractor may have a right to some relief in attempting to perform his contract. If there is, in fact, impossibility of performance under the plans and specifications, the contractor may be relieved of his contractual liability to perform and can recover his cost actually incurred in attempting to comply with the impossible requirements plus a reasonable profit. If the contractor is required to perform under new contractual terms or designs, which result from the impossibility, the contractor may be able to recover the additional costs incurred on his changed performance, plus a reasonable profit.

The basis on which a contractor may obtain relief when performance is impossible rests upon the doctrine of implied warranty by the owner of his plans and specifications. When the owner furnishes plans and specifications, normally the owner implicitly warrants that those plans and specifications are workable, that they will satisfactorily produce the result called for in the contract, and that the prescribed performance requirements can be achieved. A contractor has the right to rely on those plans and specifications without making his own evaluation that the requirements can be feasibly met. There are some exceptions: The contractor cannot rely upon the doctrine of impossibility of performance when the contractor has originated the specifications or design, or where under the circumstances the contractor may be deemed to have assumed the risk of impossibility. The contractor assumes the risk if he expressly agrees to assume it, if the contract provides for the accomplishment of a goal of performance without setting out specifications indicating how the contract should be performed, or if the risk of impossibility was obvious.

To be entitled to relief for impossibility of performance, the contractor must prove that performance of the contract was, in fact, either actually or practically impossible. Actual impossibility means that the contract could not be performed by any contractor. It is usually the result of erroneous specifications or a performance requirement which cannot be met with the equipment specified in the contract. The standard for impossibility is an objective one, and it is not met if performance is prevented only by the internal problems of the particular contractor who is a party to the contract.

Illustrative Case

Blount Brothers Construction Company was to construct and precisely align a circular rail as a part of a ship-model testing facility for the government. Blount Brothers claimed that because of an inherent flaw in the design the foundation was unsteady and the rail would not retain an alignment. Thus Blount Brothers sought to recover the cost of attempting permanent alignment until the government allegedly relaxed the specification for precision in alignment by accepting the work. The Board of Contract Appeals denied the claim, holding that the rail was capable of permanent alignment and that the contractor had simply had to go to more expense than anticipated to accomplish the alignment. This expense was not recoverable. [68]

Practical impossibility exists when performance would cause such extreme and unreasonable difficulty and expense that performance is not practicable within the existing commercial circumstances and basic terms of the contract. Hardships or greater costs than anticipated do not necessarily prove practical impossibility. The most common examples of practical impossibility occur when a contractor is unable to meet an unreasonable production schedule of work, when a building is destroyed in the course of construction, or when performance becomes illegal.

Illustrative Cases

A contractor agreed to obtain all the gravel necessary for a project from a certain parcel of land. There was enough gravel on the land, but part of it was under water. Removal of this submerged gravel would have cost ten times more than by the normal method, although removal was not strictly impossible. Although the court recognized the general rule that unanticipated extra cost is not an excuse for a failure to perform, the court held that difference in cost here was so great it made performance impracticable. [69]

Sadie Fisher and Joe Goldberg, Inc., the subcontractor, agreed on the construction of a movie theater in Chicago, assuming that the construction of such theater would be legal. After construction of the building was begun, the City halted it because the theater was being built within 200 feet of a church, in violation of a municipal ordinance. In releasing the contractor from its obligation to perform, the court cited the *Restatement of Contracts,* as follows: "[T]he essence of the modern defense of impossibility is that the promised performance was at the making of the contract, or thereafter became, [sic] impracticable owing to some extreme or unreasonable difficulty, expense, injury, or loss involved, . . . rather than that it is scientifically or actually impossible. While the mere fact that performance of a promise is made more difficult and expensive than the parties anticipated . . . will not ordinarily excuse the promisor . . . , nevertheless [it will be excused] where very greatly increased difficulty had been caused by facts not only unanticipated but inconsistent with the facts that the parties obviously assumed to exist or to be likely to continue." The important question is whether an unanticipated circumstance has made performance of the promise vitally different from

[68] Appeal of Blount Bros. Constr. Co., 1963 B.C.A. ¶ 3760 (1963).

[69] Mineral Park Land Co. v. Howard, 172 Cal. 289, 156 P. 458 (1916).

what should reasonably have been within the contemplation of both parties when they entered into the contract. If so, the risk should not fairly be thrown upon the promisor. [70]

A distinction between the general contractor and subcontractor may be drawn when a building under construction is destroyed before completion. The risk of such an occurrence is generally placed on the general contractor, for the destruction of the building makes its completion more expensive but not impossible. A subcontractor or any contractor performing work on an existing building has not promised to complete the building. The general contractor may be held to have promised implicitly that the building would remain in existence for the completion of the subcontractor's work, so that in some cases the subcontractor could recover his costs and a reasonable profit while the general contractor could not.

Illustrative Case

Schastey & Vollmer, a general contractor, agreed to renovate an existing building and subcontracted the painting and plastering to A. C. Wacker. A fire, the fault of none of the parties, destroyed the building before renovation was complete, and subsequently the subcontractor sued for the value of the work he had done. While recognizing the general rule that a contractor bears the risk of destruction when the contract is for the construction of a building, the court held that in a contract for renovation, the owner warrants the continued existence of the building, and so the subcontractor recovered. [71]

There is also a well-established doctrine of partial impossibility. If performance is only temporarily impossible, the contract time is extended without penalty to the contractor.

If a contractor contends that his contract is impossible to perform, the contractor must prove the fact of impossibility by testimony of an independent expert witness or evidence that other contractors either have been or would be unable to perform the contract satisfactorily.

When a problem of impossibility arises or is suspected, the contractor should notify the owner that he is claiming impossibility of performance. If the magnitude of the problem and the costs involved are substantial, an outside technical expert should be obtained to analyze and evaluate the suspected impossibility and to prepare a report on his findings. The contractor should keep a very detailed jobsite log to record all events associated with the claim of impossibility, such as trips, conferences, telephone calls, overtime, and technical and special problems incurred, which need to be kept daily by the job superintendent. Although it is rarely possible to record all costs and expenses completely and accurately, every effort should be made to record in detail the costs and expenses incurred by the impossibility of performance.

Only very infrequently do contractors encounter problems of impossibility of performance, and in order to successfully claim impossibility of

[70] Fisher v. United States Fidelity & Guaranty Co., 313 Ill. App. 66, 39 N.E.2d 67, 68 (1942).

[71] Keeling v. Schastey & Vollmer, 18 Cal. App. 764, 124 P. 445 (1912).

performance, the contractor must be alert to recognize the problem of impossibility of performance early and be able to prove the fact of impossibility and the related extra costs.

CHANGED CONDITIONS OR DIFFERING SITE CONDITIONS

The contract documents should always be checked *before bidding* to see if there is a "changed-conditions" or "differing-site-conditions" clause which provides for an increase in the contract price if physical conditions are encountered at the site which differ from those originally contemplated in the plans and specifications. The purpose of this changed-conditions clause is to eliminate from a contractor's price contingent costs which the contractor might include in his bid to guard against increased costs of performance because of the discovery of subsurface or latent physical conditions differing from those described in the contract or the discovery of unknown physical conditions of an unusual or differing nature from those which normally would be expected at the site.

The changed-conditions clause is calculated to be of benefit to both the owner and the contractor. It benefits the contractor because it eliminates the risk of increased cost of performance because of unknown or differing latent physical site conditions. The owner benefits because he pays for these increased costs of performance only in the event that the contractor actually encounters changed or differing site conditions. Without the changed-conditions clause, a contractor would increase his estimate to compensate for the added hazards which might be encountered other than the normal conditions, and the owner would pay the contractor's increased lump-sum price which guarded against encountering differing subsurface site conditions even if the site conditions subsequently proved to be normal.

Many claims for changed conditions are based on differing natural subsurface conditions, such as the presence or absence of rock or the existence of abnormal subsurface water or peculiarities of the soil. Other claims for changed conditions may be based upon the existence of artificial conditions which are brought about by the man-made activity, such as the encountering of unknown utilities.

The general conditions of each contract should be inspected prior to bidding to see if there is a changed-conditions clause and the exact scope and procedures for obtaining a change or an equitable adjustment for a changed condition. If there is no changed-conditions clause, the contractor assumes the risk of encountering changed conditions unless the owner has misrepresented the conditions or failed to provide information in its possession to prospective bidders.

A typical changed-conditions clause appears in AIA General Conditions (AIA Document A201, 1976 ed.) Article 12.2.1, which provides:

Article 12.2.1   Should concealed conditions encountered in the performance of the work below the surface of the ground or should concealed or unknown conditions in an existing structure be at variance with the conditions indicated by the Contract Documents, or should unknown physical conditions below the surface of the ground or should concealed or unknown conditions in an existing structure of an unusual nature, differing materially from those ordinarily encountered and generally recognized as inherent in work of the character provided for in this Contract, be encountered, the Contract Sum shall be equitably adjusted by Change Order upon claim by either party made within twenty days after the first observance of the conditions.

The government differing-site-conditions clause for fixed-price construction contracts is found in FPR Section 1-7.602-4 (May 1976) and in Standard Form 23-A, Section 4. It provides:

(a)   The contractor shall promptly, and before such conditions are disturbed, notify the Contracting Officer in writing of: (1) subsurface or latent physical conditions at the site differing materially from those indicated in this contract, or (2) unknown physical conditions at the site, of an unusual nature, differing materially from those ordinarily encountered and generally recognized as inhering in work of the character provided for in this contract. The Contracting Officer shall promptly investigate the conditions, and if he finds that such conditions do materially so differ and cause an increase or decrease in the contractor's cost of, or the time required for, performance of any part of the work under this contract, whether or not changed as a result of such conditions, an equitable adjustment shall be made and the contract modified in writing accordingly.

(b)   No claim of the Contractor under this clause shall be allowed unless the Contractor has given the notice required in (a) above; provided, however, the time prescribed therefor may be extended by the Government.

(c)   No claim by the Contractor for an equitable adjustment hereunder shall be allowed if asserted after final payment under this contract.

Both the AIA and government clauses provide for two kinds of unknown physical conditions: those which are not as originally represented on the plans and specifications and those encountered and generally not recognized as inherent in the particular type of work. To recover for the first type of changed conditions the contractor must show that the conditions expressly stated in the contract were incorrect or that the conditions implied by the contract as a whole were not, in fact, present. For example, if the method specified for performing the work necessarily requires certain conditions at the site, the contract is said to indicate the presence of those conditions. The changed-conditions clause is a warranty by the owner that the plans and specifications adequately and accurately indicate the physical conditions at the site.

Illustrative Case

Foster Construction C. A. and Williams Brothers Company, a joint venture, contracted to construct a bridge for the government. When the contractor encountered subsurface materials of high permeability and low stability which prevented excavation "in the dry," it made a claim under the changed-conditions clause of the contract. The Court of Claims held that contract provisions giving the type of concrete to be used, stating that all concrete was to be placed in the dry, and omitting to provide for a concrete seal, sufficiently indicated the subsurface condition so that the contractor had a right to rely on being able to excavate in the dry. Thus the actual condition encountered was within the changed-conditions clause.[72]

A contractor can recover for the second type of changed condition (that which is encountered and generally not recognized as inherent in the work) even if the contract gives no express or implied indication of the nature of the condition. The contractor must show that the actual condition is one that a reasonable contractor would not have anticipated, considering the contents of the plans and specifications, an on-site inspection, and the traditional assumptions made by experienced contractors.

Illustrative Case

Redman Service, Inc., a contractor engaged in reroofing a government building, encountered an unknown second roof which he had to remove. The second roof was held to be a changed condition because double roofs were unusual and the custom of the reroofing trade in conducting a site investigation did not include cutting into the roof to determine whether or not it was a double roof.[73]

A contractor cannot rely on site conditions indicated in the contract if a reasonable prebid site inspection would have revealed the true conditions. The contractor is held to know only what a reasonable site inspection would reveal to a reasonably experienced contractor. Specifications may contain exculpatory language which states that the contractor shall make his own test borings or shall verify all engineering measurements. These provisions are not normally construed to require the contractor to re-engineer the site in his prebid investigation. The contractor need not duplicate the owner's boring tests nor is the contractor responsible for discovering hidden conditions. If the contractor has no opportunity to inspect the site properly before bidding, he may rely on the plans and specifications.

Illustrative Case

The government requested bids for the clearing of trees and brush from 10,000 acres of land in Tennessee. The specifications, derived from aerial photographs rather than an actual survey, estimated that 2,800 acres were wooded. When the actual area to be cleared was discovered to be almost 4,000 acres, the overrun was held to be a compensable change because only 30 days were allowed for bidding, a period admittedly too short for intelligent on-site estimates of the wooded acreage.[74]

---

[72] Foster Constr. C.A. v. United States, 435 F.2d 873 (Ct. Cl. 1970).

[73] Appeal of Redman Service, Inc., 1963 B.C.A. ¶ 3897 (1963).

[74] Schutt Constr. Co. v. United States, 353 F.2d 1018 (Ct. Cl. 1965).

Changed-conditions or differing-site-conditions clauses normally include the requirement that a contractor must notify the owner or architect or both prior to disturbing a discovered subsurface or latent condition at a site differing materially from those indicated in the contract. It is particularly important that a contractor encountering a subsurface changed condition comply with the notice requirements of the changed-conditions clause. If a contractor proceeds with performance of the work affected by the changed condition without complying with the notification requirement to the owner and/or architect, then a contractor may have waived his right to obtain a change and equitable adjustment. If the owner is not notified of a changed condition, the owner may have been prejudiced because he would have lost his right to inspect the alleged changed conditions as it originally existed. As an example, if rock is encountered, then an owner would have lost the opportunity to verify the quantity of rock if the contractor proceeded to remove the rock without notifying the owner through the general contractor.

Illustrative Case

Coleman Electric Company claimed compensation under the changed-conditions clause for the excavation of 7,500 cubic yards of earth beyond the volume specified in the contract. The contractor had waited to inform the government until the extra work had been done so that it could present an accurate claim. The claim was denied because the government was not notified "before such conditions [were] disturbed" so that the government had no opportunity to determine whether the conditions were, in fact, changed. [75]

However, if a contractor fails to give the required notice, it is still possible that his claim may not have been lost if the owner or architect is fully aware of the changed conditions and of the difficulty experienced by the contractor and no prejudice is otherwise shown by the failure to give timely notification.

Illustrative Case

Contrary to the contract specifications, there was no material on the site suitable for the select material subbase course for the construction of a roadway. The government claimed that Peter Kiewit Sons' Company did not give notice of this changed condition before it was disturbed. It was held, however, that the government had worked closely with the contractor in solving the problem and was completely familiar with the contractor's difficulties, and that in light of this circumstance the government could hardly claim that it never had a chance to study the condition before it was disturbed.[76]

A contractor who encounters a changed condition which was unknown to him and not contemplated in the plans and specifications should follow the procedure outlined in the changed-conditions clause by giving the

[75] Appeal of Coleman Elec. Co., 58-2 B.C.A.. ¶ 1928 (1958).
[76] Appeal of Peter Kiewit Sons' Co., 60-1 B.C.A. ¶ 2580 (1960).

proper notifications usually prior to disturbing the changed condition. The contractor should then submit his claim for extra compensation for any increased cost of performance of the changed condition plus a reasonable profit. The contractor should be alert to identify and realize that he has encountered changed conditions which may be classified as subsurface rock, subsurface water, erroneous contour lines, changed or unknown utilities, and other unknown conditions.

Subsurface Rock

Encountering unknown subsurface rock is a changed condition entitling the subcontractor to an increase in the contract price. Changed conditions may come about either because of the existence of the differing subsurface rock conditions as to the quantity or quality of the rock. Generally in claims for changed conditions, the contractor's chances of success are greater if the claim concerns the quality rather than the estimated quantity of the rock. For example, if the specifications state that weathered limestone is expected to be encountered and the contractor encounters a hard limestone rock which is not weathered and which increases the contractor's excavation costs, then the contractor is entitled to an equitable adjustment for his increased cost of performance.

Illustrative Case

Where the contract described the rock to be excavated for the construction of a dike to be a solid rock formation, and in fact the rock was crumbly and unsuitable, the condition of the rock was within the changed-conditions clause.[77]

Subsurface Water

The discovery during performance of a subsurface water condition differing materially from that represented by the plans, specifications, and test borings entitles the contractor to an equitable adjustment for a changed condition for his increased costs of excavation because of the subsurface water.

Illustrative Case

Virginia Engineering Company, a contractor engaged in the construction of the Air Force Academy, struck pressurized artesian water during excavations. The government's test borings did not indicate *any* form of water at the locations in question. Many expensive and laborious methods were tried before the relentless flow of water was excluded from the work area. The contractor recovered under the changed-conditions clause. [78]

[77] Tobin Quarries, Inc. v. United States, 114 Ct. Cl. 286, 84 F. Supp. 1021 (1949).

[78] Virginia Engineering Co. v. United States, 101 Ct. Cl. 516 (1944).

The changed condition encountered must have been unknown on the date the contract was signed. Thus, even if the specifications do not indicate subsurface water or permafrost, the contractor may have discovered evidence of the condition by inspecting the site or the existence of the condition may be general knowledge at that location.

Illustrative Case

An excavating contractor, Promacs, Inc., claimed an equitable adjustment for extra work when it encountered permafrost in McKinley National Park in Alaska. There was no indication of permafrost in the contract specifications. The contractor's claim was dismissed because:

The basic concept underlying the Changed Conditions clause is that the long-term interest of the Government, in attempting to eliminate excessive contingency allowances from bid prices, justifies the government in assuming a portion of the risk concerning subsurface conditions . . . . [T]he Government assumes the risk . . . that the subsurface conditions will conform to those described in the contract, *or, if not there described, to normal conditions for the area involved.*

The contractor should have known that permafrost was prevalent throughout Alaska, and so it was not an "unknown" condition. [79]

Permafrost may pose extraordinary problems because it is difficult to excavate. In many instances it cannot be detected by a reasonable site inspection and therefore could be a changed condition if the owner's test borings do not disclose its presence and if permafrost is not prevalent throughout the locality.

Erroneous Contour Lines

It is generally recognized that there is an acceptable margin of error in contour lines. Before a contractor can successfully claim an equitable adjustment for site conditions encountered other than the contour lines indicated on the original plans, this margin for error must be taken into consideration with normal tolerances. Erroneous contour lines can be used as a basis for a claim if the contractor is put to an extra expense to excavate a greater amount of earth than that described in the specifications and drawings and if a reasonable site investigation would not have discovered it.

Illustrative Case

The government's ground-elevation survey in the specifications for a runway project indicated that the cut areas excavated at the site would provide the required amount of fill material for the finished grade. In fact, Poblete Construction Company, the contractor, was forced to bring in 75,000 cubic yards of fill. The government argued that notice was not given before the condition was disturbed, but it was held that the contractor was not required to do his own survey and that he therefore could not have discov-

[79] Appeal of Promacs, Inc., 1964 B.C.A. ¶ 4016 (1964) (italics added).

ered the changed condition until sometime after the excavations had begun. The claim was remanded to the parties for a determination of the reasonable tolerance in the accuracy of the contour lines to be allowed in calculating the amount of additional compensation owed to the contractor. [80]

Changed or Unknown Utilities

A contractor is entitled to an equitable adjustment for differing site conditions when the underground utilities are located at substantially different locations from the locations indicated on the plans and specifications. In spite of contract language in specifications which state that underground utilities are in approximate locations only, the courts have held that a changed condition is proper when the location of utility lines differ materially from that indicated on the plans and specifications.

Illustrative Case

In preparing for the construction of a courthouse, the architect furnished to Nelse Mortenson & Company, the contractor, an inaccurate survey of the position of a power conduit which was later damaged by the excavations. The court held that the contractor had a right to rely on the accuracy of this positive representation of the location of the conduit, and that normally the owner, not the contractor, would be liable for the damage. However, in this instance Mortensen's engineer had actual knowledge of the conduit's location, and therefore the contractor had a duty to take reasonable precautions to protect the conduit. [81]

Similarly, when an unknown existing utility is encountered, the contractor is entitled to a changed condition and compensation for his increased cost of performance plus a reasonable profit.

Illustrative Case

E. J. Henry, a contractor who was engaged to build an extension to a post office, was substantially delayed in his excavations by the discovery of two brick storm-sewer lines, neither of which appeared on the plans and specifications. The court held that the sewers, unknown to both parties at the time the contract was signed, were within the changed-conditions clause. The contractor received an equitable adjustment. [82]

The scope of the changed-conditions clause does not include non-physical conditions such as political, economic, or labor conditions. Nor does it include abnormal natural conditions such as hurricanes, flooding, or extension of work into winter weather. The general rule is that the physical condition must have existed at the time the contract was executed, but recovery under the changed-conditions clause has been allowed when a man-made condition has occurred after the contract was made if the owner could have controlled the situation.

[80] Appeal of Poblete Constr. Co., 68-1 B.C.A. ¶ 6860 (1968).

[81] Nelse Mortensen & Co. v. United States, 301 F.Supp. 635 (E.D. Wash. 1969).

[82] Henry v. United States, 250 F.Supp. 526 (N.D. Miss. 1965).

Illustrative Case

Lee Hoffman, a bridge contractor, discovered when he was ready to begin work that the area where some of the bridge abutments were to be constructed had been flooded when another contractor, constructing a cofferdam upstream, had diverted the course of the river. The upstream contractor's work was under the control of the government. Hoffman was delayed in beginning performance and claimed extra compensation for the cost of the delay. The court rejected the government's contentions that the condition did not exist at the time the contract was made and that the condition was man-made and therefore was not within the changed-conditions clause. The bridge contractor recovered. [83]

If, in addition to a changed-conditions clause, the owner also includes in the contract language stating that bidders must check subsurface conditions, that the specifications are not guaranteed, or other exculpatory language, the courts often attempt to find a way around the exculpatory language.

As an alternative remedy to the changed-conditions clause or in situations where the condition is not within the scope of the clause, the contractor may be able to allege that the inaccuracy of the specifications was a misrepresentation amounting to a breach of contract. The contractor must show that he relied on the untrue representation and was misled by it, but it is not necessary to prove the owner intended to deceive the contractor. The owner also breaches the contract if he fails to disclose information in his possession relating to subsurface conditions.

Illustrative Case

The specifications given to Reginald Potashnick, an excavation contractor, did not indicate the presence of blue granite at the site, although the government's test borings had revealed its presence. Potashnick relied on the specifications in preparing his bid. Consequently, he was put to great, unexpected expense to blast the blue granite. The court held that the government's misrepresentation amounted to a breach of warranty and a breach of contract, and so the contractor recovered his actual damages. [84]

EXCUSABLE DELAYS

General contractors must be aware of their rights to extensions of contract time for excusable delays and their right to claim damages for delays caused by the owner. Similarly, subcontractors have rights to extensions of contract time for excusable delays and are entitled to damages for delays caused by the general contractor or the owner. If a contractor encounters excusable delays so that his actual performance is extended beyond the original contract time, he must be able to establish sufficient excusable delays in order to avoid possible defaults for failure to complete the contract within the original completion date or to avoid

---

[83] Hoffman v. United States, 340 F.2d 645 (Ct. Cl. 1964).

[84] Potashnick v. United States, 105 F.Supp. 837 (Ct. Cl. 1952).

the assessment of liquidated damages or to establish his right to recover damages for delays caused by the owner.

In order to obtain an extension of contract time for excusable delays, there must be a clause in the contract or in the general conditions which permits an extension of the contract time for excusable delay. In the absence of an excusable delay clause, the common-law rule is that a contractor who undertakes a contractual obligation containing a time limitation which is of the essence must perform this obligation on time unless it is rendered impossible by an act of God, the law, or the other contracting party. The general conditions of most construction general contracts, which may be incorporated into the subcontract documents as well, contain an excusable delay clause which allows an extension of contract time when the contractor encounters excusable delays.

The excusable delay clause of the American Institute of Architects General Conditions (AIA Document A201, 1976 ed.) is contained in Article 8.3.1, which states:

8.3.1 If the Contractor is delayed at any time in the progress of the Work by any act or neglect of the Owner or the Architect, or by any employee of either, or by any separate contractor employed by the Owner, or by changes ordered in the Work, or by labor disputes, fire, unusual delay in transportation, adverse weather conditions not reasonably anticipatable, unavoidable casualties, or any causes beyond the Contractor's control, or by delay authorized by the Owner pending arbitration, or by any other cause which the Architect determines may justify the delay, then the Contract Time shall be extended by Change Order for such reasonable time as the Architect may determine.

In defining which delays are to be excused, the excusable delay clause generally aims to cover delays which are the fault of neither party to the contract and also delays which are caused by the owner or his representatives. The effect of such a clause, which grants an extension to the contract time of performance, is that the owner may not declare the contractor to be in default for finishing late, assess liquidated damages, or demand that the contractor, without extra compensation, accelerate performance to finish on the original completion date. The contractor may not recover for his increased costs resulting from excusable delays which are not the fault of the owner. Excusable delays which are not the fault of the owner are thus distinguished from delays caused by the owner for which compensating money damages may be recovered.[85]

Excusable delay clauses in contracts usually provide that the contractor shall advise the owner in writing within a specified time limitation of any circumstances that have delayed or potentially might delay the performance of the contractor. The contractor should follow the procedure of giving the required notice within the specified time limitations to preserve his rights. The notice requirement enables the owner to

---

[85] Damages for delays are discussed in greater detail on pp. 183–188.

investigate the situation and take whatever remedial action is needed to alleviate the causes which are delaying the contractor.

Article 8.3.2 of the AIA General Conditions (Document A201, 1976 ed.) contains a 20-day limitation for claiming an extension of time and makes the following provision:

> 8.3.2 Any claim for extension of time shall be made in writing to the Architect not more than twenty days after the commencement of the delay; otherwise it shall be waived. In the case of a continuing delay only one claim is necessary. The Contractor shall provide an estimate of the probable effect of such delay on the progress of the Work.

There are certain exceptions to the notice requirements which have been established by the courts in order to eliminate the harsh and unjust results that may occur because of the contractor's failure to give the notice. Substantial compliance with the requirement of timely written notice has been held to be sufficient where there was some written indication that the contractor was experiencing difficulty.[86] Informal communications which give enough information to appraise the general contractor or owner of the nature and extent of the reasons why delays are being experienced may be a substantial compliance with the requirement of timely written notice.[87]

Illustrative Case

Hoel-Steffen Construction Company submitted a claim to the Interior Department's Board of Contract Appeals for an increase in the contract sum under the Suspension of Work Clause of the standard federal government construction contract. The basis of Hoel-Steffen's claim was that the government had unjustifiably interfered with its work on the St. Louis Gateway Arch by giving other contractors priority of access to the work space. The Appeals Board dismissed the case because of the contractor's failure to give notice within the 20-day limitation set forth in the contract. On appeal, the Court of Claims reversed the board's decision. The rationale for the court's holding was that the notice provisions were for the benefit of the government—to permit officials to collect data and evaluate the desirability of continuing the delay-causing conduct. The court found that the proper officials had sufficient notice of the problem, albeit not the specific written notice required by the contract. The court held that the contractor was entitled to recover his extra costs because "notice provisions in contract-adjustment clauses [should] not be applied too technically and unliberally where the Government is quite aware of the operative facts.[88]

Since the obvious purpose of the requirement is to enable authorized representatives of the owner to investigate alleged causes of delay while the evidence is fresh, actual knowledge of the factual situation by the owner renders the notice requirement superfluous. This is particularly true when delay of the work of the subcontractor is caused by the actions of the owner or the general contractor.

[86] Appeal of Buchsbaum & Co., ASBCA 1215 (1953).

[87] Macri v. United States *ex rel.* John H. Maxwell & Co., 353 F.2d 804 (9th Cir. 1965).

[88] Hoel-Steffen Constr. Co. v. United States, 456 F.2d 760, 768 (Ct. Cl. 1972); *see also* Davis Decorating Service, ASBCA 17342, 73-2 B.C.A. ¶ 10107 (1973).

Illustrative Case

A controversy arose out of the performance of a subcontract for the erection of three fuel tanks on a foundation to be provided by Macri Construction Company, the general contractor. The subcontract incorporated the provision of the general contract which required timely written notice of the cause of delays. The subcontractor, John H. Maxwell & Co., experienced delays caused by defects in the foundation but failed to give written notice to the general contractor that performance would be delayed. Macri then tried to remedy the trouble but gave up and ordered Maxwell to proceed. The court said: "Under these circumstances equity does not permit Macri to assert surprise and prejudice." The notice requirement, held the court, had been waived, and Maxwell was not liable for liquidated damages for the delay attributable to the defective foundation.[89]

In some decisions, the formal requirement of timely written notice has been by-passed and the failure of the contractor to give the required notice is not fatal to the contractor's attempt to establish an excusable delay. This is particularly true when the owner is not prejudiced by the failure of the contractor to give timely written notice.[90] The owner may be deemed to have waived the technical requirements of timely written notice by considering a claim for excusable delay on its merits.[91]

A contractor must prove not only that an event within the definition of the excusable delay clause happened but also that the event caused an actual delay in his performance. The duration of an excusable delay may be substantially longer than the duration of the event that caused the excusable delay because of the impact or ripple effect in disrupting the progress and momentum of the job. A jobsite log is an invaluable aid in establishing in detail the actual effects and duration of an excusable delay.

To establish a claim for an extension of time, a contractor must show to what extent the work schedule was disrupted. In a large project which involves many subcontractors and suppliers, the effect of a delay in a single phase of performance can be highly complex. A delay in an important part of the project may alter the schedule for all remaining subcontracts to be completed. The constraints on available time and resources will be altered, and work may be shifted into a season in which the weather will extend performance times or seasonal activity will make it more difficult to find certain skilled tradesmen. Along with the time changes, there will be increases in costs of performance and overhead. If the delay is compensable, the courts generally will not accept as proof of damages the difference between the contract price and the contractor's actual cost; the contractor must prove that the extra cost caused by an excusable delay was reasonable and, in fact, was caused by an excusable delay, not by the contractor.

[89] Macri v. United States *ex rel.* John H. Maxwell & Co., 353 F.2d 804 (9th Cir. 1965).

[90] Appeal of Hensel Phelps Constr. Co., 71-1 B.C.A. ¶ 8652 (1970).

[91] Dirtmore-Freimith Corp. v. United States, 390 F.2d 664 (Ct. Cl. 1968); Callahan Constr. Co. v. United States, 91 Ct. Cl. 538 (1940).

In recent years contractors involved in large projects have utilized computers and the "critical-path method" of construction planning to achieve significant success in pursuing delay claims at reasonable collection costs. The critical-path method identifies the most critical sequence of performance and schedules the remainder of the work around critical elements of the sequence to achieve the most efficient work schedule in terms of time and cost. When a delay occurs, a computer can recalculate the work schedule to show the effect of all the constraining factors (previously placed in its data bank) which are changed by the delay. The computer can also work out the net effect on the project of two interrelated time delays. If an up-to-date critical-path schedule is maintained throughout the course of construction, the contractor has a ready-made documentation of the history of the project which the courts accept as persuasive evidence of the effects of delays. This history also provides a good negotiation tool for settlement discussions with the owner; and if resort to the courts is necessary, it may provide convincing evidence that the project would have been completed on schedule but for the excusable delays.

The specified events entitling the contractor to an extension of the subcontract time for excusable delay include: labor disputes, unusually severe weather conditions, unusual delays in transportation, and excusable delays attributed to the owner or general contractor.

Labor Disputes

Labor disputes are one common cause for excusable delay. The most common form of labor dispute which affects a contractor's performance is a "strike." Most strikes are held to be not forseeable and are considered to be excusable causes of delay within the meaning of the various exculpatory excusable delay clauses. Another labor dispute which a contractor may encounter is a "slowdown," which is generally considered an excusable delay in performance. A strike at a supplier's plant or by a subcontractor may amount to excusable delay which will bar the imposition of liquidated damages or default of the contractor for failure to make progress. However, a delay caused by the contractor's inability to obtain employees in a limited labor market is not excusable. A contractor has the duty to mitigate the effects of the strike by seeking an alternative method of performance by obtaining the supplies or services from other contractors or using alternative methods of transportation in order to perform within the contract time.

Illustrative Case

The heating plant of a medical center was to be rehabilitated by the installation of a new boiler along with other mechanical and architectural work. A steel strike delayed the acquisition of steel for the manufacture of the boiler by Arizona Plumbing & Heating's third-tier subcontractor. The contractor was given a time extension for this delay. However, delays in transmitting the order for the boiler through two intermediate subcontractors to the manufacturer, delay in the fabrication of the boiler not attributable to the strike, and delay in shipment of the boiler were risks borne by Arizona Plumbing & Heating, and no extension was allowed under the excusable delays clause.[92]

The duration of the excusable delay is a question of fact, but generally a contractor should claim an extension of the contract time for a period in excess of the duration of the strike in order to allow for its impact and delays necessitated by the remobilization of the job. In many cases the delays caused by the necessity of remobilizing a job and rebuilding the labor force may be substantially greater than the duration of the strike.

Unusually Severe Weather Conditions

Unusually severe weather is a condition beyond the contractor's control, which entitles the contractor to an extension of the contract time because of excusable delay. The weather must be *unusually* severe, and the standard on which the severity is judged must rest upon the usual conditions in that locality at that time of year. Official weather records are the best evidence of what the usual conditions are.

An excusable delay because of unusually severe weather may exist even if the delay does not constitute a substantial amount of the time allowed for contract performance. Further, the delay need not be over a period of consecutive days in order for each of the days to be considered part of the delay. The key question is whether the weather, regardless of its duration, actually delayed the performance of the contractor. The specific work delayed, and the extent to which performance of the work was prevented by the weather, must be shown in order to establish actual delay.

Illustrative Case

A claim for an extension of the performance time was made by J & B Construction Company, a swimming-pool contractor, for delay resulting from unusually severe weather. When the project was completed except for the grading and pouring of the pool decks, it rained more than twice the average for that period of the year in that location. The clay soil would not dry out so that sufficient compaction of the soil in preparation for pouring concrete could not be achieved. When the time the work would have been completed except for the severe weather was determined and taken into account, it was found that the contractor was entitled to a 7-day extension. J & B's claim for a further extension based on earlier heavy snow was disallowed because it did not show to what extent the work schedule was disrupted by the allegedly unusual conditions.[93]

[92] Appeal of Arizona Plumbing & Heating Co., 60-2 B.C.A. ¶ 2702 (1960).

[93] Appeal of J & B Constr. Co., 70-1 B.C.A. ¶ 8240 (1970).

Unusual Delays in Transportation

Another cause of excusable delay is an unusual delay in transportation, which includes delays occasioned by strikes or other delays unique to the specific means of transportation. In order to claim excusable delay for unusual delays in transportation, the contractor must have attempted to mitigate the delay by using alternative means of transportation within the bounds of reason.

Illustrative Case

A shipment of trusses to be used in construction in Panama was shipped by common carrier from Birmingham, Ala., by railroad and ship. In the process they were handled six times, and upon arrival they were so badly bent that they could not be used. The contractor, H. G. Nelson Construction Company, spent 9 days negotiating with the carrier before accepting and unloading the trusses. Another 22 days was required to straighten out the bends to make the trusses usable. The Court of Claims said: "It was not the duty of the [contractor] to do more than it did with respect to their shipment, and the record is clearly one which establishes that the injury to the trusses caused an unforseen delay for which the contractor is not liable . . . ." [94]

Excusable Delays Attributable to the Owner

The excusable delay clause provides for an extension of the contract time if the contractor is delayed at any time during the progress of the work by any act or neglect of the owner or architect. Excusable delays attributed to the fault of the owner or his representatives entitle the contractor not only to an extension of the contract time but also to damages for his increased cost of performance occasioned by such delays. [95]

There are numerous ways in which the owner or general contractor can delay a contractor. The most common delay caused by the owner arises from inadequate or incorrect plans and specifications. As discussed in the section Impossibility of Performance, the owner who furnishes plans or specifications warrants to the contractor that they are satisfactory for their intended performance. Therefore, any delay resulting from reliance on that warranty is attributable to the owner and excuses the contractor. Another common excusable delay attributed to the owner is the exercise of the owner's right to make changes from time to time which interrupt and aggravate performance of the work, extend the time of performance, and make performance more costly.

Other owner-attributed delays include delays (1) in obtaining access to the jobsite, (2) in obtaining a notice to proceed, (3) in obtaining inspection, and (4) while awaiting decisions or approvals of the owner or the architect.

---

[94] H.B. Nelson Constr. Co. v. United States, 87 Ct. Cl. 375 (1938).

[95] This is discussed in more detail in the section on Damages for Delays, pp. 183–188.

LIQUIDATED DAMAGES

The contractor cannot be assessed liquidated damages for delays incurred by the contractor which fall within the scope of an excusable delay clause. That is, if the contract contains a clause, such as Article 8.3.1 of the AIA General Conditions (AIA Document A201, 1976 ed.), excusing delays caused by the owner, formal change orders, labor disputes, fire, unusual delay in transportation, unanticipated adverse weather conditions, unavoidable casualties, or any causes beyond the contractor's control, the contractor will receive an extension of the contract time and not be liable for liquidated damages.

If the contract does not contain an excusable delay clause, the contractor assumes the risk of delays which are the fault of neither the contractor nor the owner. If the delay is caused by the owner, however, the delay is not a breach of the contract by the contractor, and therefore no liquidated damages may be assessed.

Illustrative Case

Under a subcontract for clearing a site and general excavation for a dam the government's engineers were responsible for providing M. B. Gillioz, the subcontractor, with tests and specifications necessary for the completion of the work. Gillioz also agreed to pay $250 liquidated damages for each day completion was delayed. He did his best to meet the contract deadline without the essential specifications, but they were like a blind-man's cane—without them he lost a great deal of time groping along. It was not until some time later that the subcontractor was supplied with redesigned plans and specifications which allowed him to complete the work. The court did not permit the general contractor to withhold liquidated damages for delay from the payment due to the subcontractor. [96]

If both the contractor and the owner have contributed to the cause of a delay, the contract may provide that the responsibility for the delay will be apportioned between the contractor and the owner and liquidated damages assessed against the contractor for his portion of the delay. An excusable delay clause may have this effect when it extends the contract time to cover the duration of days which are not the fault of the contractor. If the contract does not provide for apportionment, some courts have held that by contributing to the delay the owner totally waives any claim to liquidated damages; but other courts have held that the contractor is only entitled to a credit for the part of the delay caused by the owner.

Illustrative Case

United Engineering & Construction Company agreed to build a pumping plant for a government dry dock. The government delayed the work to implement changes in the plans and during periods when the dry dock was used for vessels; later, other delays were

[96] United States *ex rel.* Gillioz v. John Kerns Constr. Co., 140 F.2d 792 (8th Cir. 1944).

caused by the contractor. The contract did not provide for apportionment of the responsibility for delayed completion of the work. The United States Supreme Court held:

[I]n order to enforce such payment [for liquidated damages, the government] must not prevent the performance of the contract within the stipulated time; and . . . where such is the case, and thereafter the work is completed, though delayed by the fault of the contractor, the rule of the original contract [for liquidated damages] cannot be insisted upon, and liquidated damages measured thereby are waived.[97]

If the contractor breaches the contract by totally abandoning performance, the per diem liquidated damages provision may or may not apply. Some courts distinguish between a breach by a delay in completion and a breach by abandonment, finding that the parties intended to apply the liquidated damages clause only to delays when the contractor completes the work. In these states, the owner would recover only whatever actual damages resulting from the breach that he could prove.[98]

In other states the courts have applied per diem liquidated damages when the contract is abandoned by the contractor, but only for a certain period of time. There are two basic methods for the application of a liquidated damages clause to an abandonment: Under the first method, liquidated damages may be assessed for the number of days it would have taken the contractor to complete the work if he had not abandoned it. Under the second method, the owner may assess liquidated damages for the time it would reasonably take the owner to arrange for another contractor to complete the work and for the time within which the new contractor should be able to complete it.

Illustrative Case

A school construction contract which was to have been completed on April 1st was abandoned by the contractor, C. W. DeLano, on July 1st. The school district did not arrange for the work to recommence until November 21st, and the building was not completed until February 1st of the following year. The court awarded liquidated damages to the school district for the period between April 1st and July 1st, that is, the period the original contractor continued his work beyond the completion date. The court also awarded liquidated damages for the period from November 21st to February 1st, during which the new contractor completed the building. However, the court awarded liquidated damages to the school district only for the time it should have taken it to arrange for a new contractor. This was held to be 1 month and 21 days rather than the 3 months and 21 days actually taken.[99]

The courts will generally refuse to allow liquidated damages if the contractor's performance under the contract has been substantially completed by the date specified in the contract and only some details in the work remain. Substantial completion has been defined in the AIA Gen-

[97] United States v. United Engineering & Constr. Co., 234 U.S. 236, 242 (1914). *But cf.* Wallis v. Wenham, 204 Mass. 83, 90 N.E. 396 (1910).

[98] Village of Canton v. Globe Indemnity Co., 201 App. Div. 820, 195 N.Y.S. 445 (1922).

[99] School Dist. No. 3 v. United States Fidelity & Guaranty Co., 96 Kan. 499, 152 P. 668 (1915).

eral Conditions (AIA Document A201, 1976 ed.), Article 8.1.3, as "the Date certified by the Architect when construction is sufficiently complete, in accordance with the Contract Documents, so the Owner can occupy or utilize the Work or designated portion thereof for the use for which it is intended." The certificate of substantial completion is usually accompanied by a punch list of adjustments and final finishing to be done to the work. When the owner has possession or use of the property, an assessment of liquidated damages for trivial details in the work would amount to a penalty. A factor is the percentage of work remaining to be done; if a house is over 95 percent complete but has no heat, the owner cannot use the property and it is not substantially complete.

Illustrative Case

N. P. Severin Company's performance under an agreement with the government to build a low-cost housing project in Atlanta was 99.6 percent complete on the completion date as extended to take into consideration excusable delays. The government, however, would not accept the housing project on that day, even though the remaining work to be done on a boiler house would not have interfered with the occupancy of the houses by tenants. The government assessed liquidated damage of $200 per day, based on this technicality, totaling $11,200. The court held that the contractor was not liable for this amount. [100]

Subcontractors should be aware that they may be liable for liquidated damages even though there is no liquidated damage provision contained in the subcontract. If the general contractor's agreement with the owner provides for liquidated damages and the subcontract states that the subcontractor will be bound to the general contractor as the general contractor is bound to the owner, it may be argued that the subcontractor may be liable for liquidated damages in the same manner. To avoid this problem, subcontractors should insert in their contract a clause such as that found in the AIA Standard Contractor-Subcontractor Agreement (AIA Document A401, 1972 ed.), Article 12.7, which provides:

The Contractor shall make no demand for liquidated damages for delay in any sum in excess of such amount as may be specifically named in this Subcontract, and no liquidated damages shall be assessed against this Subcontractor for delays or causes attributed to other Subcontractors or arising outside the scope of this Subcontract.

Since subcontractors do not have any control over time periods of construction other than the number of days required to complete their own work, the subcontractor should not accept any liquidated damage provisions in the subcontract unless the amount is specifically tied to delays caused by the subcontractor.

If a contractor experiences an excusable delay, most contracts require the contractor to make claims for an extension of time in writing within a

---

[100] Continental Illinois Nat. Bank & Trust Co. v. United States, 101 F. Supp. 755 (Ct. Cl. 1952).

certain period of time in order to receive credit for the excusable delay and to avoid the assessment of liquidated damages. The AIA General Conditions (AIA Document A201, 1976 ed.), Article 8.3.2, provides that any claim for extension of time must be made in writing to the architect no more than 20 days after the delay occurs.[101] Contractors should carefully educate their supervisors and establish routine procedures to recognize excusable delays and claim them in writing so that contractors will not be held liable for any unnecessary liquidated damages.

ACCELERATION

If an authorized representative of the owner directs a contractor to accelerate performance to complete the contractor's work earlier than the required contract date, there is an obvious acceleration entitling the contractor to recover under the change clause for the contractor's increased cost of performance reasonably incurred by the acceleration plus a profit. A less obvious acceleration occurs in the situation where the owner requires the contractor to complete his work by the original contract date when there has been excusable delay entitling the contractor to an extension of the original contract time. This is a constructive change order for acceleration entitling the contractor to an equitable adjustment in the contract price.

The courts have required a minimal showing of certain key elements before allowing relief on an acceleration construction change. There must be an excusable delay for which the contractor is entitled to an extension of time. The contractor must have requested an extension of time, and the owner must have failed or refused to grant the extension to which the contractor is entitled. The contractor must have been required, either expressly or impliedly by the conduct of the owner's representatives, to complete the contract without an extension, and the contractor must have completed the contract on time and actually incurred extra cost.

If all these elements are present, then the contractor may be entitled to an equitable adjustment in the contract price equal to the increased cost (including overhead) reasonably incurred by the contractor in accelerating plus a reasonable profit. The same doctrine of constructive acceleration applies between the general contractor and subcontractors.

Illustrative Case

A subcontractor, Wallace Process Piping Company, entered into a contract with the general contractor, Martin-Marietta Corporation, for the installation of the mechanical and piping systems for Titan Complex 16 at Cape Kennedy. The subcontractor experi-

[101] For a discussion of notice requirements, see pp. 132–134.

enced two excusable delays. The first was caused when Martin-Marietta directed Wallace to suspend work while the government made test firings of Titan missiles. The general contractor agreed to compensate Wallace for its loss caused by that delay. The second delay resulted when the general contractor made change orders which forced the subcontractor to work more than the agreed upon 50-hour normal work week to meet the completion date. The general contractor ordered the additional work done without a time extension and denied Wallace's timely demand for an adjustment to the contract price for the premium and overtime work made necessary by Martin-Marietta's order. The court held that in refusing the claim the general contractor breached the contract and that the subcontractor was entitled to recover the overtime for the period of accelerated performance.[102]

A broad range of acceleration costs have been held recoverable. An obvious example is the extra cost of overtime wages which would not have been paid otherwise. Less obvious, but just as common, is the cost of labor inefficiency. The contractor's labor efficiency may suffer from acceleration because of changes in the work scheduling and the natural loss of efficiency caused by each individual's working longer hours. Another common cost of acceleration is the higher price of materials and their delivery. Any other direct cost incurred by the contractor in a reasonable effort to comply with an order to accelerate may be recoverable.

When a constructive change occurs because of acceleration, there generally are increased costs of performance of a contractor's work caused by the impact or ripple effect on work that has not been changed or accelerated. In ordering acceleration of one phase of the work, the owner may cause an impact and resulting acceleration costs in other phases of the work that must be coordinated with the work specifically ordered to be accelerated. These may be appropriate recoverable costs.

The contractor cannot recover acceleration costs if he causes delays which are not excusable and the owner subsequently directs the contractor to accelerate to finish by the original completion date. It is important, therefore, that the contractor base his bid on a realistic initial work schedule. Critical-path techniques are helpful in preparing a schedule which can be performed on time and efficiently. Records of the costs of acceleration must be kept so that the costs may be proved in detail before a court. Increased cost may be shown by comparing the normal productivity to the actual reduced productivity during the period of acceleration.

Problems may arise in establishing the elements of a compensable acceleration order at the fourth step showing that the owner has negatively responded to the contractor's request for a time extension. The owner may put off acting upon the request and force the contractor to choose between voluntarily accelerating or risking a breach of contract for late completion. The owner also may have unauthorized representatives place coercive pressure on the contractor to accelerate. The contractor may obtain recovery by showing that the processing of the claim

[102]Wallace Process Piping Co. v. Martin-Marietta Corp., 251 F. Supp. 411 (E.D. Va. 1965).

was unreasonably delayed, that the owner's actions show that he has in fact made a decision on the request, or that the owner has tried to coerce the contractor into voluntary acceleration. Unfortunately, these theories are not firmly established. The contractor should make it clear in written communications to the owner that the contractor's position is that he is being forced to accelerate.

Illustrative Case

At a meeting during construction, the resident engineer orally requested the paving contractor, Smith Engineering & Construction Company, to speed up work after floods delayed the work. Smith agreed readily because both parties wanted to complete the job before winter. The contractor thought that there was an understanding that the work would be accelerated; but when the time came to *pay* for the increased cost of quicker performance, the government contended that the request was not an order and therefore the acceleration was voluntarily undertaken and not compensable. The oral request was held sufficient to show that the government initiated the acceleration, and the contractor recovered. [103]

The courts have recognized that loss of labor efficiency is a legitimate damage which may be caused by delays. [104] An efficiency index analysis may be used to demonstrate quantitatively the cost to the contractor of a decrease in labor productivity during the acceleration period. When a contractor is ordered to accelerate, he must put extra men on the job and he generally finds that the labor productivity decreases. The efficiency index is simply a means of comparing the labor expense necessary to achieve a given progress during the normal productivity period with the labor expense necessary to achieve a given progress during an abnormal acceleration period.

To establish an average productivity index for a period of normal payroll productivity, the total progress payments received during an unaccelerated period is divided by the total payroll for the same period:

$$\text{Average productivity index} = \frac{\text{total progress payments}}{\text{total payroll}}$$

For example, if the contractor received $1 million in progress payments for an unaccelerated period during which he paid $400,000 in wages, the average productivity index would be 2.5.

To find what the contractor's payroll *should have been* during the accelerated period, the amount of progress payments for the accelerated period is divided by the average productivity index to give the average productivity payroll for the period:

$$\text{Average productivity payroll} = \frac{\text{accelerated progress payments}}{\text{average productivity index}}$$

[103] Appeal of Hyde Constr. Co., 1963 B.C.A. ¶ 3911 (1963).
[104] Luria Bros. & Co. v. United States, 369 F.2d 701 (Ct. Cl. 1966).

Thus, following the same example, if the contractor received $750,000 in progress payments during the accelerated period, by dividing by an average productivity index of 2.5, his payroll should have been $300,000.

The final step is to take the actual payroll for the accelerated period and subtract from it the amount the payroll would have been under average productivity conditions to arrive at the amount of the contractor's damages resulting from loss of labor efficiency caused by accelerating the work:

Loss of labor efficiency = actual payroll − average productivity payroll

If, in the example, the contractor's actual payroll for the period was $500,000, his damages would be $500,000 − $300,000 = $200,000. The claim should add this as a direct cost to the other direct costs of the acceleration plus a reasonable amount for overhead and profit.

DAMAGES FOR DELAYS

A contractor has the right to recover damages resulting from delays caused by the owner. Excusable delays attributed to the fault of the owner entitle the contractor not only to an extension of the contract time but also to damages for his increased cost of performance occasioned by the delays. The basis of recovery of damages for delays is the implied obligation that the owner will cooperate with the contractor and not impede the performance of the work of the contractor. A subcontractor has the right to receive damages for delays which are attributable to the general contractor or the owner if the effects of the delays are transmitted by the general contractor.

The duty to cooperate is implied between the owner and general contractor, between the general contractor and subcontractor, and between multiple prime contractors and all subcontractors. The owner has a duty to coordinate the work of multiple prime contractors, and the general contractor must take reasonable steps to protect subcontractors from interference caused by the general contractor himself and other subcontractors.

Illustrative Case

Fenestra, Inc., a general contractor, engaged Johnson Brothers Company, a subcontractor, to install C panels which were the outer skin of a building and were to be supplied by the general contractor. The panels proved to be defective and Johnson Brothers was required to remove them and wait several months for replacements. Fenestra compensated the subcontractor for the cost of removing and reinstalling panels but refused to pay for the delay costs resulting from keeping crews available and the extension of the work into winter weather. The court allowed recovery for these additional costs. [105]

[105]Johnson v. Fenestra, Inc., 305 F.2d 179 (3d Cir. 1962).

In order for the contractor to recover damages for delays, it must be shown not only that the delays were caused by the fault of the owner but also that the contractor was damaged by the delays. Similarly, in addition to proving the amount of damages caused by the delay, the subcontractor must prove that the delay was caused by the fault of the general contractor or the owner and transmitted by the general contractor.

Although the AIA General Conditions (AIA Document A201, 1976 ed.), Article 8.3.1, allow for an extension of time in the excusable delay clause, the General Conditions also state in Article 8.3.4 that the extension of the contract time for excusable delay caused by the owner does not preclude recovery for damages for delay. Article 8.3.4 of the AIA General Conditions provides as follows:

Article 8.3.4 This Paragraph 8.3 [relating to an extension of the contract time for delays] does not exclude the recovery of damages for delay by either party under other provisions of the Contract Documents.

The AIA General Conditions recognize the right of the contractor to claim additional costs which might include damages for delays in Article 12.3.1, which provides as follows:

Article 12.3.1 If the Contractor wishes to make a claim for an Increase in the Contract Sum, he shall give the Architect written notice thereof within twenty days after the occurrence of the event giving rise to such claim. This notice shall be given by the Contractor before proceeding to execute the Work, except in an emergency endangering life or property in which case the Contractor shall proceed in accordance with Paragraph 10.3. No such claim shall be valid unless so made. If the Owner and the Contractor cannot agree on the amount of the adjustment in the Contract Sum, it shall be determined by the Architect. Any change in the Contract Sum resulting from such claim shall be authorized by Change Order.

The AIA Standard Subcontract Form (AIA Document A401, 1972 ed.) in Article 11.4 recognizes the right of the subcontractor to claim damages for delays under the same procedure set out in the general contract documents and provides as follows:

Article 11.4 The Subcontractor shall make all claims promptly to the Contractor for additional work, extensions of time, and *damage for delays* or otherwise, in accordance with the Contract Documents." [Italics added.]

The owner is liable for damages for delays whenever it interferes with the performance of the contractor. Some of the situations which have allowed contractor to collect damages for owner caused delays are as follows:

• Whenever a formal or constructive change order directs the performance of extra work which necessarily extends the time needed to get the job done
• When the owner fails to provide adequate and accurate specifications or misinterprets

the specifications, and the contractor incurs delay waiting for them to be corrected or tries to perform the work using them

• When the contractor must wait an unreasonable time for the approval of drawings or of a subcontractor

• When the contractor must wait an unreasonable time for an inspection or a test, or if delay results from the owner's failure to give notice of an inspection

• When the owner fails to make the site available on time or fails to obtain title to a right of way when promised, or denies access to the site by another contractor whose work must precede the work of the complaining contractor

• When the contractor must wait for owner-furnished materials or for the owner to replace defective materials

• When the owner allows another contractor to disrupt the work

• When the owner directs the contractor to give priority to work under another contract

• When the owner directs that the work be done in a less efficient sequence or suspends the work

• When the owner directs that a less efficient method of performance be used

• When the owner unreasonably delays in making a payment due to the contractor

The contractor must prove that one of the preceding actions was taken by the owner and also that his performance was delayed by the activity.

Illustrative Case

Valentine & Littleton, a contractor, was engaged by the government to clear trees, brush, and debris from an area that was to be covered by a reservoir. After giving Valentine & Littleton less than a day's notice, the government partially closed the dam and flooded an area containing trees the contractor had felled but not yet gathered and burned. It was more expensive and time-consuming to remove these trees from under water. The court held that the flooding was a violation of the government's duty not to impede performance by the other party. If the time schedule for the dam was more important than not impeding the contractor's performance, the government, not the contractor, must bear the cost.[106]

Damages for delays caused by the owner to the general contractor or by the general contractor to subcontractors are based upon their implied promise that their own actions will not disrupt or impede the performance of the contractor, and generally damages for delays can be obtained by the contractor only for delays caused by the fault of the party with whom he contracted and which have increased the contractor's cost of performance. Excusable delays occasioned by providential conditions such as strikes or unusually severe weather will not give rise to recovery of damages for delays by the contractor because there is no interference with the contractor's performance by parties with whom he contracted.

Many contracts have a notification provision which requires the contractor to notify the owner within a stipulated time after the commence-

---

[106]Valentine & Littleton v. United States, 169 F.Supp. 263 (Ct. Cl. 1959).

ment of an event giving rise to a claim for an increase in the contract time and contract price under the change clause. The notice requirement in the contract should be complied with in order to preserve the contractor's right to submit a claim for increased costs because of the delay. However, in case the contractor fails to give the notification required under the change clause and excusable delay clause, there may be certain exceptions to the rule under which a contractor may obtain damages for delays in spite of the fact that he has failed to give the required notice. As in the case of noncompensable excusable delays, the notice requirement may be satisfied by substantial compliance short of formal written notice or when the owner or general contractor had actual knowledge of the problem and was not prejudiced by the lack of written notice.[107]

Often in the fine print of the general contract with the owner (or the subcontract with the general contractor) there may be a clause that the contractor give up his right to damages for delays caused by the owner or general contractor and be content with an extension of the contract time of performance. The waivers are called "no damages for delay" clauses. Contractors should refuse to include such waivers in the general contract or subcontract because express waivers of the right to damages for delay are generally enforced by the courts. Since owner-caused delays can cost the general contractor and subcontractors a great deal of money as well as time and a waiver of damages for delays can have harsh consequences, the courts have construed such clauses narrowly. Two exceptions allow the contractor to collect damages despite the presence of a waiver of damages in the contract. These occur when the owner actively interferes with the performance of the contractor and when the delay is too long.

Active interference by the owner has been found in cases relating to delay in procuring a right of way, having the site available, or furnishing materials, and delay caused by the furnishing of defective materials, by furnishing defective specifications, by suspending work, by not accepting the work, by denial of access to the site by another contractor, and by changing the normal sequence of work.[108]

Illustrative Case

Gasparini Excavating Company, a contractor working on a turnpike was ordered to begin work but was prevented from working because another contractor was still on the site which delayed the excavation. The excavating contractor sued for money damages for the ensuing delay, relying on the Turnpike Commission's promise in the

---

[107]For a full discussion of notice provisions, *see* pp. 132–134.

[108] United States v. Spearin, 248 U.S. 132 (1918) (specifications); Wood v. City of Ft. Wayne, 119 U.S. 312 (1886) (owner-furnished materials); Pitt Constr. Co. v. City of Dayton, 237 F.305 (6th Cir. 1916) (right of way); Lichter v. Mellon-Stuart Co., 193 F.Supp. 216 (W.D. Pa. 1961), *aff'd* 305 F.2d 216 (3d Cir. 1962) (sequence of work); Continental Illinois Nat. Bank & Trust Co. v. United States, 121 Ct. Cl. 203, 101 F.Supp. 755 (1952) (suspension of work); Grant Constr. Co. v. Burns, 92 Idaho 408, 443 P.2d 1005 (1968) (site availability); F.N. Lewis Co. v. State, 132 Misc. 688, 230 N.Y.S. 517 (1928) (acceptance of work); Gasparini Excavating Co. v. Pennsylvania Turnpike Comm'n, 409 Pa. 465, 187 A.2d 157 (1963) (denial of access).

contract that it would coordinate the project. The Commission relied on the waiver of damages clause:

> No claims for damages or extra costs due to delay to the Contractor's work caused by the work of slushing contracts will be allowed and it is hereby agreed that the contract prices are submitted on this basis.

The court held that denial of access to the site after ordering Gasparini to begin work was an affirmative or positive interference on the part of the owner justifying an award of damages despite the contract language.[109]

The same exceptions should apply to a waiver of damages clause in a subcontract. If the clause is in the subcontract only by *reference* to the prime contract, an *express* provision in the subcontract requiring the general contractor to deliver material or make a site available would be held to be inconsistent with and controlling over the waiver of damages clause and controlling, thereby allowing the recovery of money damages.

Any delay in the performance of a construction contract can have a ripple effect on the cost of the work remaining to be done. When owner-caused delays force the contractor into more costly operations, the owner is liable for damages for the resulting additional outlays. The possible extent of the additional expense caused by an owner-caused delay is demonstrated by the following case.

Illustrative Case

The government provided faulty specifications to J. D. Hedin Construction Company, a contractor engaged in building a Veteran's Administration Hospital. Substantial delay was caused by the faulty specifications and the government's failure to correct them within a reasonable time. These delays extended into bad weather; the exterior work would otherwise have been completed before the bad weather. A strike occurred, 17 days of which would have been after the completion of the work but for the government's delays. Hedin was forced to maintain temporary roads for a longer period at additional cost. The extension into bad weather brought increased costs for heating and snow removal. The contractor shifted into a period of higher wages for laborers under their collective bargaining agreement during the delay extension. The contractor was forced to take over the work of a subcontractor who did not perform because of the delay. The Court of Claims held that all these effects were caused by the government's delays with respect to its faulty specifications and awarded damages plus job and home office overhead to the contractor. The final damage figure due to Hedin was $518,000.[110]

The contractor should keep accurate records to be able to establish the time, duration, and cost of the delay. A jobsite log which outlines the various delays encountered on the job and accurate cost records are invaluable aids in pursuing a claim for damages for delays.

Overhead, an indirect cost which is increased by an owner-caused delay, is a recoverable damage for delay. The method of computing over-

---

[109]Gasparini Excavating Co. v. Pennsylvania Turnpike Comm'n, 409 Pa. 465, 187 A.2d 157 (1963).

[110]J.D. Hedin Constr. Co. v. United States, 347 F. 2d 235 (Ct. Cl. 1965).

head damages accepted by the federal government and some state courts is called the "Eichleay formula," from the case in which Eichleay Corporation successfully established its right to apportion general overhead.[111]

The rationale of Eichleay as developed and accepted by federal procurement decisions and apparently now starting to be recognized by state jurisdictions is the fact that overhead costs, including main office expenses, cannot ordinarily be charged to a particular contract. They represent the cost of general facilities and administration necessary to perform all contracts undertaken by a company. It is therefore necessary to allocate these costs to specific contracts on some rational basis of proration. Overhead rate does not increase during the performance of a contract, but expenses do continue during the period of suspension or delay. Generally, specific direct amounts expended in performance of a specific contract cannot be established, and it has been held that it is sufficient to demonstrate by the mere fact of prolongation of time of performance and continuation of main office expense that more of such expense was incurred during the performance than would have been except for the suspension or delay.

The formula developed by Eichleay is computed by determining a daily overhead dollar amount and multiplying it by the number of days of delay. The allocation for delay damages is accomplished as follows:

1. Overhead allocable to contract =
$$\frac{\text{contract billings}}{\text{total billings for contract period}} \times \text{total overhead for contract period}$$

2. Daily contract overhead = $\dfrac{\text{allocable overhead to contract}}{\text{days of performance}}$

3. Overhead allocable for delay period = daily contract overhead × number of days of delay

Delays caused on jobs by the owner and delays caused by the general contractor to subcontractors can subject the contractor and subcontractors to costs for delays which can be and frequently are very substantial amounts. Contractors and subcontractors should be alert to recognize the causes of delays and consider claiming damages for delays when they are caused by the owner or general contractor.

WARRANTIES

Either by contract or by operation of the law, a contractor's responsibilities may be extended beyond the time of acceptance of the work. The contractor may give the owner an express warranty of the quality of the materials used or the workmanship performed, or in certain situations such warranties may be implied in the construction contract. As modern technology advances, many contractors who install complicated equip-

[111]Appeal of Eichleay Corp., 60-2 B.C.A. ¶ 2688 (1960). *See* Dewey Jordan, Inc. v. Maryland-Nat'l Capital Park & Planning Comm'n, 258 Md. 490, 265 A.2d 892 (1970).

ment now offer the owner service contracts under which the contractor provides preventive maintenance and extends warranty-type protection beyond the original contract warranty. A warranty clause distributes between the parties the risk of defects which may arise in the work. A contractor must be cognizant of the amount of risk which he assumes under a warranty, and the contractor must add enough to the contract price to cover that risk assumed. Pricing warranties or service contracts, which is similar to pricing on an insurance basis, involves determining as accurately as possible the average risk so that the losses resulting from defects in some jobs are balanced out by the charges collected on jobs which are defect-free, leaving the contractor with a fair profit on the average.

The legal doctrines and exceptions discussed herein may vary according to applicable law and contract clauses. Therefore, legal advice on warranties should be sought from an experienced attorney in specific fact situations.

Express Warranties

Most construction contracts provide for some guarantee of the work, and these contract provisions are valid and will be enforced by the courts. The risks which the contractor assumes may vary greatly according to the scope of the express warranty clause. A contractor who is only installing equipment furnished by the owner may guarantee only his workmanship, while the contractor who agrees to construct the work to meet certain performance standards may be responsible for defects in the design provided by the contractor as well as defects in materials and workmanship.

The AIA General Conditions (AIA Document A201, 1976 ed.) contain warranty provisions in Articles 4 and 13:

4.5.1. The Contractor warrants to the Owner and the Architect that all material and equipment furnished under this Contract will be new unless otherwise specified, and that all Work will be of good quality, free from faults and defects and in conformance with the Contract Documents. All Work not conforming to these requirements, including substitutions not properly approved and authorized, may be considered defective. If required by the Architect, the Contractor shall furnish satisfactory evidence as to the kind and quality of materials and equipment. This warranty is not limited by the provisions of Paragraph 13.2.

13.2.1 The Contractor shall promptly correct all Work rejected by the Architect as defective or as failing to conform to the Contract Documents, whether observed before or after Substantial Completion and whether or not fabricated, installed or completed. The Contractor shall bear all costs of correcting such rejected Work, including compensation for the Architect's additional services made necessary thereby.

13.2.2 If, within one year after the Date of Substantial Completion of the Work or designated portion thereof or within one year after acceptance by the Owner of designated equipment or within such longer period of time as may be prescribed by law or by the terms of any applicable special warranty required by the Contract Documents, any of the Work is found to be defective or not in accordance with the Contract Documents, the

Contractor shall correct it promptly after receipt of a written notice from the Owner to do so unless the Owner has previously given the Contractor a written acceptance of such condition. This obligation shall survive termination of the Contract. The Owner shall give such notice promptly after discovery of the condition.

These AIA warranty clauses provide the owner with a reasonably comprehensive guarantee of the work for 1 year, considering that the term "work" is defined elsewhere in the General Conditions to include all labor necessary to produce the construction required as well as all materials and equipment incorporated into the construction.

The AIA Contractor-Subcontractor Agreement (Document A401) sets out the subcontractor's warranty to the general contractor:

11.9 The Subcontractor warrants that all material and equipment furnished and incorporated by him in the Project shall be new unless otherwise specified, and that all Work under this Subcontract shall be of good quality, free from faults and defects and in conformance with the Contract Documents. All Work not conforming to these standards may be considered defective. The warranty provided in this Paragraph 11.9 shall be in addition to and not in limitation of any other warranty or remedy required by law or by the Contract Documents.

If the subcontract incorporates the general contract documents by reference, the subcontractor's warranty clause provides that the subcontractor may also be bound by the terms of warranties in the general contract documents.

The contractor should carefully study the scope of any warranty clause which he is asked to sign so that he can price it accurately according to his past experience with the defects which are likely to arise. Another important part of a warranty clause is the designation of the time from which the warranty period will run. If there are other contractors on the job, or if a subcontractor who gives a warranty performs his work early in the life of the total project, the work may be done and the equipment will have been installed for a substantial period of time before the final acceptance by the owner of the total project. If the contractor's warranty starts to run at the time of substantial completion or acceptance of the project as a whole, equipment may be used or lie idle to age or deteriorate for a long period before the warranty period even begins. Therefore, the contractor should try to ensure that his warranties begin to run at the time his performance is substantially completed or accepted. A wise policy is to coordinate warranties given on equipment and materials so that the contractor's warranties are coextensive with the warranty period of the manufacturer of the equipment and materials. If the contractor gives a longer warranty to the owner than the manufacturer gives to the contractor, the contractor should be sure that the added risk that he is assuming is reflected in the contract price.

Occasionally a type of warranty is found in construction contracts which provides that work will be performed to the satisfaction of the owner. Most courts take the position that this language means that the performance must be satisfactory to a reasonable person. A few courts have rejected this objective test, holding that the contractor has promised to satisfy the subjective opinion of the particular owner, but these courts have said uniformly that a rejection by the owner must be made in good faith. In practice, the results of cases under either view have tended to reach the same results. The owner's right to reject the work under a "satisfaction" warranty may be waived if the owner takes possession of the work and uses it, makes a partial payment for it (in limited circumstances), or unjustifiably prevents completion of the work.

Illustrative Case

The contract for the construction of the building included a provision that the owner, Howard Sheehan, would not be bound under the contract unless the work was satisfactory to him. He rejected the building on the grounds that it was not satisfactory. The court held that the warranty should be construed as one to furnish such a building as ought to reasonably satisfy the owner and as not permitting the owner to express dissatisfaction merely for the purpose of repudiating the contract.[112]

If the contractor expressly warrants both that the work will be free of defects and that the work will be completed in accordance with the plans and specifications furnished by the owner, the contractor will not be liable under his warranty for defects in the work which result from faulty specifications. The owner impliedly warrants the adequacy of plans and specifications furnished by the owner, and the contractor can be expected only to follow the plans and specifications using sound materials and workmanship.

Illustrative Case

MacKnight Flintic Stone Company guaranteed to erect a courthouse in New York in perfect order and also guaranteed that the basement would be absolutely watertight for a term of years. The work was to be performed in accordance with specifications prepared by the city engineer, who also supervised the work. Although the quality of materials and workmanship was never in question, the City refused to pay the contractor because the basement would not remain dry. The court upheld MacKnight Flintic's right to payment because the contractor had no right to depart from specifications provided by the owner, even if departures would have produced a waterproof basement. The warranty was construed by the courts to make the basement watertight only so far as the City's plans and specifications would permit.[113]

Under a majority of express warranty clauses, such as the AIA warranty provisions, the contractor guarantees the work only against defects and does not guarantee that work will survive normal wear and tear for the duration of the warranty period. In a particular case the contractor may, if he desires, agree to maintain the work and guarantee that it will

[112] Allred v. Sheehan, 54 Cal. App. 688, 202 P. 681 (1921).

[113] MacKnight Flintic Stone Co. v. City of New York, 160 N.Y. 72, 54 N.E. 51 (1899).

perform up to a certain standard for the period of the warranty. The cost of assuming the risk of wear and tear of the equipment should be included in the contract price. This type of warranty may have many of the characteristics of a service contract.

To establish a claim under an express warranty the owner need show only the existence of the defect in materials or workmanship. The contractor may escape liability by showing that the problem with the work was caused by the owner, such as by defective materials supplied by the owner or by defective plans and specifications supplied by the owner. If the contractor agrees to correct defects appearing within 1 year of the date of substantial completion, and then the owner, if required, gives prompt notice to the contractor of the discovery of the defect, the owner will have the normal period of the statute of limitations allowed for any breach of contract action in which to bring suit. However, the owner must give the contractor an opportunity to correct the defects under the terms of the contract before filing suit.

Implied Warranties

Not only must the contractor comply with the express warranties contained in his contract or subcontract, but he may also be liable for warranties which are implied by law. The implied warranties may have a greater scope and a longer duration than the express warranties. Under the Uniform Commercial Code, implied warranties of merchantability and fitness for a particular purpose have become uniformly implied in contracts for the *sale of goods*. An implied warranty of merchantability requires that the goods would pass without objection in the trade under the contract description and that they are fit for the ordinary purposes for which such goods are used. An implied warranty of fitness for a particular purpose arises when the seller at the time of contracting has reason to know that the goods are required for a particular purpose and that the buyer is relying on the seller's skill or judgment to select or furnish suitable goods for that purpose.

Since construction contractors furnish services as well as goods to the owner, their contracts do not fall strictly within the Uniform Commercial Code. The courts of some states, however, have taken the precedent and the theories of the Uniform Commercial Code and applied them to the construction contract situation, especially when the contractor is a builder-vendor selling a residence to a homeowner rather than selling to another businessman.[114] Other state courts have explicitly rejected opportunities to apply the principles of the Uniform Commercial Code to construction contracts.[115]

[114]Humber v. Morton, 426 S.W.2d 554 (Tex. 1968).
[115]Tison v. Eskew, 114 Ga. App. 550 (1966).

Illustrative Case

A plumbing contractor, Hobbs-Sesack Plumbing Company, was hired by James P. Aced to install a radiant hot-water heating system in the floor of a building. The tubes used by the contractor soon corroded and leaked, and Aced sued, claiming a breach of implied warranty because the tubing was not suitable for its ordinary use. The court held that although the transaction was not a sale, an implied warranty of merchantability would be implied in other types of contracts where justified. The court read into the contract a warranty that the tubing would be of a quality allowing its use without corrosion for a reasonable time. [116]

In most states, even those which do not apply the UCC to construction contracts, a contractor is held to have given the owner an implied warranty to carry out the specifications using good workmanship and following the general practices of the trade. The courts have reasoned that if the contractor was not required to use skillful, average work conforming to industry standards, his promise under the contract to complete the work would mean very little. To determine the standards of workmanship in a particular trade, the courts may refer to that trade's code of workmanship standards, such as the National Electric Code, if one is available.

Illustrative Case

A contract provided that the provisions of the National Electric Code were to govern the installation of permanent wiring and electrical equipment at a construction site. The National Electric Code provided that the junction boxes were to be installed so that the wiring contained in them could be rendered accessible without removing any part of the building and that such junction boxes should be securely fastened in place. The contractor, Mishara Construction Company, installed conduits in front of the junction boxes in such a way as to make them inaccessible, and the junction boxes hung free without attachment to the structure. The government directed rework in the form of repositioning each box and fastening it securely to a structural member of the building. The contractor was not allowed compensation for this rework because the initial installation was found to be a violation of both the standard of good workmanship and the requirements of the National Electric Code. [117]

If the owner inspects the work or has an opportunity to inspect and then accepts the work, he may not use the warranties implied in the contract to sue the contractor for defects which should have been discovered by a reasonable inspection. [118] On the other hand, the owner's remedy under implied warranties is not waived by acceptance with respect to latent defects in the work. Partial payment of the contract price by the owner has been held by some courts to be a waiver of defects of which the owner has knowledge. However, the AIA General Conditions expressly state that partial payments will not be acceptance of defects in the work.

[116]Aced v. Hobbs-Sesack Plumbing Co., 55 Cal.2d 257, 12 Cal. Rptr. 257, 360 P.2d 897 (1961).

[117]Mishara Constr. Co., 66-1 B.C.A. ¶ 5308 (1966).

[118]Barnard v. Kellogg, 77 U.S. (10 Wall.) 383 (1870); Elliott Consol. School Dist. v. Busboom, 227 F. Supp. 858 (S.D. Iowa 1964); City of Osceola v. Gjellefald Constr. Co., 279 N.W. 590 (Iowa 1938).

If the owner points out the defects to the contractor and the contractor agrees to correct them, a partial payment of the contract price will not amount to a waiver of those defects.

Illustrative Case

Helms Construction Company agreed to construct a house for James and Nellie Langley in a workmanlike manner and in accordance with the plans and specifications. The Langleys accepted the work and paid the contract price then later sued the contractor for breach of contract based on defects in the work. The court held that defects in the gutters, downspouts, and molding on the porches of the house were discoverable defects and that the Langleys had waived their right to complain of them by accepting the house. There was sufficient evidence, however, that defects in the vent over the stove, kitchen cabinets, and kitchen floor covering were latent defects of which the owners were ignorant at the time of acceptance. The jury verdict for the Langleys therefore was upheld. [119]

Similarly, an express warranty to correct defects appearing within 1 year does not apply to patent defects existing at the time of acceptance which should have been discovered by a reasonable inspection.

Illustrative Case

Wallace Diteman, Inc., a contractor, built a school gymnasium under a specification which required the surface of the gym floor to be within a tolerance of plus or minus $1/16$ inch from the established plane of the floor. After a prefinal inspection, the school district objected to the condition of the floor because of its unevenness. The school district conditionally accepted the building subject to the contractor's agreement to correct the defects in the floor. Wallace Ditemen corrected the floor to the satisfaction of the architect, and final payment was made, the school district then relying upon the contractor's express warranty to remedy any defects due to faulty material or workmanship appearing within 1 year of the date of final payment. The court held that the defects in the floor which were the subject of the subsequent suit against the contractor were not latent defects but defects existing at the time of the acceptance of the work. The school district knew of the condition of the floor but elected to accept the work and make final payment, and so there was no breach of the contract by the contractor. [120]

The few courts which have considered the issue of whether implied warranties cover latent defects in materials supplied by the contractor to meet contract specifications have arrived at different conclusions. Some courts have said that if the contractor has not expressly assumed the responsibility for latent defects in materials, he is not liable if he had no knowledge of the defect and if he acted in good faith and with reasonable care and skill in selecting the material.

[119]Langley v. Helms, 12 N.C. App. 620, 184 S.E.2d 393 (1971).

[120]Grass Range H.S. Dist. v. Wallace Diteman, Inc., 465 P.2d 814 (Mont. 1970).

> The specifications of a masonry subcontract provided for Masonry Contractors, Inc., to use a certain kind of brick which was manufactured solely by one company. The subcontractor installed the brick in a proper manner but, because of a defect in the manufacture of the brick, the mortar failed to adhere to the brick and the wall leaked water. The court held that such latent defects were not the responsibility of the subcontractor under any implied warranty theory if he selected the materials with care and skill from a reputable dealer. Furthermore, these bricks did not fall within the subcontractor's express warranty to provide materials of good quality because under the contract Masonry Contractors had no freedom of choice either as to the selection of the type of brick it would furnish or the manufacturer from whom such material could be bought. [121]

The courts of one state have held to the contrary that with respect to the purchase of a home from a builder, the builder is liable for latent defects in materials under a theory of implied warranty of fitness, which in that state amounts to strict liability.[122]

The law allows the parties to decide who will bear the risk of defects in the construction, and therefore a contractor may place in the contract a disclaimer provision excluding implied warranties from the transaction. The Uniform Commercial Code has established specific requirements for disclaimers of warranties to ensure that they are clearly stated and understood by both parties. It is a sound policy for construction contractors to follow these requirements even if they are dealing in a state which has not applied the UCC to construction contracts. The UCC requires that a disclaimer of an implied warranty of fitness be conspicuous and in writing. A disclaimer of an implied warranty of merchantability must be conspicuous and must mention the word "merchantability." For an effective disclaimer of implied warranties, the contract should contain a paragraph such as the following immediately after the express warranty provision:

THE EXPRESS WARRANTIES CONTAINED HEREIN ARE *IN LIEU OF* ALL OTHER WARRANTIES, EXPRESS OR IMPLIED, INCLUDING ANY WARRANTIES OF *MERCHANTABILITY* OR *FITNESS FOR A PARTICULAR USE.*

The presence or absence of a disclaimer of implied warranties may have a significant effect on the time within which the owner may bring suit against the contractor based on a defect in the work. If implied warranties are excluded, the owner may bring suit only for those defects which appear during the 1-year period specified by the express warranty. The state statutes of limitations which control suits based on implied warranties are typically 4 to 8 years. The contractor should be aware of clauses such as one found in AIA Subcontract, Document A401, which provides:

[121]Wood-Hopkins Contracting Co. v. Masonry Contractors, Inc., 235 S.E.2d 548 (Fla. App. 1970).

[122]Clark v. Campbell, 492 S.W.2d 7 (Mo. App. 1973).

The warranty provided in paragraph 11.9 shall be in addition to and not in limitation of any other warranty, or warranty required by law or required by contract documents.

This language explicitly reserves implied warranties. To disclaim implied warranties, however, the contractor must do more than delete this language from the contract; he must insert a disclaimer.

Government Construction Warranties

Warranties in government construction contracts may be controlled by both the warranty clause and the inspection clause in the contract, an example of which is found in ASPR 7-604.4:

7-604.4 Warranty of Construction (1974 APR)

In addition to any other warranties set out elsewhere in this contract, the Contractor warrants that work performed under this contract conforms to the contract requirements and is free of any defect of equipment, material or design furnished, or workmanship performed by the Contractor or any of his subcontractors or suppliers at any tier. Such warranty shall continue for a period of one year from the date of final acceptance of the work, but with respect to any part of the work which the Government takes possession of prior to final acceptance, such warranty shall continue for a period of one year from the date the Government takes possession. Under this warranty, the Contractor shall remedy at his own expense any such failure to conform or any such defect. In addition, The Contractor shall remedy at his own expense any damage to Government owned or controlled real or personal property, when that damage is the result of the Contractor's failure to conform to contract requirements or any such defect of equipment, material, workmanship, or design. The Contractor shall also restore any work damaged in fulfilling the terms of this clause. The Contractor's warranty with respect to work repaired hereunder will run for one year from the date of such repair or replacement.

(b) The Government shall notify the Contractor in writing within a reasonable time after the discovery of any failure, defect, or damage.

(c) Should the Contractor fail to remedy any failure, defect, or damage described in (a) above within a reasonable time after receipt of notice thereof, the Government shall have the right to replace, repair, or otherwise remedy such failure, defect, or damage at the Contractor's expense.

(d) In addition to the other rights and remedies provided by this clause, all subcontractors', manufacturers', and suppliers' warranties expressed or implied, respecting any work and materials shall, at the direction of the Government, be enforced by the Contractor for the benefit of the Government. In such case if the Contractor's warranty under (a) above has expired, any suit shall be at the expense of the Government. The Contractor shall obtain any warranties which the subcontractors, manufacturers, or suppliers would give in normal commercial practice.

(e) If directed by the Contracting Officer, the Contractor shall require any such warranties to be executed in writing to the Government.

(f) Notwithstanding any other provision of this clause, unless such a defect is caused by the negligence of the Contractor or his subcontractors or suppliers at any tier, the Contractor shall not be liable for the repair of any defects of material or design furnished by the Government nor for the repair of any damage which results from any such defect in Government furnished material or design.

(*g*) The warranty specified herein shall not limit the Government's rights under the Inspection and Acceptance clause of this contract with respect to latent defects, gross mistake or fraud.

1-7.102-5 (*d*)   The inspection and test by the Government of any supplies or lots thereof does not relieve the Contractor from any responsibility regarding defects or other failures to meet the contract requirements which may be discovered prior to acceptance. Except as otherwise provided in this contract, acceptance shall be conclusive except as regards latent defects, fraud, or such gross mistakes as amount to fraud.

The government warranty clause is similar to the warranty in the AIA General Conditions, except that under it the contractor's warranty begins to run again for 1 year on work repaired or replaced under the initial warranty period, and the general contractor may be required by the government to enforce all subcontractor's manufacturers' and suppliers' warranties, expressed or implied, which pertain to the work and materials contained in the project. The effect of the government inspection provision is that the contractor expressly takes responsibility for latent defects which are discovered after acceptance of the work, while the government expressly agrees that its rights as to patent defects are waived with the acceptance of the work. It has been held that when the contract contains both an inspection clause and a warranty clause, the government has a cause of action on latent defects under the inspection clause even after the period of the express warranty has expired.[123]

Federal Regulation of Warranties

In July 1975, the Magnuson-Moss Consumer Product Warranty Act, 15 USC Section 2301, became effective to regulate written warranties in the sale of all consumer goods. This covers tangible personal property and fixtures attached to real property if normally used for personal, family, or household purposes manufactured after July 1, 1975. If an item may be purchased for either commercial or personal use, the person who supplies such a product to the public must comply with the requirements of the Act. The Federal Trade Commission, in interpreting the Act, has stated: "Where an appreciable portion" of a product category is normally sold to customers for personal or family use, all warranties and service contracts applicable to such products must conform to the Act, but the Act does not cover products whose use is purely commercial.

The applicability of the Act to construction contractors applies mainly when they install consumer products in buildings. The construction of a building itself, even if it is intended for personal, family, or household use, does not appear to fall within the coverage of the Act.

A contractor who installs a consumer product must clearly and conspicuously disclose the terms and conditions of any written warranty,

[123]Appeal of Cottman Mechanical Contractors, Inc., 67-2 B.C.A. ¶ 6566 (1967).

stating the coverage of the warranty, what the warrantor will do in the event of a defect, malfunction, or failure to conform with the warranty, who will bear the expense of correcting such a defect, the procedure which should be followed by the consumer in order to obtain performance of any obligation under the warranty, a brief, general description of the legal remedies available to the consumer, and how quickly the warrantor will remedy the defect after being notified of it by the consumer. Warranties will be automatically extended according to rules to be prescribed by the FTC when the consumer is unable to use the product for extended periods of time due to defects covered by the warranty. The warrantor may not require the consumer to purchase any other particular product to use in connection with the product under warranty in order for the warranty to be valid.

A warrantor must designate his written warranty as either a "full" or a "limited" warranty. If a warranty is designated as full, it automatically extends to the consumer the federal minimum standards set out in the Act. These standards require that the warrantor remedy any defects within a reasonable time and without cost to the consumer. The warrantor may elect to either repair the product, replace it, or refund the purchaser's money if the consumer agrees to refund or if replacement and repair are not possible. A full warrantor may place no limit on the duration of implied warranties on the product under state law, and any limitation by the warrantor of the consequential damages arising from a breach of the warranty must be conspicuously noted on the face of the warranty. The warrantor must give the consumer an option to elect a refund or replacement of the product after a reasonable number of attempts to repair it; he must place only reasonable duties beyond notification of defects upon the consumer, and he must extend the protection of the warranty to transferees who obtain the product from the initial consumer during the warranty period. However, the full warrantor need not correct the defect if he shows that the damage was caused by unreasonable use by the consumer, including a failure to provide reasonable maintenance.

Any warranty which does not satisfy the federal minimum standards must be designated as a "limited" warranty. Under certain circumstances, both full and limited warranties could apply to the same product if clearly differentiated by the warrantor. No designation of a warranty is required if the contractor merely expresses its general policy that it will satisfy its customers without giving any specific limitations. These expressions of policy, however, remain subject to FTC rules regarding unfair trade practices and deceptive advertising. They must apply to all the contractor's work, not just to one particular product.

The Magnuson-Moss Warranty Act restricts the right of suppliers of consumer products to disclaim warranties implied by state law, such as an implied warranty of merchantability or fitness. If the supplier gives a written warranty on the product or a service contract executed at the time of sale or within 90 days of sale, implied warranties may not be disclaimed except as to their duration, and the duration may be limited only if there is a written warranty, if the duration is at least as long as that of a reasonable written warranty, and if the duration is conscionable and prominently indicated.

The Act also provides remedies for consumers. First, the Act encourages warrantors to set up informal dispute settlement procedures and requires the FTC to set up minimum requirements for these procedures. If a proper procedure is established by a warrantor, consumers would have to resort to it before filing a civil suit. Consumers may sue a warrantor in state court for violation of the Act or for a breach of a warranty or a service contract, and they may sue in federal district court if the suit involves individual claims of at least $25 aggregating to at least $50,000. Consumers must give the warrantor an opportunity to cure a failure to comply with his obligations of the warranty before an action may be brought. The FTC is also given the power by the Act to sue warrantors to enjoin them from giving deceptive written warranties and for failure to comply with the Act.

Consequential Damages

Consequential damages are damages which result upon the breach of a construction contract but are not the type of damages which would usually follow a breach of that contract. They are damages to a party which accompany a breach because of special circumstances existing when the contract was made. The general rule is that consequential damages may be recovered only if the owner and contractor had reason to know that the consequential damages would follow a breach because of the special circumstances. Either the contractor or the owner may provide in the contract that it will not be liable for any consequential damages resulting from known special circumstances; but, to be effective, such a limitation on liability must be placed in the contract and show an affirmative understanding between the owner and contractor that the possible damage recovery has been limited. Therefore, if the owner's contract form is used, the contractor must *add* a clause in order to exclude consequential damages.

Illustrative Case

Under a contract for the installation of an elevator in an apartment house, Otis Elevator Company, which installed the elevator, stipulated in the contract that it was not to be liable for consequential damages resulting from any breach of the installation contract. There was a delay in the installation of the elevator which constituted a breach of the contract and caused the owner, Boylston Housing Corporation, to lose rent of apartments during the period the elevator was inoperative. The court held that the loss of rent was a consequential damage and not recoverable under the limitation on consequential damages in the contract. [124]

[124]Boylston Housing Corp. v. O'Toole, 321 Mass. 538, 74 N.E.2d 288 (1947).

As noted previously, the Magnuson-Moss Warranty Act requires that any limitations on consequential damages in full warranties with consumer products must appear conspicuously on the face of the warranty. The philosophy of the UCC with regard to limitation of consequential damages is that they may be limited or excluded unless the limitation or exclusion is unconscionable. Limitation of consequential damages for injury to the person in the case of consumer goods is said to be prima facie unconscionable, but limitation of damages where the loss is commercial is not necessarily unconscionable.

SERVICE AGREEMENTS

Installation of complicated machinery such as air-conditioning equipment, refrigeration units, elevators, or even computers has become an important part of the business of many construction contractors, and the specialty contractor's role in the continuing maintenance of those machines has expanded. There are several advantages to the owner of such equipment in placing the equipment under a service or maintenance contract. A service contract avoids the necessity of the owner setting up his own preventive maintenance program, ensures that the equipment will be maintained in an operating condition of high efficiency, and extends the life of the equipment. A very important consideration for the owner of the equipment is that a service contract allows him to budget a fixed amount for maintenance expenses and to minimize unexpected large bills resulting from failures of the equipment under some types of service contracts. In effect, the owner is budgeting the proper maintenance of the equipment. There are also advantages in service contracts for the construction contractor. They may lead to more satisfied customers and provide a number of potential buyers of the contractor's new equipment; service contracts can become a profitable part of the contractor's business.

Service agreements arise in two basic situations: the "service warranty," the cost of which is included by the contractor in the cost of the equipment and its installation; and the "service contract," entered into between the owner and the contractor to provide service and preventive maintenance beyond the terms of the original warranty.

Service Warranties

A service warranty given as part of the original purchase and installation differs from most construction warranties in that the contractor guarantees the performance of the equipment for a certain period rather than guaranteeing that the materials and workmanship will be free from defects. The following is an example of a service warranty:

The contractor shall furnish maintenance and 24-hour callback service of the equipment provided by him for a period of 3 months after completion and acceptance of his work. This service shall include regular examination of the installation by competent and trained employees of the contractor, and shall include all necessary adjustments, greasing, oiling, cleaning, supplies and parts to keep the equipment in proper operation, except such parts made necessary by misuse, accidents, or negligence not caused by this contractor.

It is to the advantage of both the owner and the contractor when a service warranty is made an integral part of a construction contract for the installation of equipment because they have provided in advance for any service calls needed to work out problems with the equipment in the initial period of use. When a subcontractor installs the equipment and the subcontract includes a service warranty, the provision should clearly state that the *owner,* not the general contractor, is entitled to the promised service starting when the owner accepts and begins to use equipment, not starting when the equipment is installed and the general contractor is still on the job. If the general contractor needs to use the equipment, a special interim service agreement should be placed in the subcontract charging for the general contractor's use on a per diem basis and making the general contractor liable for all costs of correcting any damage or abuse caused by his use of the equipment.

Service Contracts

Although there are a myriad of variations of service contracts, there are four basic types of service contracts which may either take up coverage at the expiration of a service warranty or provide repairs and maintenance beyond the scope of a warranty which covers only defects in material and workmanship. The four types of service contracts are inspection, time and materials, full labor, and full coverage.

An inspection contract provides only labor and miscellaneous materials such as lubricants needed to make regularly scheduled inspection calls, which provide the basic maintenance that the manufacturer of the equipment may require under a defects warranty, and the inspection will hopefully head off major problems with the equipment. Labor and materials for making any repairs necessitated by problems found during the inspection are at extra cost to the owner and may or may not be provided at a discount by the contractor. The contract usually provides for a schedule of maintenance calls and should contain a detailed list of the cleaning and inspection to be done each time. An example of an inspection type of service contract is as follows:

This agreement includes complete cleaning and inspection to be provided on the following schedule: *twelve* regularly scheduled maintenance calls during the *year* on a *monthly* basis. Oiling and adjustment of equipment at the time of inspection is provided when necessary. Each inspection will include the following: check air-handler filters, check for adequate refrigerant charge, check for refrigerant leak if system is short, check condensor and clean if necessary, lubricate condensor fan and motor, etc.

The contractor would be liable for damages caused by problems which were not discovered because the inspection was negligently carried out, or for damages caused when inspectors left the equipment out of adjustment, or in an otherwise improper condition.

Under a time and materials service contract, the contractor normally offers the owner a discount on labor and materials for repairs and emergency service provided during the duration of the contract. This type of service contract normally also includes a lump-sum price for inspection calls such as are provided under a pure inspection service contract. Thus the owner pays only for such service as he actually receives and for an assurance of prompt service by the contractor. He is not insured, however, against the cost of major repairs. The operative language of a time and materials service contract may be as follows:

The purchaser shall receive _____ percent discount on all materials or parts required. The purchaser will receive a _____ percent labor discount from current noncontract labor rates for all labor required to perform regularly scheduled maintenance, emergency service, or any unnecessary repairs. Labor rates will be subject to change without written notice.

The full-labor service contract provides the owner with all labor required for maintenance and repairs for a fixed price. He may also receive a discount on materials. The full-labor agreement is often complimentary to a lengthy manufacturer's warranty against defects in the equipment. A full-labor service contract may provide:

The purchaser will receive all labor necessary to perform the scheduled maintenance cost, repairs, and emergency service. The purchaser will receive a _____ percent discount on all material or parts not included in this agreement.

The full-coverage service contract is perhaps the most widely used. For a fixed price, it offers the owner inspection, preventive maintenance, and all labor and parts for repairs and emergency service during the term of the agreement. The contract may contain a promise by the contractor to maintain the equipment in good working order or in an economic operating condition or to guarantee operation at the level of the original specifications. The full-coverage service contract may exclude from its coverage replacements of certain high-risk components of the equipment. A detailed description of the coverage in the contract is imperative, and it is particularly important for a full-coverage service contract to except what it does not cover. The price charged the owner should reflect the average risk to the contractor of carrying a large volume of such service contracts so that equipment which requires little or no repair will counteract large cost to the contractor from equipment which requires major repair, and in the end the contractor will be left with a reasonable profit. The operable language of a full-coverage agreement may be as follows:

The contractor shall provide scheduled maintenance on the equipment. The purchaser will receive all materials and parts necessary to maintain the system in economical operating condition, or the condition at the time of acceptance of this agreement. The purchaser will receive all labor necessary to perform the scheduled maintenance costs, repairs, and emergency service, and those optional services listed. We assume no responsibility for the following items of equipment, which are not included in this contract. . . .

There are several problem areas concerning service contracts of which the contractor should be aware from both a legal and a practical standpoint. The condition of the equipment at the beginning of the contract period, for example, is very important. Although few problems may be encountered if the contractor has sold and installed the equipment, if the equipment was installed by some other contractor, the service contractor *must* make a very thorough inspection of the equipment to make sure that it is maintainable and therefore that the contract has some prospect of being profitable. If parts of the equipment are worn, the condition of the equipment may be noted in the contract and the fraction of the lifetime of the part which has already passed may be apportioned to the customer as in the following example:

The items listed on the schedule all show wear. To provide you with the maximum service from these items, we are accepting them in their present condition with the understanding that you are to pay, in addition to the base amount of this contract, an extra at the time the items listed are first replaced. The charge for this replacement would be determined by prorating the total cost of replacing the individual items. You are to pay for that portion of the life of the items used prior to the commencing date of this contract, and we are to pay for that portion used since the commencing date of this contract.

It is important that each service contract provide enough preventive maintenance to keep the equipment at peak operating condition in order to save the contractor emergency repair costs.

In a service contract, the contractor should be very careful to delineate and limit the exact coverage of the agreement. It should be made clear that any labor contracted for does not include overtime work unless this is specially priced. Repairs should not be covered by the agreement if caused by acts of God, fire, power failures, problems with electrical supply lines or plumbing lines, modifications required by insurance companies or government agencies, or the actions of other third parties. The coverage should exclude any necessary alteration of a building or structure and should exclude any work which amounts to a change in the original design because of obsolescence. The following illustrative provisions are taken from a typical service agreement on air-conditioning systems:

The contractor's responsibility will not include changes, repairs, or corrections to equipment due to design, government code, or insurance requirements. The purchaser will assume responsibility and pay extra for all service and materials required due to electrical power failure, low voltage, burnt-out main or branch fuses, low water pressure, or other work excluded from this contract. The contractor shall not be liable for any damages due to labor, destruction by fire, commercial delays, spoilage, loss of business, or condition, and/or acts of God where circumstances are beyond his control, and it is expressly agreed that the contractor assumes no liability for negligence, misuse or failure whatsoever other than the contractor's failure to perform the service herein set forth, nor shall the contractor be liable for consequential damages. The contractor shall not be required to remove or replace or alter any part of the building structure in the performance of this agreement. The contractor shall not be responsible for replacement of parts when they are obsolete or when original design changes are necessary.

The following provisions are taken from a service contract to maintain elevators:

We shall not be required to make other safety tests nor to install attachments on the elevators whether or not recommended or directed by insurance companies or by governmental authorities, nor to make any replacements with parts of a different design. It is agreed that we are not required to make renewals or repairs necessitated by reason of negligence or misuse of the equipment or by reason of any other cause beyond our control, except ordinary wear and tear.

The contractor may also provide in the contract that he will not be liable for damages caused by any delays in service or repair caused by the contractor or by forces beyond his control, such as the availability of parts, strikes, or other causes. The contract should provide that the contractor will not be liable for damages resulting from any fault in the original design or installation of the equipment, damages to person or property caused by equipment failure which was not the direct result of the contractor's negligence, and all consequential damages. For example:

The contractor shall not be liable for loss, damage, or injury caused by failure or delay in performing services hereunder when such failure or delay arises from causes beyond his control. The contractor shall not be liable for loss, damage, or injury arising from a performance of service hereunder, unless caused by his negligence, nor shall he be liable, under any circumstances, for consequential damages.

It may be advantageous for the contractor to provide in the contract for liquidated damages to be paid to the owner in the event the owner is damaged when the contractor fails to perform his obligations of maintenance and repair under the service contract. Service contracts are appropriate subjects for liquidated damages because it is difficult or impracticable to fix the actual damages resulting from such a breach of contract.

Illustrative Case

A burglar-alarm service contract contained a liquidated damage provision which was held by a court to be a reasonable estimate of a fair compensation for any loss that might be sustained because of a breach. The parties had arrived at a valid and enforceable liquidated damages figure of $50. Thus, when the alarm failed to transfer the signal to the police, the owner collected $50 and the burglar collected $35,000. [125]

[125] Better Food Markets, Inc. v. American Dist.Tel. Co., 40 Cal.2d 179, 253 P.2d 10 (1953).

The responsibilities of the owner with respect to the equipment should be carefully delineated in the contract. The owner should be required to notify the contractor promptly of problems with the equipment or any unusual occurrences. The owner should be required to provide free access by the contractor to the equipment during normal hours for inspection and repair, to use high-quality supplies in connection with the equipment, to accept the contractor's judgment with respect to what repairs are needed, to never physically move the equipment, to use the equipment normally and as the manufacturer recommends, and to never alter the equipment or let any party service it other than the contractor.

The contractor should be aware of the maintenance credit concept. Some owners, notably the government, may bargain for or demand a provision in the contract which requires the contractor to give the owner a maintenance credit of a specified amount to compensate the owner for losses due to delay when the contractor does not provide service or repair promptly after being notified by the owner.

A service contractor has a duty to carry out inspections and repairs using ordinary care, and he will be liable for the foreseeable harm caused to persons or property by a negligent repair job. The contractor who repairs equipment will be liable for leaving the equipment in a dangerous condition to any persons who might foreseeably be injured as a result of the dangerous condition, not just to the owner.

Illustrative Case

Mr. Morgan, a contractor, installed a furnace for Mr. Floyd, a homeowner, and later repaired it by installing a new transformer and advising the owner that the furnace was in good condition and would give another 10 years of service. But the contractor had failed to complete the installation and failed to securely connect the wires which provided electrical contact from the transformer to the furnace electrodes. Upon Floyd's complaints that the furnace was not working correctly, on several occasions Morgan sent his employees to repair the furnace, but the defect was never corrected. On one occasion when Floyd was trying to adjust a loose wire, the furnace exploded. The court held that Morgan should have known of the defect and the danger involved and had a duty to warn persons of the dangerous condition of the furnace. Morgan was held liable for Floyd's personal injuries.[126]

The Magnuson-Moss Warranty Act applies to service contracts covering consumer products as well as to written warranties on such products. The service contract is defined by the Act to be a written contract to perform over a fixed period services relating to maintenance, repair, or both of a consumer product. The Act requires that the terms of a service contract be disclosed clearly and conspicuously in understandable language and the duties imposed upon the owner must be reasonable. A supplier of a consumer product or equipment who enters into a service contract with the owner within 90 days of the sale of the product may not disclaim im-

---

[126]Floyd v. Morgan, 106 Ga. App. 332 (1962).

plied warranties resulting from the sale of the product, but he may limit the duration of implied warranties to the same term as that of a reasonable expressed warranty. This provision of the Act is in contrast to the authority of one case where a state court held that the execution of a service agreement between the buyer and seller after the sale of the product was a waiver of any implied warranties attaching to the product. The court reasoned that the owner's agreement to pay the contractor to repair and service the product was inconsistent with the owner's claim that the contractor should pay for repairs because of a breach of an implied warranty.[127]

[127]B.H. Tureen Hotels, Inc. v. Nachman & Co., 317 S.W.2d 422 (Mo. 1958).

6 INSURANCE

INTRODUCTION

Contractors must know the special risks of financial loss which may be covered by insurance, and they must be aware of the additional hazards of construction which require special endorsements to a general liability insurance policy. Insurance policies are contracts under which the insurer agrees to pay the insured or a beneficiary designated by the insured an agreed-upon amount of money should certain contingencies occur. The importance of insurance cannot be overemphasized in the uncertain world that surrounds construction general contractors and subcontractors. Nearly everyone recognizes the grim possibilities of automobile accidents, serious illness, and death and the crippling financial burdens these sudden events can cause. Few responsible individuals attempt to go through life without insurance coverage to protect against these possibilities. No responsible businessman in construction should attempt to conduct his business without adequate insurance coverage to protect against the very real risks that face his business.

A contractor once commented to the author, "You really don't know what kind of insurance coverage you have until you have a loss." His philosophy was not only wrong, but he was flirting with financial disaster because it normally takes only one major uninsured loss to put a contractor out of business.

Contractors encounter many high risks of personal injury and property damage that can and should be protected against with adequate insurance. Unfortunately, contractors face many unusual risks which are not normally covered by general liability insurance policies and many such risks which are expressly excluded. These excluded risks are very real risks to the contractor and must be protected against. Most good insurance companies can provide various types of supplemental insurance to cover these gaps in the standard general liability insurance policy. This chapter will discuss the major forms of supplemental insurance that a contractor should investigate to make sure he is covered. These forms of supplemental insurance include: contractual or hold harmless coverage; completed operations coverage; broad-form property damage and installation floaters; explosion, collapse, and underground (XCU) coverage; workmen's compensation coverage; comprehensive automobile liability and aircraft coverage; and builder's risk insurance. The standard insurance policy conditions are cited along with their limitations and exclusions, and the additional insurance coverage, which is available to extend the contractor's basic general liability contract, is also discussed. In most contexts, the interests of general contractors and subcontractors with respect to the necessary insurance coverages are substantially identical, and so the discussion of this chapter generally applies to both, except as noted.

The purpose of this chapter is to present a general review of the considerations involved in obtaining adequate insurance coverage. It is not intended as legal advice, nor can it be relied upon in interpreting any particular insurance policy or condition. It is not a substitute for competent handling of the contractor's insurance affairs by a professional agent or broker who is familiar with the insurance requirements of contractors or for specific legal advice from a competent attorney.[1]

COMPREHENSIVE GENERAL LIABILITY INSURANCE

A comprehensive general liability insurance policy can cover known, existing liability hazards at the start of the policy and, if written properly, can automatically cover unknown and new hazards that may develop while the policy is in force. Although called "comprehensive," such insurance policies are far from complete, as this chapter will demonstrate.

A good comprehensive general liability insurance policy not only covers the costs of legally determined damages due to negligence but also provides for legal services. Insurance companies like to keep control over litigation in which they might ultimately be found liable. As a result, they write general liability insurance policies that provide for the insurance company to employ its own lawyers and investigators and to control all aspects of the litigation. This is actually a substantial benefit to the contractor. There may be no negligence involved at all and consequently no legal liability on the contractor's part; however, should a claim be brought or a suit instituted for an injury, the contractor will need the trained personnel to investigate, negotiate, and if necessary, litigate. To have the expenses involved covered by the insurance premiums the contractor has already paid can be a great benefit. Contractors usually carry comprehensive general liability insurance on an annual basis or for another set time period, such as a 3-year basis. Comprehensive general liability insurance is a standard form of insurance available in all states. Some carriers have introduced variations of their own that in many cases provide broader coverage than the basic form discussed here.

A comprehensive general liability policy includes premises and operations coverage, elevator liability, independent contractors' protective lia-

---

[1] For an in-depth discussion of insurance requirements for contractors including scope of policies, exclusions, specific endorsements, rating systems and other related subjects, *see* W. Derk, *Insurance for Contractors* (4th ed., 1974); *see also* *Risk Management in Building Construction* by Georgia Chapter, C.P.C.U., The National Underwriters Co., 420 East Fourth St. Cincinnati, Ohio 45202 (1976).

bility, and can usually be extended to include owner's protective liability. It covers all sums which the insured becomes legally obligated to pay as damages because of (a) bodily injury or (b) property damage in each of these areas. Premises and operations coverage consists of protection for liability arising out of bodily injury and property damage caused by an incident on any premises owned or occupied by the contractor anywhere in the United States or Canada if all exposures are properly noted at the time of inception of the policy. Most states have now developed rules that include elevator liability in the premises and operations coverage. However, whether elevator liability must be paid for separately from premises and operations liability will depend on the state. Independent contractors' protective liability covers the insured's legal liability for bodily injury and property damage arising from the operations of any subcontractors the contractor might employ.

A contractor should also have an endorsement to his comprehensive general liability policy which protects against personal injuries such as libel, slander, and false arrest. These risks are not remote to contractors. False arrest could arise when the contractor mistakenly has someone arrested for stealing his material or equipment on a jobsite, and a subcontractor could be sued for libel or slander for giving the erroneous credit information that a general contractor was not paying his bills. A personal injury endorsement should also be broadened to cover suits for libel or slander that are brought against the contractor by an employee or former employee, which might arise when the contractor gives an adverse recommendation of an employee or former employee.

Owner's protective liability coverage protects the owner from bodily injury and property damage claims arising from the operations of the subcontractor or any of his sub-subcontractors. Although this coverage is of no particular direct benefit to the contractor, the owner often insists on the contractors having such coverage. It is a frequent practice in the construction industry for contractors to own or use airplanes or watercraft. Any contractor who owns or uses aircraft or watercraft in his operations should have separate liability insurance policies by adding aircraft or watercraft owned or nonowned coverage.

A comprehensive general liability policy will include, in addition to the named insured, any executive officer, director, or stockholder while acting within the scope of his duties as such. Consideration should be given to expanding the additional named insureds to cover all employees, which can be done for a nominal premium.

The extent of coverage under a typical, comprehensive general liability insurance policy leaves large areas of a contractor's business risks unprotected. Even more important, every comprehensive general liability insurance policy specifically lists areas of exclusion. It is not unusual for a policy to list well over a dozen such exclusions. Unfortunately for contractors, many of these exclusions are in precisely those high-risk perils which contractors encounter frequently. As a result, if a contractor has only a basic general liability insurance policy, he faces very real financial risks. The result of a loss in an excluded area could be a legal and financial catastrophe. To avoid such a catastrophe, a contractor should be sure to supplement his comprehensive general liability policy. This chapter will consider the major exclusions in typical general liability insurance that contractors should seek to cover with supplemental insurance.

CONTRACTUAL OR HOLD HARMLESS COVERAGE

Of particular importance to contractors is the exclusion in the general liability policy for the contractual liability of the contractor. A comprehensive general liability policy covers liability for a contractor's acts or omissions of negligence, but it does not cover the liability that might be incurred under a hold harmless agreement. Contractual hold harmless agreements are encountered everywhere, including service, delivery, and maintenance-work contracts. Often they are signed as part of a whole contract without a realization of their potential impact. For purposes of this discussion, hold harmless clauses typically found in general contracts will be used for illustration. Similar hold harmless clauses appear in subcontracts in which the subcontractor holds the general contractor harmless.

Although hold harmless clauses are far from uniform and difficult to classify precisely, they do seem to fall into three general categories. The first type of hold harmless clause is the limited-form hold harmless clause that covers indemnification of the contractor's own negligence. A typical limited-form hold harmless clause provides:

The contractor agrees to indemnify, defend, and hold harmless the Owner from and against all loss or expense (including costs and attorneys fees) by reason of liability imposed by law upon the Owner for damages because of bodily injury, including death at any time arising therefrom, sustained by any person or persons or on account of damage to property, including loss of use thereof, arising out of or in consequence of the performance of the contract, provided such injury to persons or damage to property is due or claimed to be due to the negligence of the contractor, his employees, or agents.

Under such a clause, the contractor is bound to cover the costs of defending and paying any judgments against the owner arising solely from negligent acts or omissions of the contractor.

The second type of hold harmless clause is the intermediate-form indemnification under which the contractor must indemnify the owner for damages arising from the joint negligence of the contractor and owner. A typical intermediate-form indemnification hold harmless clause reads as follows:

The contractor agrees to indemnify, defend, and hold harmless the Owner from and against all loss or expense (including costs and attorneys fees) by reason of liability imposed by law upon the Owner for damages because of bodily injury, including death at any time arising therefrom, sustained by any person or persons or on account of damage to

property, including loss of use thereof, arising out of or in consequence of the performance of this contract, whether such injuries to person or damage to property is due or
claimed to be due to the negligence of the Contractor, the Owner, their agents, and employees, except only such injury or damage as shall have been occasioned by the sole
negligence of the Owner.

Under such a clause, the contractor is bound to cover the costs involved in
dealing with a claim whenever he is chargeable with any portion of the
negligence that led to the injury. Only where the injury is solely due to
the negligence of the owner is the contractor relieved of financial responsibility.

The third type of hold harmless agreement is the broad-form indemnification under which the contractor agrees to indemnify the owner even
when it is the owner that is solely responsible for the loss. A typical
broad-form indemnification hold harmless clause is as follows:

The contractor agrees to indemnify, defend, and hold harmless the Owner from and
against all loss or expense (including costs and attorney fees) by reason of liability imposed by law upon the Owner for damages because of bodily injury, including death at
any time arising therefrom, sustained by any person or persons or on account of damage
to property including loss of use thereof, whether or not caused by or contributed to by
said Owner or others.

Under such a clause, the contractor agrees to bear the financial burden of
any and all claims regardless of whether he is chargeable with any negligence at all. In many states such hold harmless agreements are limited in
application because they have been declared by statute or have been held
by the courts to be in violation of public policy. Yet they are often still encountered.

One frequently encountered hold harmless indemnification clause is
that provided in Article 4.18 of the AIA General Conditions (A201 1976
ed.). The hold harmless clause that appears in the AIA Standard Subcontract Form (A401 1972 ed.) in Article 11.20 is similar but adds the
general contractor as a party indemnified by the subcontractor. AIA
General Conditions, Article 4.18, reads as follows:

4.18 Indemnification

4.18.1 To the fullest extent permitted by law, the Contractor shall indemnify and hold
harmless the Owner and the Architect and their agents and employees from and against
all claims, damages, losses and expenses, including but not limited to attorneys' fees,
arising out of or resulting from the performance of the Work, provided that any such
claim, damage, loss or expense (1) is attributable to bodily injury, sickness, disease, or
death, or to injury to or destruction of tangible property (other than the Work itself) including the loss of use resulting therefrom, and (2) is caused in whole or in part by any negligent act or omission of the Contractor, any Subcontractor, anyone directly or indirectly
employed by any of them or anyone for whose acts any of them may be liable, regardless
of whether or not it is caused in part by a party indemnified hereunder. Such obligation
shall not be construed to negate, abridge, or otherwise reduce any other right or obliga-

tion of indemnity which would otherwise exist as to any party or person described in this Paragraph 4.18.

4.18.2 In any and all claims against the Owner or the Architect or any of their agents or employees by any employee of the Contractor, any Subcontractor, anyone directly or indirectly employed by any of them or anyone for whose acts any of them may be liable, the indemnification obligation under this Paragraph 4.18 shall not be limited in any way by any limitation on the amount or type of damages, compensation or benefits payable by or for the Contractor or any Subcontractor under workers' or workmen's compensation acts, disability benefit acts or other employee benefit acts.

4.18.3 The obligations of the Contractor under this Paragraph 4.18 shall not extend to the liability of the Architect, his agents or employees, arising out of (1) the preparation or approval of maps, drawings, opinions, reports, surveys, change orders, designs or specifications, or (2) the giving of or the failure to give directions or instructions by the Architect, his agents or employees providing such giving or failure to give is the primary cause of the injury or damage.

Under this clause, an intermediate-form indemnification clause, a contractor would be financially liable for any accident in which his fault or negligence had a contributing part. However, his liability under this intermediate-form hold harmless clause does not extend to injury or loss caused primarily by the architects' professional responsibilities.

Illustrative Case

Upson-Walton Company hired a building contractor, the Leonard H. Krill Company, to construct an office and factory building. The building contractor hired a steel subcontractor, Kilroy Structural Steel Company, to do the steel work. During the steel work, a high-voltage powerline snapped. The live wire seriously injured one of the steel subcontractor's employees, who sued the owner to recover damages for his injury. Upson-Walton's insurance companies settled the claim and then sued the subcontractor for the amount of the settlement plus the attorney's fees they had expended in the settlement. Because Kilroy had signed a subcontract containing a hold harmless clause with provision for indemnification and the injury occurred incidentally to the execution of the subcontract, the court held the subcontractor fully liable even though his employee had sued only the onwer.[2]

In order to protect himself from such liability, the contractor should supplement his general liability insurance policy with broad-form hold harmless insurance coverage. This type of endorsement which covers his contracts is known as "broad-form blanket contractual liability coverage" and protects the contractor from liability imposed under hold harmless clauses in his contracts.[3]

[2] New Amsterdam Casualty Co. v. Kilroy Structural Steel Co., 159 N.E.2d 797 (Ohio App. 1959).

[3] See The Hold Harmless Agreement by Georgia Chapter C.P.C.U., The National Underwriters Co., 420 East Fourth Street, Cincinnati, Ohio 45202, for an in-depth discussion of the insurance aspects of hold harmless agreements.

COMPLETED OPERATIONS COVERAGE

A general liability insurance policy covers liability while the contractor is actually on the job, but it does not cover him after he leaves the jobsite for any damage resulting from the completed work at the jobsite. Unless the contractor supplements his basic general liability insurance policy with completed operations coverage, he will be liable for an insured loss if his work subsequently fails. The term "products liability coverage" is occasionally used to include traditional completed operations coverage. Completed operations coverage usually excludes liability incurred because of an error in design by a contractor who also designs the work.

It is often difficult to determine precisely when a contractor's operations have been completed and his completed operations coverage takes over from his premises and operations coverage under this general liability policy. Legal problems can be avoided if the completed operations coverage is purchased from the same company that is responsible for the general liability policy and in the same amount of protection. Generally, actual completion of work rather than acceptance of the work by the general contractor, owner, or architect is the line drawn.

Completed operations coverage covers damage to property other than the cost of replacing the contractor's own work. It should also cover the entire cost of the contractor's legal defense when there is damage to both the contractor's own work and damage to other property. One of the important benefits of having completed operations insurance is that it covers the costs of defending claims. For example, the completed operations insurance carriers for several of our clients have assumed the entire cost of defense of roof-failure cases even though the substantial portion of the damage alleged in the cases was the replacement of the roof, which is not covered under completion operations coverage, and repairing the interior water damage, only a small part of which was covered under the completed operations coverage. In the case of completed operations coverage, those benefits can be especially great because of the investigative nature of insurance carriers when there is a substantial argument about exactly whose work caused the building failure or other damage.

Illustrative Case

In 1913 the roof and balcony of the Orpheum Theater in New York collapsed while in the stage of plastering operations. Since the failure occurred 20 minutes after quitting time, no one was hurt; but the damage to property was considerable. The New York City Building Department had examined and approved the plans and determined that the materials and workmanship were good. No fewer than six independent investigations were carried on, including one sponsored by the steel subcontractor, in an attempt to pin the legal and financial burdens on someone. The issue was never completely resolved since deficiencies in many areas were uncovered.[4]

[4] *Engineering News-Record,* January 30, 1913, p. 234; January 1, 1914, p. 203; March 26, 1914, p. 689.

In the preceding case completed operations coverage would have handled the subcontractor's expenses of investigation and defense and protected from an adverse judgment if he had been found liable for the whole thing.

In a case where a ceiling collapsed, the investigation by the completed operations carrier discovered that the mechanical contractor had cut a substantial number of the wires suspending the ceiling in order to reroute some ductwork above the suspended ceiling. The ceiling contractor, who did not know that the wires had been cut, was completely exonerated for very substantial damages when thorough investigation by his completed operations insurance carrier showed that the wires had been cut.

There are other somewhat less dramatic examples of how the contractor's completed work could cause trouble for him. For example, a plumbing subcontractor could complete all of his work in a high-rise apartment project but then find that one of his pipes has started leaking, damaging the walls, ceiling, woodwork, and carpeting in many apartments. A roofer could finish his work on a warehouse only to find that the roof starts to leak and damages the materials stored inside. A short in electrical wiring that causes a fire after the electrical work is completed, damage caused by a ceiling falling, or structural damage if foundation work proves to be defective would all be covered under an adequate completed operations coverage insurance policy.

BROAD-FORM PROPERTY DAMAGE AND INSTALLATION FLOATERS

The typical comprehensive general liability insurance policy contains another type of exclusion, which provides:

Excluded is property damage to

1. Property owned or occupied by or rented to the insured
2. Property used by the insured
3. Property in the care, custody, or control of the insured or as to which the insured is for any purpose exercising physical control

This exclusion may be the source of more debate and discussion than any other single provision of the comprehensive general liability insurance policy. This exclusion stops the insured from collecting on damage he does to another person's property while working on it or with it as well as excluding coverage for damage to the insured's own property. Legal liability insurance is not intended to cover damage to one's own property. There are other types of building and equipment insurance to compensate for such losses. But one would normally expect his general liability policy to cover damage to other property that arises in the course of his occupation. Unfortunately, that is not always the case.

If a piece of equipment that belongs to someone else is in the contractor's care, custody, or control and is damaged, the contractor's general liability insurance policy will not cover the loss. The exclusion from coverage by the words "care, custody, or control" are frequently broadly construed and the phrase "which the insured is for any purpose exercising physical control" is also one with potentially great application. Contractors are frequently in positions where they are exercising "physical control" or some degree of "care, custody, or control" over property that belongs to the owner or another contractor or subcontractor. If a crane were damaged while it was being leased by the contractor or if property of the owner which was being installed were damaged, the contractor would have to pay for that loss out of his own pocket unless he had taken steps to eliminate the gap in coverage resulting from the care, custody, or control exclusion.

A contractor might attempt to eliminate the care, custody, or control exclusion from his insurance policy by prevailing on the insurance carrier to eliminate the care, custody, and control exclusion and paying a higher premium. However, insurance companies probably will resist that attempt and rarely agree to elimination of the care, custody, and control exclusion. An effective way to deal with the problems presented by the care, custody, or control exclusion is to use broad-form property-damage coverage, a broad-form installation floater, or direct-damage equipment floater to narrow the extent of the care, custody, or control exclusion.

A broad-form property-damage-coverage endorsement defines specific instances of care, custody, or control that are meant to be excluded, thereby including everything else. This endorsement is designed to narrow the question of just how much of the property being worked on is subject to the care, custody, and control exclusion. While continuing to exclude liability for damages to property being worked on, the broad-form property-damage endorsement deletes coverage for only that particular part, provided the accident occurs away from the insured premises.

"Floaters" receive their title from the fact that they cover mobile or floating goods and equipment and were originally offered by marine insurers to cover cargo before and after it was on ship. An installation floater would provide coverage for damage to machinery and other prefabricated or preassembled equipment until it is actually installed, tested, and accepted on the jobsite. Adequate installation floater coverage is very important to cover equipment and materials in transit or stored at the jobsite for installation by the contractor. Installation floaters should be coordinated with builder's risk insurance to avoid gaps in coverage and to hold down the cost of the floater by providing that it should be in excess of any applicable builder's risk insurance. An equipment floater would cover equipment used by the contractor except that intended for vehicular use on the highways.

Illustrative Cases

International Derrick & Equipment Company contracted to procure and install a metal tower and antenna mast for a broadcasting company, and after erecting the supporting tower, contracted with a subcontractor, Tower Erection Company, to raise the mast. The subcontractor's workers negligently broke the antenna. International Derrick & Equipment sued the subcontractor and subcontractor's insurer. Tower Erection was found liable for the $4,500 damage to the antenna, but because the antenna was considered to be in Tower Erection's care, custody, or control at the time of raising, the subcontractor's insurance policy did not cover the loss.[5]

S. Birch & Sons Construction Company contracted with Alaska Towing Company, the lessee of a barge, to transport some heavy construction equipment for it. The actual unloading of the barge was Birch's responsibility, and it had rented wharf and gridiron space to do the job. One of Birch's employees supervised the unloading operations. Through the negligence of one of Birch's employees, the barge was damaged and sank. United Pacific Insurance Company, with which Birch had a liability policy, refused to pay for the loss because it said the barge was in the care, custody, and control of Birch at the time of the damage. The court agreed, leaving Birch to pay for the loss out of its own pocket.[6]

Losses or damages which occur to property which is in the care, custody, and control of a contractor can frequently be of catastrophic proportions and will put the contractor out of business unless these losses are covered by insurance. One of the author's clients who is an electrical contractor dropped an electrical generating turbine while it was being lowered into position into a powerhouse of a dam in Tennessee. The damaged turbine belonged to the Tennessee Valley Authority, and the damages were very substantial. Fortunately the electrical contractor had undergone a thorough review of his insurance plan just a few months before and had an installation floater covering the turbine; his insurance company picked up all damages for repair of the turbine.

It is easier to sense the lurking danger of a care, custody, and control loss than to know from what quarter it will come. The author and his wife bought a crystal chandelier to be hung in the stairwell of their house recently completed in Atlanta, Ga. The chandelier which had remained totally intact for over 175 years did not last 15 minutes in the hands of the electrical contractor. The owner of the electrical company who broke the chandelier assured the author he had plenty of insurance to cover it. He didn't. The chandelier was in his care, custody, and control, and he did not have installation floater coverage. The author's insurance company paid for the broken chandelier and then subrogated against the electrical contractor, who was uninsured for the loss.

EXPLOSION, COLLAPSE, AND UNDERGROUND COVERAGE

For many classifications of work, the comprehensive general liability insurance policy excludes damages caused by explosion, collapse, and underground operations. This exclusion is oftentimes unclear, being worded something like the following:

[5] International Derrick & Eqpt. Co. v. Buxbaum, 240 F.2d 536 (3d Cir. 1957).
[6] S. Birch & Sons Constr. Co. v. United Pacific Ins. Co., 324 P.2d 1073 (Wash. 1958).

This insurance does not apply to property damage included within:

1. The explosion hazard in connection with operations identified in this policy by a classification code number which includes the symbol "X"

2. The collapse hazard in connection with operations identified in this policy by a classification code number which includes the symbol "C"

3. The underground property damage hazard in connection with operations identified in this policy by a classification code number which includes the symbol "U"

The use of symbols "X," "C," and "U" give this type of exclusion the nickname "XCU exclusion." The X exclusion applies to all property damage arising out of blasting or explosion including explosion of pressure vessels and the like. The C exclusion applies to all property damage to adjacent structures other than the work project itself brought on by collapse resulting from work operations. The U exclusion applies to all property damage to buried conduits, pipe mains, sewers, telephone wires, and the like resulting from excavating or grading operations.

A large variety of contracting work is subject to the XCU exclusion. Typical examples of applicable exclusions include full XCU exclusion of pipeline, powerline, or conduit construction work, pile driving and caisson work, contractors' equipment rented to others with operations, excavation and land-grading operations, dam, subway, and tunneling work, telephone, telegraph, and fire-alarm line construction, street and road construction, and paving. Quarrying, welding, and sand and gravel digging are normally excluded by the X exclusion. Plumbing and septic tank installation are usually excluded by the U exclusion. Wrecking operations, building moving, and salvage work are generally excluded from coverage by the comprehensive general liability insurance policy under both the X and C exclusions.

Obtaining supplemental insurance coverage to remove the XCU exclusion can be fairly expensive. Nonetheless, any contractor doing underground work should investigate eliminating the XCU exclusion. Grading, foundation, and excavation contractors should have explosion and underground coverage to protect themselves and may want to consider collapse of building coverage.

Illustrative Case

In the early morning of July 4, 1925, the Pickwick Club in Boston collapsed, killing forty-four persons and injuring many others. The collapse was attributable to excessive vibration in the old building caused by thunderous dancing of the Charleston and by the loss of lateral support due to excavation operations for a large garage next door. Unless the excavation subcontractor had collapse coverage, he might have been personally liable for the property damage contributed to by the lack of lateral support.[7]

[7] *Engineering News-Record*, July 16, 1925, p. 115; August 20, 1925, p. 319.

Every state, as well as the District of Columbia, requires employers to pay compensation benefits to their employees for job-related injuries pursuant to the workmen's compensation statute of each state. The most common way of fulfilling that obligation is through the purchase of a workmen's compensation and employers liability policy which will pay benefits to the injured employee on behalf of the employer to whatever extent is called for by the law of that state. Such coverage is specifically excluded from the typical general liability insurance policy, and it is necessary for the contractor to supplement his general liability insurance with a workmen's compensation and employer's liability policy. There are many variations which arise from the variations and technicalities of the Workmen's Compensation Act of the various states. Benefits vary considerably from state to state. In the few states that have a limitation on medical benefits for injured employees, additional medical benefits should be considered.

If a contractor has employees working in the states of Nevada, North Dakota, Ohio, Washington, West Virginia, or Wyoming, which have what are called "monopolistic state funds," he is required to purchase the workmen's compensation insurance from the state fund rather than a private insurance company. In these states a contractor should purchase employer's liability from a private insurance carrier because the state funds only provide the workmen's compensation.

Desirable coverage extensions to the workmen's compensation and employer's liability policy include an all-states endorsement, recommended if a contractor does work in more than one state. Every state in which the contractor has employees working or domiciled should be noted on the policy. An endorsement for voluntary compensation can extend compensation benefits to classes of employees that are excluded from coverage under the state workmen's compensation law such as executive officers.

If a contractor has employees who work on or near navigable streams or waterways, they may be entitled to United States longshoremen and harbor workmen's compensation benefits should they be injured on the job. This is a separate endorsement that has to be added to the policy. It's a very innocuous exposure; but if a contractor is involved with bridge or pier work or has employees involved with loading or unloading a vessel or barge, the contractor probably has an exposure and needs to be sure he has proper protection. In addition, should any employees be members of the crew of a vessel, including a floating barge which operates on a navigable stream or water, the contractor may become subject to the Jones Act and needs maritime voluntary compensation as well as legal protection which can be included by policy endorsement.

A contractor with a good safety record will save substantial premium dollars, and a contractor with an adverse loss record will have to pay larger premiums. In this regard, it is important for the contractor to place his workmen's compensation insurance with an insurer that will offer top-quality loss-prevention services as well as prompt and equitable claims handling. Under workmen's compensation experience rating system, a contractor with a good safety record saves money and a contractor with a poor safety record is penalized.

COMPREHENSIVE AUTOMOBILE LIABILITY AND AIRCRAFT COVERAGE

Specifically excluded from the comprehensive general liability policy is coverage of:

Bodily injury or property damage arising out of the ownership, maintenance, operation, use, loading, or unloading of

1. Any automobile or aircraft owned or operated by or rented or loaned to the named insured

2. Any other automobile or aircraft operated by any person in the course of his employment by the named insured

Given the frequency of accidents to automobiles and the fact that every businessman is subject to such accidents, contractors should be sure to investigate available comprehensive automobile liability coverage.

Comprehensive automobile liability coverage covers any vehicle that fits into one of three categories: (1) owned automobiles, including long-term leased vehicles; (2) hired vehicles; and (3) nonowned vehicles such as employees' personal automobiles used in connection with business. A comprehensive automobile liability policy like the comprehensive general liability policy contains many exclusions, some of which the contractor may want to cover. The most important one flows from the definition of automobile. Generally included are passenger cars, trucks, trailers, semitrailers, and other land motor vehicles designed for travel on public roads. Excluded are pieces of "mobile equipment," which include land motor vehicles not subject to motor vehicle registration, maintained for use exclusively on the insured's premises, designed for use principally off public roads, or designed or maintained for the sole purpose of affording mobility to certain specified types of equipment. Use of such mobile equipment, however, is generally covered by the contractor's comprehensive general liability policy.

If the contractor obtains his comprehensive automobile liability coverage from the same source as his comprehensive general liability policy with the same period of coverage and the same limits of liability, he can save himself from a lot of potential legal trouble and worry.

Comprehensive automobile liability coverage provides for legal defense and payment of damages resulting from damage to persons or property from automobiles owned by the contractor's business. Frequently, contractors hire trucks or other vehicles. Comprehensive automobile liability coverage protects the contractor from liability arising out of any accidents his employees may have with any hired vehicle. Finally, it protects the contractor from liability arising out of any accidents his employees, but normally not partners, may have with their own vehicles while those vehicles are being used in the course of the contractor's business. This protection, called "employers' nonownership liability coverage," does not protect the employee, but it does cover the contractor himself should his employee be either uninsured or underinsured.

An employer is also liable if an employee has an accident while "acting on behalf of the employer." The law fixes liability not only on an employee that is negligent in the operation of this automobile but also on his employer when the employee is using his personal automobile in the employer's business.

Illustrative Case

A foreman of a contractor had an accident while driving his personal automobile to the jobsite in order to post a required work permit. The passenger in the other car was seriously injured with a broken back, which required long hospitalization and rehabilitative recovery including medical specialists, therapy, and numerous operations. He was without income for a substantial period of time. The injured passenger obtained a jury verdict both against the foreman individually and against the contractor-employer in the amount of $125,000. The employer was held liable because the employee was acting on behalf of his employer for the employer's benefit. The contractor was not carrying nonowned astomobile liability coverage, and his employee carried only $20,000 liability insurance limits. The contractor was liable for the payment of the balance of the judgment without any insurance coverage.[8]

To require evidence of insurance certificates on all personal automobiles of employees is impractical for contractors in the construction industry. It is imperative that a contractor include nonownership contingent automobile liability coverage as part of his overall liability insurance program. This will protect him against liability incurred by his employees while they are operating vehicles "on his behalf."

LIMITS OF LIABILITY COVERAGE

The limits of liability coverage on a contractor's comprehensive general liability insurance policy should contain multimillion-dollar limits for each occurrence. Such high dollar figures of coverage can be obtained relatively cheaply in comparison with the protection they ultimately afford through umbrella excess liability coverage.

Umbrella excess liability coverage serves two major functions: First, it backs up the contractor's comprehensive general and automobile liability policy by covering any loss insured under it that exceeds the limits of the policy. The umbrella policy picks up the difference between the amount of the damages and the limit of the underlying comprehensive general liability policy up to the umbrella policy's stated limits. Second, the

---

[8] *Walls & Ceilings*, January 1975, p. 10.

umbrella excess liability coverage provides coverage for some of those areas omitted by the general liability policy once the damages in one of those areas have exceeded a large deductible. The areas of exclusion under the general liability policy that should be covered have been outlined previously.

Under umbrella liability coverage, it is still necessary for the contractor to keep up his basic comprehensive general liability policy, and there are still insurance exclusions. But, the benefits of such a policy should not be overlooked. A $100,000 to $300,000 liability limit is grossly inadequate in the days of six- and seven-figure lawsuits. A contractor is risking ruin if he fails to have both adequate insurance coverage and adequate insurance limits.

Adequate insurance coverage with adequate limits is expensive. But the expense of adequate insurance should be passed on as a business expense to those for whom the contractor works. In addition, there are several things a contractor can do to keep the cost of his insurance down without sacrificing too much in the area of coverage.

It is important to be insured by a reputable company that is in a strong financial position, but the insurance industry is competitive. The contractor should find a few agents or brokers who know the construction industry insurance requirements to make presentations of insurance programs for the contractor. Once a contractor has found a good agent or broker who offers good service as well as competitive prices, it will pay to cultivate the relationship. A contractor cannot afford to have his brother-in-law handle his insurance unless his brother-in-law is a professional agent or broker who is thoroughly familiar with the insurance requirements for contractors.

The contractor is usually ill-equipped or not knowledgeable enough to prescribe his insurance needs, and his best bet is to be careful in selecting his agent or broker and to let the agent or broker outline the insurance protection program for the contractor's approval. Agents or brokers are paid on a commission basis, which comes out of the contractor's premium. Most states allow an agent or broker to reduce his commission, and every insurance company allows it as well. However, after the insurance has been placed at a stated price, rebates of a part of the agent's or broker's commission are usually illegal in most states. As an alternative to a commission basis of compensation, the agent or broker or contractor should consider contracting with an agent or broker on a fee basis to compensate the agent or broker for his time and expertise and pay for his insurance coverage at the net cost to the agent or broker.

Contractors should make intelligent use of deductibles and self-insure low-dollar risks. When a contractor agrees to a deductible, he relieves the insurance company of the burden of small but ultimately costly claims. In return, the insurance company can reduce the premium rate. In the long run, the savings in premiums should make up for the contractor's occasional picking up of petty claims. For example, a $250 deductible collision premium may be substantially less than $100 deductible premiums. Thus the contractor should consider self-insurance of reasonable deductibles and insuring the shock losses with an excess limits policy. Uninsured losses are tax-deductible so that the state and federal governments would pick up a good portion of the uninsured loss.

Finally, although it is important for contractors to insure against risks that they face, money can be saved by their not insuring against risks that are small or extremely remote. Coverage for the theft of inexpensive tools or office supplies is generally superfluous. Premium dollars should be put where they are really needed.

BUILDER'S RISK INSURANCE

The term "builder's risk insurance" is often used to refer to all types of normal coverage, both property and liability. This type of insurance primarily protects against certain perils to property during construction of the project.

The General Conditions of the Contract for Construction, AIA Document A201, states that unless otherwise provided, the owner is to purchase and maintain property insurance upon the entire "work" at the site. The term "work" includes all labor necessary to produce the construction required by the contract documents and all materials and equipment incorporated or to be incorporated into the construction. The interests of the owner, contractor, subcontractors, and sub-subcontractors are included, and the insurance is to protect against loss by fire, extended coverage (for example, windstorm, explosion, riot, vehicles, aircraft, and smoke), vandalism, and malicious mischief.[9]

The general contractor should make sure that he knows upon whom the burden of carrying insurance rests. As noted, AIA Document A201 (1976 ed.) states that the owner is responsible; however, this can be changed by agreement. Always check for modifications of these sections of the contract. The AIA General Conditions provide for the basic building risk coverage in Article 11.3 as follows:

11.3 PROPERTY INSURANCE

11.3.1 Unless otherwise provided, the Owner shall purchase and maintain property insurance upon the entire Work at the site to the full insurable value thereof. This insurance shall include the interests of the Owner, the Contractor, Subcontractor and Sub-subcontractors in the Work and shall insure against the perils of fire and extended coverage and shall include "all risk" insurance for physical loss or damage including, without duplication of coverage, theft, vandalism and malicious mischief. If the Owner does not intend to purchase such insurance for the full insurable value of the entire Work, he shall inform the Contractor in writing prior to commencement of the Work. The Contractor may then effect insurance which will protect the interests of himself, his Subcontractors and the Sub-subcontractors in the Work, and by appropriate Change Order the cost thereof

---

[9] See B. Rothchild, Construction Bonds and Insurance Guide (1974) for a detailed discussion of the insurance requirements of the American Institute of Architects Documents. This book is obtainable from American Institute of Architects, 1735 New York Avenue, Washington, D.C. 20006.

shall be charged to the Owner. If the Contractor is damaged by failure of the Owner to purchase or maintain such insurance and to so notify the Contractor, then the Owner shall bear all reasonable costs properly attributable thereto. If not covered under the all risk insurance or otherwise provided in the Contract Documents, the Contractor shall effect and maintain similar property insurance on portions of the Work stored off the site or in transit when such portions of the Work are to be included in an Application for Payment under Subparagraph 9.3.2.

11.3.2   The Owner shall purchase and maintain such boiler and machinery insurance as may be required by the Contract Documents or by law. This insurance shall include the interests of the Owner, the Contractor, Subcontractors and Sub-subcontractors in the Work.

The terms of the insurance contract govern the extent of coverage and the period of coverage. Standard insurance contracts are tailor-made to fit the particular project and desires of the insureds by means of endorsements, riders, and other attachments. A builder's risk form attached to a standard fire insurance policy, for example, will describe the property being covered. Property insurance forms cover the building during the course of construction as well as additions, attachments, and other permanent fixtures belonging to and constituting part of the building. This coverage also applies to temporary structures, supplies, equipment, and materials incident to the construction and may also cover tools, equipment, and machinery owned by those insured or for which the insured is legally liable when any of these items are on the premises or within 100 feet of the premises. Thus, property being transported to the site or property stored off the site would not be covered.

The absolute necessity for careful examination of the contract documents and any builder's risk policy cannot be emphasized too greatly. Since the insurance contract defines the coverage, it is necessary for every contractor to make sure that coverage is provided for the possible risks that will be encountered on a specific job. For example, if materials are to be fabricated off the jobsite, it would be necessary to obtain coverage for losses sustained in transit or where the fabrication occurs. If the owner prepays for materials and these materials are stored off-site, separate coverage may be necessary. If the risk of theft is great, a separate endorsement should be requested and obtained. All-risk insurance, which is required by AIA General Conditions, has some exclusions, and the contractor should be aware of them. For example, although insurance against theft of materials is required by Article 11.3.1 to be included in the all-risk policy, losses due to shortages discovered on taking inventory and unexplained or mysterious disappearance of materials most likely will not be covered.

The general contractor and subcontractor should be aware of the requirements for presenting claims and the time limits within which claims must be made. A claim for theft of materials, for example, may require substantiation in the form of police reports.

Adequate insurance coverage should never be presumed to exist. A high deductible may destroy what otherwise would be adequate coverage. If a contractor's presumptions are incorrect, he may become the insurer instead of the insured. For any construction job, contractors should request the insurance documents, examine them, and ask questions if necessary. They should consult with their insurance counsels to determine if there are coverage gaps that should be plugged. Only then will contractors be sure that they have considered the contingencies and weighed the risk of loss properly.

CONCLUSION

There may be other areas of exclusion from the basic comprehensive general liability insurance policy that any particular contractor may want to cover. This chapter has discussed only the major ones that affect most contractors. Contractors all too often make the mistaken assumption that they are fully covered when they should be reviewing their insurance programs with their broker or agent and attorneys. Contractors should deal with brokers or agents who are familiar with the construction industry and have handled insurance programs for contractors before. A contractor cannot afford to have an insurance agent or broker who applies insurance principles and coverage that would be fine for a manufacturing company but totally inappropriate for a construction company.

In reviewing his insurance coverage, a contractor should consider not only the cost of the insurance but more importantly the scope of the coverage and the extent of services that he receives from the insurance company and agent. For example, claims should be handled expeditiously and fairly. Engineering and safety services calculated to minimize losses on each project should also be offered.

Insurance carriers should be notified immediately of every occurrence or incident that might lead to a claim. Most comprehensive general liability policies have exculpatory clauses that allow the insurance carrier to deny liability if they are not properly notified of an incident that could result in a claim. Many insurance companies will provide a set of standard incident report forms upon request.

This chapter has discussed some areas of concern and have attempted to introduce the contractor to some of the insurance industry's terminology. The chapter cannot take the place of competent, specific professional insurance advice and professional legal advice. However, it can offer perhaps the best advice of all: Contractors should review their insurance coverage, and they should do it *now*!

7 REMEDIES

INTRODUCTION

Settling disputes which arise during the performance of construction contracts can be a costly and time-consuming process. This chapter presents a general discussion of the remedies which may be available to a general contractor or subcontractor when he performs the work specified by the contract and is unable to obtain by informal settlement "his due" under the contract—the contract price, additional compensation for extra work, or a time extension following an excusable delay.

A characteristic common to the remedies discussed in this chapter is that the effectiveness is diminished without careful thought and preparation by the contractor in his contract and during the performance of the job. Some of the remedies are not even available unless they are provided by the parties in the contract. The contractor who trusts the other party's good intentions until it is too late, who does not make sure he understands the available options in the event of a dispute, and who does not take the steps necessary to place himself in the best position to recover the money he has earned may be sorry when things do not occur as smoothly as he had hoped.

Drafting and checking of contracts for legal pitfalls is the first and most important stage of pursuing a remedy or avoiding the need to pursue it. In order to have the benefit of a tight-payment clause, fair disputes and arbitration clauses, or a right-to-stop-work clause, they must be bargained for and put in the contract. Important lien and bond rights must be preserved and not waived in the contract. The next stage is systematic on-the-job documentation of extra work, change orders, and unexpected conditions and costs encountered. The importance of these accumulated facts in proving what happened, whether for a disputes procedure, in arbitration, or in court, cannot be overemphasized. A systematic approach is also necessary for strictly following the claim and notice requirements under the disputes clause. To make documentation systems work, the contractor must educate key personnel so that they will carry out procedural matters in a timely fashion and know which orders and actions constitute significant events. Of course, the contractor must file his liens and bond claims in time to make them an available remedy.

Even better, contractors should establish standard procedures which prevent major disputes from arising in the first place. One of the best ways is to have a tough, consistent collection system—a bill collected now cannot turn into a bad account or a lawsuit later. The contract is never complete until the contractor's payment is collected for his performance. In the contract the contractor should establish a date certain for payment to him of amounts as they become due. If payment does not arrive on that date, the followup procedure should be *immediate*. Accounts should be systematically "aged," with notices sent and collection procedures initiated every time. A reputation for collecting fairly and consistently can be of great value in this regard.

One of the author's clients is a construction subcontractor who does a business of $2 to $3 million per year and never builds up more than $300 to $400 worth of bad debts! His approach is simple: He calls the account immediately after the payment date and demands payment. He is not interested in why payment has not been made. If an excuse is offered, he says: "I have heard all the excuses before and I am not interested in your excuses. I am sending a man over to pick up the check this afternoon!" And he gets it.

This general summary is designed to point out some of the remedies available to construction contractors to collect their money. The legal doctrines and exceptions discussed herein may vary according to the applicable law and contract clauses. Be sure to seek competent legal advice in the specific fact situation, and seek this advice early so as to avoid legal disputes.

DISPUTES CLAUSES

As a general rule, it is certainly in the best interests of the owner and general contractor or the general contractor and subcontractor to settle their differences amicably under the contract without having to resort to legal remedies. However, there are occasions on which it is not possible to negotiate or compromise differences. One of the parties may be stubborn or completely out of touch with his contractual obligations so that the dispute may have to be decided by a third party. Private and public construction contracts typically recognize that disputes will arise during the performance of a complex construction project, and most public and private general contracts contain procedures for handling these disputes.

Of course, the parties should attempt to solve the dispute without resorting to the formal proceedings of invoking the disputes clause or to litigation or arbitration. In any contract disputes procedure, settlement at the first level is always preferable because it avoids the costly delays of further attempts to settle or avoids the cost of arbitration or litigation. An additional advantage is that the parties at the first level are more familiar with the work and are thus able to evaluate the merits of any claim if each is fully informed on the other's position.

Private Contracts

Most construction general contracts contain a clause specifying the method by which the general contractor can make a claim for additional compensation. A claim is necessary whenever the contractor incurs extra cost, whether through change orders, changed conditions, constructive change orders, or delays.

Not only is a *claim* necessary, but the contractor must give written *notice* of his intent to make a claim, usually within a specified time (*see* pp. 132–134 for a discussion of notice requirements).

Prompt notice should be given of claims for extensions of time as well as claims for adjustment of the contract price to protect the contractor's right to extend performance beyond the original completion date without being assessed for liquidated damages for a delay in completion of the work. The written notice sent to the owner should include a description of the extra work ordered, claims for extra compensation and time to be calculated and forwarded at a later date, and a statement that the contractor will not be responsible for damages resulting from the delay caused by the extra work ordered.

This disputes procedure contemplated by most private contracts includes contract procedures similar to those established by the American Institute of Architects's documents, which contemplate that the initial dispute will be handled by or through the design professional. The AIA General Conditions (AIA Document A201, 1976 ed.), Article 12.3.1, provide that if the owner and the contractor cannot agree on the amount of adjustment to the contract sum, then it shall be determined by the architect. The General Conditions further provide (Article 2.2.6) that the architect is the interpreter of the requirements to the contract documents and the judge of performance thereunder by both the owner and the contractor. All claims, disputes, and other matters in question between the contractor and the owner relating to the execution, progress of the work, or interpretation of contract documents are referred initially to the architect for decision. Under Article 2.2.9 of the AIA General Conditions, the architect must render a decision within a reasonable time.

The architect's decision is subject to arbitration by written demand of either party within 30 days after he renders a decision in writing. The architect's decisions in matters "relating to artistic effect" will be final if they are consistent with the intent of the contract documents. However, the architect's decisions on other matters in dispute are not final and are subject to arbitration. Either party may demand arbitration from the official decision of the architect. In order for a decision to be final and binding, the AIA General Conditions, Article 2.2.12, require that the decision be in writing and must state that it "is final but subject to appeal." Article 2.2.12 stipulates that the decision will become final and binding if no demand for arbitration is made within the 30-day period after the date on which the party making the demand received the architect's decision. However, this article also provides that a party may seek arbitration 10 days after a claim has been presented to the architect if the architect has not rendered a decision prior to that date.

Often General Conditions will state that a decision by the design professional, either an engineer or architect, will be final and binding on the parties. This provision is extremely dangerous because the design professionals cannot be counted upon to render a completely impartial decision since their fees are being paid for by the owner, and typically the subject matter of the dispute may involve alleged defective plans and specifications or other fault of the engineer or architect. Many states interpret as "final" decisions of architect or engineers rendered under a contract clause giving decision-making power to these arbiters. The different states use different standards in determining whether or not the engineers' or architects' decisions may be overturned. Many states follow the rule that an architect's or engineer's decision is "final" within the meaning of the contract unless the arbiter acts outside the authority conferred by the contract, or if his decision is arbitrary, dishonest, or fradulent.

Illustrative Case

In the leading decision defining the legal definition of an "arbitrary decision" the court stated: "A decision or finding may be held to be arbitrary when existing important facts, conditions and expressed contract provisions should obviously have been considered and given due and proper weight, but were not. A decision may be found to be arbitrary when the person given the authority to decide took the position that the matter involved was a matter to be disposed of in his discretion when such was obviously not the case and he was required by the contract to consider and weigh facts, circumstances and conditions as well as to interpret and to be governed by certain standards contained in the terms of the contract."[1]

Although disputes clauses typically provide initial determinations of suits faster than litigation, they may involve a considerable amount of time. If the contractor is required to perform while the dispute proceeds, then he will be out of pocket for the cost of performance, which may create a substantial cash-flow problem for him. If a dispute arises concerning the cost of the change order, Article 12.1.4 of the AIA General Conditions requires that the owner pay at least what the architect certifies is the value of the work based upon the contractor's reasonable expenditures and savings and a reasonable allowance for overhead and profit. A contractor should not allow the owner to attempt to starve the contractor into submission when there is a dispute about the value of a change order. Under the AIA change clause, the contractor is entitled to at least what the architect says the value of the work is and can then go to arbitration to argue about the excess. Article 12.1.4 provides as follows:

12.1.4 If none of the methods set forth in Clauses 12.1.3.1, 12.1.3.2 or 12.1.3.3 is agreed upon, the Contractor, provided he receives a written order signed by the Owner, shall promptly proceed with the Work involved. The cost of such Work shall then be deter-

[1] Needles v. United States, 110 Ct. Cl. 535, 603 (1944).

mined by the Architect on the basis of the reasonable expenditures and savings of those performing the Work attributable to the change, including, in the case of an increase in the Contract Sum, a reasonable allowance for overhead and profit. In such case, and also under Clauses 12.1.3.3 and 12.1.3.4 above, the Contractor shall keep and present, in such form as the Architect may prescribe, an itemized accounting together with appropriate data for inclusion in a Change Order. Unless otherwise provided in the Contract Documents, cost shall be limited to the following: cost of materials including sales tax and cost of delivery; cost of labor, including social security, old age and unemployment insurance, and fringe benefits required by agreement or custom; workers' or workmen's compensation insurance; bond premiums; rental value of equipment and machinery; and the additional costs of supervision and field office personnel directly attributable to the change. Pending final determination of cost to the Owner, payments on account shall be made on the Architect's Certificate for Payment. The amount of credit to be allowed by the Contractor to the Owner for any deletion or change which results in a net decrease in the Contract Sum will be the amount of the actual net cost as confirmed by the Architect. When both additions and credits covering related Work or substitutions are involved in any one change, the allowance for overhead and profit shall be figured on the basis of net increase, if any, with respect to that change.

Government Contracts

Contracts with the federal government and other public bodies typically contain administrative remedies which are available to the government, general contractors, and indirectly to subcontractors in some instances. Under the disputes clauses contained in most federal government contracts, the contracting officer will make an initial decision as to the matter in dispute. However, the contracting officer's decision is typically reviewable by a higher authority such as the head of the agency, the board of contract appeals, and ultimately the courts. Although it is subject to a number of exceptions and rules, the contracting officer's decision will be determinative if it is supported by substantial evidence and if it is not contrary to law. Obviously it is better to settle the dispute at the contracting officer level, and a contractor should make a maximum effort in preparing and presenting his claim to the contracting officer. Presenting a claim to the contracting officer demands the same degree of thoroughness as preparing for litigation, and a thorough preparation coupled with a solid presentation to a contracting officer generally avoids litigation.

The contract and the courts dictate that "the contracting officer must act impartially in settling disputes. He may not act as a representative of one of the contracting parties but as an impartial unbiased judge."[2] As the initial disputes decision maker, the contracting officer is the judge and jury. However, as a practical matter, a contractor should always consider the fact that the government pays the contracting officer's salary. He also has many other factors that control his decision, such as budget. Most contracting officers recognize the probability that the contractor may appeal from his decisions and that there will be an administrative hearing relative to the merits of the matters in dispute. Accordingly, in

[2] Penner Installation Corp. v. United States, 116 Ct. Cl. 550, *aff'd,* 340 U.S. 898 (1950) (per curiam).

rendering a decision the contracting officer should be conscious of his responsibility and also should be continually reminded by the contractor that it is his responsibility to be an impartial and unbiased judge.

Most government contract forms provide a remedy to the general contractor who disagrees with the decision of the contracting officer, and the general contractor is permitted to appeal from the final written decision within a stated period of time to the head of the agency or to his representative, which is usually a board of contract appeals. In an administrative appeal hearing, the contractor has a chance to present his case in an attempt to overturn the decision of the contracting officer. Further appeals to the courts may be permitted if the decision of the board of contract appeals is not supported by substantial evidence or is contrary to law.

Administrative Remedies Available to Subcontractors

The general contract usually stipulates that the disputes procedure under the contract is between the owner and the general contractor. However, a subcontractor whose dispute is ultimately with the owner may obtain the general contractor's agreement to provide cooperation and contract privity to provide the subcontractor with indirect access to the disputes procedure through the general contractor. Although direct appeals in the name of the subcontractor are generally not available for a direct appeal of disputes with the owner under the disputes clause, a subcontractor's claim can be prosecuted either by the general contractor on behalf of the subcontractor or by the subcontractor using the general contractor's name and privity.[3]

The procedure of indirect appeals in the name of the general contractor is one of form because the general contractor need not be actually involved in prosecuting the subcontractor's claim. The general contractor typically is motivated to extend to the subcontractor indirect appeal rights because it would result in all the parties' rights being adjudicated in one forum at one time by the owner and the subcontractor who are the real parties in interest. If the general contractor does not grant to the subcontractor the right to an indirect appeal through the general contractor's disputes clause, the result may be that the general contractor and his surety may be sued in court by the subcontractor while the general contractor is required to pursue his administrative disputes remedy against the owner.

In many instances the subcontract will incorporate by reference all the boilerplate of the general contract, and it may be argued that it also includes the disputes clause. This often creates an issue as to where the subcontractor is bound to proceed under the disputes article and is bound by an administrative decision which the general contractor may

---

[3] Appeal of The Boeing Co., 67-2 B.C.A. ¶ 6693 (1067); Appeal of Traylor Bros. Inc., 65-2 B.C.A. ¶ 4968 (1965); Appeal of Tidewater-Kiewit-P.E.C., 61-2 B.C.A. ¶ 3178 (1961).

institute under the article on behalf of the subcontractor. However, it is typically argued that because all disputes are between the owner and the general contractor, the conduit clause in a subcontract is not meant to be applicable to encompass any disputes arising under a subcontract.

Courts have generally permitted the subcontractor to sue the general contractor or its surety directly, regardless of the general contractor's disputes clause, *unless* the subcontract expressly provides that the subcontractor is bound to the administrative remedy.

Illustrative Case

Prepakt Concrete Company, a subcontractor that performed piling work for construction of a United States postal facility in San Juan, Puerto Rico, brought suit against the original general contractor, Beacon Construction Company, and its assignee to recover the contract price and the value of additional work requested. Beacon moved to stay the proceedings pending pursuit of the administrative remedy under a Post Office disputes clause. Though the court found that Prepakt had notice because the subcontract had included an agreement to do work in accordance with Post Office Department General Conditions, one of which was the disputes clause, the subcontractor was not bound. The court found that in the absence of an *express contractual provision,* only the general contractor has a right to present factual issues to the contracting officer; and under the usual form of general contract, the government's liability runs only to the general contractor with whom it is in privity. The court noted that the interest in having all disputes decided in a single forum could easily be protected by a proper clause in the subcontract expressly making the disputes-clause procedure applicable to the subcontractor.[4]

The subcontractor is not required to pursue the administrative remedy in the general contract if the claim of the subcontractor is for breach of contract which is not within the purview of the disputes article.[5] Disputes clauses relate to questions of fact such as equitable adjustment, not to actions for contract damages.[6] Even the board of contract appeals may not take jurisdiction over breach of contract claims, even if the claims are directly related to the contract between the government and the general contractor.[7]

Since an indirect appeal is technically in the name of the general contractor, the general contractor obviously would be bound by the decision, but it does not necessarily follow that the subcontractor is also bound. The legal relationships between the general contractor and the government may be substantially different than the legal relationship between the subcontractor and the general contractor. The government may have certain defenses against the general contractor which the general contractor may not have against the subcontractor. Moreover, a dispute may be solely between the general contractor and the subcontractor but may not involve any substantial issues concerning or any liability to the govern-

---

[4] Beacon Constr. Co. v. Prepakt Concrete Co., 375 F.2d 977 (1st Cir. 1967).

[5] Callahan Constr. Co. v. United States, 91 Ct. Cl. 538 (1940).

[6] Boomer v. Abbett, 121 Cal. App.2d 449, 263 P.2d 476 (1953).

[7] Silberblatt & Lasker, Inc. v. United States, 2 CCF ¶ 253, 101 Ct. Cl. 54 (1944).

ment. Therefore, the dispute would be beyond the jurisdiction of the disputes clause between the government and the general contractor. There also may be disputes between the general contractor and the subcontractor which solely relate to a matter of law, in which case the administrative remedies under the disputes clause may be inapplicable because the jurisdiction of a disputes clause typically is limited to adjudications of questions of fact or mixed questions of law and fact.[8]

Since the subcontractor's indirect appeal must proceed through the offices of the general contractor, it is vital that the general contractor preserve the subcontractor's right of indirect appeal and not take any action that would destroy the possibility of appeal, such as the general contractor executing a release to the government or not giving timely notice of a subcontractor's indirect appeal.

There is a lurking trap that may cut off a subcontractor's rights to indirectly appeal to the government. If the subcontractor agrees to exculpatory language which releases or eliminates any liability that the general contractor may have to the subcontractor, the government may argue that the government cannot be liable to the general contractor who has released any liability to the subcontractor under a doctrine that arose in the case of *Severin v. United States,* 99 Ct. Cl. 435 (1943), *cert. denied,* 322 U.S. 733 (1944). The *Severin* doctrine basically held that an exculpatory clause which relieved the general contractor of liability to the subcontractor precluded the general contractor from suing the government on the subcontractor's behalf. Fortunately, the Armed Services Board of Contract Appeals and even the Court of Claims have subsequently limited the application of the *Severin* doctrine in indirect appeals to the Board, and there are specific exclusions where the *Severin* doctrine does not apply.

The way to ensure that the *Severin* doctrine does not apply on an indirect appeal is to provide that the general contractor remains liable to the subcontractor for any amounts recovered pursuant to the indirect appeal of the subcontractor. Subcontractors and general contractors should be careful to see that any exculpatory clauses in subcontracts or in supplemental agreements are drawn so that they do not completely release the general contractor and fall into the *Severin* trap. A conditional release can be achieved by having the general contractor agree to remain liable to the subcontractors for any monies that are received by the government on the subcontractor's appeal.

The subcontractor does not have to take an indirect appeal unless there is specific language in the contract, providing that it is his exclusive remedy and that he is bound thereby. In the absence of specific language which binds the subcontractor to pursue an indirect appeal under the general contract's disputes clauses, the subcontractor can proceed directly against the general contractor in court in the absence of a binding arbi-

---

[8] Appeal of C.W. Schmid Plumbing & Heating, 1962 B.C.A. ¶ 3458 (1962).

tration clause. In government claims the subcontractor may also proceed against the general contractor's bonding company under the Miller Act in federal court. A subcontractor's claim against the general contractor under the Miller Act may also be based upon actions by the government which were indirectly transmitted by the general contractor.[9] State court actions may also be available to the subcontractor under subcontracts in governmental and private work.

ARBITRATION

Arbitration can be an expeditious and inexpensive method for resolving most disputes arising in the construction industry, but, surprisingly, arbitration is a relatively unfamiliar process to most contractors. An insight into the procedures and techniques of arbitration as well as its relative advantages and disadvantages can be helpful in choosing a remedy for a dispute. Though arbitration is not always the best forum in which to resolve a dispute, it certainly is one alternative that the contractor should consider. It has been stated that arbitration is a "simple proceeding voluntarily chosen by parties who want a dispute determined by an impartial judge of their own mutual selection, whose decision, based on the merits of the case, they agree in advance to accept as final and binding." Others have characterized arbitration as "an expensive detour on the way to the courthouse." Two questions must first be answered: (1) How is arbitration initiated? and (2) What are the legal effects of the arbitration process?

The Agreement to Arbitrate

The first step in any arbitration procedure is the agreement to arbitrate. This agreement may come in the form of a provision within a construction contract, or it may be reached after the dispute arises. An agreement to arbitrate is found in the AIA General Conditions (AIA Document A201, 1976 ed.), Article 7.9:

7.9 Arbitration

7.9.1 All claims, disputes and other matters in question between the Contractor and the Owner arising out of, or relating to, the Contract Documents or the breach thereof, except as provided in Subparagraph 2.2.11 with respect to the Architect's decisions on matters relating to artistic effect and except for claims which have been waived by the making or acceptance of final payment as provided by Subparagraphs 9.9.4 and 9.9.5, shall be decided by arbitration in accordance with the Construction Industry Arbitration Rules of the American Arbitration Association then obtaining unless the parties mutually agree otherwise. No arbitration arising out of or relating to the Contract Documents shall include, by consolidation, joinder or in any other manner, the Architect, his employees or consultants except by written consent containing a specific reference to the Owner-Contractor Agreement and signed by the Architect, the Owner, the Contractor and any other person sought

[9] Wallace Process Piping Co. v. Martin-Marietta Corp., 251 F. Supp. 411 (E.D. Va. 1965).

to be joined. No arbitration shall include by consolidation, joinder or in any other manner, parties other than the Owner, the Contractor and any other persons substantially involved in a common question of fact or law, whose presence is required if complete relief is to be accorded in the arbitration. No person other than the Owner or Contractor shall be included as an original third party or additional third party to an arbitration whose interest or responsibility is insubstantial. Any consent to arbitration involving an additional person or persons shall not constitute consent to arbitration of any dispute not described therein or with any person not named or described therein. The foregoing agreement to arbitrate and any other agreement to arbitrate with an additional person or persons duly consented to by the parties to the Owner-Contractor Agreement shall be specifically enforceable under the prevailing arbitration law. The award rendered by the arbitrators shall be final, and judgment may be entered upon it in accordance with applicable law in any court having jurisdiction thereof.

7.9.2 Notice of the demand for arbitration shall be filed in writing with the other party to the Owner-Contractor Agreement and with the American Arbitration Association, and a copy shall be filed with the Architect. The demand for arbitration shall be made within the time limits specified in Subparagraph 2.2.12 where applicable, and in all other cases within a reasonable time after the claim, dispute or other matter in question has arisen, and in no event shall it be made after the date when institution of legal or equitable proceedings based on such claim, dispute or other matter in question would be barred by the applicable statute of limitations.

7.9.3 Unless otherwise agreed in writing, the Contractor shall carry on the Work and maintain its progress during any arbitration proceedings, and the Owner shall continue to make payments to the Contractor in accordance with the Contract Documents.

When the construction contract provides for arbitration, the first threshold question is whether the agreement is enforceable. In the overwhelming majority of states agreements to arbitrate future disputes are enforceable. However, under certain state laws, agreements to arbitrate all future disputes arising under a construction contract are not enforceable.[10] In such states, if one of the parties to the contract does not wish to arbitrate, he may be able to defeat any attempt to arbitrate. However, even in those states where arbitration agreements are not enforceable under *state* law, it is possible the agreement would be enforceable under *federal* law. The Federal Arbitration Act provides that an agreement to arbitrate in a contract evidencing a transaction involving commerce is valid and enforceable. The arbitration agreements in such contracts must be enforced by both state and federal courts.

It should be noted that these minority state laws only prevent enforcement of arbitration clauses against nonwilling parties: should both parties agree and proceed to arbitrate, all states will uphold and enforce the arbitration decision.

Even in the absence of a prior agreement to arbitrate future disputes, the parties may wish to submit the dispute to an independent arbitrator for a private resolution of the dispute without going to court.

[10] Wright v. Cecil A. Mason Constr. Co., 115 Ga. App. 729, 155 S.E.2d 725 (1967).

Illustrative Case

A plastering contractor followed specifications for plastering a section of a transcept vaulted ceiling of a large church. The contractor contended that the plaster failed to adhere to the ceiling because of a defective specification in the mix of plaster specified by the architects. The architect, who was the representative of the owner, contended that the contractor guaranteed the performance and that the plaster specifications were not defective and ordered the contractor to replaster the section of the ceiling. When no agreement between the owner and the plastering contractor could be reached on the reimbursement for the cost of replastering the ceiling, the parties agreed to submit the dispute to private arbitration under the rules of the American Arbitration Association. The plastering contractor prevailed in the arbitration. However, both parties prevailed in getting the dispute settled privately and expeditiously without having to go to court, which is what both the contractor and church wanted. [11]

The matters which must be determined by arbitration are fixed by the scope of the arbitration clause in the contract. Thus, for example, if the clause provides for "arbitration of disputes which may arise in connection with the *performance* of this agreement," the owner may not be able to enforce arbitration of a dispute involving the payment clause. [12]

Generally the courts will not reconsider the decision of the arbitrators applying the law to the facts of the dispute. However, they will vacate the arbitrators' award if it was procured by fraud, corruption, or partiality, if the arbitrators acted beyond the authority granted to them by the contract, or if the arbitrators manifestly disregarded the law which defines the rights of the parties. [13] But if the contractor has reason to know before the arbitration that one of the arbitrators is likely to be biased in his consideration of the decision of the engineer or architect, the contractor should object to the arbitrator's qualifications before submitting the dispute to arbitration.

Illustrative Case

An arbitration agreement between a subcontractor, Commonwealth Coatings Corporation, and a general contractor provided that disputes would be settled before three arbitrators, one to be appointed by each of the two parties and a third to be elected by the two appointed arbitrators. The elected arbitrator, the supposedly neutral member of this arbitration panel, was an engineering consultant for various concerns, and one of his regular customers in his consulting service was the general contractor. As a consultant to the general contractor, the third arbitrator had a repeated and significant relationship with the general contractor, having received substantial amounts in fees over a 5-year period, and, in fact, the relationship even went so far as to include services on the very project in dispute. The relationship of the third member of the panel and the general contractor was not revealed until after an award had been made. Commonwealth Coatings challenged the award on this ground, and the case reached the United

---

[11] Unpublished arbitration case.

[12] Galt v. Libbey-Owens-Ford Glass Co., 397 F.2d 439 (7th Cir.), *cert. denied,* 393 U.S. 925 (1968) (italics supplied).

[13] Amicizia Societa Navegazione v. Chilean Nitrate & Iodine Sales Corp., 184 F. Supp. 116 (S.D.N.Y. 1959), *aff'd,* 274 F.2d 805 (2d Cir.), *cert. denied,* 363 U.S. 843 (1960); 9 U.S.C. § 10.

States Supreme Court, which analogized the position of a neutral arbitrator to that of a foreman of a jury or a judge in a court. Although the Court recognized that arbitrators could not sever all their ties with the business world, the Court felt that it would not hinder the arbitration process for arbitrators at a minimum to disclose to parties any dealings that might create an impression of possible bias. Because of the nondisclosure of the relationship between the general contractor and the supposedly neutral arbitrator, the Court allowed the arbitration decision to be vacated even though the third arbitrator was not alleged to be guilty of actual fraud or bias in deciding the dispute. The Court stated:

> This rule of arbitration and this canon of judicial ethics rest on the premise that any tribunal permitted by law to try cases and controversies not only must be unbiased but also must avoid even the appearance of bias. We cannot believe that it was the purpose of Congress to authorize litigants to submit their cases and controversies to arbitration boards that might reasonably be thought biased against one litigant and favorable to another.[14]

A party may also entirely waive the right to arbitration by participating in court action without insisting upon arbitration.[15]

General contractors and subcontractors working on government projects should note that arbitration agreements in their subcontracts do not conflict with the rights granted to subcontractors by the Miller Act. Thus, a subcontractor must comply with the arbitration provision of the subcontract before bringing a Miller Act suit to enforce a payment bond.[16] However, if the subcontract only incorporates by reference the arbitration procedure of the General Conditions of the general contract, the subcontractor may bring a Miller Act suit without first going to arbitration.[17]

Arbitration Procedure

The procedures for arbitrating may be as varied as the imaginations of the participants. Probably the most frequently used procedure is that set out by the American Arbitration Association (AAA). The AAA is a public service, nonprofit organization whose sole function is to resolve disputes through the use of arbitration. The rules of the Association for the settlement of disputes in the construction industry are incorporated into the AIA General Conditions and Standard Subcontract Form A401 and are particularly structured for settlement of disputes in the construction industry. To better understand the arbitration procedure, the following will describe an arbitration utilizing the rules of the AAA.

When an aggrieved party initiates arbitration, he should first give written notice to the other party of an intention to arbitrate. The notice

---

[14] Commonwealth Coatings Corp. v. Continental Casualty Co., 393 U.S. 145 (1968).

[15] Burton-Dixie Corp. v. Timothy McCarthy Constr. Co., 436 F.2d 405 (5th Cir. 1971).

[16] United States *ex rel.* Capolino Sons, Inc., v. Electronic & Missile Facilities, Inc., 364 F.2d 705 (2d Cir.), *cert. denied,* 385 U.S. 924 (1966). The rights of the parties under the Miller Act are discussed in this chapter under Bond Rights.

[17] Fanderlik-Locke Co. v. United States *ex rel.* Morgan, 285 F.2d 939 (10th Cir. 1960).

should set forth a statement of the nature of the dispute and the remedy sought. Simultaneously, the initiating party should file with the regional office of the AAA three copies of the notice to arbitrate, together with a copy of the contract or agreement containing the arbitration provision. The notice to the adverse party as well as to the AAA should contain "the claim," setting forth the pertinent facts giving rise to the dispute. The claim is the equivalent of the "complaint" in a court suit. It is important to note that under the rules of the AAA, the claim may not be changed subsequent to the appointment of arbitrators unless the arbitrators allow for an amendment to the claim. Within 7 days of receipt of the demand for arbitration, the opposing party may file an answer, or "counterclaim." If the opposing party fails to file an answer to the claim, for the purposes of arbitration, the opposing party is deemed to have denied the claim.

When the regional office of the AAA receives the claim, a panel of arbitrators is selected by the AAA and their names are forwarded to each party. This list will usually consist of seven to fifteen prospective arbitrators. Together with the list, the AAA forwards instructions to each party requesting each party to strike the names of those arbitrators listed who are for some reason unsatisfactory. No reason need be given for striking the name of any arbitrator. Each party is instructed further to list in order of preference those arbitrators who have not been stricken and to return the list to the AAA within 7 days. The respective parties do not exchange their list of preferred arbitrators; instead, the AAA receives the respective lists prepared by the opposing parties. If either party fails to submit his preference as to arbitrators, it is deemed that all members of the panel are acceptable to the party failing to respond. Should any party strike the names of all the arbitrators on the panel, the AAA will request each party to select one name from the panel of arbitrators and submit it to the AAA. The AAA will then select a third panel member to serve.

Often the arbitration agreement itself will specify the number of arbitrators to be used. In cases involving substantial sums of money, it is usual that the panel consist of three arbitrators. In the event the agreement does not so specify the number and the parties fail to mutually agree as to the number of arbitrators, the AAA will initiate procedures for the appointment of a single arbitrator. The procedure is similar: Each party selects his preferences from the panel of arbitrators, and the AAA selects that arbitrator whose name is most preferred.

Arbitrators normally do not make their living by arbitrating; instead they usually come from the ranks of lawyers, contractors, architects, engineers, or educators. In order to become an arbitrator, certain prerequisites prescribed by the AAA must be met; once approved by the AAA, the individuals certified as arbitrators are randomly placed upon panels for arbitrations. Under the rules of the AAA, each arbitrator agrees to serve without compensation for a single day of hearing. Should the hearing go beyond 1 day, the arbitrators require the payment of a fee, which is normally in the range of several hundred dollars per day per arbitrator. Under the rules of the AAA, both parties share the expenses of the arbitration, including the administrative fees of the AAA and compensation to the arbitrators.

Simultaneously with the selection of arbitrators, the AAA requests each party to advise when they will be available to arbitrate the dispute. From the dates commonly preferred by both parties, the AAA selects the arbitration date. If there is need for discovery by the opposing parties, the date for hearing will generally be postponed until discovery is completed. After the arbitrators are selected, the postponement or selection of a hearing date is within the discretion of the arbitrators rather than the administrative personnel of the AAA.

As in courts, parties have the right to conduct discovery in the form of depositions or written interrogatories. If the opposing party refuses to respond, a court order can be obtained to enforce a response or deposition from the opposing party.

A significant difference between arbitration and litigation is in the power to compel witnesses to appear at the hearing. The arbitrator has no subpoena power, which is available in courts of law. Generally, however, witnesses are willing to appear. However, in those situations where the arbitration is conducted by court order, subpoenas may be available through the court.

The hearing itself resembles a court proceeding. Witnesses are usually, though not always, sworn, and the arbitrators sit as judges. Unlike courts of law, the rules of evidence are relaxed; the panel of arbitrators have broad discretion to allow any testimony they believe relevant or of probative value, including hearsay. The moving party first presents its case and is followed by the opposing party. At the end of the proceeding, each party is allowed a closing statement, which resembles the closing argument in a court of law. The arbitrators will frequently request that the closing argument be made in written form. This procedure allows each party to argue both the facts presented as well as the law each party contends to be applicable. After the hearing has been completed, the arbitrators will commonly announce that the record will remain open for a definite period of time to allow either party to submit additional evidence or briefs.

The closing briefs mentioned are very important in that they must educate the panel or arbitrators as to the pertinent law. The closing argument in an arbitration is considerably more important to present the applicable law than in a court proceeding where a judge has a working knowledge of the applicable law. Most commonly, the arbitrators sitting on the panel may have little or no understanding of the technical rules of law applicable to the situation.

After all closing arguments, oral or written, are submitted and the record is closed, the arbitrators enter their decision. Under the rules of the AAA, the decision must be entered within 30 days of the closing of the record. The decision of the arbitrators is binding and has the effect of a judgment in a court of law. Should the losing party fail or refuse to comply with the arbitrators' decision, the prevailing party may obtain a court order forcing the losing party to carry out its obligations.

A Comparison with Litigation

Arbitration has particular advantages and disadvantages when compared with litigation. An important advantage to arbitration is that it can be fast and relatively inexpensive, and the arbitrators can utilize any type of remedy a court could use. From the time the demand for arbitration is filed until a final decision is rendered, it may take no longer than 5 to 6 months. In comparison, litigation can seldom be completed in a period shorter than 12 months. Another advantage to arbitration is that the expenses of arbitration are relatively small. The initial filing fee for an arbitration claim is $50, and for most claims under $10,000 the total expense will not exceed $400, excluding any private attorney's fees.

Another important consideration is the fact that arbitrators for construction disputes have technical expertise in the field at issue. As indicated previously, it is common that contractors or architects or engineers will sit on the panel deciding the case, and certainly in technical construction matters it is helpful to have people with expertise determining the issues. Moreover, in arbitration there is little chance for procedural delays in that there are no court dockets to postpone the proceeding. The informality of arbitration is very conducive to getting to the facts of the case without unnecessary delay or hindrances by technical evidentiary arguments. Conversely, in arbitration, the panel often has little or no legal expertise. As a result, the arbitrators may tend to look to the equitable rather than the legal side of the argument. In short, an individual may be defeated in an arbitration proceeding even though he is in technical compliance with his legal obligations.

It is impossible to generalize as to whether or not arbitration is preferable to litigation. Certainly, where an expeditious remedy is important, arbitration should be considered. Similarly, where the dispute involves technical issues requiring expertise by the party determining the case, arbitration has definite advantages. On the other hand, where there are technical rules of law which will determine the issues of the case, a court of law seems preferable. The contractor should consult his attorney for advice as to whether the contractor is already legally bound to submit disputes to arbitration and as to which alternative is preferable in each individual case if arbitration is not mandatory.

COURT ACTION

A great number of construction contract disagreements can be resolved through negotiations between the owner and general contractor or between the general contractor and the subcontractor; but when negotiation fails, the injured party must seek other means or redress. One of his alternatives is court action through a lawsuit. Litigation is civilized society's substitute for violence, and it should be realized that even lawyers consider it a last resort in the resolution of disputes. A lawsuit is risky. It may be compared to an old western walk—the parties start at opposite ends of the street and meet in the middle with guns blazing. Both may get "killed."

While the litigation is proceeding, the parties are left in limbo and with unsettled expectations. It is time-consuming, expensive, and acrimonious. Not least important, litigation substitutes the often unwieldy machinery of the court for consensual and flexible agreement of the parties. The process can be a disagreeable one for those involved, and certain factors should be assessed before a lawsuit is launched.

Delay

The first consideration may well be the delay which litigation involves. Court calendars are increasingly congested, with delays consequently becoming more extended and irksome to the parties involved. The postponement of cash award, first while awaiting trial and then through possible appeals, can sometimes be of crucial importance to the general contractor or subcontractor who is operating on a tightly stretched budget. In contrast, a well-managed and cooperative arbitration can often be completed in a relatively short amount of time.

Precedent

Another consideration is that the dispute is made public and the court's decision will be precedent for future resolution of factually similar situations. The moving party should consider whether he wishes the outcome —an outcome which at commencement he does not know will be favorable to him—to be public knowledge and possibly to become the standard for future lawsuits.

Expense

Court proceedings can be troubling and expensive for *both* parties. Preparation for trial frequently involves more of the attorney's time than the general contractor or subcontractor optimistically anticipated. Thorough preparation is the benchmark for successful litigation, and that essential preparation results in escalating legal fees.

Lay Jury

A factor often overlooked by an angry would-be litigant is that he will be presenting his case to a jury of laymen who know little or nothing about the construction industry. Should the facts be highly technical or should the situation be governed by the customs of the industry, the contractor may find difficulty in conveying the intricacies of engineering data or construction accounting (on which his case depends) to a lay jury.

It is obvious, however, that there are situations where court actions represent the best and perhaps the only avenue to settlement. There are important advantages to court action.

Discovery

An advantage to court action is the availability of discovery procedures: depositions of involved parties, interrogatories, and motions to compel production of essential documents. The litigants also have the right to subpoena witnesses, documents, and records. Such procedures may well result in a more thorough uncovering of essential facts and consequently produce a better base for decision. Whether this additional investigation is necessary depends, of course, on the particular facts of the case.

Multiple-Party Practice

The goal of modern court procedure under the Federal Rules of Civil Procedure and similar state court rules is to settle all the controversies between all the persons involved in a particular dispute in the same court proceeding. The person bringing the suit, therefore, may join as defendants all persons who may be liable to the plaintiff with respect to a single transaction or occurrence if any question of law or fact common to all the defendants will arise in the suit. Defendants may bring into the suit "third-party defendants" who are those who may be liable over to the defendant for all or part of the plaintiff's claim against the defendant. Multiple-party arbitration is much more restricted. The policy of the AAA is to refuse to hear disputes arising under separate contracts containing arbitration clauses in a joint arbitration if one of the parties objects to such a consolidation. Some courts, however, have ordered consolidated arbitration between the owner, architect, and a contractor,[18] between the owner, general contractor, and a subcontractor,[19] or between the owner and several prime contractors.[20] Many courts have also refused to consolidate arbitration in construction cases.[21]

Enforcement

Another important advantage of court action is that it carries with it an efficient and certain means of enforcement. The judgment makes unequivocally clear which parties are bound and to what extent. In con-

[18] Robinson v. Warner, 370 F. Supp. 828 (D.R.I. 1974).

[19] Uniroyal, Inc. v. A. Epstein & Sons, Inc., 428 F.2d 523 (7th Cir. 1970).

[20] Children's Hospital v. Am. Arb. Ass'n, 331 A.2d 848 (Pa. Super. 1974).

[21] See, e.g., Stop & Shop Companies v. Gilbane Bldg. Co., 304 N.E.2d 429 (Mass. 1973).

trast, the specific enforcement of an arbitration clause or award against a nonwilling party can be trying and difficult.

It is obvious that court action offers less flexibility than other alternatives, such as arbitration: Evidence must be presented within the formal and sometimes restrictive limits of the rules of evidence; once the suit is commenced, room for maneuvering and give and take on the part of the parties is restricted; and the parties are bound to the often ponderous schedule of the court. The decision to pursue court action must rest on an assessment of the advantages and disadvantages of the legal process in relation to the particular facts and problems of the individual situation.

LIEN RIGHTS

Stated most simply, a "lien" is a security interest in the real estate improved for payment for labor or materials used in its improvements; the lien provides for a right to sell the property to which the lien attaches if the debt is not paid. Liens were not recognized at common law, and they were created in this country solely by statutory enactment. The right to assert a lien is a right granted and therefore defined by statute; the general contractor, subcontractor, or supplier must comply with the statute if his lien is to be enforceable. Lien laws have been enacted in every state and differ in their terms; this discussion is prefaced with advice that the general contractor, subcontractor, or material supplier should consult with his attorney to ascertain the intricacies and requirements of the local law.

The right to assert a lien derives from equitable considerations. When a building is constructed on land, the law of fixtures says that it becomes a part of that land; those who have provided labor, materials, and services in the construction, therefore, have increased the value of the land on which the building is constructed. Once the labor and materials have been incorporated into the project, the contractor, subcontractor, or materialman cannot repossess them if he is not paid. Thus the only protection that a person furnishing labor or material for construction has is an assurance of a meaningful security interest in the land to secure payment for the value of labor and materials furnished to improve that land. The lien laws evolved, in part, to encourage participation in construction of real estate improvements.

Increasingly, work and materials today are provided for a construction project on a credit basis. The supplier furnishes goods to the subcontractor and bills him; the subcontractor installs the goods in the construction and bills the general contractor; when construction has reached a certain level, the general contractor is entitled to a progress payment from the owner. That progress payment then filters down to the various levels of subcontractors and suppliers in satisfaction of the credit obligations incurred. This pyramid of credit is secured, not by the net worth of the person or firm to whom it is extended, but by the land on which the construction occurs.

Construction lien laws benefit two different types of participants in the construction process: First, the general contractor, who has directly contracted with the owner and directly helped to make the owner's land more valuable, is protected by the lien law. Second, the persons who have no direct contractual relationship with the owner but who have nonetheless furnished labor or material for the project—subcontractors, suppliers, and laborers—are given a secured interest in the owner's land to protect them should the person with whom they *have* contracted default in payment.

The requirement of offering protection to all levels of those involved in the construction project can sometimes result in multiple liability for the owner. The owner may pay his general contractor in full only to find out that the general contractor, because of dishonesty or insolvency, has failed to pay his obligations; the owner subsequently is faced with lien claims from remote subcontractors or suppliers of whom he was not even aware. Thus the owner is faced with the unenviable choice of paying twice or losing his newly improved land and building.

As a result of this dilemma, the careful owner wants proof, before making payment, that there are no outstanding lien claims to subcontractors or suppliers. Hence some lien laws include a requirement that potential claimants give notice to the owner of their interest in claiming a lien. The owner is likely to pressure his general contractor to obtain written waivers of lien rights, so that the owner is assured that no possible claims await him. The problem is a complex one: The general contractor, typically operating on a low-capital position, finds he needs to obtain lien waivers before receiving the progress payment from the owner necessary to pay his subcontractors and suppliers; but those subcontractors and suppliers may understandably be reluctant to sign waivers of their lien rights until they are paid. Lien laws in their notorious diversity reflect different resolutions of these competing interests.

Waivers of Liens

A contract containing a provision waiving any lien rights presents a serious danger: If a general contractor or subcontractor signs such a contract, the laws of most states will give him no further lien protection. Accordingly, the prudent general contractor or subcontractor should strike such a clause from any contract or subcontract he executes. Any possible objection from the owner or general contractor to such a change should be outweighed by the realization that a contract with a waiver clause strips the general contractor or subcontractor of any recourse should the owner or general contractor be unable to pay. Not only may he lose his right to file a lien, but he may, in addition, have to remove at his own cost any liens which may have been placed against the property as a result of his work. For example, if the subcontract also contains a clause in which the subcontractor agrees to indemnify the general contractor and the owner from liens arising out of the subcontractor's work, the subcontractors may have to remove those liens placed by his materialmen and subcontractors. Should the general contractor fail to pay the subcontractor, the subcontractor would find himself faced not only with loss of his own lien rights, but also with the obligation to remove the liens of others.

Similarly, the general contractor or subcontractor should never sign a lien waiver or affidavit stating that he has been paid, when, in fact, he has not yet received payment. If such a waiver is requested, the general contractor or subcontractor should make sure that the waiver or affidavit is contingent on his actually receiving payment for the amount due. Most waivers of liens for final payment can be easily modified by inserting the prefatory words "Upon receipt of $___," followed by the waiver of lien language in which the general contractor or subcontractor waives his lien rights and acknowledges receipt of all monies due him. Should he not receive payment, the lien waiver and acknowledgment of receipt thus will not be effective.

On an interim waiver of lien the general contractor or subcontractor should be quite careful to waive his lien rights only for the money he has received; lien rights for future work should always be preserved. An interim standard waiver of lien that has been recommended by both the Associated General Contractors of America and the American Subcontractors Association contains the following language, which waives lien rights only to monies actually received:

Furthermore, in consideration of the payments received, and upon receipt of the amount of this request, the undersigned does hereby waive, release, and relinquish all claim or right of lien which the undersigned may now have upon the premises above described except for claims or right of lien for contract and/or change-order work performed to extent that payment is being retained or will subsequently become due.

In some states, a general contractor can waive or discharge subcontractors' and material suppliers' lien rights by signing a final affidavit stating that all materialmen and subcontractors have been paid. However, a general contractor who signs a false affidavit certifying that all lower levels have been paid when, in fact, they have not is subject to *criminal* penalties.

Finally, it should be noted that because of the drastic consequences of lien waivers, the legislatures of several states recently have passed laws invalidating any purported waivers of liens.[22]

---

[22] Mass. Ann. Laws ch. 254, § 32 (Michie/Law. Co-op 1968 Supp. 1975); N.Y. Lien Law § 34 (McKinney's 1966); N.Y. Acts 1975 (Bill No. S. 947-A).

Amounts Recoverable by Lien

Lien laws can be divided into two broad categories, generally known as the "New York system" and the "Pennsylvania system," and differentiated by the ceiling on the amount the lien claimant may recover. Under the New York system, the lien depends on and is limited by the amount remaining due to the general contractor at the time the subcontractor serves notice that he has furnished labor or material for the project. Under this system, the lien is described as "derivative"; that is, the lien claimant is subrogated to the rights of the general contractor. To recover a given sum, the subcontractor or materialman must show that at least the amount of his claim was owing to the general contractor, and the owner generally may not be forced to pay more than in the contract price.

Under the Pennsylvania system the rights of lien claimants do not depend at all on the existence of any indebtedness due from the owner to the general contractor; claimants enjoy a so-called direct lien. Statutes of this type follow one of two forms: one which imposes unlimited liability on the owner's property, or another by which the owner may limit his lien liability to the contract price.

Perfecting the Lien

The potential claimant should consult his attorney about the intricacies of the procedures required by local statute for obtaining a lien. The subcontractor or general contractor, in compliance with the statutory requirements of some states, should give notice to the owner of his intention to perform services or furnish materials or notice that he has already furnished them; he must give notice of his intention to claim a lien; and he must then file a claim of lien in the manner and within the time prescribed.

Notice to owner.   Many jurisdictions require, in addition to filing of the lien claim, that a claimant serve notice on the owner or his agent within a specified time. Some jurisdictions make the notice requirement conditional on the owner's being a resident of the city or county and provide that where he is a nonresident, the notice may be posted or published. Still other jurisdictions provide that notice may be given the owner by providing him with a copy of the filed claim. In many jurisdictions, however, notice must precede the filing of the claim and must apprise the owner of the claimant's intention to file. The statute should be examined for the timing requirements of the individual jurisdiction.

The general contractor is usually exempt from this requirement of notice because of his direct contractual relation with the owner; the rationale is that the contractor's existence and the services he performs are known to the owner. Similarly, notice typically is not required when the labor or material are furnished by a subcontractor or materialman on order of the owner.

The contents of the notice are prescribed by individual statutes.

Generally, the notice must be sufficient to fully acquaint the owner with all of the facts bearing on the claim. For example, the lien should state the nature and kind of work done or materials furnished, the time when furnished, and the amount of the claim. Exhaustive technical adherence to a particular form of notice is not required; however, a substantial compliance in good faith with the provisions of the statute will usually suffice. The statutes typically provide that notice must be written and signed by the claimant or his authorized representative.

Various jurisdictions prescribe different methods of service. Some require personal service on the owner; others accept service by registered mail; some permit the claimant to choose either method.

The claim. In the overwhelming majority of states, the claimant must file for record with some designated public official, such as the county clerk, a verified statement of his claim in a form prescribed by the statute. This claim is not a complaint or a pleading; instead, it is merely notice of the claim so that owners and prospective purchasers of the property may have notice of the amount, nature, and claimant of the lien.

The statutes prescribe various timing requirements for the filing of the lien claim. Some jurisdictions have held that a lien notice prematurely filed prior to substantial completion of a contract is ineffective to create a lien; in contrast, other courts have held that the claim may be filed before or after completion. The statutes generally require that the claim must be filed within 60 or 90 days after completion or termination, although some are as short as 30 days and others may permit filing as long as 6 months after completion of the claimant's work.

Lien rights are lost by many general contractors, subcontractors, and material suppliers because they failed to file their notice and claim within the time limitations provided in the lien laws. General contractors, subcontractors, and material suppliers should realize that there is no element of insult to an owner or a general contractor in filing a lien; instead it is an approved statutory way of protecting legal rights. The general contractor, subcontractor, or material supplier should contact his attorney well before expiration of the statutory period so that the attorney can obtain a proper legal description of the property involved (a requirement in many states) and possibly negotiate payment without the necessity of filing the lien.

Enforcement of Liens

Should the general contractor, subcontractor, or material supplier not be paid, he must file suit to commence legal action for the recovery of the amount of his claim and foreclosure of his lien. The mechanic's lien statutes set forth the time within which an action or suit must be brought to enforce the lien, and often the time is short, typically between 3 months and 1 year. If the action is not brought within the prescribed time, the lawsuit is barred. Some jurisdictions provide that the period during which suit may be brought may be shortened on written demand of the owner that the claimant commence action, a procedure which provides a quick method of clearing the cloud on the owner's title. Also, bonds can discharge claims of lien in most states to clear up title. However, the subcontractors and material suppliers then have an action against the bond.

BOND RIGHTS

The courts have commented often on the advantages to the public which result from bonds to protect subcontractors, materialmen, and laborers for public work; indeed, they have noted that public bodies are under a moral obligation or public duty to protect persons furnishing materials and labor to their contractors against the default of such contractors. Since ordinarily liens cannot be claimed against property owned by governmental entities, such protection is necessary to prevent subcontractors and suppliers from suffering injustice and loss because of the failure of irresponsible contractors to pay for the labor and material used in making public improvements.

Miller Act Bonds

The current statutory expression of this viewpoint is the Miller Act,[23] which requires a government prime contractor to provide two separate bonds: a performance bond for the sole protection of the government and a payment bond to protect those persons supplying labor and materials to the contract project. The Act requires the performance bond to be "in such amount as [the contracting officer] shall deem adequate," a figure usually fixed at 100 percent of the contract price.

Public works.   The Miller Act requires bonds for "public works" of the United States, a term which can occasionally create confusion in a time of pervasive federal aid to state and local governments. The factor of title alone (to buildings or improvements or to the land) has not been of primary significance in determining whether the project is a "public work" within the meaning of the Act.

Illustrative Case

The construction of a library building at Howard University in the District of Columbia—a project for which federal funds were appropriated under the National Industrial Recovery Act of 1933—was held to be a "public work" since it was a project carried on with public aid to serve the interests of the general public.[24]

[23] 40 U.S.C. § 270 (1969).

[24] United States *ex rel.* Noland Co. v. Irwin, 316 U.S. 23 (1942).

However, neither does the mere use of federal funds, in itself, make a project a public work. Accordingly it becomes important to determine who the "owner" of the project is in order to assess its public nature. Where there is a contract for a public building or public work of the United States, if the person or agency making the contract on behalf of the United States had authority to so contract, it is immaterial whether the contract was made in the name of the United States or of such person or agency: The contract is one involving a "public work."

Persons entitled to protection. The Miller Act states that the payment bond protects those who supply *material and labor* to the prime contractor for use on a public work. There has been concern among subcontractors and suppliers and resulting litigation over how far down the tiers of subcontractors and suppliers the protection extends.

Illustrative Case

Clifford F. MacEvoy Company, a government contractor, executed a payment bond pursuant to the Miller Act to cover the construction of a Defense housing project. The contractor purchased building materials from a supplier, James H. Miller & Company, who, in turn, had procured them from yet another supplier, Calvin Tomkins Company. Upon failure of Miller to pay for the goods, Tomkins instituted action on the Miller Act payment bond. The Court held that a person supplying materials to a materialman of a government contractor is too remote to recover on the payment bond executed by the contractor.[25]

The preceding case established that the Miller Act bond provides protection only for *those who have a direct contractual relationship with the prime contractor or with a subcontractor.* Thus it becomes important to determine the definition of "subcontractor" under the Miller Act. The cases seem to have limited that definition to the meaning generally accepted in the building trades: one who performs for and takes from the prime contractor a specific part of the labor or material requirements of the original contract. Thus those who contract to furnish goods or services to materialmen, or third-tier subcontractors, would not be covered by the Act, as the preceding case indicates.

Services and goods entitled to protection. The courts occasionally have had trouble defining the extent of the "labor and materials" the Miller Act purports to protect. For example, they have excluded from the Act's coverage:

1. Repair parts which add materially to the value of construction equipment and render it available for other work
2. Repairs to machinery made *after* completion of the work
3. Rental of a subcontractor's equipment during a period when it was not being used because the government stopped the work

[25] Clifford F. MacEvoy Co. v. United States *ex rel.* Calvin Tomkins Co., 322 U.S. 102 (1944).

In 1966 the Miller Act was amended to cover Social Security and withholding taxes which a contractor might fail to pay. The contractor is also responsible for health and welfare contributions.

Illustrative Case

Carter Construction Company entered into a collective bargaining agreement under which it was required to pay contributions into a health and welfare fund. When the contractor was delinquent in its contributions, the court held the trustee of the fund could maintain an action against the contractor's surety.[26]

One hotly contested area of surety-ship law has been whether the Surety on a Miller Act Bond is liable for a subcontractor's delay damages. The sureties argue that a Miller Act Bond covers only the cost of "labor and material" used in performing the contract, and thus excludes recovery for delayed damages. In some cases, Miller Act sureties successfully argued that the type of damage being sought, for example, lost profits, did not constitute "labor and material" and were thus not recoverable on the bond.[27] Recently, however, several courts have recognized that delays can result in a subcontractor being required to furnish additional labor and material or increase the cost of the labor and material. In such cases the courts have required the surety to pay the costs of these "delay damages."[28]

Notice and filing suit. Subcontractors in direct privity with the general contractor are not required to give notice of their intent to sue; the contractor knows or should know whether he is indebted to the subcontractor with whom he deals. But if the subcontractor is a second-tier subcontractor and does not have a direct contractual relationship with the general, he must give formal written notice to the general contractor within 90 days after he furnished or supplied the last labor or material for which he is making a claim. If he fails to give such notice, his right to action is defeated. Although the notice required by the statute is not a formal document, it should contain sufficient information to enable the contractor to identify the claim with reasonable certainty: It should state the name of the recipient of the labor or materials and the amount of the claim with substantial accuracy. Service of such notice can be made by registered mail directed to the general contractor at his office, place of business, or residence.

[26] United States *ex rel.* Sherman v. Carter, 301 F.2d 467 (9th Cir. 1962).

[27] United States *ex rel.* Pittsburgh-Des Moines Steel Co. v. MacDonald Constr. Co., 281 F. Supp. 1010 (E.D. Mo. 1968).

[28] United States *ex rel.* E & R Constr. Co. v. Guy H. James Constr. Co., 390 F. Supp. 1193 (M.D. Tenn. 1972).

The Miller Act was amended in 1959 to provide that no suit could be maintained on the bond after the expiration of 1 year after the day on which the last of the labor was performed or material was supplied by the claimant. This 1-year requirement is jurisdictional in nature and cannot be waived; it can defeat an action, no matter how meritorious the claim. A claimant cannot rely on a surety to grant an extension of time to file suit because such a waiver is unenforceable.

Nonfederal Public Bonds

Almost all states require contractors to provide performance bonds and to pay for labor, materials, and supplies required for state public improvements. Since the duties and liabilities arising out of such bonds are controlled by state statute, any contractor who considers a state or local project should check his state's laws to determine the extent of his liability in executing the required bond; the subcontractor or supplier can determine his rights against the contractor by similar examination.

Many state statutes are modeled after the Miller Act. In such states, decisions interpreting the Miller Act have been the lodestone for local courts in construing the state statute.

Private Bonds

Some jurisdictions have enacted statutes permitting or requiring a private property owner to exact from the contractor a bond protecting subcontractors, materialmen, and laborers. Those statutes *permitting* rather than compelling an owner to do so have met with general approval by the courts as an efficient method of protection and enforcement of liens. These statutes usually provide that where the owner files with his contract a bond of the contractor, recovery against the owner by materialmen and others would be limited to the amount due on the contract.

Obligation to require bonds. Those statutes *requiring* the owner to exact a bond have met with more mixed results. Some cases have held that such statutes are invalid, at least where the owner's failure to exact the bond results in personal and individual liability of the owner to the subcontractors, materialmen, laborers, and others sought to be protected by the statute.

Illustrative Case

A Florida statute amended the mechanic's lien law to provide that the owner should procure a surety bond from the contractor; alternatively, the owner, upon the contractor's failure to furnish the bond, should make no payments to the contractor prior to the visible commencement of operations and should withhold 20 percent of the progress payments and contract price as a penalty. Upon failure to meet these requirements, the owner would be rendered personally liable in the full amount for all outstanding bills on the project. The court held the statute invalid under the Florida

Constitution; while the Constitution required the legislature to provide for an adequate lien by mechanics and laborers on their work, this statute was viewed as an excessive and arbitrary exercise of the powers of government, unauthorized by the established principles of private right. [29]

However, there are cases holding such statutes valid.

Illustrative Case

A Utah statute provided that on any project exceeding $500 in price, the owner must secure a bond equal to contract price; the statute also provided that any person furnishing labor or material had a direct right of action against the surety for the amount due. Should the owner fail to procure the bond, he was liable for payment of such obligations. The court held that the statute could not be regarded as an unreasonable regulation, much less a violation of constitutional provisions. [30]

Several states require by statute bonds in private work, at least insofar as certain housing projects are concerned. Such legislation may either supplement the supplier's right to a mechanic's lien or provide that the bond rights shall be in substitution for the lien right.

Statutes requiring the owner to withhold, under specified circumstances, payments from the contractor for the express purpose of protecting subcontractors, materialmen, and laborers have been held valid in a number of cases. Some statutes have provided that a certain percentage of the contract price be withheld for a required period (for example, 35 days) after completion to protect and benefit lien claimants.

Illustrative Case

A California statute ordered such delay in the amount of 25 percent of the total contract price. A contract failing to conform with the requirement was held void, although the owner argued that the statute unconstitutionally circumscribed the right of private contract within the usual pursuits of business and was an unreasonable restriction on the owner of his rights in regard to use of his property. The court held the statute did not enlarge the rights of lien claimants and, rather than infringing on the owner's rights, provided a remedy whereby in certain situations his lien liability would be curtailed. [31]

Persons entitled to recovery. The vast majority of courts have supported the general rule that a person furnishing materials or labor is entitled to recover on a contractor's bond to the owner if the bond contains a condition for the benefit and protection of laborers and materialmen; this right is afforded even though the owner is the only obligee named in the bond. This rule is an outgrowth of the doctrine that a third person may enforce a contract entered into between others for his benefit. The right exists regardless of the existence of a statute giving such a remedy or requiring such a bond.

[29] Greenblatt v. Goldin, 94 So.2d 355 (Fla. 1957).

[30] Rio Grande Lumber Co. v. Darke, 50 Utah 114, 167 P. 241 (1917).

[31] Stimson Mill Co. v. Nolan, 5 Cal. App. 754, 91 P. 262 (1907).

Where a private contractor's bond is made for the benefit of laborers, materialmen, and subcontractors, it is not necessary that they be named in the terms of the bond; indeed, they need not even be known at the time of execution of the bond. Nor are those beneficiaries excluded from seeking recovery by the fact that they did not know of the existence of the bond at the time they furnished goods or services.

However, because of the general contract principle that the intention of the parties shall control, in the situation where the terms of the bond make it clear that the bond is designed solely for the benefit of the formal parties thereto, subcontractors, materialmen, and laborers cannot sue on the bond, notwithstanding that they might derive some benefit from its enjoyment. Bonds can be drafted to provide an indemnity to the owner or general contractor for performance only; where the bond is conditioned merely to indemnify and hold harmless the owner from any pecuniary loss resulting from the breach of any of the terms of the contract, the courts have held that they do not provide a direct right of action by third-party beneficiary subcontractors and suppliers.

Illustrative Case

Kelly Engineering Company contracted to furnish materials and labor to completely air-condition a building in Little Rock, Ark. The bond furnished by the contractor contained a provision: "[T]he Principal indemnifies the Obligee against loss or damage directly arising by reason of the failure of the Principal faithfully to perform the above mentioned contract. . . ." Even though the original contract called for a performance bond *with* third-party beneficiaries (a requirement not met by the bond actually procured), the court found the wording of the actual bond to indicate that it was a mere indemnity bond. [32]

Because there are no statutory requirements for private bonds, the exact wording can frequently be crucial. Although in interpreting bond terms the courts will examine the circumstances surrounding the bond and the contract accompanying it, it is important that the bond expressly states, if it is so intended, that the subcontractors and suppliers may maintain a direct right of action.

Bonding Requirements for Subcontractors

Private contractors increasingly insist that their subcontractors furnish performance and payment bonds: Such bonds provide protection for the contractor against liability on its own bond for claims of various tiers of subcontractors, materialmen, and laborers. The considerations discussed previously apply equally to subcontractors' bonds. Because of the distinction between and differing legal treatment of the indemnity bond and third-party beneficiary payment bonds, it is important that the subcon-

[32] Employers' Liability Assurance Corp. v. A.W. Johnson Co., 234 Ark. 806, 354 S.W.2d 733 (1962).

tractor's bond provide the same protection for the prime contractor and the prime contractor should check the subcontractor's bond to ensure that its wording is sufficiently clear to show that it permits a direct right of action by the subcontractor or supplier. If he does not, the contractor may find himself defending an action under his own bond, with the resulting trouble and expense of seeking indemnification from the subcontractor's surety.

The American Institute of Architects has prepared forms, for example, AIA Document A311 (1969 ed.), which generally balance the interest of the competing parties. The AIA bond form as drafted is between the owner and the prime contractor, but subcontractors can easily modify it to serve their own bonding needs.

It is helpful if the bonds specifically provide for indemnification of all legal and attorney's fees resulting from default or nonpayment. Sureties are reluctant to acknowledge liability for attorney's fees under a contract provision, but there is little room for dispute if the liability has been clearly indicated in the bond as well.

The subcontractor should be careful to condition his payment bond upon liability of the owner. Otherwise he may find that he has assumed a greater scope of liability than has the owner or the prime contractor. For example, a materialman may have let his rights expire under the Miller Act payment bond, or he may be too remote for coverage under the contractor's bond; but under a carelessly drafted subcontract bond, he may still have a right to recover against the subcontractor. The bond should expressly state that if the claimant cannot recover against the owner or obligee, *for whatever reason,* he cannot recover under the subcontract bond.

Checklist for Subcontractors

Although every government construction job and many private projects require the general contractor to furnish a payment bond, many subcontractors fail to take the necessary steps to protect themselves under the provisions of those bonds. The following steps are recommended on *all* jobs:

1. The subcontractor should determine if the project is bonded. Some subcontractors are working on bonded jobs without knowing they are protected against default.

2. When the job *begins,* it is wise to obtain a copy of the bond from the owner. The insurance company who underwrites the bond sends the bond directly to the owner. The owner is generally quite cooperative in furnishing a subcontractor with a copy of the bond.

3. Should the subcontractor not be paid on time, he should do *exactly* what is required by the terms of the bond and within the time stated in the bond. For example, if the bond requires that notice be given to the insurance company within 30 days of any default by the general contractor and that such notice must be sent by certified mail to a particular address, then all these conditions must be complied with if the subcontractor is not to lose his right to payment under the bond.

Some state laws provide that bond claimants can compel the surety to pay a penalty and claimant's attorney's fees should the surety refuse in bad faith to honor its obligations under a payment bond within a specified period of time after receipt of a notice of default.[33] Such legislation typically results in sureties being more responsive in paying off their obligations under such payment bonds.

RIGHT TO STOP WORK

The operations of most general contractors and subcontractors of whatever size are predicated on an uninterrupted cash flow. As expenses for labor and material and equipment are incurred, they must be matched by an equal amount of income. Few, if any, general contractors or subcontractors can wait until the end of a project for payment. When a contractor does wait until the end of a project for payment, he is financing or "banking" the project, a function which should not be the contractor's obligation.

For these reasons the construction industry long ago adopted the practice of paying general contractors and subcontractors monthly, based upon the ratio of work completed to total contract work, i.e., the "percentage of completion." This method of payment should be specifically set forth in the contractor's subcontract. The typical "progress payments" clause provides for monthly payments based upon the percentage of work in place plus the cost of materials stored on the jobsite. A percentage of the amount due each month may be withheld from the payment as retention. Because of the necessity of having income meet expenses on a month-to-month basis, most contractors bid their projects so that the progress payment less retention covers the hard costs which must be funded on a current basis.

Although there is some variation in the progress payment clauses of different contracts, a typical clause appears in Standard Subcontract Form, AIA Document A401, Article 12.3, and provides:

Unless otherwise provided in the Contract Documents, the Contractor shall pay the Subcontractor each progress payment and the final payment under this Subcontract within three (3) working days after he receives payment from the Owner. The amount of each progress payment to the Subcontractor shall be equal to the percentage of completion allowed to the Contractor for the work of this Subcontractor applied to the contract sum of this Subcontract, plus the amount allowed for materials and equipment suitably stored by the Subcontractor, less the aggregate of previous payments to the Subcontractor and less the percentage retained as provided in this Subcontract.

Thus, the subcontract often adopts the provisions of the general contract relative to the percentage to be withheld as retention, time of payment, and whether or not stored materials are paid for. The general contractor incorporates his subcontractor's applications for payment with his

---

[33] See, e.g., Ga. Code Ann. § 103–210 (Supp. 1975).

application to the owner. Upon receipt of payment from the owner, the general contractor pays off his own debts and pays each subcontractor its share of the monthly payment. The owner, or the lending institution, retains control over the retention withheld from the monthly payment.

A construction project reaches the crisis stage if the general contractor or subcontractor is not given his monthly progress payment. The general contractor or subcontractor is placed in the position of having incurred great expense without gaining the compensating income, and, often worse, he is faced with the prospect of continuing work, thus incurring greater expense, without knowing if it will be reimbursed.

Viewed from the subcontractor's position, a missed progress payment is usually the result of one of three causes: (1) For some reason, the owner or lending institution has refused to pay the general contractor; (2) the subcontractor's work is defective, and the general contractor refuses to make payment until the work is corrected; (3) the general contractor has been paid but has applied the full payment to its own debts and thus does not have any money to pay the subcontractor.

In the first case, where the owner refuses to pay the general contractor (assuming that the refusal to pay is not based on any default of the subcontractor), the subcontractor's legal rights and remedies flow to the party with which it has contracted, the general contractor. The dispute between the general contractor and the owner does not affect the subcontractor's right to payment. Although many subcontracts state that the subcontractor will be paid within a certain or reasonable time after the general contractor is paid by the owner, this does not mean that payment to the subcontractor depends absolutely on payment by the owner.

The AIA Standard Subcontract Form (AIA Document A401, 1972 ed.), contains a payment savings clause (Article 12.5) that stipulates that the subcontractor be paid if the owner does not pay the general contractor or if the architect does not approve the work for any reason not the fault of the subcontractor. Even in the absence of a payment savings clause, in construing contingent payment clauses, the courts have consistently held that such a provision merely establishes a *time* for payment of the subcontractor and is not construed to mean that payment by the owner is a *condition precedent* to payment of the subcontractor.[34]

Illustrative Case

A. J. Wolfe Company, a subcontractor for electrical work on a Cambridge apartment house, sued Baltimore Contractors, Inc., the general contractor, for amounts due under the subcontract calling for periodic payments. The contractor asserted the defense that it had not received its progress payments from the owner. The court held that the clause providing that the contractor should pay his subcontractor within ten days of receipt of its own payments from the owner did not establish a condition precedent for payment; in the absence of a clear provision that payment to the subcontractor is

---

[34]*See* pp. 70–75 for a discussion of the cases involving subcontract contingent payment clauses.

directly contingent upon receipt by the general of payment from the owner, such a provision would be viewed only as a postponing payment by the general for a reasonable time after requisition and completion of the subcontractor's work.[35]

Although the general contractor's first line of defense is to assert that he is not liable to the subcontractor until payment is made by the owner, the subcontractor must clearly stipulate this to be the case before a court will uphold the general contractor's point of view.

In the second case, where the general contractor has been paid but withholds payment claiming that the subcontractor's work is defective, the resolution of the dispute will depend upon the merits of the general contractor's claim of defect. If the subcontractor's work is defective, he is not entitled to full payment, but the general contractor's remedy (and the architect's) is to refuse *approval* of the pay request—not to withhold payment of previously approved funds. Legally, the general contractor is faced with the immediate problem of overcoming the presumption that the subcontractor's work was acceptable. The general contractor previously has forwarded the subcontractor's application for payment to the architect, thereby implying that the general contractor approved of the subcontractor's work. The architect has inspected the subcontractor's work, has inventoried the materials stored on site, and has approved the application for payment. The owner, relying on the architect's approval, has paid the general contractor for transmittal of the funds to the subcontractors, suppliers, and materialmen and expects these people to be paid in order to avoid mechanic's liens.

If the general contractor's claim of defective work is not justified, then the general contractor has no legal excuse for withholding payment and the rights and remedies of the parties are the same as in the third case.

In the third case, where the general contractor fails to make payment without excuse, he is clearly in breach of the subcontractor but the subcontractor's rights and remedies may vary according to the particular facts of each case.

The general contractor or subcontractor should not stop work if he does not have the legal right to do so. On the other hand, neither should he continue to work and finance the project if stopping work is a legally valid remedy. One of the toughest legal problems in the field of construction law is whether a contractor or subcontractor can stop work where a progress payment is missed. If the party continues work, he runs the considerable risk of incurring great expense for which he may never be reimbursed. If he stops work, without the legal right to do so, he runs the even greater risk of incurring damage liabilities if the project is delayed or if someone else is hired to complete the project at a greater price.

In determining the legal ramifications of a missed progress payment, the contractor and his attorney should review the problem along the lines

---

[35]A. J. Wolfe Co. v. Baltimore Contractors, Inc., 244 N.E.2d 717 (Mass. 1969).

of the following proposed analysis. First, what rights to stop work are contained in the general contract or subcontract, either expressly or implicitly by reference? The general contractor or subcontractor should insert a stop-work clause in every contract before it is signed. What "notices" are required, and have they been given? If the general contract or subcontract contains a standard stop-work clause and proper notices are given, the general contractor or subcontractor may stop work at the specified time.

Second, assuming that there is no stop-work clause, the general contractor or subcontractor must determine whether the failure to pay is a "material breach" of the "entire" contract. The important factors in this analysis are:

1. The size of the overdue payment, both in terms of percentage and dollar amount

2. The amount of work remaining to be performed, both in terms of percentage and dollar amount

3. Whether the owner or general contractor has any legal justification for withholding payment

4. Whether the general contractor or subcontractor is *prevented* from continuing performance by the cessation of his cash flow

Often the contract or subcontract itself will set forth the subcontractor's right to stop work, either expressly or implicitly. A typical right-to-stop-work clause appears in the Standard Form Subcontract, AIA Document A401, Article 12.6, as follows:

The Contractor agrees that if he fails to make payments to the Subcontractor as herein provided for any cause not the fault of the Subcontractor, within seven days from the time payment should be made . . . the Subcontractor may, upon seven days' additional written notice to the Contractor, stop his Work without prejudice to any other remedy he may have.

In addition to this express definition of the right to stop work, the AIA General Conditions (AIA Document A201), Article 9.7.1, also recognize the right of the general contractor to stop work after 7 days following written notice to the owner and architect. If the General Conditions are incorporated into a subcontract giving the subcontractor the same rights, redress, and remedies against the owner, then the subcontractor might rely on the language in the General Conditions for contract authority to stop work.

If the general contractor or subcontractor decides to exercise a right to stop work that is either explicitly or implicitly made a part of his contract, he should comply with the *notice* provisions contained in the subcontract or the General Conditions. For example, note that in the contract clause quoted previously, the subcontractor cannot stop work immediately after the progress payment is due. First, the general contractor is allowed 7 days after the due date in which to make payment. Second, if payment is not made within 7 days, the subcontractor can give *written notice* of his intent to stop work but may not actually stop work until an additional 7 days after such written notice is given. Therefore, the subcontractor may not actually stop work until at least 14 calendar days from the due date. Naturally, the subcontractor will not want to incur any unnecessary expenses during this 14-day period.

Illustrative Case

A subcontractor has a subcontract with the general contractor. Monthly progress payment is due from the general contractor to the subcontractor on August 10 but is not paid. The general contractor has at least until August 24 to make payment. If the subcontractor gives written notice on August 13, then he cannot stop work until August 24 because the general contractor is entitled to 7 days plus 7 days "additional." If the subcontractor gives written notice on August 21, then he cannot stop work until August 28. [hypothetical case]

Where these notices are required by the contract, they are vitally important and should not be overlooked. Stopping work is the most drastic remedy which a contractor or subcontractor has, especially where his action will shut down a major project. The general contractor or subcontractor should proceed cautiously to ensure that he has covered every legal issue, especially any required notices.

Often, however, the contracts make no mention of the right to stop work. This is especially true when the subcontract is executed on a form drafted by the general contractor or the general contract is on a form drafted by the owner. In these cases the right to stop work depends upon the application of the common-law concepts of "material breach," "entire-severable contracts," "prevention," and "rescission/restitution." Again, the general contractor or subcontractor should seek legal advice and closely examine his legal position before he stops work.

The law has always favored the completion and fulfillment of contracts. In a society such as ours, which depends so heavily upon commercial relationships, the law must be designed to encourage fulfillment of contractual obligations and discourage nonperformance. This basic principle has been adhered to since the inception of Anglo-American common law and is at the root of a general contractor's or subcontractor's dilemma in determining whether he has the right to stop work.

With this principle in mind, the courts have adopted the rule that a small or immaterial breach of a contract will not justify the injured party's ceasing performance of his obligation. When a party is faced with an insubstantial breach of contract, he is expected to complete his performance and then sue for whatever damage he has suffered as a result of the breach. The other side of this coin is that the injured party *may* cease performance and sue immediately for his damages *if* the breach is a "material breach" which goes to the root of the contract.

Therefore, the general contractor or subcontractor is not justified in stopping work unless nonpayment of the progress payment (or payments) constitutes a material breach of his contract. Whether a particular nonpayment is such a breach is not a matter of *law* which can be decided the same way in every case. Rather, the question of material breach is a *fact* issue which must be determined on the individual merits of each case.

To fully understand the significance of this material breach issue, one must first examine the legal distinction between an "entire contract" and a "severable contract": Basically, an "entire contract" is one in which complete performance by one party of all of its obligations under the contract is expected in return for complete performance by the other party of its obligations. For example, a subcontract for the plaster work in a house when the work is to be paid for when fully complete is an entire contract. The subcontractor is expected to perform all of the plaster work, his entire obligation, before he is entitled to payment.

A "severable contract" is one in which each party agrees to perform a *series* of obligations and the other party agrees to perform a corresponding series of obligations. For example, where a subcontractor purchases materials from his supplier and the purchase order provides for delivery of specific quantities on specific dates and that after each delivery the subcontractor shall make a specific payment for the materials delivered the parties have executed a severable contract. The obligations of each party depend upon the prior completion of the other party's obligation.

The distinction between entire and severable contracts is important because a breach of an entire contract will not justify stopping work unless the failure to perform is a material breach of the *whole* contract. With a severable contract, a material breach of one series of concurrent obligations will justify refusing to perform the remaining series of obligations. Obviously, it often requires a greater breach of contract to justify ceasing performance on an entire contract than on a severable contract.

Although a construction general contract or subcontract, providing for periodic payments based upon the amount of labor and material expended, closely resembles an installment or severable contract, most courts hold that such a contract is an entire contract.

Illustrative Case

A contract for construction of a building on an Indian reservation provided that the contract price was to be paid in payments representing 80 percent of the value of the work executed and actually in place to the satisfaction of the government at the expiration of each 30 days. One of the specifications required the contractor, Augustus W. Boggs, to be responsible for all damages to the building from fire or other causes during prosecution of the work. Boggs failed to complete the building by the specified date, and while the building was still in his possession (the government having rejected the work and materials), it was completely destroyed by fire. The court held that the government was entitled to recover from the surety on the contractor's bond for progress payments made to Boggs during the course of the work because under this contract, a completed building was the thing bargained for. [36]

The rationale of decisions such as the preceding one is that the parties have basically agreed to complete performance of the construction contract in return for payment of the full amount due on the contract. The agreement to pay the full amount in periodic installments merely sets forth the *time* for payment and does not contemplate a series of concurrent obligations.

Some courts, however, have construed a contract with periodic payments as being severable, especially where the facts show that the parties intended it to be so.

Illustrative Case

A contract to grade and build 2 miles of road in accordance with plans and specifications provided that the contractor, Dillon & Harrison, was to be paid at the rate of $3,000 per mile; that estimates of the amount of work completed in a satisfactory manner were to be made every 2 weeks; and that the owner, Suburban Land Company, would thereupon pay the amount due less 10 percent retention. The contract was held apportionable because it provided in specific terms for estimates and partial payments every 2 weeks. The contractor was held able to recover the value of his labor and materials even though it had only partially completed the work. [37]

The characterization of a construction contract or subcontract as an entire contract has a significant effect on the general contractor's or subcontractor's right to stop work. When a progress payment is missed, the general contractor or subcontractor cannot stop work unless that particular failure to pay constitutes a material breach of the *whole* contract. Accordingly, it would appear that failure to pay a small progress payment on a very large job would *not* constitute a material breach, and the general contractor or subcontractor would not be justified in stopping work. As we shall see, this is not necessarily true in every case, but the first step in determining whether the general contractor or subcontractor is justified in stopping work is to determine whether the missed progress payment constitutes a material breach of his particular contract.

Illustrative Case

A subcontractor has a subcontract with the general contractor to perform masonry work for a total contract price of $100,000. The general contractor is to make periodic payments based upon the percentage of work in place and materials stored on the jobsite. The subcontract does not contain any provisions authorizing the subcontractor to stop work if the general contractor misses a payment. The general contractor misses a payment of $10,000. The subcontractor's work has been good, and the general

---

[36] United States v. United States Fidelity & Guaranty Co., 236 U.S. 512 (1915).

[37] Dillon & Harrison v. Suburban Land Co., 73 W. Va. 363, 80 S.E. 471 (1913).

contractor is not justified in withholding payment. The general contractor has previously met every pay request and has paid a total of $60,000, which covers all of the material necessary for the project. The remaining portions of the subcontract are primarily labor. The general contractor breached the contract by failing to make payment when due. Is this a "material" breach which would justify the subcontractor in stopping work? There is no definite answer to this question. [*hypothetical case*]

In a case much like the preceding one, the United States Supreme Court affirmed a lower-court decision to the effect that the subcontractor was justified in refusing to continue work and was allowed to sue for damages without completing its work.[38] The rationale behind this decision was that, by continuing the work after a missed payment, the subcontractor, in effect, would have been *financing* the project and such an arrangement was not part of the subcontract. The court pointed out that in a contract calling for the performing of labor and furnishing of materials covering a long period of time and involving large expenditures, a stipulation for progress payments must be deemed so material that a substantial failure to pay would justify the contractor in declining to proceed. This, of course, restates the troublesome question "What constitutes a 'substantial' failure to pay?" This decision has provided the precedent in many other cases holding that a missed progress payment constituted a material breach, thereby justifying the general contractor or subcontractor in stopping work.[39]

It is important for the subcontractor or general contractor to note that a missed progress payment is not *automatically* a material breach which would justify stopping work. Although some courts have held, almost as a matter of law, that a failure to make a progress payment "indubitably" constitutes a material breach, other courts have examined the particular facts of each case to determine whether the failure to pay was "so substantial and fundamental as to go to the very root of the contract."

Illustrative Case

Pickard Engineering Company agreed to perform plumbing and heating work for the general contractor, Southern Construction Company, which agreed to make monthly progress payments, withholding 10 percent retention. The subcontract did not expressly or implicitly authorize the subcontractor to stop work if the general contractor missed a payment. At the time when the Pickard's work was 90 percent complete, Southern failed to make a progress payment without legal excuse. Because the remaining portion of work consisted entirely of purchasing material from the subcontractor's supplier, which would then be turned over to the general contractor, Pickard would have been required to use all the money in the missed progress payment and

---

[38] Guerini Stone Co. v. P.J. Carlin Constr. Co., 248 U.S. 334 (1919).

[39] *See, e.g.,* Autrey v. Williams & Dunlap, 343 F.2d 730 (5th Cir. 1965); United States *ex rel.* F.E. Robinson Co. v. Alpha-Continental, 273 F. Supp. 758 (E.D.N.C. 1967); Rosenberger v. Hutchinson, 143 So.2d 604 (La. App. 1962); S.T. Grand, Inc. v. Cedar Bay Park Corp., 14 Misc.2d 428, 182 N.Y.S.2d 747 (1958).

all future progress payments to repay the supplier for these materials. Pickard stopped work on the project while the supplier continued to supply material directly to Southern without immediate payment. After the project was completed Southern made full payment to the supplier, but this payment exceeded the contract price to which Pickard was bound. The subcontractor sued the general contractor, not for breach of contract, but for the value of the labor and material which Pickard supplied to the project prior to stopping work. This value exceed the contract price. The general contractor countersued for the money which the general contractor was required to pay to the supplier. The key issue in both the suit and countersuit was whether the subcontractor was justified in stopping work. Under the facts, out in the preceding case, the court held that the subcontractor was not *not* justified in stopping work.[40]

The rationale for this decision was that because the subcontractor would have paid the entire progress payment to the supplier, and because the supplier continued to provide the materials without being paid, the subcontractor had not been damaged by the general contractor's failure to pay and was, therefore, not justified in stopping work.

The *Restatement of Contracts,* published by the American Law Institute, sets forth the general rules of contract law which are usually followed by the federal and state courts. The *Restatement* has adopted the following rules for determining the "materiality" of a failure to perform:

In determining the materiality of a failure fully to perform a promise the following circumstances are influential:

(a) The extent to which the injured party will obtain the substantial benefit which he could have reasonably anticipated;

(b) The extent to which the injured party may be adequately compensated in damages for lack of complete performance;

(c) The extent to which the party failing to perform has already partly performed or made preparations for performance;

(d) The greater or less hardship on the party failing to perform in terminating the contract;

(e) The willful, negligent or innocent behavior of the party failing to perform;

(f) The greater or less uncertainty that the party failing to perform will perform the remainder of the contract.[41]

Of these rules, the ones which have the greatest applicability to the construction contracts and progress payment situation are (a), (c), (d), and (f). These four rules read together indicate that the most important facts to examine in determining whether a general contractor or subcontractor has the right to stop work are: (1) the amount of work remaining to be done on the contract, both in terms of percentage and in terms of dollars to be paid; and (2) the size of the progress payment, or payments

---

[40] United States *ex rel.* Pickard v. Southern Constr. Co., 293 F.2d 493 (6th Cir. 1961).

[41] *Restatement of Contracts* § 275.

overdue, both in terms of percentage and dollar amount. Again, no absolute rule can be predicted on these factors.

Since the rationale behind the general contractor's or subcontractor's right to stop work is that he is not expected to *finance* the project by continuing to provide labor and material after his cash flow is cut off, a missed progress payment early in the project, even though small in amount, may be a material breach, whereas a large missed progress payment later in the project may not be. This analysis is implicitly supported by the *Restatement:*

Where the failure is at the outset, a very slight failure is often sufficient to discharge the injured party. But even in that case, and more obviously if the failure of a promisor occurs after part performance by him, the question becomes one of degree. Both the amount that he has done and the benefit that the injured party has received are considered. The question then to be answered is: Will it be more conformable to justice in the particular case to free the injured party, or, on the other hand, to require him to perform his promise, in both cases giving him a right of action if the failure to perform was wrongful?[42]

A review of the cases considering a general contractor's or subcontractor's right to stop work indicates that the courts have never really broken down their analysis of this problem in order to examine specifically the relationship of the missed progress payment to the total contract price. However, these cases do indicate that default on a progress payment which is a significant *percentage* of the total contract amount will support a finding of material breach. What constitutes a significant percentage, of course, is a factual determination made by the court in the individual case; in the few cases discussed here, the percentage sufficient to constitute a material breach has a range from 7.17 to 37 percent.

The exception to the analysis outlined above is where the failure to pay actually *prevents* further performance by the general contractor or subcontractor. "Prevention" of performance has the same legal effect as a material breach. Theoretically, therefore, a default which is too small to be a material breach will still justify stopping work if the default prevents further performance. As a practical matter, it may be difficult to prove that a small default did prevent performance. At least one court has held that, *as a matter of law,* a general contractor's failure to pay did not prevent further performance even though the subcontractor lacked working capital.[43]

Assuming that the general contractor or subcontractor is justified in stopping work, he has two remedies for his damages: The first is an action on the contract, and the second is an action for the value of labor and materials supplied.

The measure of the general contractor or subcontractor's damages in an action for breach of the contract would be the unpaid installments of the contract price that have become due and payable as a contract debt

---

[42] *Restatement of Contracts* § 275, Comment (a).

[43] Palmer v. Watson Constr. Co., 121 N.W.2d 62 (Minn. 1963).

for work completed, and, in addition, the money damages caused by the total breach of the contract by the owner or general contractor, i.e., "lost profits." These damages include all other unpaid installments of the contract price less the cost of completion of the work that is saved to the subcontractor by reason of the default of the owner or general contractor, with additional compensation for any other injury that could not be reasonably avoided by the general contractor or subcontractor and that the owner or general contractor has reason to foresee when the contract was made.

If the general contractor or subcontractor is not able to show the cost to complete with specificity, he may still seek damages for the value of labor and materials supplied. This remedy is known as "restitution," and the measure of damages is the reasonable value of all labor and materials supplied to the project less the amounts actually paid in previous payments.

The difference between these two remedies is that in restitution the general contractor or subcontractor is not awarded "lost profits" or "consequential damages." This difference is based upon the underlying distinction between contract damages and restitution which is summarized by the *Restatement of Contracts*.

When the remedy given for breach of the contract is money damages, the amount awarded is determined with the purpose of putting the injured party in as good a position as he would have occupied, had the contract been fully performed by the defendant. In granting restitution as a remedy for breach, however, the purpose to be attained is the restoration of the injured party to as good a position as that occupied by him before the contract was made. [44]

Although restitution seems to offer the general contractor or subcontractor a smaller recovery, it is an advantageous remedy where there is difficulty or uncertainty in proving the cost to complete the project or, more importantly, where the actual expenditures for labor and material exceed the contract price.

The right to stop work is one of the most important remedies a general contractor or subcontractor has; but, due to its drastic results, it cannot be exercised in every case. The general contractor or subcontractor must analyze his particular case and weight the relative *economic* disadvantages of stopping work (risking a law suit) and continuing work (becoming the "banker" for the job). Where the legal rights and economic advantages demand stopping work, the right should be exercised.

[44] *Restatement of Contracts* § 347, Comment (b).

INDEXES

Table of Cases

Subject Index

TABLE OF CASES

SUBJECT INDEX

Changes, constructive changes, misinter-
    pretation of specifications (*Cont*):
      reasonableness of interpretation,
        151–152
        specific provisions control general,
          153
        technical meanings, 152
        voluntary performance, 155
      origin of, 143
      overinspection, 155–157
        authority of inspector, 156
      owner-furnished property, defective,
        161–163
        damages, 162
        models and patterns, 162
        unreasonable attempts to make
          conform, 162–163
      rejection of conforming work, 157–159
        custom and usage, 158
        damages for nonconformity, 159
        standard of workmanship, 158–159
      rejection of "or equal" substitutes,
        159–161
  damages for delay, 186–191
    documentation, 190
    noncompensable damages, 188
    notice, 189
    overhead, 190–191
    ripple effect, 190
    waiver of, 189–190
  documentation, 139–140
    custom and usage, 140
    delay damages, 190
    experts, 140
    jobsite log, 139
    photographs, 140
    written memoranda, 139
  excusable delays, 173–179
    attributable to owner, 179
    duty to mitigate, 177, 179
    labor disputes, 177–178
    liquidated damages, 180
    necessity for clause concerning, 174
    noncompensable delays, 174
    notice, 174–175
    ripple effects, 176
    transportation, delays in, 179
    weather, unusually severe, 178
  fixed-price contracts, 33–34
  general contracts, 57–58
  impossibility of performance, 163–166
    actual impossibility, 163–164
    assumption of risk, 163
    destruction of building, 165
    implied warranty, 163
    notice, 165
    partial impossibility, 165
    practical impossibility, 164–165
  liquidated damages, 180–183
    absence of clause concerning, 182
    apportionment, 180–181
    breach by abandonment, 181

Changes, liquidated damages (*Cont.*):
    excusable delays, 180
    substantial completion, 181–182
  notice, 132–134
    absence of harm from failure to give,
      134
    function of, 133
    provision in general contract, 133
    waiver of, 133
  oral order, 129
  pricing, 136–139
    architect's certificate of value, 138
    data, 142
    disputes, 136
    general contract, 57–58
    overhead and profit, 137–138
    subcontract, 83–84
    timing of, 137
  scope of work, 129, 134–136
    cardinal change doctrine, 135
    refusal to perform work out of scope,
      135
    (*See also* General contracts, scope of
      work; Subcontracts, scope of work)
  unit-price contracts, 35
  (*See also* Subcontracts, changes)

Disputes (*see* Remedies, disputes clauses)

General contracts, 31–66
  change clauses, 57–58
    disputes, 57
    pricing, 57–58
    retention on price of changes, 58
    (*See also* Changes)
  conduit clause, 33
  default and termination, 63–66
    architect's certificate, 63–64
    minor violations, 64–65
    right to remedy deficiency, 65
    termination for convenience of govern-
      ment, 65–66
  lien rights, 32
    (*See also* Remedies, lien rights; Sub-
      contracts, lien rights)
  payment, 32–54
    ensuring, 32
    methods of computing, 32–41
      cost-plus contracts, 36–41
        allowable costs, 36–40
        maximum cost provision, 36, 41
        reimbursable costs and base-cost
          figure distinguished, 36
        unreasonable expenses, 40
      fixed-price contracts, 33–34
        changes in contract requirements,
          33–34
        escalation clause, 33
        unit-price payment in combina-
          tion with, 35